RUSSIA AND AZERBAIJAN

RUSSIA AND AZERBAIJAN

A Borderland in Transition

Tadeusz Swietochowski

COLUMBIA UNIVERSITY PRESS

NEW YORK

Columbia University Press
New York   Chichester, West Sussex
Copyright © 1995 Columbia University Press

Library of Congress Cataloging-in-Publication Data

Swietochowski, Tadeusz, 1934–
     Russia and Azerbaijan: A borderland in transition /
     Tadeusz Swietochowski
        p.   cm.
     Includes bibliographical references and index.
     ISBN 0–231–07068–3
     1. Azerbaijan—History.   2. Azerbaijan (Iran)—History.
     3. Nationalism—Azerbaijan—History.   4. Nationalism—Iran—
     Azerbaijan—History.   5. Russia—Relations—Azerbaijan.
     6. Azerbaijan—Relations—Russia.   7. Iran—Relations—Iran—
     Azerbaijan.   8. Azerbaijan (Iran)—Relations—Iran.   I. Title.
     DK695.4.S95   1995
     327.47055'3—dc20   94–48574
                                                                                              CIP

Casebound editions of Columbia University Press books
are printed on permanent and durable acid-free paper.

Printed in the United States of America

c 10 9 8 7 6 5 4 3 2 1

CONTENTS

PREFACE

This book is an inquiry into the past of the people living in the quintessential borderland, many times over: between Europe and Asia, Islam and Christianity, Russia and the Middle East, Turks and Iranians, Shi'a and Sunni Islam. The book deals with a divided people in a divided land and a split that has resulted from European conquest of a frontier region of the Middle East. It examines the last two centuries of Azerbaijan's history, beginning with the Russian seizure of the northern part of the country in the early nineteenth century, and concluding with the achievement of independence by the post-Soviet Azerbaijani Republic in the 1990s.

Although the discussion will deal with the Azerbaijan on each side of the Russian-Iranian border, this is not a comprehensive history of both. Indeed, much of the history of the two Azerbaijans during this period has been omitted. The focus is on what they held in common, on what forces divided them even more deeply than did foreign conquest, and on the new bonds that developed after—and sometimes despite—the conquest.

The very existence of a country divided between two states engenders questions with international ramifications, yet this book is not a study of a region's diplomatic history. Indeed, it attempts to keep this aspect to a minimum, concentrating instead on the evolution of the identity of Azerbaijan's people on both sides of the frontier.

Although a sizable entity in terms of territory and population, Azerbaijan has attracted remarkably little attention in historical writing, not merely in comparison with neighboring countries but with any part of the Middle East. Only in recent years as the formerly Soviet

Azerbaijan began to appear in the news has interest grown and the number of monographs increased. Yet the history of the two Azerbaijans has never been examined in one monograph. Apparently the assumption has been that since each of the two parts has been enmeshed in the fabric of such diverse states as Iran, Russia, and the USSR, they have become as dissimilar as the proverbial apples and oranges, no matter how much common history, language, religion, trade, and migration they share. Another reason, which is even more discouraging, is that the topic is replete with pitfalls. Primarily, treatment of the southern part of Azerbaijan is inseparable from the larger history of Iran. Tabriz has always been incomparably more closely integrated with Iran than Baku has been with Russia, and there is no room for asymmetrical treatment of both Azerbaijans within their respective state structures. Azeri national aspirations and movements were more fully articulated in the Russian-ruled part, while the other part expressed its particularistic concerns along with Iran as a whole.

This book expands on some of the themes covered in my previous work on Azerbaijani history and politics. The organization of the present work was set by the rhythms of history—periods of slow change alternating with times of acceleration and upheaval. The first chapter focuses on the century of gradual administrative and economic transformations that followed in the wake of the Russian conquest of the land north of the Araxes River and the growth of Russian influence across the Iranian border. The second chapter considers the intellectual changes resulting from the contact with Europe, mainly through Russia. Chapter 3 deals with a shorter period of revolution on both sides of the border and World War I. The assertion of independence by Russian Azerbaijan for two years, and autonomy by the Iranian part for a few months, forms the fourth chapter. Establishment of Soviet rule over one part of Azerbaijan and of the Pahlavi dynasty over the other, both of which promoted the rift between the two sections of the country, is the focus of the fifth chapter. Chapter 6 addresses the World War II Soviet occupation of northern Iran and the rise of an autonomist regime in Tabriz under its aegis, a development that was also seen as an attempt to stop assimilation and assert the Azeri identity. The seventh chapter covers the long period stretching from the downfall of the autonomist regime in Tabriz to the overthrow of the Shah, during which both the USSR and Iran, strongly attempting to isolate the two parts of Azerbaijan, resorted to vigorous assimilation policies. During this period the declining empires were otherwise unable to control the forces changing the societies under their rule. The final chapter deals with the crumbling of the colonial grip on Soviet Azerbaijan, the revival of national aspirations, and the country's gradual homecoming to the Middle East through the renewal of links with Turkey and Iran. The chapter ends with the election of the post-Soviet non-Communist president of an independent Azerbaijani republic. The epilogue covers the rule of the post-Communist People's Front regime, which ended with the Summer of 1993 coup that brought the republic's former Communist party leader back into power and the one-year period that followed.

The mass of publications from the former Soviet Azerbaijan—books, collections of documents, articles—includes the source material from the great eruption of hitherto suppressed information in the glasnost era. Likewise some of the primary sources came from the State Archives of Azerbaijan. Other sources came from depositories outside of the former Soviet Union, notably from the Public Records Office of Great Britain, the National Archives of the United States, and the Archives of the Ministry of Foreign Affairs of Poland.

Of the many problems encountered in writing this book, the most intractable was that of names, of countries as well as of individuals. Frequent changes of names reflect the kaleidoscopic upheavals of recent history in this part of the Middle East, and changes such as *Ottoman State* to *Turkey*, and even more *Persia* to *Iran*, are inconvenient and confusing. In Azerbaijan these changes are bedeviling, all the more so for being politically charged. The very name *Azerbaijan*, when used to denote the land north of the Araxes, has been known to raise the objections of some natives of Iran, although this usage has now been accepted by all sides. But the use of the adjective Azerbaijani to refer both to the language and the people has become controversial; indeed, some see it as a vestige of the Stalinist epoch. In the age of freedom, according to this view, the correct ethnonym should be Azeri or Azeri Turk. Likewise, the language that they speak should be called Azeri or Azeri Turkish, yet the adjective referring to the country remains Azerbaijani, and no one would say Azeri exports, economy, or administrative system. The question of terminology is one to be settled by the people of Azerbaijan and, one hopes, soon. As to the name for the people of Iranian Azerbaijan, the diversity of the ethnonyms used—Azeris, Azerbaijanis, Azeri Turks, Turks—is even greater; one author has remarked that it is as difficult to agree on their appellation as it is to agree on their numbers. The inference may well be that the people of Azerbaijan are not given to fixation of compartamentalizing by ethnonyms; perhaps they even instinctively find such vagueness convenient. It is not the purpose of this book to promote the use of one particular name, and therefore I opted for the lack of consistency in the use of ethnonyms, a reflection of a continuing state of affairs. In many cases the context was the guide for the use of the particular version of the name for the country and its people.

Remarkable confusion also surrounds the matter of personal names. North of the border, the use of family names was a feature attendant on Russian rule, and it thus smacked of colonialism. Typically, names would take Russian endings: Mammädov, Hajinskii, Aghayev, and so forth. Yet changed political circumstances led to native-sounding versions of family names. Patriotic-minded historians even have changed the names of long-dead public figures. Other Azeris, having emigrated to Turkey, turkicized their names: Rustambäkov was changed to Rustambäyli, Khasmammädov to Hasmehmetli; Aghayev became Agaoğlu. This book uses only the name by which a given person began his public life in Azerbaijan, regardless of any later versions, although subsequent changes might be indicated in parentheses. Still, I am well aware that I fell short of a satisfactory level of consistency in this matter and again leave it to the context to determine the version of the name.

In the spelling of names and foreign terms, the transliteration systems are those of the Library of Congress for Russian, Persian, and Ottoman. For the Azeri Cyrillic, transliteration is based on the tables of Edward Allworth.

ACKNOWLEDGMENTS

Now that this work has come to its end, my pleasant task is to express appreciation and thanks to the institutions and persons that generously extended me their assistance. Travel to foreign archives and libraries was indispensable and was made possible by short-term grants from the International Research and Exchange Board-IREX, National Endowment for the Humanities, American Philosophical Society, and the Olin Foundation. The work in American depositories was assisted by a short-term grant from the Kennan Institute for Advanced Russian Studies. The writing of the book was greatly facilitated by a one-year Fellowship from the Columbia University Harriman Institute for Advanced Soviet Studies, a summer grant from the National Endowment for the Humanities, and Monmouth College Creativity Grants. Among the foreign-based institutions that were helpful in my research, I wish to express special appreciation to the staff of Baku's Azerbaijani Akhundov State Library, the Institute of History at the Azerbaijani Academy of Sciences, the Radio Liberty Research Institute in Munich, the Azerbaijani State Archives, and the Archives of Political Parties and Social Movements in Baku.

Many individuals generously assisted me in completing this book, and some even anonymously. I wish to convey to them all my heartfelt gratitude. My special thanks go to Evan Siegel, Cosroe Chaqueri, Ramiz Abutalibov, Hasan Javadi, Elizabeth Fuller, Shövkät Taghiyeva, 'Ali Rasizadä, Bahtyar Rafiev, Audrey Altstadt, Nasib Nasibzadä, Raul Motika, George Bournoutian, and many other friends and colleagues.

Azerbaijan

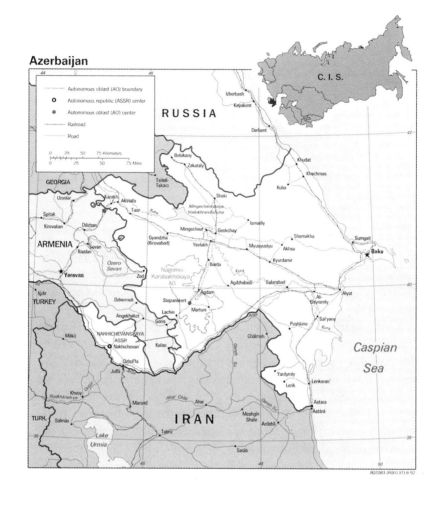

C. I. S.

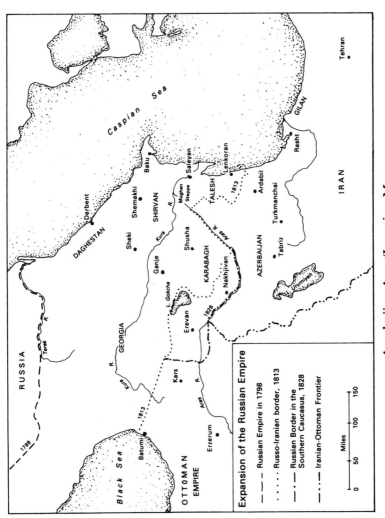

Azerbaijan Area/Location Map

Expansion of the Russian Empire

- – – – Russian Empire in 1798
- · · · · · Russo-Iranian border, 1813
- –··– Russian Border in the Southern Caucasus, 1828
- ·–··– Iranian-Ottoman Frontier

Miles

0   50   100   150

RUSSIA

Terek R.

Kura R.

Ares R.

GEORGIA

Batumi

Black Sea

OTTOMAN EMPIRE

Erzerum

Kars

1813

1798

1828

Erevan

L. Gokcha

Ganje

Nakhjivan

KARABAGH

Shusha

Sheki

DAGHESTAN

Derbent

Shemakhi

SHIRVAN

Kura R.

Baku

Saleyan

Mughan Steppe

Caspian Sea

Lenkoran

1813

TALESH

AZERBAIJAN

Tabriz

Urumiyeh

IRAN

Ardabil

Turkmanchai

Rasht

GILAN

Tehran

RUSSIA AND AZERBAIJAN

ONE

The Parting of the Ways and the New Links

The Land of Azerbaijan and the Conquest by Russia

Azerbaijan is the name of the land populated today by the Azeri Turks, the people who inhabit the region stretching from the northern slopes of the Caucasus Mountains along the Caspian Sea to the Iranian plateau. As a political or administrative unit, and indeed as a geographic notion, Azerbaijan's boundaries were changing throughout history. Its northern part, on the left bank of the Araxes River, was known at times under different names—Caucasian Albania in the pre-Islamic period, and, subsequently, Arran.

From the time of ancient Media and the Achaemenid Kingdom, Azerbaijan usually shared its history with Iran. According to the most widely accepted explanation, its name derives from Atropatenes, an Iranian satrap who was retained by Alexander the Great and eventually established a line of local rulers. A more popular theory traces the origin of the name to the Persian word *azer*, "fire." Azerbaijan is the Land of Fire because the fires in its numerous Zoroastrian temples were fed by plentiful sources of oil. Azerbaijan maintained its Iranian character after conquest by the Arabs in the mid-seventh century and the subsequent conversion to Islam, when it was a separate province under the early Islamic caliphate. Only in the eleventh century, with the influx of the Oghuz Turkic tribes under the Seljuk dynasty, did the country acquire a significant proportion of Turkic-speaking inhabitants. The original population began to be fused with the immigrants, and gradually the Persian language was replaced by a Turkic dialect that evolved into a distinct Azeri Turkish language. Turkification was slow and complex, sustained by successive waves of incoming nomads from Central Asia. After the Mongol invasions in the thirteenth century, Azerbaijan became a part of the empire of Hulagu and his successors, the Ilkhanids, then passed under the rule of the Turkmens who founded the rival Qara Qoyunlu and Aq Qoyunlu states. In the fifteenth century a native Azeri state of Shirvanshahs flourished north of the Araxes. The post-Mongol period brought the first flowering of Azeri as a literary language used far beyond Azerbaijan, a process that culminated in the poetic works of such writers as Nesimi (d. 1404), Khatai (d. 1525), and Fuzuli of Baghdad (d. 1556).

At the end of the fifteenth century Azerbaijan became a power base of another native dynasty, the Safavids. Through a series of conquests and vigorous politics of centralization, they built a new Iranian kingdom. Shah Ismail I (1501–1525), known also as a poet under the pen name Khatai, whose capital was Tabriz, made the Shi'ite branch of Islam the official religion of his empire, an act that set the Azeris firmly apart from the Ottoman Turks. Under the early Safavids, their homeland was frequently the battleground in the wars between Shi'ite Iran and Sunni Turkey, and because of the threat of Ottoman incursions, the capital was moved from Azerbaijan to Qazvin, and then, under Abbas the Great (1588–1629), to Isfahan. A strategically vital province, Azerbaijan remained under the authority of a *bäylärbäy*, a governor who usually combined his administrative position with the highest military rank of *sepahsalar*. Safavid rule, which gradually lost its Azeri character, lasted for more than two centuries. Undermined by internal strife and the Afghan invasion, it came to an end in 1722.[1]

In 1747 Nadir Shah, a strong ruler who had established his hold over Iran eleven years earlier, died in a palace coup, and his empire fell into chaos and disintegration. These circumstances effectively ended Iran's suzerainty over Azerbaijan, where indigenous principalities emerged. These local centers of power were virtually independent, although some maintained tenuous links to the weakened Zand dynasty. Most of the principalities took the form of khanates, including Karabagh, Sheki, Baku, Shirvan, Ganja, Derbent, Kuba, Talysh, Nakhichevan, and Erivan in the north, and Tabriz, Urumi, Ardabil, Khoi, Maku, Karadagh, and Maragin in the south.

Internally, the khanates were miniature replicas of the Iranian monarchy, and their socioeconomic structure was based on state ownership of land, an outgrowth of the medieval institution of *iqta*. Plots were distributed to landholders, *bäys* and *aghas,* as nonhereditary grants for services rendered to the ruler, the khan. The khanates were often subdivided into *mahals* (regions), territorial units inhabited by members of the same tribe, a reflection of the strong residue of tribalism.[2]

Azerbaijan lacked a tradition of unity within an autochthonous statehood, and likewise not all the khanates were ethnically homogeneous, some of them including Kurds, Talyshis, Lesgins, or Armenians. A possibility of creating such a state through the expansion of one of the khanates at the costs of others appeared twice in the wars waged by the rulers who were respectively natives of the southern and northern parts of Azerbaijan. In the mid-eighteenth century, Fath 'Ali Khan Afshar of Urmia subordinated to himself the khanates of Karadagh, Maragin, and Tabriz, but in 1761 was defeated by Karim Khan Zand, allied with Panah 'Ali Khan of Karabagh. In the later part of the century, Fath 'Ali Khan of Kuba succeeded in extending his control over a large part of northeast Azerbaijan, but his ambitions aimed even higher: he wanted to replicate the feat of the Safavids who had used Azerbaijan as a base for establishing their hegemony throughout Iran. His schemes came to grief in 1784, when Russian armies deployed in the Caucasus Mountains against Turkey threatened his rear. The Russians had become concerned that Kuba's expansion would create an undesirably strong power center in the region they regarded as their future sphere of influence, and Fath 'Ali Khan found himself forced to relinquish most of his conquests.[3]

Russia's interest in the Caucasus and the land beyond was longstanding and its roots were diverse. There was the lure of lucrative trade with Iran and Asiatic Turkey; the desire for local raw materials, notably silk, cotton, and copper; and the drive for colonization of sparsely populated regions. But the overriding attraction was the strategic value of the Transcaucasian isthmus. Russian military involvement in Transcaucasia dated back to the time of Peter the Great (1683–1725), whose abortive Persian Expedition of 1722 aimed at extending the Russian presence toward the Indian Ocean. Russia's southward drive resumed in a more extensive and sustained manner under Catherine II (1763–1796). After the seizure of the Crimea and the Kuban River territory in 1785, Russian administration was established in most of the Caucasus Mountains. By that time Russia had already begun to impose itself in Transcaucasian politics. Insecure on his throne, in 1783, the Georgian king of Kakheti-Kartli, Irakli II, was the first to sign a treaty accepting Russian protection. Another Georgian monarch, Solomon I of Imeretia, followed suit, as did Murtazali, the Daghestani ruler of Tarku. In due time, hegemony turned into outright conquest, beginning in 1801 when Tsar Alexander I (1800–1825) proclaimed the formation of the Georgian *guberniia* (province) consisting of the lands of the former Kakheti-Kartli kings. The new province also included the sultanates of Kazakh and Shamshadil, the first Azerbaijani territories to be joined to Russia.[4]

To secure a strategic hold on Georgia, the Russian commander-in-chief in the Caucasus, General Pavel Tsitsianov, in a classic exercise of the domino theory, deemed it necessary to extend his control over Azerbaijani khanates eastward to the Caspian coast and southward to the Araxes River. In carving out a part of Azerbaijan for Russia, his goals were primarily military; Tsitsianov was seeking the imposition of vassalage treaties on the khanates. In some cases—notably Karabagh, Sheki, and Shirvan—this acceptance occurred peacefully. The treaties left the khans unrestricted authority in the internal affairs of their states and guaranteed their rights of succession. In return, they had to admit Russian garrisons, to pay tribute—in cash or in kind, which invariably included silk—and most important, to surrender their rights to wage wars and conduct foreign policy. Tsitsianov applied armed persuasion toward those khans who were reluctant to peacefully accept his terms. In 1804 his forces laid siege to Ganja, where in a memorable show of resistance the khan, Javad, was killed in the battle. Javad's realm was immediately incorporated into Russia as the *uezd* (county) of Elizavetpol, a new name given to Ganja in honor of Tsar Alexander's wife. The prolonged fighting in the mountainous area of Jar-Belokan was another act of defiance to Tsitsianov's policy of intimidation. Tsitsianov himself paid with his life for the arrogance of personally bullying into submission Huseyin Qulu Khan of Baku, who had him killed during an audience in 1806. The Russian general's posthumous reward was that history recognized him as one of the chief architects of the conquest of Transcaucasia.[5]

By this time, Azerbaijani resistance to Russia had been strengthened by Iran's recovery from its long period of weakness and instability. With the ascension of the new dynasty of the Turkmen Qajar tribe, Iran experienced both a revival of centralizing policies and the willingness to contest Russia for sovereignty over what had been Iran's northern marches. Symbolizing this region's importance for the Qajars was their practice of appointing the kingdom's crown prince, Vali'ahd, as the viceroy of Azerbaijan. His place of residence was Tabriz, which now became virtually the second capital of Iran, and even diplomatic missions chose to set up their quarters in the city. The first to receive the title of the viceroy, in 1799, was Abbas Mirza, one of the 160 sons of Shah Fath 'Ali (1797–1834).

In 1804 Abbas Mirza, with reinforcements from the khans of Erivan and Nakhichevan, moved against the Russians, only to be defeated in the battle of Etchmiadzin. The Iranians reappeared in the spring of 1806, arousing insurrectionary fever in Karabagh and Sheki, two khanates that only recently had accepted Russian overlordship. The war went on for several years, although at a sluggish pace. The Russians faced intermittent rebellions and subjugated the khanates of Baku and Kuba in 1806, and Talysh in 1809. Only in 1812, having ended the concurrent war with Turkey, did they engage in vigorous fighting against Iran.[6] The brief and successful Russian campaign of 1812 was concluded with the Treaty of Gulistan, which was signed on October 12 of the following year. The treaty provided for the incorporation into the Russian Empire of vast tracts of Iranian territory, including Daghestan, Georgia with the Sheragel province, Imeretia, Guria, Mingrelia, and Abkhazia, as well as the khanates of Karabagh, Ganja, Sheki, Shirvan, Derbent, Kuba, Baku, and Talysh.

A special feature of the treaty was Russia's involvement in Iranian succession politics—by the commitment to help the heir to the throne appointed by the shah to retain his position in case of an attempt "from outside to deprive him thereof." Should discord occur among sons of the shah, Russia would refrain from intervening "until the shah himself requests it."[7]

The Turkmanchai Settlement

The Gulistan treaty proved to be merely the end of the first round in the two powers' contest for Transcaucasia. Thirteen years later, Shah Fath 'Ali ventured to challenge the Russian hold over the region and sent his army across the Gulistan Treaty frontier on the war that the Shi'te clergy proclaimed as the holy. In May 1826 the Iranians seized Lenkoran, Shemakha, and Nukha, and laid siege to the Russian garrison in Shusha. Abbas Mirza, again at the head of the army, marched into Russian-held Azerbaijan expecting wide support from a population disaffected with Russian domination as well as from the khans who felt humiliated as Russian vassals and exiled rulers whose rights the Qajars claimed to be championing.

In fact, the khan of Talysh at once mounted a rebellion against the Russian garrison, and in Karabagh, Shirvan, and Sheki the population welcomed the returning khans or their descendants.[8] Yet in Azerbaijan of that period, instances of natives fighting on the side of the Russians were not exceptional. Apart from the country's tradition, which for centuries had supplied recruits for the shah's elite forces, there surfaced a current of pro-Russian orientation among some bäys and aghas, who faced a choice between subjection to Russia and the ruthlessness of the Qajars. Chronically short of manpower in Transcaucasia, the Russians drew the natives into the ranks of their militias and auxiliary troops, even though they regarded the Christian Georgians as more reliable than the Muslims. Still, in the first war with Iran, units of native volunteers were formed; in the second war, one of these squadrons distinguished itself in the decisive battle of Ganja.[9]

After the Iranian defeat at Ganja, the newly appointed commander-in-chief of the Russian forces in the Caucasus, General Ivan Paskevich, soon brought the war to a victorious end when his troops seized Tabriz. The Russians did not intend to limit their conquest to the northern part of Azerbaijan and were bent on exploiting anti-Qajar sentiments all over the province. An Iranian chronicler recounts that in their advance the Russian armies were guided by some Tabrizis who "were angry with Abbas Mirza." A cleric, Mir Fattah, "seduced the inhabitants of Tabriz to obey the Russians" and, together with some notables, welcomed their entry and offered prayers for the prosperity of the tsar. Paskevich entrusted him with the government of the city.[10]

After the loss of Tabriz, Fath 'Ali sued for peace. The negotiations proceeded from Russia's position of strength, which was more overwhelming than during the negotiations for the 1813 Gulistan treaty. In contrast to 1813, the central issue was no longer Transcaucasia, but Azerbaijan, most of which already in the grip of Russian forces. On February 10, 1828, a treaty was signed in the village of Turkmanchai. Its chief architect was the playwright and Oriental-scholar-turned-diplomat Alexandr Griboedov.

Although the Treaty of Turkmanchai provided for the immediate transfer of only two khanates, Nakhichevan and Erivan, to Russian sovereignty, it stipulated also that Iran was to pay an indemnity of twenty million silver rubles. Failure to produce the amount within six months, the annexed protocol said, would result in all of Azerbaijan's passing under Russian rule. This likely prospect was staved off with the aid of the British, who, sufficiently alarmed by the Russian expansion, came up with a subsidy. As a result, the division of Azerbaijan went into effect.[11] The new frontier, for the most part, followed the Araxes River and split the territory of Arran from the historical core of Azerbaijan. The area populated by Azeris was divided into equal parts, but a larger proportion of the Azeri-speaking population remained in Iran. Unlike the Georgians, the Azeris did not have the benefits of territorial-ethnic unity, a fact that would be seen as an impediment for their evolution into a nation. The Treaty of Turkmanchai was concluded without hearing the voice of the Azeris, presumably of the khans. One day, the treaty would turn into the symbol of national bitterness, a black day of historical injustice in the eyes of the twentieth-century Azerbaijani national movement.[12]

The frontier across Azerbaijan was drawn for strategic reasons, with a view to facilitating Russian penetration of Iran and to outflanking Turkey. When Tsarist officials restored the southern half of Azerbaijan to the Shah's sovereignty, they might have done so with the conviction that not only this part but possibly most of Iran would in time fall under Russian rule or domination. Closing the period of the Russo-Iranian wars, the Turkmanchai settlement also established Russia as the chief geopolitical fact confronting Iran.

The treaty also had profound and long-range economic impact. The loss of the wealthy Caucasian provinces diminished the income of the Iranian treasury, and the Qajar regime tried to alleviate its chronic financial predicament by selling the crown lands (*khaliseh*) to the *mulkadars*, who often were rich town-dwellers willing to invest in land to maximize their profits. For the peasantry, now faced with higher rentals, the restructuring of land tenure led to drastic deterioration of their condition, and the increased burdens reduced many to the status of agricultural laborers. A mass of people searching for employment emerged, but their condition was not alleviated by the incipient industrial revolution. Iran, a buffer zone between the Russian and British empires, did not even experience the benefits of colonial, one-sided, industrialization.[13]

The plight of the rural masses had some parallel among a large part of the town population, mainly because of the capitulatory rights that guaranteed Russia preferential treatment for its exports, which were not competitive in European markets. By lowering the tariff barriers first for Russian and then for British products, Iran became flooded with cheap foreign imports, a process that ruined a large number of native craftspeople and merchants. Inhabitants of Tabriz felt particularly endangered, and popular discontent helped turn the city into a major center of religious factionalism in the 1840s. Among the groups that flourished in this decade, a strong support gained the religious-social movement of Babism, which expressed the restiveness of the economically suffering middle classes. Sayyid 'Ali Muhammad, the merchant-saint who proclaimed himself the *Bab* (gateway) to the Hidden Imam, the only true sovereign in the Shi'ite doctrine, called in his teachings for justice, along with such politically charged ideas as safeguarding of freedoms, defense of private property from taxation and confiscation by the government, and the rights of the provinces vis-à-vis the center. In 1848 Babism officially seceded from Islam, and among the disturbances caused by its growing militancy was the 1850 uprising in Zinjan, which held out against the forces of Shah Nasr ul-Din for a year. By 1852 the movement was ruthlessly suppressed following the execution of Sayyid 'Ali Muhammad in Tabriz.

Although Babism did not spread across the Araxes, the first academic treatment of the Babid phenomenon came from an Azeri-born scholar at Kazan University, Kazim Topchibashev.[14] The Babid upheaval did little to alter the ruinous pattern of foreign trade: between 1833 and 1847, Russian exports to Iran amounted to 250 million paper rubles, while Iranian exports to Russia only reached slightly more than a third of this amount, 90 million.[15] The importance of Iranian markets for Russia would increase dramatically with the industrialization that followed the Great Reforms of the 1860s.

While Iran as a whole suffered economic and social consequences of these capitulatory treaties, Tabriz was not in a state of unrelieved gloom. The city adapted itself to the role of an entrepôt for the influx of European products coming from the West via Trebizond or from Russia across the Araxes.

The bazaar of Tabriz deserves attention because of its extent and the number of its shops; "for a Persian bazaar it is fairly broad," wrote a Russian traveler at mid-century:

> The variety of goods available in it is hardly matched in any other Persian town except for Teheran; as for the quantity of goods, in this respect Tabriz has undoubtedly no rival in Persia. As regards commercial relations this town is an important center in Persia:

for the bigger half of the country it serves as the main fair and it is primarily from there that European goods received from Constantinople through Trebizond are distributed over Persia.[16]

Tabriz, through which passed a quarter of Iran's foreign trade, grew in population, despite outbreaks of cholera in 1866 and 1871. The city's merchant class enjoyed a measure of prosperity enhanced by steady contacts with the outside world and a level of educational progress higher than throughout the rest of Iran. Among its schools, Tabriz could boast of one run by American missionaries.

The construction, in the Russian-held territory, of the Batum-Baku railroad in the 1880s initially diverted Western merchandise from the Trebizond route, but this door was soon closed to imports of non-Russian origin. Although the link to the West via Turkey continued, the trade with Russia became dominant. Within a half a century of the Turkmanchai Treaty, the northern regions of Iran, and Azerbaijan in particular, were perceived as being in Russia's orbit, on the verge of inevitable absorption. Lord Curzon, a British observer with a keen sense of geopolitics, sharpened by the experience of the Great Game, the Anglo-Russian rivalry in Asia, expressed this view:

> Russia regards Persia as a power that may be temporarily tolerated, that may even require sometimes to be humored or caressed, but that in the long run is irretrievably doomed. She regards the future partitions of Persia as a prospect scarcely less certain of fulfillment than the achieved partitions of Poland. . . . It would be safe to assert that no Russian statesman or officer of the General Staff would pen a report upon Russian policy towards Persia and the future of that country that did not involve as a major premise the Russian annexation of the provinces of Azerbaijan, Gilan, Mazanderan, and Khorasan. . . . I do not doubt that the steps to be taken, in the event of war, disorder, or some equally favorable chance, for the realization of these ambitions have been authoritatively discussed and approved. Russia covets the splendid province of Azerbaijan for its 40,000 square miles of rich and varied country, its stalwart Turkish peasantry, the military aptitudes of its population, and its great commercial capital of Tabriz. Contiguous over a long stretch of frontier with her Transcaucasian dominions and within easy reach from her military capital, Tiflis, it could be invaded with ease and annexed without difficulty.[17]

In this description Lord Curzon was faithful to his opinion, which he expressed elsewhere, of the history of Russia as the state that never retreats. "She may say, 'J'y suis, j'y reste.' But neither can she stand still. . . . Ambition, policy, Nature itself, call her on: and she is powerless, even if she is willing to resist the appeal."[18]

The Conquest and Demographic Change

The Turkic-speaking Muslims of Russian-held Azerbaijan, commonly known as Shirvanis and sometimes even by the medieval name Arranis, differed from their ethnic siblings south of the Turkmanchai border in one essential respect: a large proportion belonged to the Sunni branch of Islam. The Russian estimates from the 1830s, although based on incomplete data, showed that the ratio of the Shi'ites to Sunnis was almost even, with a slight edge in favor of the latter.[19] While the sectarian distribution did not correspond with the territorial divisions of the khanates, the Sunnis tended to concentrate in the northern and western parts of the country, subject to religious influences from the mountainous citadel of Sunnism, the Caucasus.

The statistics of 1848 record still the same roughly fifty-fifty ratio, but the figures for the 1860s indicate that the proportion of the Sunnis had substantially declined. The ratio subsequently stabilized at the level by which the Shi'ites of the Jafarite rite held a clear majority of two to one among Azerbaijan's population north of the Araxes. The waning strength of the Sunni element was the effect of their migrations to Turkey; what began as a trickle turned into torrent after the final suppression by Russia of the armed struggle of the Caucasian mountaineers.[20]

The Shi'ite-Sunni split found its reflection in divergent Azeri attitudes toward the nineteenth-century Russian wars. The Tsardom was able to use Shi'ite volunteers against Turkey, not only in 1828–1829 but also in 1853–1855, and even against the anti-Russian *ghazavat* (crusade) in Daghestan headed by Shamil. By contrast the Sunnis showed restiveness at the time of Russo-Ottoman conflicts and tended to support Shamil, in some cases arms in hand. Many of them demonstrated their feelings by joining the outflow of the Muslim emigrants from Russia.

The conquest altered not only the sectarian but also the ethnic makeup of the population of Transcaucasia, a Russian possession that was conceived on lines that one day would be emulated by France in

Lebanon: a strategic foothold in the Middle East with the large proportion of Christians as the mainstay of the colonial rule. The outmigration of the Sunnis was offset by the reverse trend, the inflow of Russians, Germans, and the Armenians from Iran and Turkey, the last coming in the largest numbers. The Tsarist regime encouraged what, in effect, was a population exchange. In 1834 an imperial decree established the Armenian *oblast'* (district) comprising territories of the former Erivan and Nakhichvan khanates, an act which some saw as restoring to Armenians their ancient lands of Eastern Armenia. Recent research by George Bournutian confirms that

> prior to the Russian conquest the Armenians accounted for some 20 percent of the total population of Eastern Armenia, and the Muslims 80 percent; following the Russian annexation, 57,000 Armenian immigrants arrived from Persia and the Ottoman Empire and 35,000 Muslims emigrated from Eastern Armenia. By 1832, therefore, the Armenians formed ... half of the population.[21]

The Armenian immigrants settled down mainly on the crown lands, but in some cases displaced the Muslims by buying out their lands, a practice that held the potential for ethnic tension. Remarkably, relations between the two groups appeared for a long period to be free of major instances of violence. These Christian immigrants were not European settlers, but newcomers from the familiar Middle Eastern environment.

Another area of Armenian concentration where they had formed for centuries a substantial part of the population was Karabagh. The Russian figures from the 1830s put the number of Armenians at approximately 19,000, against 35,000 Muslims.[22] The Armenians inhabited the mountainous portion of the former khanate.

Reporting in 1845 on conditions in Karabagh, an army officer summarized Russian officialdom's view of the Armenians: appreciation for their economic attainment and political usefulness mixed with unmistakenly hostile prejudices:

> All Armenians live settled lives. . . . They are hardworking and well-to-do people; among those who dwell in towns not a few are rich, some possessing as much as 30,000 to 80,000 gold rubles. They have been able to achieve such prosperity only under the present period of Russian rule, whereas forty years ago they lived

in a state of abject destitution and were victims of abuse and robbery by the khans. Armenians are devoted to the Russian government and certainly will not betray us. They live peacefully and except for extremely rare cases do not take to banditry; only their passion for cheating, greed and all kinds of shady deals—vices common to all Armenians, are not foreign to those of Karabagh.[23]

The influx of the Armenians to Transcaucasia experienced major increases after each of the nineteenth-century Russo-Turkish wars: their population surged after the Crimean War of 1853–1856 and the 1876–1878 War. In addition, the mid-1890s massacre by Kurds under the Abdulhamid II (1876–1909) regime in Anatolia caused an influx of Armenians. By the turn of the century, the number of Armenians in Transcaucasia had reached 1,243,000.[24]

Colony or Province?

Still in the early stage of the conquest, in 1816, a Russian commander by the name of Marquise Philippe Paulucci penned down remarkably straightforward suggestions on how to deal with the peoples of the newly acquired lands beyond the Caucasus:

> 1. Refrain from anything that could weaken their perception of our power, the principal source of our strength in these regions.
> 2. Establish commercial relations so as to generate among them needs that they still do not feel.
> 3. Maintain continuous state of dissension among their diverse nations and never forget that their unity could be fatal for us.
> 4. Introduce among them the light of Christianity.
> 5. Absolutely prevent them from the possibility of links with Turkey and Persia.[25]

With the conquest of Transcaucasia, Russia became the first European power to extend its rule over a part of the Middle East. This part, situated on the rim of the Middle East and separated from Russia by a mountain range, was seen, by virtue of its geographical location, as a bridgehead for further expansion, rather than as a region to be closely integrated with the Russian state. In fact, use of the term *colony* in reference to Transcaucasia gained acceptance among Tsarist officials, who took as their model the French rule of Algeria. Finance Minister

T. K. Kankrin defined the meaning of the term and elaborated on its implications for the policy that he proposed to Nicholas I:

> When Transcaucasia is described as a colony, the assumption is made that the government would stop short of incorporating this region into the state outright. It is not expected that Transcaucasia would be made into a part of Russia or of the Russian nation in so far as its way of life is concerned; rather, these lands should be left in their position of Asiatic provinces, but hopefully governed more efficiently than in the past.[26]

His vision was to turn Transcaucasia into a "Russian East India."

Initially, the conquest made only minor changes to the region's traditional forms of government. Cases of outright abolition of the khanates, such as Ganja or Baku, were exceptional, and the tsardom preferred to adopt indigenous institutions to its purposes, inasmuch as the retention of a khanate's administrative machinery alleviated the shortage of Russian officials and promised financial savings. Only gradually did the commander of the Caucasus, General A. P. Ermolov, begin disposing of the khanate regimes altogether, seeing them as a disruptive and potentially pro-Iranian forces. He barred the rights of Ismail, successor to the khan of Sheki, and in 1818 proclaimed his domain a Russian oblast'. The next year, the khanate of Shirvan was abolished, and its ruler Mustafa, was forced to flee to Iran to avoid arrest on conspiracy charges. A similar stratagem was employed on the khan of Karabagh, Mahdi Qulu, and produced the same effect. The khanate of Talysh, on the other hand, continued to exist nominally until 1844, although it had passed under the military government in 1826, when its ruler had defected to the invading Iranians. Likewise, the khanate of Nakhichevan survived until this late date. A French diplomat, commenting on the khans taking refuge across the border, wrote: "Almost all the khans dispossessed by Russia are today on Persia's pay. . . . Persia keeps many pretenders, who will not fail to reclaim their ancient rights if the opportunity presents itself."[27]

The removal of a khan did not entail the end of the old ways in which the population had been ruled. During the 1820s seven Russian provinces were created—Baku, Derbent, Sheki, Karabagh, Shirvan, Talysh, and Kuba—each under a military *nachal'nik* (provincial commander), each one in essence a khanate without a khan. Their government, which was staffed by native officials, was based on local laws and customs. Persian was retained as the official language of the local administration, and justice was dispensed by the *shari'a* courts. The powers of the nachal'nik closely resembled those of a khan, though he had no right to pass death sentences or order corporal punishment.[28]

The situation bred rampant corruption and, combined with the notorious brutality of the military personnel, provided fertile ground for the popular unrest in the 1830s. The unsettled condition of the Russian domains in the Caucasus and beyond fueled a controversy within the Tsarist bureaucracy on the question of what should be the long-range administrative policy toward the region.

Of the two schools of thought that emerged, one, more pragmatic, favored quasi-autonomous regionalism, with implicit accommodation to indigenous traditions and interests, in keeping with Kankrin's definition of colonial status. The other emphasized the need for centralization, uniformity, and, ultimately, Russification. The two schools differed especially with regard to the Muslim parts of Transcaucasia. The first school counseled a gradual and slow dismantling of the remains of the khanate system, while the second school aimed to quickly abolish the extant khanates and to integrate their territories into the fabric of the Russian state.[29] The echoes of this debate would henceforth resound in every subsequent shift of Russia's Transcaucasian policies.

As an experiment in integration, the Baron P. V. Hahn reform of 1841 abolished the military government, obliterating all vestiges of the khanate system. In its place the system of division into uezds was introduced, their boundaries drawn without regard to the khanates' territories. The reform also abolished the residual tribalism of the mahals, superseding them with the smallest territorial units, *uchasteks*. This act, which ended the age-old fragmentation of Azerbaijan in one stroke, also led to a massive dismissal of native officials. Moreover, in the spirit of full integration with Russia, there followed an attempt at tampering with the economic structure: some of the *tül* holdings—land grants awarded to bäys and aghas—were to be confiscated, with the view of eventually redistributing them to Russian settlers.[30]

Within less than a year, the Hahn reforms were scuttled for going too far, and although the khanate system was not restored, the pendulum swung the opposite way. Another reorganization took place that resulted in the establishment of the viceroyalty of the Caucasus. In 1845, all military and civil responsibilities for the region passed from the central government to the Viceroy, who reported directly to the tsar. Count (later Prince) Mikhail S. Vorontsov received the appointment as first viceroy of the Caucasus.[31]

Vorontsov's preferred policy was co-optation of the native elites to Russification and integration. In Azerbaijan, where the impoverished bäys and aghas had seen their social status eroding, he favored, in effect, creation of a new elite by upgrading their legal status to the level of the Russian *dvorianie* (gentry). On Vorontsov's recommendation, Nicholas I issued the December Rescript of 1846, which formally bestowed hereditary and inalienable rights of the Muslim holders of the tül lands. A centuries-old institution, legal state ownership of most land, came to an end with the massive transfer of property titles into private hands.[32]

In addition to the December Rescript, the tsardom took steps to solidify its alliance with the newly created Muslim gentry by offering access to civil service careers to "all sons of bäys and aghas, who can present proof of noble birth." The government bureaucracy, after one more territorial reorganization in 1846, was able to absorb the subsequent influx of native employees. This time Transcaucasia was divided into four guberniias—Tiflis, Kutais, Shemakha, and Derbent—an arrangement that greatly increased the number of civil service vacancies.[33] For those who belonged to the "Muslim privileged estate," and who wished to acquire qualifications for civil service, the viceroyalty extended aid in the form of Caucasian Educational Grants. In this manner, the 1840s witnessed the rise of a native class of professional bureaucrats with a modicum of European education from Russian, or "Russo-Tatar," schools, a new element in the traditional society.[*]

Vorontsov's retirement in 1865 started the gradual reversal of his accommodating policies. While the period of the 1860s and 1870s was notable elsewhere for liberalization and decentralization, in Transcaucasia, it saw a transition toward the "organic merger" with Russia. In step with this new integrationist disposition there came a series of changes in territorial administration, with the effect that by 1867 the bulk of Azerbaijan was consolidated into two guberniias, Baku and Elizavetpol, which jointly came to be called Eastern Transcaucasia.[34]

---

[*]The term *Tatar* was used by Russians to refer to various Turkic-speaking peoples of the empire. As a misnomer with regard to the Azeris, it will be put hereafter in quotation marks.

Even though the organic merger was meant as a departure from the Kankrin-type colonialism, the logic of *divide et impera* prevailed in drawing the borders of the new guberniias. A large proportion of the "Tatars" remained outside of Eastern Transcaucasia, and its two provinces also included sizable minorities. According to 1871 figures, in the Elizavetpol guberniia, the relation of "Tatars" to the Armenians was 878,000 to 292,000. In the Baku guberniia, there were 465,000 "Tatars"; they were followed in population by the Russians (77,000), Caucasian Mountaineers (63,000), Armenians (52,000), Jews (8,000), and others (137,000). The Azeris found themselves included in the provinces outside Eastern Transcaucasia: in the four of five uezds of the Erivan guberniia, they accounted for 32 to 57 percent of the population. In 1883 the Muslim population of the guberniia amounted to 211,000 against 286,000 Armenians.[35] In the Tiflis guberniia, the proportion of the Azeris was smaller, 63,000 out of the population of 558,000.[36]

The familiar correlation between the tsardom's centralization policy and Russification reemerged in the 1860s. The same act that established the Elizavetpol guberniia did away with the division of uezds into uchasteks. The effect was a drastic reduction of native personnel at the lowest levels of bureaucracy, with most of the positions in territorial administration ending up in the hands of the Russians and Armenians. These kinds of changes reached their high point under Alexander III (1881–1894). Soon after acceding to the throne, the tsar denied the special status of Transcaucasia by replacing the office of viceroy with that of a simple governor-general, while at the same time restoring the authority of central government departments over the local affairs of the region.

For all the built-in pitfalls in Russian administrative reforms, it was also apparent that these reforms had enhanced the internal consolidation of Azerbaijan in at least two important respects: the dismantling of the khanates weakened deeply rooted local particularisms, and the formation of the two guberniias of Eastern Transcaucasia resulted in a territorial block that the "Shirvanis" or "Arranis" would regard as the core of their homeland. Even the term *Azerbaijan*, although seldom used for the territory north of Araxes, began to appear in the works of European scholars or journalists. Administrative integration was in turn reinforced by economic and social changes that came, albeit at a slower pace, in the wake of the conquest.

Oil Revolution and the World of Baku

Russia's conquest of the land north of the Araxes is regarded as a momentous event in several centuries of Azerbaijan's history inasmuch as it brought one part of its population under European rule and ushered them onto a path of historical development different from that of their compatriots who remained within Iran. Yet in the early nineteenth century, it was a case of one preindustrial society conquering another, and for half a century Russian changes remained limited to administrative reforms. The conquest's initial impact on the economy of Azerbaijan north of the border was on the whole slight; in some ways, it was retrogressive. Again, it was Kankrin who spelled out the guidelines for the Russian economic interests in the region. The land beyond the Caucasus, in his words, should remain "a colony producing the raw materials of a southern climate."[37] Until the mid-nineteenth century, Azerbaijan received almost no Russian investments. Meanwhile, despite the access to the Russian market, agricultural production in this land of southern climate remained stagnant, apparently because of the ineffectiveness of alien rule.

The military government neglected the vital task of maintaining irrigation works in the countryside. In the towns, even seemingly beneficial effects of the conquest, such as the termination of internecine warfare, had mixed economic impact. While some towns, such as Baku, Ganja, Shemakha, and Nukha, revived and grew to the size of ten thousand or more inhabitants, others, such as Shusha, Kuba, and Derbent, suffered a decline in population after 1830.

On the opposite side of the balance sheet, the conquest initiated or accelerated some developments of long-range significance. The transition to a money economy was stimulated by the requirement that peasants pay rentals in cash rather than in kind for land formerly leased from the khans and now from the Russian treasury. The break-up of the khanates gave impetus for economic integration of Russian-held Azerbaijan, a process that gained further momentum with the replacement of diverse local currencies by the ruble in the 1830s. Yet the Tsarist regime was in no hurry to do away with the old custom barriers crisscrossing the country, because it continued to derive income from tolls between the defunct khanates.

Not until the second half of the century, when the country had become sufficiently integrated with the Russian market, did the signs of economic vitality began to emerge. Even before the advent of the great oil boom of the 1870s, some advances were discernable in such export-oriented branches of the economy as cotton and tobacco growing, wine-making, copper mining, and carpet weaving. Yet even these advances did not materially alter the fact that the Azerbaijani economy was overwhelmingly agricultural, and that agriculture methods remained primitive.[38] The Agrarian Reform that went into effect in the Elizavetpol, Baku, and Erivan guberniias in 1870 did not unleash a torrent of social and economic transformations. In Eastern Transcaucasia close to 70 percent of the peasantry lived on lands the Russian crown had taken from the khanates and thus had been exempt from the obligations that the reform abolished. Otherwise, the peasants were allotted five *desiatins* per adult male (1 desiatin is equivalent to 2.7 acres), an amount of land so small that an average villager had to rent an additional one-third of the acreage from either the crown or the local landlord. Unlike in central Russia, the government did not extend credits to the peasants for purchasing their plots of land. As for the bäys and aghas, the great majority owned plots averaging 6.3 desiatins and lived an existence hardly distinguishable from their peasant neighbors, even though they continued to exercise their leadership through village assemblies and elective courts. Barely 4 percent of landlords possessed estates averaging 1,500 desiatins, from which was drawn the pool of land available for leasing. Overall, the Azerbaijani countryside remained unshaken in its tradition-bound way of life, and there was little social stratification and mobility.[39]

The progress of urbanization was slow, and by the end of the century 89 percent inhabitants of the Elizavetpol and 70 percent of inhabitants of the Baku guberniias, respectively, still lived in the countryside. The lower proportion of rural population in the latter province reflected the special case of the city of Baku, its size swollen by immigrants from outside Eastern Transcaucasia.[40]

While the degree of economic and social change throughout most of the century of the Russian rule was modest and its pace not markedly faster than south of the Araxes, the coming of the industrial age to the Russian-held part created essential differences between the two Azerbaijans. Even so, the scope of the changes was limited.

After a long period of stagnation, during which the extraction of crude oil hovered at a minuscule level, production began to gain momentum in 1859, with the building of the first kerosene refineries

in Baku. The turning point came as the result of the most consequen-
tial government act the Russian bureaucracy ever issued in Azerbaijan. In 1872 the practice of granting oil concessions on state lands was
changed to long-term leasing to the highest bidder. The door was
thrown open wide to native, Russian, and foreign investors, with substantial capital, and the readiness to engage in large-scale mechanized
production.

Within a year of the reform, the first successful drilling replaced
the old method of well-digging, and a spectacular gusher inaugurated
the ascent of Baku to the position of a major world oil producing center. "The time when the eastern part of Transcaucasia was regarded as
almost plague-infested had lasted long," reminisced the native writer
Hasan bäy Zardabi:

> Then, in the rocky fields around Baku oil fountains shot high up,
> and all watched with fascination these marvelous phenomena of
> nature. As the owners of the fountains were quickly piling up
> their millions, capitals and expertise began to flow in from every-
> where, what used to be in effect the place of administrative exile,
> now began to bubble with life.[41]

Among the foreign investors, foremost was the Nobel Brothers
Company, which would come to control more than half of the Baku oil
output. Their chief competitors became the Paris Rothschilds, who in
1883 completed the construction of the Batum-Baku railroad, a feat
that brought the oil to the Western markets.

As the Baku oil fields continued to throw up fountains, the
extraction and processing of oil grew on an unparalleled scale, with
Baku's 1898 output surpassing that of the United States.[42] But the
ways that the oil industry was allowed to operate soon began to claim
prohibitive costs, the perennial feature for all the period of the Russian rule. Chaotic or sloppy drilling and extraction led to decline in
productive capacity. In the long run the result was irreversible damage in the fields around the city, hastening exhaustion of resources,
and after 1905 Baku ceased to be a major factor in the world oil market.[43] All the same, the effects of this growth had led to virtually revolutionary transformations, albeit confined geographically to the
Baku oil belt. It generated employment for tens of thousands of nona-
gricultural workers, it produced such attributes of economic modernization as labor migrations and railroad and steamship transportation,

and it brought about the rise of an urban metropolis of Baku. The overall result of the "oil revolution" was a dichotomy not uncommon in a colonial situation: a generally traditional but lopsided economy, with a single rapidly growing industry based on mineral resources rather than on manufacturing, geared to external markets, owned largely by foreign investors, and operated by nonnative skilled labor. Typical also was the contrast between the city rising out of the industrialization and the countryside unshaken from its timeless pattern of existence.

Still a sleepy harbor on the Apsheron Peninsula at mid-century, in the 1870s Baku turned into bustling boom city with the highest rate of population increase in the Russian Empire. The number of inhabitants rose from 14,000 in 1863 to 206,000 in 1903, making it the largest city in Transcaucasia.[44] Commenting on its growth, an English visitor in the early twentieth century noted:

> Baku lies under the heavy disadvantage of having become "civilised" too quickly. In rough outline it is quite shapeless, though this is due in great measure to the peculiar formation of the Apsheron Peninsula on which it lies. Everywhere houses are packed together in squalor and deformity. With the exception of the Nikolaevskaia, with its magnificent golden-spired cathedral and quite respectable town hall, few of the streets are worthy of the name. Along this main thoroughfare there are mansions looking down on the sea. . . . Along the promenade are gardens and pavilions and avenues of electric light typical for our South Coast resorts of fashion. There is at least one first-class hotel—the Metropole—and several unutterable ones.[45]

Baku grew into a polyglot urban center in which no single ethnic element predominated. The three largest groups were the Russians, the Armenians, and the Muslims. The latter often held a plurality oscillating between 35 and 45 percent, although their statistical designation included the natives of Eastern Transcaucasia as well as the immigrants from northern Iran, Daghestan, and even the Volga region. Most of the Muslims retained close links to their villages and adjusted poorly to urban life. They accounted for more than half of the labor force in the oil industry, and their unskilled labor commanded correspondingly low pay. The better jobs, requiring skills or training, were held by Russians and Armenians.

This vibrant industrial metropolis was hardly a melting pot. Rather, in a manner typical for an immigrant city, ethnic communities lived their separate lives in distinct neighborhoods. The differences in their economic status accentuated the barriers of culture, religion, and language; naturally, there was a significant amount of intercommunal tension. Baku had developed in three concentric belts of population. The center, in which oil extraction and processing was banned, was inhabited by the wealthy: merchants, businessmen, and professionals, among whom few were Muslims. Surrounding the city proper were the industrial suburbs, Chernyi Gorod, Belyi Gorod, Zlykh, Akhmadly, and Kish, and the more distant oil field districts with the villages of Sabunchi, Bibi-Eibat, Ramany, Zabrat, and Balakhany. It was here, in the derrick-studded, pollution-darkened landscape, that the majority of the poorest and least educated inhabitants, mainly Muslim workers, lived in hastily built shantytowns.[46]

Remarkably, the advent of the industrial age in some ways strengthened the bonds with the part of the country south of the Araxes. The gravitational pull was stronger in one direction than the other. "Russian commercial and oil wealth attracted the people of Iran. They brought back money, chiefly, but also some knowledge," reminisced a prominent native of Tabriz, Hasan Taqizadeh.[47] The lure of higher wages drove workers from Tabriz province across the Araxes border. They accounted for a sizable proportion of the labor force in Eastern Transcaucasia—15 and 12 percent in the guberniias of Baku and Elizavetpol, respectively. Like most Muslim laborers, these immigrants were predominantly unskilled, and if employed seasonally, as was often the case, they would return home after their work had ended. Official statistics show that there was a significant amount of emigration across the Araxes: the Russian consulate in Tabriz issued 312,000 visas between 1891 and 1904. Historian Cosroe Chaqueri estimated that if one added the legal immigrants to the large number of illegal immigrants, 20 to 50 percent of males between the ages of 20 and 40 in the northern parts of Iran spent some time working over the Russian border, most in Transcaucasia, some in Central Asia.[48]

The contemporary writer Ahmäd bäy Aghayev (Agaoğlu) described the heavy transmigration in other terms: he recalled that in his youth the links between the two Azerbaijans were so close that whenever a new folk song, fable, or story (*dastan*) was born on one side of the border, it would soon be known on the other.

These poor fellows were employed in the heaviest jobs for little pay. It could be said that the prosperity displayed by Transcaucasian firms was the product of the toil of these miserables. At the railroads, factories, oil wells, streetcars' maintenance, at harvests in the heat of the summer, in such jobs as carrying heavy loads—they were always there. Patient, hard-working, enduring, and at the same time deprived of any protection, suffering all kinds of hardships so that they could earn a little money to help their families. But their despotic ruler would put guards at the frontier at the time of their crossing and would forcibly take away most of this money.[49]

Although the influx of immigrants from Tabriz province was large, their integration into Eastern Transcaucasian community was minimal. In Baku, the *hamshahris* from Iran, who lacked the vital benefits of extended family ties, lived in slums separated from their slightly better off northern compatriots.

With its multilingual population, urban sprawl, and fast pace, Baku was an alien enclave in Eastern Transcaucasia, but the city irresistibly drew the enterprising, the ambitious, and the educated from all over the country. Their concentration turned Baku not only into the virtual capital of Azerbaijan but also into the fountainhead of the rising native entrepreneurial class. The oil boom made it possible for some Muslims who had previously owned oil wells, kerosene refineries, or land in the Baku area to accumulate quick fortunes. In the initial stage of the industry's expansion, which lasted until 1872, they still controlled most oil-related enterprises. But even then, as the figures for 1870 indicate, although 88 percent of all wells were in the hands of the "Tatars," their small operations accounted for only half the oil output in Baku. As soon as the regulation on bidding for oil leases went into effect, Muslim entrepreneurs began to lose out to their nonnative competitors, not only to the big Russian and even bigger Western European companies but also to smaller Armenian investors.

In the 1872 auction the funds invested in the leases by the "Tatars" did not exceed 5 percent of the total, while the share taken by the Armenians was ten times as large. The position of the Armenian families—the Mirzoevs, Mailovs, Liazonovs, Aramiants, Tavetosyans, and Mantashyans—expanded over the years, and by 1900 they owned close to a third of industrial companies in the Baku guberniia, with only 18 percent belonging to the "Tatars." Small as this might appear, it was still sufficient for some—Taghiyev, Naghiyev, Asadullayev, Mukhtarov, and the Sultanov family—to accumulate great wealth.[50]

Even though the Muslims lost control of much of oil industry, and even though this situation repeated itself in activities such as wine making, fish processing, and tobacco growing, there were some areas where they retained their strength. The lucrative investments in Baku real estate, the simplest and safest use of capital under the boom conditions, remained largely in the Muslims' hands.[51] Similarly, Caspian Sea shipping was dominated by the "Tatars." They succeeded in building up for themselves a powerful position as the middlemen in Baku's growing trade with Iran in general and with Azerbaijan in particular, another link between the two parts of the country, enhanced greatly by kinship ties. Likewise, a few Muslim families controlled most of the silk spinning in Nukha, Karabagh, and Ordubad. Concentrated mainly in Baku, the native entrepreneurial class was numerically small— one estimate puts it at five hundred persons[52]—its growth impeded by colonial rule and foreign competition. Its political influence was limited by the restriction on the non-Christian representation to the Baku *Duma* (assembly) to one-third of the deputies. Only at the turn of the century did this restriction cease to be rigorously applied, and the proportion of Muslim deputies grew quickly to almost a half. By this time, the city duma, apart from native entrepreneurs, included also politically articulate professionals and intellectuals, among them the lawyer 'Ali bäy Topchibashev and the journalist Ahmäd bäy Aghayev.

Increasingly, the Azeri capitalists made their impact felt on the community's life outside of strictly business activity. In this respect, the figure of Zeynal 'Abdin Taghiyev stood out. A quintessential self-made man, Taghiyev was reputed to be the richest man in Transcaucasia. Starting with a small oil-bearing plot of land, he multiplied his fortune by investments in kerosene refining and branched out into extensive land and stock market speculations. With time he extended his interests beyond the oil industry: he founded the first cotton mill in Azerbaijan and invested in tobacco and cotton plantations. Although barely literate, Taghiyev financially supported a wide range of educational and philanthropic ventures, among them schools, scholarships, newspapers, and theater, in Azerbaijan as well as in other Muslim centers of Russia. The Araxes frontier was no obstacle to his philanthropy, and he financed the first modern high school in Tabriz, as well as the liberal

Persian-language newspaper in Calcutta, *Habl-i matin*.[53] At home, Taghiyev's backing benefited especially the endeavors of the native cultural revival. A pivotal force in this revival was the intelligentsia—another group that emerged from the changes taking place in traditional society.

TWO

From the Enlightenment Movement to Political Programs

The Rise of the Intelligentsia and the Azeri Literary Revival

While in some ways the two parts of Azerbaijan drew closer after the Russian conquest, in other respects they began to drift apart. A signal manifestation of the growing divergence was the rise of the intelligentsia north of the Araxes. A social force as well as a cultural phenomenon, it emerged from the contact of the two civilizations—the traditional Islamic and the comparatively modern European, as represented by Russia. The very term *intelligentsia* in the context of Azerbaijan's history carries a somewhat different meaning from that in European languages. In Russia, where the word gained wide currency, its classic definition was that of a group formed of individuals from various social classes and held together by ideas, not by a shared common profession or economic status. Indeed, intellectuals, with their inclination to skepticism, did not easily fit this description, though they were not excluded. In the languages of Muslim peoples in Russia on which the term was grafted, it also referred to those who had acquired the ways of the Infidel and therefore were no longer entirely a part of us. The intelligentsia was thus a foreign body issued from the fabric of the native community, and its traditionalist opponents criticized its members by such labels as assimilators and even renegades.

As a group, the intelligentsia shared a set of beliefs, attitudes, and opinions that made it a conduit for European ideas and, in time, the main agent of change within Azeri society. In striking disproportion to their numbers, they were destined to have an increasingly greater impact on the course of Azerbaijani history. Although the notion of the intelligentsia differed from that of intellectuals, it did imply some achievement in European-style education. Conversely, people with a background of traditional Islamic schooling, except those who accepted the reformist outlook, were not counted among the intelligentsia.

Initially, the Azeri intelligentsia was comprised of those few who had acquired a familiarity with the Russian environment, for the most part by way of military or civil service. Their numbers grew in the Vorontsov years, when access to government positions was thrown open to Transcaucasian Muslims. They usually had attended Russian military schools or the "Russo-Tatar" schools in existence since the 1830s. In the second half of the nineteenth century, when the civil service was largely purged of the native element, the intelligentsia came to be dominated by graduates of Russian universities and of the Transcaucasian teacher's seminaries in Gori and Tiflis. In fact, by the end of the century, schoolteachers, some of whom took to journalism or other literary endeavors, became one of the intelligentsia's largest professional components.[1]

The Azeri intelligentsia made its appearance around mid-century, soon after its Russian counterpart, on which it was closely modeled, to the extent that even the westernizers and *Narodniks* (populists) found their local equivalents. In a stroke of good fortune the intelligentsia produced in its early stages a man of intellectual brilliance and artistic accomplishment, who expressed the group's typical concerns for the future. Mirza Fath 'Ali Akhundzadä (Akhundov, 1812–1878), a translator in the Chancellery of the Viceroy of the Caucasus, gained fame primarily as the author of the first European-style plays in Azeri. The "Tatar Molière," as Vorontsov fondly called Akhundzadä, wrote a series of comedies between 1850 and 1855 that satirized the ills and flaws he saw in the contemporary society—all of which, in one way or another, were rooted in ignorance or superstition.[2]

While his play writing made him a pioneer of the theater in the Turkic-speaking world as well as in Iran, he was a tireless campaigner for the simplification of the Arabic alphabet, a reform he saw as "a medicine with the effect that the letters of this script dating back to the barbarian era would be written jointly, . . . that the letters would be distinguished one from another by their shape without recourse to the dots. Then, everyone in a short time and without much exertion would be able to read in his native language."[3] In his later writings—essays, articles, and the philosophical treatise *Three Letters of the Indian Prince Kamal al-Dovleh to His Friend the Iranian Prince Jalal al-Dovleh and*

Jalal al-Dovleh's Reply—Akhundzadä turned from gentle satire to aggressive social criticism. Akhundzadä's writings reflected the typical preoccupations of the nineteenth-century intelligentsia. First and foremost was the spread of learning, as the aspirations of the modernizers were still primarily those of an enlightenment movement. Linked to this movement were secularism and the Azeri literary revival.

In the case of Akhundzadä, secularism was an outgrowth of his agnostic proclivities, even though these were far from consistent. Above all, he regarded Islam's grip on all facets of life as an obstacle in the path of learning. Secularism became a distinguishing trait of many in the intelligentsia because of an even more compelling reason: they saw it as a means of blunting the edges of the Shi'a-Sunni strife and as a precondition for instilling the sense of community into the Muslims of Transcaucasia.

Because the Azeri literary revival stemmed from the need to communicate the ideas of the enlightenment to as many as possible in their own language, the issue touched on the emergence of a new group identity. Akhundzadä himself epitomized the contradictions inherent in the uncertain identity of the Azeris of his time. Even while being a Tsarist official of impeccable loyalty, he called himself "almost an Iranian." He felt closer to Iran than to any other country, and his philosophical writings reveal the intensity of his preoccupation with all things Iranian. He placed his hopes for essential transformations in what came to be known as the Qajar renewal, with its symbol the Shah Nasr al-Din (1848–1896), who enjoyed the reputation of being reformminded. With this in mind, Akhundzadä offered a statement of his views on the ideal of enlightened statecraft in Iran:

> The stability of kingship and the continuity of the dynasty go hand in hand with learning and the freeing of the people from superstitions. Having fulfilled this precondition, the Shah ought to set up Free Masonic Lodges and representative assemblies, and to effect concord with the people, so that he would be of one mind and heart with them. He should not regard the kingdom as his property, but rather see himself as the people's trustee. . . . He should act in accordance with the requirements of the law and have no right to a willful action. . . . The people, knowing his excellent qualities, will love him, and will pay no heed to anyone claiming his rights . . . mindful that the Shah has given them secu-

rity, public order, justice, and well-being. In such a way they will become patriots: in his name, they will sacrifice their lives and property for the country.[4]

In his glorification of the pre-Islamic greatness of Iran, before it was destroyed at the hands of the "hungry, naked, and savage Arabs," Akhundzadä was one of the forerunners of modern Iranian nationalism, and of its militant manifestations at that. Nor was he devoid of anti-Ottoman sentiments, and in the spirit of the age-long Iranian-Ottoman confrontation he ventured into historical writing on the victory of Shah Abbas I over the Turks at Baghdad. Akhundzadä is counted as one of the founders of modern Iranian literature, and his formative influence is visible in such major Persian-language writers as Malkum Khan, Mirza Agha Khan Kirmani, Zein ul-'Abdin Maraghai, and Mirza 'Abd ul-Rahim Talibof. All of them were the advocates of reforms in Iran.[5]

If Akhundzadä had no doubt that his spiritual homeland was Iran, Azerbaijan was the land where he grew up and whose language was his native tongue. His lyrical poetry was written in Persian, but his works that carry messages of social importance are written in the language of the people of his native land, which he called *Turki*. With no indication of a split personality, he combined larger Iranian identity with the Azerbaijani—he used the term *vatan* (fatherland) in reference to both—and in this "fatherland of fatherlands" frame of mind he became a major figure of the Turkic literary renaissance, a process that, ironically, would lead to the emancipation of Russian Azerbaijan from centuries-long Iranian cultural domination. The hold of Persian as the chief literary language would be broken, followed by the rejection of the classicist Azeri, a heavily Persianized idiom that had been in use along with Persian, though in a secondary position. De-Iranization found a measure of support from Russian officials anxious to neutralize the Azeris' identification with Iran. But their encouragement was neither wholehearted nor long-lasting. After the retirement of Vorontsov, this support was reduced to reluctant tolerance and would subsequently be replaced by attempts at linguistic Russification in the years of Alexander III's reign.

Meanwhile, the literary revival had come of age in the 1870s with the second generation of the intelligentsia. No longer a scattered number of individuals, they now formed a group of some cohesion. A disproportionately large number of this group was drawn from the Sunni minority, perhaps because of the less restrictive influence of the Sunni religious establishment. Also, the Sunnis were more receptive to the Azeri-Turkic revival, in view of their cultural gravitation toward Turkey. Among the intelligentsia, these affinities were reinforced by the attraction to the spirit of the *Tanzimat*, the period of Ottoman constitutional reforms then under way (1856–1876). From the Azeri perspective, Turkey, more than Iran, became an example of a Muslim country open to modernizing ideas, an image that was to persist ever after. Typically, for all his anti-Ottoman prejudices and his appreciation for Nasr ul-Din, Akhundzadä traveled to Istanbul in 1863, where he expected to find a "better climate" for changes such as his alphabet reform project.

The intelligentsia's prime concern became the building of communications through which to spread their ideas to the tradition-bound society, and the literary revival expressed itself in the new media of modern theater and the press. Akhundzadä believed that "the purpose of dramatic art is to improve people's morals" and that the theater was an appropriate vehicle for conveying a message to the largely illiterate public.[6] Yet only toward the end of his life were his plays shown on the native stage, through the efforts of a Baku *gymnasium* teacher named Hasan bäy Zardabi. In time these efforts resulted in the rise of the theater as an important cultural institution.[7]

Almost simultaneously with the rise of the theater came the birth of the Azeri press—also the fruit of Zardabi's endeavors. In 1875 he launched the Baku newspaper *Äkinchi* (Ploughman), the first Turkic-language press organ in Russia. In tune with the Narodnik views of its publisher, the heritage of his student years in Moscow, the *Äkinchi* was intended to promote the native *Volksgeist* embodied in the peasantry, but it ended up as a forum for the intelligentsia. Circulated also in Iran, where its Rasht correspondent, Hasan ul-Gavaid, was one of its chief contributors, the newspaper became the focus of controversies among the Azeris on both sides of the border. Characteristically, the issue of language was a chief source of the friction. Those literati whose language of expression was Persian reacted with hostility to Zardabi's use of the "unprintable idiom of the common folk." Others objected to his identification of the native Turki with Ottoman. Zardabi expressed his views on the language as follows: "It is true that Ottoman is not the same as our language, but the differences are not such as to need translations from one into the other. What is needed only is to read Ottoman books carefully, because that language contains many Arabic, Persian, and other nations' words, which makes it difficult to follow."[8] As the circle of the *Äkinchi* contributors included Sunnis, like Zardabi himself, their innuendos on fanaticism in Iran provoked indignation.

Furthermore, *Äkinchi* failed to elicit the same benevolent response from Tsarist officials that native writers of the previous generation had enjoyed. Zardabi was suspect because of his Narodnik views, and even more so for his pro-Ottoman sympathies. The authorities feared that the process of de-Iranization could lead to an even less desirable awakening of pro-Turkish sentiments among Azeris, and in the midst of the Russo-Ottoman War in 1877 *Äkinchi* was ordered to close down.[9]

Response to the Challenge of the West: Pan-Islamism and Turkism

While Zardabi marked the incipient articulation of Turkic identity in Azerbaijan, his position was still representative of a small minority, even among the intelligentsia, and it continued to be an unusual position well into the next generation. The Paris-educated Ahmäd bäy Aghayev in his writings of 1890s revealed identification with Iran and anti-Ottoman bias, noteworthy traits in a man who one day would become a prominent Turkish nationalist.[10] He referred to the Azeris as the *societé persane* and spoke harshly of those who, like Zardabi, had questioned this view in the past:

> Having completed their studies, they tried to spread among the peasants their nihilist ideas and non-Asiatic, European ambitions through the newspaper *Äkinchi*. The natives called them "good for nothing" or "lost men," appropriate descriptions considering their dissolute morals and the contempt these individuals showed for their country.[11]

That country was Iran under the "bold reformer, His Majesty the Shah," Nasr al-Din. A quarter-century after Akhundzadä, Aghayev still put hopes in the aging shah, who was soon to be assassinated by a more reform-minded intellectual, Agha Kirmani. In the Islamic renaissance that would be inspired by the impact of the West, Aghayev saw Iran playing a role comparable to France in Europe, but "Turkey, which has been making extraordinary efforts to regenerate itself, will not succeed because individualism is dead there."[12] At this stage,

Ahmäd bäy was still a devotee of the Pan-Islamic thinking that domi-nated the Azeri intelligentsia.

With its call for the unity of the world's Muslims in response to encroachments of the West, a cause that could claim a broad mass appeal, Pan-Islamism addressed itself to the collective consciousness of the *'umma*, the worldwide community of believers in Islam, regardless of their ethnic distinctions.[13]

Primarily a defensive reaction to pressures of the outside world, Pan-Islamism failed to develop into a uniform doctrine. There was, in actuality, more than one version of Pan-Islamism. The call for the world's Muslims to close ranks around the Ottoman sultan, who also used the title caliph, was in fact a foreign policy instrument of the Abdulhamid II regime. Yet its thrust was aimed at the Western pow-ers, a circumstance that helped Pan-Islamism to gain acceptance in Shi'ite Iran. Here the Qajar dynasty was increasingly blamed for sell-ing the country to the British and Russians, and popular protest, led by the *'ulama*, erupted in mass demonstrations against the Tobacco Monopoly in 1891–1892, the first instance of successful political mobi-lization in Iran.

Hajji Sayyid Jamal al-Afghani, an Iranian-born itinerant orator, journalist, teacher, and political activist, preached a liberal variety of Pan-Islamism. He believed in Islam's compatibility with reason, sci-ence, and technology and urged Muslims to adopt, albeit selectively, Western techniques and methods. Al-Afghani exhorted his coreligion-ists to rid their thoughts of dogmatism, superstition, fatalism, and pas-sivity and to overcome sectarian divisions. At the same time that he advised Muslims to use nationalism as a weapon against colonialism, he believed in eventual unification of all Islamic peoples under one rule, which would be constitutional and liberal rather than despotic, as was the Ottoman State. Young Azeris, such as Aghayev, found al-Afghani's brand of Pan-Islamism appealing and were especially drawn by the prospect of a Shi'ite-Sunni reconciliation in an ecumenical spirit of modernized Islam.[14] Furthermore, it made it easier for them to culti-vate the historical bond to Iran. With time, the voices from the north began to find echoes south of the Araxes River, and here too the last decade of the century witnessed the coming of a reform-minded gen-eration, even though educated in *maktabs* (primary schools) and *madrassas* (secondary schools) and often wearing clerical garb. As Taqizadeh reminisced:

Modern civilization came to Azerbaijan primarily from two sources: through knowledge of the Turkish language there were intellectual ties, first with Istanbul and Ottoman territories, and second with Russian territories, especially Transcaucasia and to a degree with Haji Tarkhan (Astrakhan) and Ashkabad.[15]

For many of his contemporaries the travel across the Araxes became a formative experience, and, increasingly, Tabriz reformists switched their sights from Istanbul to Baku, which was geographically, ecclesiastically, and linguistically closer. Among those inspired with new ideas by the sojourn in Transcaucasia was Hasan Rushdiyeh. With the help of Taghiyev's money, he established in Tabriz the first modernized, or *jadidist*, high school, which would become a model throughout Iran. Hasan Taqizadeh, together with Russian-educated brothers Mirza Muhammad 'Ali and Mirza 'Ali Muhammad Tarbiyat, founded in 1895 a literary circle. Its members extended their pursuits to founding another jadidist school, a periodical *Gangina-yi funun* (Treasury of Knowledge), and a library-bookstore that doubled as a meeting place for political activists. In the early 1900s these activists began to coalesce into secret or semi-secret groups devoted to constitutional and reformist goals.[16] Generally, the intellectual movement in Iranian Azerbaijan differed from its equivalent north of the Araxes in two major ways: its language of expression continued to be Persian and therefore it appeared as a part of the assimilationist process of Persianization. Second, it was comparatively devoid of secularism; in fact it remained under the influence of the Shi'ite clergy, a factor that contributed to its strongly Pan-Islamic bent.

Pan-Turkism found its parallel in other "Pan" movements of the age, its name evoking the models of Pan-Germanism and in particular Pan-Slavism. The new movement had its roots in nineteenth-century European turcology and in the writings of such authors as Arminius Vambery. In the Russian state, it initially spread with the efforts of the Crimean "Tatar" Ismail Gasprinskii (Gaspirali), who in his newspaper *Tarjuman* (Interpreter), published in 1883 in Bakhchisaray, again with support from Taghiyev, preached the unity of all Turkic peoples within the empire. He was careful to emphasize his loyalty to Russia, a generous and civilized nation that was bringing progress to the Muslims under its rule, unlike selfish and conceited Britain. At the same time, he was alert to the dangers inherent in policies of Russification, especially those inspired by Pan-Slavism. Largely in response to Pan-Slavism, Gasprinskii presented defensive programs for the unity of the Turkic peoples within the Russian Empire, Turkism and Pan-Turkism. The first term conveyed concern with the ethnic identity of Turkic-speaking peoples; the second expressed its striving for their cooperation and solidarity. Pan-Turkism and Pan-Islamism were not mutually exclusive, as Islam was the common religion for almost all Turkic peoples. Some Pan-Turkists considered themselves also Pan-Islamists and easily overlooked the potential contradictions between the two ideologies. The roots of Pan-Turkism lay in the ethnic and linguistic awareness of a particular group of peoples, and those of Pan-Islamism in their purely religious identity. While Gasprinskii spoke of one great nation (*qavm*) of all the Turks, he stopped short of calling for political action. It would have been an unrealistic proposition in any case, given the repressive climate of the period.[17]

The Turkic unity he preached had spiritual, linguistic, and cultural qualities, expressed in the famous slogan: *Unity of language, thought, and work*. The first step toward this goal would be the creation of a literary idiom that served all Turks, from the Balkans to the Great Wall of China. Such a language was in fact forged in the columns of the *Tarjuman*. It was based on the Turkish of Istanbul, that is, Ottoman, though purged of excessive Arabic and Persian elements and written in simplified syntax. Apart from the *Tarjuman*, the common idiom was promoted in the curricula of an expanding network of jadidist Muslim schools. The writing in this idiom was understood by the educated in most of the Turkic lands, but for the average reader it was easily intelligible only among the Oghuz Turks of the Crimea and Azerbaijan. The Volga "Tatars" understood it with some effort, while most eastern and northern Turks found it difficult to comprehend without special study. Even in Azerbaijan, the Ottomanization effort was criticized as leading to artificiality, yet the trend surfaced in the post-*Äkinchi* Azeri press. Linguistic Ottomanization was noticeable in all the magazines of the period, the small-circulation and short-lived *Ziya* (Aurora, 1879–1881), *Ziya-i Kafkasiyyä* (Aurora of the Caucasus, 1881–1884), and *Käshkül* (Darwish bowl, 1884–1891).[18] The writers for these publications consciously moved away from the native vernacular and initiated a process that eventually would be regarded as a setback for the development of a native literary idiom.

All the same, the rise of Turkism, rather than of Pan-Turkism, stimulated the Azeris' search for self-awareness. The most sophisticated of post-*Äkinchi* journals, *Käshkül* was the first to draw a clear distinction between the notions of a local religious community and a nationality, both of which continued to be called *millät*. *Käshkül* ridiculed those who, in answer to the question "What is your nationality," would respond "I am a Muslim." Going a long step further, the newspaper proposed the use of the term *Azerbaijani Turks* for the people on the both sides of the Araxes. "Separately we are *bi-janli*" (a play on words in which this distorted form of "Azerbaijani" means "soulless"[19]).

This type of literary approach to the budding national consciousness, the sense of Turkishness blended with the Azeri identity, signaled that the intelligentsia who began their public lives in the last decade of the century were fundamentally different from their forebears: they had begun to become politically inspired.

One of the first Muslims of Russia to make the transition from educational and cultural Pan-Turkism to political action was an Azeri, 'Ali bäy Huseynzadä. Like Gasprinskii, Huseynzadä became acquainted with Pan-Slavism and was impressed with its threatening dynamism. In 1889 he left his medical studies in St. Petersburg and set out for Istanbul to spread the idea of one Turkic nation.[20]

Because the Ottomans were still strangers to Pan-Turkism, it was the task of immigrants from Russia to work for their conversion. Such missionary pursuits went against the grain of the official state doctrine, Ottomanism, which, by proclaiming the unity and equality of all the subjects of Turkey, downgraded their ethnic distinctions. The absolutist Sultan Abdulhamid II (1876–1909) was suspicious of any manifestations of nationalism, Turkish included, regarding them as disruptive for the state. In Istanbul, Huseynzadä addressed his efforts to those who were disaffected with the regime by becoming one of the founders of the underground opposition group *Ittihad-i Osmaniyye* (Ottoman union), from which the latter-day Young Turkish movement was to evolve. Yet at this stage even Abdulhamid's opponents could not shed their Ottomanism. He was somewhat more successful in influencing a handful of intellectuals through his writings, which he published under the pseudonym *Turan* (Land of Turks), after the title of one of his poems. Among those indebted to him was the future Ottoman prophet of Turkism, Ziya Gökalp, who acknowledged 'Ali bäy as one of his most important teachers.[21] Even so, Huseynzadä had little reason to be satisfied with the reception of his ideas in Turkey under Abdul-hamid, and when with the 1905 Russian Revolution more promising circumstances suddenly arose in Baku, he hurried home and became a moving spirit of the daily newspaper *Hayat* (Life). The paper was inaugurated with a statement that synthesized Azeri political thinking at this juncture:

> As Muslims and subjects of Russia we want progress within the framework of economic and political conditions of the Russian state. As Muslims we desire the progress for all our coreligionists and with all our heart wish for their well-being in any corner of the world. We are also Turks, and that's why we wish progress, flourishing, and happiness for all Turks anywhere.[22]

In the pages of the same newspaper, Huseynzadä spelled out what would later be a famous slogan: *"Turkläshtirmak, Islamlashtirmak, Avrupalashtirmak"* (Turkify, Islamicize, Europeanize). Subsequently adopted and slightly modified by Ziya Gökalp, this slogan became the battle cry of Turkism in the Ottoman State. In Azerbaijan, one day these three words would be symbolized in the tricolor flag of the independent republic.

Ideological Adaptation: Azeri Liberalism and Socialism

Among the rising ideological currents, liberalism and socialism had a more European frame of reference than did Pan-Islamism or Turkism. Azeri liberals viewed themselves as part of a broadly defined Russian liberal movement, whose goals were expansion of local self-government and gradual reforms leading to the establishment of a constitutional regime. The nucleus of Azeri liberalism was in the Muslim representatives in the Baku Duma, which consisted largely of merchants and industrialists. Outside of this municipal assembly, they made their voice heard through the newspaper *Kaspiy*, a highly successful experiment in adopting a Russian press organ for the purposes of the native elite. The use of the Russian-language publication was in keeping with the views of much of the intelligentsia, whose leading figures, beginning with Akhundzadä, were on record as having long called for learning Russian as a way of overcoming their countrymen's insulation from the non-Muslim world.

The owner of *Kaspiy* was Taghiyev, and its editor-in-chief 'Ali Mardan bäy Topchibashev, a lawyer with close links to Russian liberals. In the 1905 Russian Revolution, the Azeri liberals allied themselves closely with the local Russian *Kadet* (Constitutional-Democrat) Party, and from their ranks came almost all the native deputies to the First (1906) and Second (1906–1907) State Duma. In the Russian parliament, the deputies from Eastern Transcaucasia joined with other Muslim representatives to form the *Ittifaq* (Union) parliamentary group.[23]

As much as the liberals were linked with the *Kadets*, the Azeri socialists were affiliated to the Baku chapter of the Russian Social Democratic Workers Party (RSDWP), although the relationship was never clearly defined. A handful of the native members and sympathizers of the RSDWP formed in 1904 the first Azerbaijani political association, *Himmät* (Endeavor), a name derived from its clandestine newspaper. Among its founders were Sultan Mäjid Äfandiyev and Mämmad Hasan Hajinskii. Mämmad Ämin Räsulzadä, later one of the leading figures of twentieth-century Azerbaijani history, also began his public life in the ranks of the Himmät. As he reminisced many years later, the association consisted of the young Muslims studying in Russian secondary schools. "We tried to awake in the members of our organization national feelings, studied the native language and literature, read the works of our poets condemning the Tsardom and distributed among workers tracts with revolutionary and national contents."[24]

With the outbreak of the Russian Revolution in January 1905, the Himmät's following grew rapidly as the Muslim proletariat proved to be receptive to the socialist slogans used by their coreligionists, the more so because the attacks on the autocracy and capitalism could be understood as aimed at the Infidel. Early that same year, two capable organizers joined the Himmät, strengthening its leadership. Both members of the RSDWP, they were Mäshadi Äzizbäkov, an engineer turned professional revolutionary, and Nariman Narimanov, a man of diverse talents, known as a journalist, playwright, and educator, and recently engaged in medical studies with support from Taghiyev.[25]

The Himmät organized strikes and mass meetings and incited agitation among workers, including immigrants from Iran. Yet for all the personal links with the RSDWP, it did not evolve into a closely knit, centralized structure on the Bolshevik model. Rather, it remained a loose association of individuals inclined toward radicalism, but concerned less with doctrine than with action.[26] As the Russian Revolution gained momentum, socialist agitation was overshadowed by the eruption of ethnic violence, which was intertwined with social grievances.

THREE

The Age of Revolutions and Political Awakening

Ethnic Violence and Political Mobilization

As the 1905 Russian Revolution unfolded, and the nonnative population of Baku was infected with revolutionary fever, the Muslims remained conspicuously inactive, as though insulated by cultural and psychological barriers from the turmoil of the Infidel's world. Yet they were soon to be shaken from their passivity by an outbreak of inter-communal violence that was so extensive that it became known as the Tatar-Armenian War. Antagonism between the two ethnic groups, which had been growing over a long period, now transcended cultural and religious differences. Similar differences existed between the Azeris and Georgians, but there was no antagonism between them: the two peoples did not view each other as a threat. "The Armenians have two points in common with Jews," wrote a Western diplomat from Transcaucasia. "These are their extreme dispersion and their general superiority in education, industry, and enterprise over the population among whom they live and this has made them both weak and strong. They have been disliked and feared by their neighbors, and are defenseless against their attack."[1] This opinion clearly expresses a Eurocentric view; observers with a Middle Eastern perspective have been inclined to notice greater similarities with the Maronites or Copts. Like other Christian minorities in the Middle East, the Armenians developed a special relationship with a European power, in the given case with Russia.

The Armenians' association with Russia turned into one of the most fateful alliances in history, even though Russia did not lack generosity toward the Armenians, who clearly enjoyed preferential treatment among the peoples of Transcaucasia. The alliance was based as much on religious affinity as on long-range political calculations—restoration of Armenia in some form, at the expense of Turkey. The alliance, however, was flawed by its great imbalance between the power of Russia and that of Armenian nationalism. Russia's far-flung interests and commitments often did not coincide with Armenian aspirations, and during times of trial Russia was unwilling, unable, or just too distant to come to the aid of its small ally. At the same time, the friendship with Russia helped poison the Armenians' vital coexistence with Turkey, whose territory most of them inhabited.

Meanwhile, in Transcaucasia, Muslim-Armenian antagonism had developed into a complex, multifaceted problem. Most historians agree that apart from the perception of the Armenians as a privileged group under the Russian rule, there were economic and social factors at play. For example, the fledgling Muslim bourgeoisie was hard-pressed by Armenian competition. Moreover, there were conflicts of interest between unskilled "Tatar" laborers and Armenian entrepreneurs and merchants, and the animosity of the predominantly rural Muslims toward the more urbanized Armenians. These interpretations, in the view of one author,

> do not recognize the areas of Azerbaijani strength. In fact, public disorder conflicted with the substantial commercial and civic interests of the Azerbaijani Turkish upper classes. . . . The root of conflict must be sought in historical differences manipulated over decades by Tsarist colonial policies meant to incite jealousy, perhaps even violence, as a means of control. . . . Both communities wished to alter the status quo but in different ways. The Azerbaijanis wanted to alter it at the Russian expense; the Armenians, at the Azerbaijanis[' expense].[2]

The differences in social structure were most obvious in the degree to which each community was politically organized. Unlike the Muslims, the Armenians had produced a dynamic nationalist movement spearheaded by the Armenian Revolutionary Federation, the *Dashnaktsutiun*.

The Dashnaktsutiun's avowed objective was the creation of a free and autonomous Armenian state in the Ottoman provinces of Eastern Anatolia, and the group saw its enemy in Abdulhamidian Turkey, not in Russia. Yet in the 1890s Armenian nationalism found itself on a collision course with the Tsardom, in a dramatic reversal of the friendship with Russia. The immediate reason was the Russian assimilationist drive that led to closing Armenian schools and put pressure on the Gregorian Church to join the Orthodoxy. Against this backdrop even more essential causes were discernible. The Armenian national movement, though aimed at Turkey, was nonetheless revolutionary, and the Dashnaktsutiun professed commitment to the especially explosive mixture of nationalism and socialism; meanwhile the tsardom was passing through one of its most reactionary phases. Moreover, the Russian government did not contemplate renewing its expansion into the Middle East in the foreseeable future, a circumstance that diminished the value of an Armenian ally. The failure to intervene in defense of the Armenians during the 1894 massacres by the Kurds in Anatolia was a sufficient indication of the Russian disposition.

The culminating stage in the Russo-Armenian confrontation came in 1903 with the confiscation of the properties of the Gregorian Church at the order of the governor-general of the Caucasus, Prince Gregorii Golitsyn.[3] Armenian reactions included terrorist attempts on the lives of Tsarist dignitaries, among them Golitsyn. By this time the Russian authorities had already made a series of gestures calculated to win over the Muslims.

While there is no doubt that Russian officialdom tried to use ethnic antagonism for the regime's benefit, no firm proof exists that they engineered mass violence; sufficient hostility had developed between the two peoples to set off the explosion without external prodding.

The intercommunal violence broke out first in Baku, on February 6, 1905. Clashes continued in successive waves well into the next year, spreading to the other parts of Transcaucasia having closely mixed Muslim and Armenian populations. Although many instances of indiscriminate killings occurred, the term *Tatar-Armenian War* aptly describes the nature of the conflict.[4] While the world press gave extensive and pro-Armenian coverage of the events, there was no resemblance to the Anatolian massacres of the past decade. Writing with the benefit of historical perspective, an Armenian author stated: "The Tatars, though numerically superior to the Armenians, and having the sympathetic support of the Tsar, were not a match for the superior and organization and leadership of the Dashnaktsutiun. . . . Though the years 1903–1905 were among the bloodiest in Armenian history, they resulted in unqualified Armenian victory."[5]

The clashes were not confined to the towns, and, according to an Armenian estimate, 128 Armenian and 158 Muslim villages were destroyed or pillaged.[6] The rugged, mountainous countryside of Nagorno-Karabagh was the major center of the fighting. This area of the Elizavetpol guberniia, with its slopes, rivers, and valleys that opened toward the east, which once had been part of the Karabagh khanate, was traditionally an area of seasonal coexistence for Armenian farmers and seminomadic pastoralist Muslims who brought their flocks to the mountain meadows each summer.

The overall estimates of lives lost vary widely, ranging from 3,100 to 10,000. All the data available suggest that the Muslims suffered higher losses than did the Armenians, confirming the truth that the more modernized the society, the more effective its fighting force. More than any other event in this revolutionary period, the blows from the *Dashnakist* armed squads were the catalyst for consolidating the Muslim community of Transcaucasia. The Tatar-Armenian War generated Muslim unity for a cause that transcended local or sectarian loyalties, and henceforth such divisions ceased to be a serious impediment to political action. The impulse to draw together also reached across the Araxes, where solidarity with the "Caucasians" was reinforced by the fact that among the victims of the fighting were immigrants from Iran. It was feared that anti-Armenian violence could spread to Tabriz even though the Armenians did not represent nearly as great a threat to the native interest groups. In the end the violence did not occur, largely because of the political acumen of the Armenian leaders in Tabriz. "They declared themselves Iranians and expressed disgust at the behavior of their people in the cities of the Caucasus," noted Ahmad Kasravi, a historian who was also a witness to the epoch.[7]

In response to the superior effectiveness of the Dashnakist forces, various Azeri groups hitherto engaged in chaotic fighting began to coordinate their efforts, and in time the intelligentsia became involved. In the fall of 1905 a clandestine political association under the name *Difai* (Defense) sprang up in Ganja. The initiative came from some local notables who thereby started careers in politics: Shafi Rustambäkov, the brothers Alakpär and Khalil Khasmammädov, Ismail Ziyatkhanov, Nasib Ussubakov (Yusufbayli), and Hasan Aghazadä. From Baku they were joined by Ahmäd Aghayev.

Remarkably, the leaders of the Difai tried to blunt the edge of ethnic strife. Aghayev publicly condemned the violence committed by

Muslims, and Ziyatkhanov, speaking in the State Duma, pointed an accusing finger at the government. There are indications that some prominent members of Difai maintained contacts with their opposite numbers in the Dashnaksutiun, and both organizations had links to the liberal wing of the Young Turkish movement. The main enemy in the eyes of the Ganja group was the devious and zigzagging Russian policy. Following the spring 1905 appointment of I. I. Vorontsov-Dashkov to the restored position of the viceroy of the Caucasus, the Tsarist bureaucracy took an increasingly pro-Armenian stand. Vorontsov-Dashkov considered the Armenians as a people attached to property, family, and religion, and as such natural supporters of law and stability. Moreover, he was a proponent of a new war with Turkey in which he saw the Armenians resuming their role of Russia's advance guard.

In its proclamations, the Difai blamed Russia for the recent bloodshed, but it warned the Armenians that violence on their part would be answered by force. The Difai sponsored the organization of Muslim fighting squads, most notably a group of 400 fighters in Shusha, the site of some of the war's most violent clashes. Members of the party were engaged in acts of individual terror, mainly against Tsarist officials, police, and military personnel suspected of encouraging the Armenians. A product of the Tatar-Armenian War, this protonationalist Azeri organization broke the long spell of passive acquiescence to Russian rule.[8]

While one of the landmarks of the 1905 Revolution was the intelligentsia's assumption of the Transcaucasian Muslim community's leadership, this momentous development occurred somewhat by default: no other group was capable of filling the needs of the moment. No other sector of society was able to produce election candidates, publish newspapers, organize meetings, write petitions, or deliver parliamentary speeches. Even though the intelligentsia, the first to develop idea of an Azerbaijani statehood, proved to be quite adept in these tasks, they did not enjoy active endorsement by the population. In fact, the prevailing attitude of the masses was one of passivity and indifference, a cause of unending frustration for the intelligentsia. One of its luminaries, Uzeir bäy Hajibäkov, vented this feeling in "An Open Letter to the Caucasian Muslims":

> Russians, Armenians, Georgians, and Poles all try to elect and send to the Duma their best representatives. But you, Muslims,

do not so much as give a thought to it. It does not befit you to join
the Russians and Armenians in getting deputies ready for the
Duma. What is there in common between you and the Duma?
The Duma—that's something born of the Russians, and you,
thanks to God, are Muslims. That's why you have no business
associating yourself with the Russians and Armenians, who only
want to invent new tricks—you'd better take care of your own
affairs. You do not give a second look to the Russians and Armenians; they are shameless, impudent breeds, who bathe naked in
the *hamam*, who do not respect old age. And now they want to set
up the Duma. . . . This is not your concern, let them do what they
want.[9]

The Two Azerbaijans and the Constitutional Revolution in Iran

While Transcaucasian Muslims largely viewed the changes in
Russia with indifference bred of alienation, the upheavals that followed soon afterward in Iran and then in Turkey became for them a
matters of intense concern. These two revolutions across the border
were taking place in the context of cultures and societies with which
they were able to identify more closely.

The Russian Revolution of 1905 left its imprint on Iran in two different ways. On one hand, it temporarily restricted tsardom's capacity
for military intervention abroad; on the other hand, it provided Iranians
with an example that encouraged them to launch their own reforms.
Pressure for change had been mounting for many years under the Qajar
regime, which had failed to develop on the lines of Akhundzadä's advisory. Instead, its hallmarks became stagnation, oppression, and corruption. At the same time, Britain and Russia, competing for economic concessions from Iran, gradually reduced the country to semicolonial status.

The crisis in Iran came to a head in December 1905, when the
Russian Revolution had already crested. A long series of disturbances,
including the *bast*, an act of taking sanctuary, in this case on the
grounds of the British legation, forced the Shah, Muzaffar al-Din
(1896–1907), to yield to popular demands, much as Nicholas II had to
do in Russia: on August 5, 1906, he signed a law proclaiming a constitution under which the *Majlis* (parliament) was to be elected on the
basis of a restricted franchise that benefited primarily the interests of
the clergy and the bazaar merchants. The constitution included the

provision that made Persian the official language, an acknowledgement of the historical rivalry of Persian and Turkic elements and a departure from the long tradition of their symbiosis in Iran.

The concessions granted to some groups led to the call for broadening of reforms, and those who intended to carry the revolution further began to organize. There sprang up the associations known as *anjumans*, a term describing people's councils and political clubs, as well as fighting organizations such as the republican-minded *fida'iyan* (self-sacrificers) and of the militant Islamic *mujtahid*, all of which grew particularly strong in Tabriz.[10]

Although the constitutional movement had started in Teheran, its principal stronghold soon became Tabriz, which was the second city of Iran and in many ways rivaled the capital. When the Majlis met, the twelve-member Tabriz delegation headed by Hasan Taqizadeh formed the core of the liberal parliamentary group. Another contributing factor in Tabriz's political importance was its proximity to revolutionized Russia, in particular to the other Azerbaijan. From the Russian Azerbaijani perspective, there were two meanings to the term *Iran*: one referred to a large, multilingual kingdom to which they were linked by religion, cultural heritage, and—until the nineteenth century—common history. The other, narrower meaning connoted Iranian Azerbaijan, the land of common language and closest ethnic kinship. The Iranian constitutional revolution brought a new dimension to the links between the two Azerbaijans: the political cooperation between those who opposed the status quo in their respective states on both sides of the border. This cooperation found a stimulus in the incipient, seldom-articulated sense of Pan-Azerbaijanism, the notion of solidarity and unity of the divided land. It was primarily a spontaneous phenomenon, rather than a program of political action, and would henceforth continue to resurface at various junctures of history as a constant, if subdued, feature of Azerbaijani politics.

The feelings surrounding Pan-Azerbaijanism could coexist with the sense of Iranian identity. Hasan Taqizadeh, who visited Baku at that time, recalls that "the Muslims of the Caucasus considered themselves quite as Iranians . . . since the Ottoman influence had not yet advanced into areas of Shi'a population."[11] The channels of communication between the two Azerbaijans, each in the grip of turmoil, were numerous. In Baku the mass of the immigrants from Iran became a special concern for the Himmät; in their poverty and alienation they not only accepted the lowest wages, but they shunned labor unions and strikes, allowing themselves to be used as scabs. There was an urgent need to integrate them into the common front, and in 1906 Narimanov set up the first organization of Iranian workers under the name *Ejtima-i Amiyyun* (Social democracy), beginning the tradition of close, organic ties between the workers' movements in both Azerbaijans. Any member of Himmät could belong to *Ejtima-i Amiyyun*, and Äzizbäkov sat on the Iranian organization's Central Committee, which resided in Baku. *Ejtima-i Amiyyun* soon branched out to Tabriz, where its local executive body headed by 'Ali "Musyo" became known as the Secret Center. In the same year, Narimanov founded in Tiflis a secret committee in charge of supplying the Tabriz revolutionaries with contraband arms, ammunition, and printed matter.[12]

The fate of the Iranian revolution was not the concern of the socialists alone, and support was forthcoming from other quarters and in different forms. In the words of a Baku scholar, the literary output in Russian Azerbaijan that dealt with the upheaval on the other side of the Araxes would fill more than ten volumes.[13] Intellectual contacts were extensive, and the Baku newspapers that circulated in Tabriz province were instrumental there in stimulating interest in the Russian transformations. Once the crisis in Iran was under way, the Baku press, which reacted to the Russian Revolution with bewildered reserve, seemed to be more aroused by what was happening across the Iranian border. "The people of the Caucasus did not stint in their support and enthusiasm," wrote Kasravi, "and as we have said, the newspapers there, such as *Irshad*, published by Ahmäd bäy Aghayev, *Tazä Hayat*, by Hashim bäy, *Molla Nasr al-Din*, by Mirza Jalil (Mammad Quluzadä), and several others valued the Iranian movement, and would write about whatever happened in Iran and discuss it. So these papers had many readers in Iran, particularly in Azerbaijan."[14] For those who did not read Azeri, *Irshad* put out a Persian-language edition written by the Persian writer Sadeq Mamalek. Aghayev himself wrote articles for Iranian newspapers, which, modeled after the Baku press, began to mushroom as the revolution gained momentum. The most striking example of journalistic inspiration from across the border was the founding in Tabriz by Mirza Agha Biluri of the literary-satirical magazine *Azerbaijan*, the local equivalent of the Tiflis-based Azeri language *Molla Nasr al-Din*.

Of all publications from Transcacasia, the most widely read was

Molla Nasr al-Din, "the newspaper, the memory of which," in the words of Kasravi, "must go down in history. The paper had a good poet, a good artist, and several good writers. It denounced the evils of the time in its own joking language, and its writing was effective. There is a whole range of evil deeds which can be eliminated faster by humor and satire."[15] Because of the ban imposed on *Molla* by the Viceroy Mirza Muhammad 'Ali, its circulation was clandestine until the restriction was lifted under pressure by the Majlis deputies from Azerbaijan. Of the contributors to *Molla,* the greatest impact on fueling revolutionary sentiments was provided by the poet Mirza Alakpär Sabir of Tiflis, the bard of the Azeri *Sturm und Drang.* His diatribes against despotism and denunciations of the rich and powerful were recited at political meetings as well as by fighters on the front lines of the Iranian revolution.

The violence began on June 23, 1908, when the successor to the deceased Muzaffar al-din, Muhammad 'Ali, staged a counterrevolutionary coup. Troops under the Russian commander of the Persian Cossack Brigade, Colonel Liakhov, bombarded and dispersed the Majlis, after which came the formal restitution of the absolutist regime. As it turned out, the coup's chief effect was to trigger civil war: some provincial centers, foremost among them Tabriz, refused to acquiesce in the Shah's seizure of power. A special reason for Azerbaiijan's hostility to Muhammad 'Ali was the harshness of his rule as viceroy of the province. The Tabriz constitutionalists took control of the city and organized a militia. Its commander was Sattar Khan, a professional horse dealer who possessed extraordinary bravery and energy. The European press compared him with Zapata of Mexico; the Russian newspapers compared him with the eighteenth-century peasant rebel Pugachev. The second in command was master bricklayer Bagher Khan. The folklore of both Azerbaijans, beginning with the poetry of Sabir, elevated Sattar Khan into a legend, a distinction all the more deserved because he was one of the few Azeri leaders in his century to take up arms.[16]

The Iranian revolution also marked the onset of the Ottoman involvement in Azerbaijan, whereby the province was made into the hub of a triangular relationship of Iran, Russia, and Turkey. Initially, this involvement consisted of the Abdulhamidian regime's actions in support of the Shah Muhammad 'Ali against the rebellious province. The sultan not only encouraged the shah to resist concessions to the constitutional movement, but he also sent Kurdish tribesmen across the border in an attempt to intimidate opposition to Qajar absolutism through pillaging and occupying frontier villages. Abdulhamid feared that the advance of the constitutional movement in Iran would strengthen the hand of his own opponents at home. The interventionist forays met with condemnation of the Young Turkish Committee of Union and Progress (CUP), which proclaimed full solidarity with the Iranian constitutionalists. The Young Turkish coup d'etat of July 1908, which put an end to the Abdulhamidian despotism, itself encouraged the Tabriz insurgents. They issued declarations, some in the name of "the nation of Azerbaijan," threatening separation unless the constitution was restored or stating that in such a case, "the Sultan would be as good as the Shah."[17] If one source of revolutionary influence on Tabriz was Baku, the other was Istanbul, the more so that the age-old Shi'ite hostility toward the Ottomans was losing its edge. The new regime in Istanbul was sympathetic to the aspirations of the Turkic-speaking liberals in northern Iran, and in the long run the Young Turks would help infuse an element of ethnic tension into the disputes between Azerbaijan and Teheran.

For the moment, though, the CUP support for the Tabriz rebellion remained limited to military incursions across the frontier, especially in the vicinity of Urmia. The troops operating there encouraged the inhabitants to accept Ottoman citizenship, a practice that provoked strong protests from Russia. Overwhelmed by a host of more pressing contingencies, the Young Turks could devote only scant attention to the crisis in Iran. Nonetheless, the perceived link between Sattar Khan and Istanbul alarmed Tsarist officials, who feared that an independent socialist republic might emerge in Tabriz province.

These apprehensions were fed by the presence in Tabriz of political émigrés from Transcaucasia. As the new phase of the Iranian upheaval coincided with the mounting wave of post-1907 repressions in Russia, revolutionaries migrated across the Iranian border, at the invitation of the Tabriz Secret Center. Their number included Georgian and Russian Social Democrats and a contingent of battle-hardened Dashnakists, but the majority were Muslims, mainly Himmätists. The Tabriz uprising offered a platform for the cooperation of members of hostile ethnic groups. A French consular report from the end of 1908 noted that "the revolutionary party dominates Azerbaijan and is in constant touch with the Committee of Union and Progress in Constantinople and also with the Tiflis Revolutionary Committee (sic) in which the Armenians have a preponderant influence."[18]

In October 1908 forces loyal to the shah closed in on Tabriz, beginning a siege that would last more than half a year. Social conflict was evident in the Tabriz fighting: the middle-class sections of the city became the strongholds of the revolution, while the slums turned into bastions of reaction. The poor were aroused against the liberals and saw them as apostates, unbelievers, enemies of the religion or as Bahais. Even after clearing the city of enemy fighters, the constitutionalists faced the blockade by the Shahseven tribesmen and the hostile peasantry. Growing starvation led to cases of people eating grass, but the defenders successfully resisted their ineffectual adversaries. Western newspapers reported that in the later stages of the siege most of the fighting was done by the Transcaucasians while the Tabrizis remained passive.

In April 1909, under the pretext of bringing food supplies to the foreign community of Tabriz, the Russian army entered the city and were received by the population with feelings of relief. The surviving Transcaucasian revolutionaries succeeded in making their way home.[19]

The suppression of Tabriz did little to salvage the throne of Muhammad 'Ali. As his troops were bogged down in Azerbaijan, a rebel force that included another contingent of Transcaucasian volunteers moved from the Caspian province of Gilan toward Teheran. After the capital fell into the hands of the insurgents, Muhammad 'Ali was forced on July 16, 1909, to renounce the crown in favor of his twelve-year-old son Ahmäd, and the constitution was restored under the regency of Asad ul-Mulk.

In the second constitutional period, one of the émigré Himmätists, Räsulzadä, rose to political prominence throughout Iran. The man who one day would become the standard-bearer of Azerbaijani nationalism north of Araces at this stage of his public life easily embraced the national cause of Iran, proving how vividly this cause still was identified with the historical homeland of the Azeris. In August 1909, Räsulzadä founded the Teheran daily *Iran-i nou* (New Iran), in the words of E. G. Browne, "the greatest, the most important and the best known of all Persian newspapers."[20] *Iran-i nou* became the organ of the Democratic Party of Iran, a left-of-center group that attracted reform-minded intellectuals.

Most of the twenty-seven Democrats in the Majlis came from

northern Iran, notably from Azerbaijan, and their number included such prominent political figures as Hasan Taqizadeh and Muhammad Tarbiyat. Outside of the parliament, the party was run by Räsulzadä and his close associate at that time, Haidar Khan Amuoghli. The latter, one of the more colorful figures in the Iranian and Azerbaijani revolutions, was born and raised in Ganja and settled in Iran. He began his political activity in the *Ejtima-i Amiyyun*, where he acquired the nickname *Bombi* (Bomber) because of his skill in using high explosives against reactionaries. In his more moderate phase he joined the ranks of the Democrat Party, but ended up as one of the founders of the Communist Party of Iran.[21]

In his editorials in *Iran-i nou*, Räsulzadä tried to acquaint the public with the notions of socialism, but he placed greater stress on the Jacobin-sounding call for a speedy and radical centralization of the state. Such a centralizing process would lead to the integration of all peoples inhabiting Iran: Turkic and Persian speakers, Muslims, Jews, Christians, and Zoroastrians. Together, they would forge an Iranian nation made of free and equal citizens.[22]

Inevitably, Räsulzadä became a thorn in the Russian side, an experience about which he reminisced: "I was working at that time in *Iran-i nou*, the first Iranian daily newspaper of European type, around which the Russian embassy began immediately to weave all possible intrigues. Then the embassy put pressure on the Iranian government to have me leave the country. The reason was that they did not like the interview which I made with Mr. Shuster, who had come to Iran the heal its financial condition."[23]

The newspaper remained in his hands until May 1912, when Iran was no longer in the position to resist the demands for his deportation. Hastily, he left for Istanbul, the capital of the only victorious revolution of the three in this epoch. The city became the favorite place of refuge for Iranians after another military intervention by Russia had brought the constitutional revolution in Iran to a brutal close.

After a reign of terror in Tabriz, which an American witness, Morton Shuster, described as "unrestrained shootings, hangings, tortures, blowing of men from cannon," Iranian Azerbaijan effectively came under the Russian occupation.[24] This condition brought the two parts of Azerbaijan under the umbrella of one power, and its natural by-product was the expansion of the old links: commerce, migration, and travel. In the years 1911–1915 Azerbaijani products accounted for almost all of Iran's 34.5 million rubles' worth of exports to Russia: at 4.5 million rubles, Russia's share in the external trade of Iranian Azerbaijan hovered around 90 percent. In the same period, Russia gave up its opposition to the railroad construction in the Iran frontier regions, no longer fearing the penetration by its potential enemies, Britain and Germany. Work on the often-postponed Russian concession of the Julfa-Tabriz rail line began in 1913 and was completed in three years. The effect was that the province of Azerbaijan became more integrated with the transportation system of Russian Transcaucasia than with Iran's. The volume of the commercial exchange took now a leap forward, although due to the war Azerbaijan achieved a favorable balance of trade. Likewise, the labor migrations grew after 1911, when 191,000 workers legally crossed the Iranian-Russian frontier; at the eve of World War I, immigrants from Iran accounted for the largest segment of the Baku proletariat. As for individual travel, the biographies of Azerbaijani public figures of the period show that many of them spent some time north of the Araxes.[25]

The Russian occupation was to be a temporary arrangement, but it showed signs of continuing indefinitely. Still, the possibility of outright annexation remained unmentionable, and the Russians ruled through a highly unpopular reactionary, Prince Samad Khan Shoja al-Dovleh.

Revolution on the Bosphorus and the Turks of Russia

In contrast to the drawn-out upheavals in Russia and Iran, the third revolution in as many years seemed like a surgical operation in its swiftness and permanence of effect. The despotic regime of Abdulhamid II was toppled by a well-coordinated military coup. On July 24, 1908, the sultan was forced to restore the constitutional regime, under which the dominant group became the Committee of Union and Progress.[26] The crisis involved no volunteers from abroad, no prolonged violent confrontation, and no exodus of political activists, yet in the long run the Young Turks' revolution produced deep and enduring consequences for the Azeris. A sensitive poet, Sabir, hailed it with an outburst of hope along with a warning:

Oh, Ottomans, do not get deceived as the Iranians were, for God's love
Do not get burnt out as the Iranians have, for God's love.[27]

Under the new liberal regime in Istanbul, the Ottoman apostles of Turkism found freedom for their activities, and this included pursuit of their concern for ethnic cousins abroad. The Ottoman public became fully aware that more Turks lived in Russia than in Turkey. Intellectuals took the lead, and in December 1908 the first association devoted to promoting Turkism, the cultural-academic *Türk Derneği* (Turkic circle), was established. Turks from Russia were encouraged to participate, and soon their representatives made an appearance on the Bosphorus. Some of them even assumed political or governmental positions: Huseynzadä, Gasprinskii, and the Tatar leader Yusuf Akchurin (Akçuraoğlu) were invited to join the Supreme Council of the CUP, and Ahmäd Aghayev was appointed inspector of the Istanbul school district.

The Azeri contingent was particularly strong. In the same manner that the Himmätists had been finding their way to revolutionary Iran to carry on their struggles, the luminaries of the Azeri intellectual elite were emigrating to Turkey, now the land of promise for their political aspirations and literary ambitions.

Once accepted in Turkey, Pan-Turkism, which so far had been an amorphous cultural movement, coalesced into organized forms. Associations and clubs enjoyed the support of the press and, increasingly, of the government. Furthermore, Pan-Turkism began to assume a political color. Its leading theoretician became Ziya Gökalp, who preached the Turkish national awakening in the Ottoman State, and this call dovetailed with his vision of Turan, the homeland of Turks and cradle of their history.

The extreme Pan-Turkists claimed that people inhabiting Turan would one day be united under the leadership of Turkey and bound together by language, religion, and the benefits of modern European civilization. Yet Turan was a far-off ideal, the crowning fulfillment of the Pan-Turkish dream, and for the foreseeable future Gökalp put forward the more realistic alternative of uniting the peoples of the Oghuz subgroup of Turkic languages, the Azeris and Turkmens, as those most closely related to the Ottoman Turks. Furthermore, for the time being, their unity would not be of a political but rather of a purely cultural nature. Thus was added to Pan-Turkism a new strain, Oghusianism, which singled out the Azeris as the object of the Ottoman Turks' special attention.[28] The immigrants from Azerbaijan were responsive. Some, notably Aghayev, who had been known for their identification with Iran redirected their intellectual vigor and switched their commitment to the Young Turkish cause, because it offered a more promising prospect for change and progress. Henceforth, Ahmäd bäy would link his political life to Turkism and, in the end, to Turkish nationalism.

Always a prolific writer, he now became one of the leading contributors to the journal *Türk Yurdu* (Turkic homeland), which stated that its goal was to "serve Turkism and to benefit the Turks." Aghayev's writings for *Türk Yurdu* bore the imprint of his particular Azerbaijani perspective, notably with regard to the Shi'ite-Sunni split. Indeed, he saw the sectarian split as one of the three factors accounting for the weakness of the Turkic world, the other two being the lack of political unity and an absence of national consciousness. "How could this consciousness have taken root among a people who are constantly preoccupied with sectarian quarrels, who have always lived under foreign influence? . . . When the teachings of Bab appeared in Iran, the Azeri Turks more than anyone else sacrificed themselves for the new faith despite the fact that the founders of Babism were Persians. Likewise, today it is the same Turks who are doing most of the fighting for Iranian freedom and constitution."[29] Also the Ottomans deserved the blame for their persistence in confusing nationality with religion or sect: "Even today in Istanbul, we call our brothers, the Azeri Turks, Persians, although they speak a language which is only slightly different from the dialect spoken in Istanbul."[30]

While Aghayev and Huseynzadä had linked their political fortunes with Turkey, other émigrés from Eastern Transcaucasia chose to return home. They brought with them reinforced ideas of Turkism, which after 1908 had become the dominant current in Azeris political thinking. Even the conservatives, suspicious of nationalism and inclined toward the Shi'ite prejudice against Turkey, were swept up by the surge of solidarity with the Ottomans, who had become the target of a series of European invasions in the Tripolitanian War of 1911 and the Balkan Wars of 1912 and 1913. Vorontsov-Dashkov, in his 1913 report to the Nicholas II on "Eight Years of Governing the Caucasus," admitted to a possibility of an "outburst of religious fanaticism" fed by the proximity of the region to Muslim countries. In his view, the Muslim population of Transcaucasia was the only, albeit the most numerous, group that might confront Russia with a separatist movement. As preventive policies, he recommended efforts to "influence the Muslims by familiarizing them with Russian civilization and instilling in them the notions of Russian jurisprudence."[31]

Seeds of the Future: The Rise of the Musavat Party and the Politics of the Literary Language

Among those returning from Turkey was Räsulzadä, whose political odyssey also included the transition from identification with Iran to Turkism. In 1913, he took advantage of the Tsarist amnesty on the three-hundredth anniversary of the Romanov dynasty. Soon afterward, he joined a clandestine association that had existed in Baku since October 1911 and was to grow into the largest and longest-lived Azerbaijani political party. The founders of the association were a handful of the former Himmätists, led by Karbalai Mikailzadä, Abbas Kazimzadä, and Qulam Rza Sharifzadä, all of whom shared disillusionment with the Russian Revolution, but felt affected by the worldwide political stirrings among Islamic peoples.

According to one of the founding members, the name *Musavat* (Equality) signified the desire to achieve equal rights for Muslims, while at the same time it indicated striving for the freedom of the whole Islamic world.[32] Musavat had announced its birth with a manifesto that—despite the radical past of its authors—ignored social issues. Moreover, the party that would eventually be the main force of Azeri nationalism couched its first proclamation entirely in terms of the 'umma consciousness by appealing to Pan-Islamic rather than Pan-Turkic sentiments. Recalling that "the noble people of Islam had once reached with one hand to Peking ... and with other built at the far end of Europe the Alhambra palace," the manifesto deplored the Islamic world's current weakness.

In 1912 the Musavat put forward the program of political action that called for the unity of all Muslims, regardless of nationality or sectarian affiliation, restoration of the lost independence of Muslim countries, and moral and material assistance to Muslim peoples struggling for the preservation of their independence. The Musavat was ready to cooperate with all who followed these goals.[33] The program was notable for its generalities, and it clearly intended to accommodate a broad spectrum of the public. The only clues to Musavat's political coloration at this early stage was the emphasis on "Muslim progress," suggesting the readiness to eschew conservative elements. Reference to the development of "commercial, industrial, and economic life" seemed to address the native middle classes. In fact, the Musavat was to draw a large part of its following from the ranks of the intelligentsia, students, merchants, and entrepreneurs, and its natural base of support became the metropolitan area of Baku. For reasons of security, its members were organized into three-person cells spread over Transcaucasia and Iran. The concealment seemed to be so effective that the Musavat, which began to call itself a "party," gave few signs of life. The dearth of evidence of its early activity prompted one Soviet historian to express doubt as to whether the party had existed before 1917, although other scholars did not accept this view.[34]

On joining the Musavat, Räsulzadä became its guiding spirit and unchallenged leader. Yet under tsardom his main field of activity was journalism. In an article published in the journal *Diriliq*, he tackled the relationship of the notions 'umma and millät, arguing that an essential difference existed between the two. In his view, 'umma carried a purely religious meaning and expressed the collective consciousness of believers in Islam worldwide. Millät, on the other hand, referred to a community based on common language, civilization, territory, *and* history, as well as religion, the last being only one of its elements.[35] Coincidentally or not, this definition of a nation resembled another, given in the same year, 1913, by his erstwhile personal friend and political companion, Joseph Stalin, in the article "Marxism and the National Question."

Räsulzadä argued that the term *millät*, in its proper sense, could not be used to denote a religious group: its meaning was primarily secular, and its attributes were clearly those of a nation, though distinct from the *qavm* by its connotation of territoriality. A secular meaning of nationalism was the foundation of the latter-day ideology of Musavatism, but at the moment Räsulzadä stopped short of naming the nationality of his compatriots and did not offer so much as a suggestion of Azerbaijani national identity. More clearly than in the political discussions, the issue of this identity emerged in the great debate on the literary language of Azerbaijan.

Among the multitude of questions that absorbed the press during the post-1905 years, the literary language became the focus of an especially persistent and intense controversy, all the more so because it touched on the essence of the still-unanswerable but increasingly relevant question: what is the nationality of the Transcaucasian Muslim? There was no historical tradition of an Azerbaijani statehood, the idea of millät was still vague and confusing, but there was the Azeri language and literature, the ultimate criterion of group identity. As the consciousness of belonging to a Turkic-speaking family of peoples, *qavm,* filtered down to many, especially the educated—indeed, they began openly to call themselves Turks—another question emerged: how should they qualify their Turkishness, and, more specifically, to what extent, if at all, should they identify themselves with the Ottomans? The debate between the partisans of the Azeri literary language, the *Azärijilar,* and the Ottomanizers reflected the controversy between the native particularism and a broader vision of Azerbaijan's future. It also signaled Azeri self-assertion vis-à-vis Ottomanization after the emancipation from the hold of the Persian language. A leading literary journal of the post-1905 period, *Füyuzat* (Abundance), held the view that the Azeris, as the Oghuz Turks, were basically the same as the Ottomans, and differences between the two peoples were of minor significance. The journal's editor and chief contributor, 'Ali Huseynzadä, criticized the inclination toward parochialism that could lead to the eventual rise of a separate nation, a millät among whom he called the "Caucasian Turks." He believed that history was entering the age of large states bound by common religion, language, and culture. He made it abundantly clear that his preference was for an Azerbaijan unified in some way with the Ottoman State, "the spiritual and political head of the Islamic world." *Füyuzat*'s position, like that of Gasprinskii, was that all Turkic peoples should adopt the same literary idiom, a modified Ottoman. Their arguments stressed the benefits for intellectual advancement among the Caucasian Turks, whose language had failed to develop the ability to express abstract concepts and complex reasoning. "What we call the native language has for centuries been cut off from progress in politics, philosophy, and science, and consequently it had been arrested in its natural evolution."[36]

The opponents to Ottomanization were motivated at first by a concern that the public would be alienated from the press and that literature would be written in a language not easily comprehended by the majority. Understandably, the *Azärijilar* came primarily from populist-leaning groups, but their concern was also with access to readers in Iran. Their mouthpiece became *Molla Nasr al-Din. Molla* was inaugurated with the pledge of its publisher, Jalal Mammad Quluzadä, to write in a simple language accessible to anyone. A satirical journal, it reveled in showing how Ottoman grammar and expressions produced comic effects in Azeri. Other organs of the *Azärijilar* were *Täräqqi* (Progress) and *Iqbal* (Felicity). The Ottomanizers promoted their views in the journals *Yeni Füyuzat* (New abundance), *Shälälä* (Cascade), and *Diriliq* (Vitality).

The rise of linguistic particularism was not limited to Azerbaijan; it was a manifestation of a broader process under way in other Turkic communities of Russia. The opposition to Ottomanization produced in some of these communities the equivalent of the *Azärijilar* in *Tatarchiliq* (Tartarism) and *Qazaqchiliq* (Kazakhism), distant flickers of the language-based nation-forming ideas that arose in a later historical period.[37]

The language debate acquired still another dimension after the 1908 revolution in Turkey, when, with the rising spirit of Turkism, some writers in Istanbul launched their own campaign for purifying Ottoman of its Arabic and Persian elements. They called Ottoman an artificial idiom, little understood by Turks. The reverberations of this nationalistically minded reform movement, which assumed the name *Yeni Lisan* (New language), soon began to have an impact on the Azerbaijani scene. Curiously, the arguments of the Turkish writers strengthened both sides in the controversy. The *Azärijilar* contended that Ottoman, corrupted as it was by foreign admixtures, did not deserve to be called a Turkic language. "The place where the language is most Arabized is Istanbul," wrote *Molla Nasr al-Din*, pointing to the contrast with Azeri, which used a vocabulary largely drawn from native vernacular. For their part, the Ottomanizers also made use of *Yeni Lisan*'s ideas. In 1912 the magazine *Shälälä*, written entirely in reformed Ottoman, became their main press organ. The magazine's aim was to work for "the unification of the Turkic languages on the basis of the Ottoman." The *Azärijilar* were quick to point out that even *Yeni Lisan*'s version of Ottoman, although purged of Persian and Arabic grammatical forms, failed to decrease the proportion of non-Turkic words, which still amounted to some 70 percent.

At the height of the debate, Faridun bäy Kochärli, the literary historian, came forward with a memorable statement linking the issue of language to that of national identity, vis-à-vis outside influences. Language, he wrote, "is the basic attribute of every nation [millät]: a nation could lose its wealth, its government, even its territory, and still survive; but should the nation lose its language, not a trace of it would remain." That was the threat hanging over the Caucasian Turks, who have just recovered their written language after a long period of domination by Persian but now are being pressured to replace it with Ottoman. The language of the Caucasian Turks has become full of Ottoman words and expressions, and Kochärli compared the efforts of the Ottomanizers to the attempts at Russification in the past. "In our opinion such aping, such conduct, amounts to national treason."[38] This forceful assertion of native identity, in a quest for emancipation from outside cultural domination, foreshadowed the emergence of Azerbaijanism, the latter-day political program of the Azerbaijani nation state.

Characteristically, the politician Räsulzadä had held back from endorsing the *Azärijilar* in his writings at the eve of the Great War. To promote a separate literary Azeri, he insisted, would run contrary to the idea of the unity of Turkic peoples, although he rejected outright the position of the Ottomanizers. In his view, which echoed the opinions of the *Yeni Lisan* movement, Ottoman, an artificial language, should be replaced by purified Turkish, still in the process of formation among the young generation of writers in Turkey.[39]

World War I and the Two Azerbaijans

Within barely three months after the World War began, its fires spread to the Middle East, when, at the end of October 1914, the Ottoman state joined the fray by attacking Russian naval installations in the Black Sea. Turkey entered the war by proclaiming it a *jihad*, and Mehmet VI, as the sultan and caliph, called on Muslims throughout the world to support the cause of the Ottomans fighting against one group of Infidel states on the side of another.

A CUP circular was more specific on Turkey's reasons for joining the war against "our sworn, irreconcilable, eternal enemy. . . . We should not forget that the reason for our entrance into the World War is not only to save our country from the danger threatening it. No, we pursue an even more immediate goal—the realization of our ideal, which demands that having shattered our Muscovite enemy, we lead our empire to its natural boundaries, which would encompass and unite all our related peoples."[40] The hostilities on the Caucasus front began in early November, with the Ottomans' penetration in the direction of Batum, where the local Muslim Lazes and Ajars welcomed them by rising up against the Russians. Simultaneously, the Ninth and Tenth Ottoman Army Corps fought a successful frontier battle at Köprüköy. These initial victories were sufficiently encouraging for Enver Pasha to order a major offensive, and he personally took command of the Third Army, which consisted of eleven of the forty divisions available in Turkey.

His immediate objective was to destroy the bulk of the Russian Caucasus-front forces between Kars and Sarikamish, after which would follow the conquest of Transcaucasia. The operation was to be aided by a flanking movement into Iranian Azerbaijan and then to Baku. A task force of three understrength divisions was assigned for this grandiose purpose and placed under the command of Enver's young uncle, Halil Pasha. The main battle began on December 22, and the Ottomans' attacks were at first successful. At the front's northern section, the Russians had to abandon Ardahan. As the Russian officials were hastily readying themselves for the evacuation of Transcaucasia, the tsar's government appealed to its Western allies to launching a diversionary attack, a request that planted the seeds of the Gallipoli operation.

The critical situation was nonetheless resolved in favor of the Russians, with the bold counterattack at Sarikamish that destroyed the Ninth Corps by mid-January. Decimated as much by cold, disease, and hunger as by battle fatigue, the Ottoman Third Army lost 85 percent of its original contingent of 90,000. The outcome at Sarikamish set the future course of the war on the Caucasus front, in which Turkey lost the strategic initiative and would be unable to recover it until the closing months of the conflict.[41] In the spring of 1915, the Russian forces, with the help of Armenian irregulars, entered eastern Anatolia. The fear of Armenian disloyalty led the Ottoman government to order mass deportations that were accompanied by fighting and killings. In addition to considerations of military security, the CUP regime might have wished to eliminate the ethnic barrier between the Turkic peoples of Russia and Turkey.

The estimates of Armenian lives lost in 1915 exceed one million.[42] The effects of the violence in eastern Anatolia were soon felt throughout Transcaucasia; Armenian refugees began to settle in towns and cities throughout the region, including Baku.

After an extended lull in the fighting, the Russians, who had been unable to prevent the sufferings of the majority of Armenians, in February 1916 captured the fortress of Erzerum. Two months later they occupied the Black Sea port of Trebizond. Just as the Ottomans were preparing for a counteroffensive, a well-aimed Russian blow wiped out much of the reconstituted Third Army. In July the Russians reached their farthest point of advance in Anatolia, Erzincan. On their southern wing they were making preparations for a thrust toward Mosul to achieve a link-up with the British, who were converging toward the same point from central Mesopotamia.

At almost the same time as the sultan proclaimed the jihad, the shah issued a *farman* (decree) declaring neutrality, a dubious commitment in view of Iran's weakness and the presence of Russian troops in the province of Tabriz. The Ottoman government protested this presence but promised to respect Iranian neutrality if the Russian troops were withdrawn. As Russia refused to evacuate, Turkey found justification for launching raids across the Iranian border. Thus, as the Battle of Sarikamish hung in the balance, the Ottomans carried out the first of their forays into Tabriz province. With the Halil's force at the last moment reassigned to fill the thinned out ranks of the Third Army, only a detachment of 3,000 largely auxiliary Kurdish cavalry could be mustered, and the expedition carried more political weight than strategic importance. The force also included refugees from Tabriz, notably of the *Mujahidin-i Azarbaijan* group, who had moved to Turkey and were now seeking to return home with Ottoman help. The *Mujahidin's* contribution to Turkey's war effort was modest, but their propaganda value was of some significance, because their number included prominent Tabrizis Majd al-Saltaneh, Biluri, and Tufangchi, as well as Haidar Khan Amuoghli, who gave an example of close cooperation with Turkey.[43]

Having seized an undefended Tabriz in early January 1915, the Ottomans stood at the doorstep of Russian Azerbaijan. A prominent Young Turk, Ömer Naji, regarded as the driving spirit of Turkey's Caucasus policy, was appointed CUP inspector general for Azerbaijan and East Caucasus. He began at once to enlist the Shahseven tribesmen for the march on Baku, but by the end of January had to abandon Tabriz. The Ottomans had succeeded in taking the city only because of the temporary withdrawal of Russian troops for the defense of Kars and Sarikamish. Once the great battle had ended, the Russian corps of General Chernozubov, assisted by the Armenian volunteers, quickly reoccupied the province and the city of Tabriz.

Of the two Azerbaijans, the Iranian part, although not a prime strategic goal in itself, was more profoundly affected by the hostilities, because it served as a corridor for flanking or diversionary movements aimed at Baku. In the spring of 1915, Halil Pasha, who finally had an expeditionary force at his disposal, moved from Mosul toward Tabriz but was forced to retreat to Anatolia when a large Armenian uprising broke out in the region of Van. On two other occasions, Ömer Naji tried to carry anti-Russian insurgency into Iranian Azerbaijan where, by all indications, the Ottomans would be treated as friends. In the fall of 1915, he briefly seized Sudjubulak, and repeated this operation the following spring, just before his death. In no instance, however, did Ottoman incursions threaten Russia's hold on Tabriz. "There was an opportunity to attack Russian forces occupying certain points in the province," wrote the American Consul from Baghdad. "However, the more important purpose is believed to have been that of reaching the Caspian Sea and controlling it for the purpose of facilitating the Pan-Turanian movement across Turkestan."[44]

As for Ottoman designs toward Iranian Azerbaijan, these were clearly subordinated to the exigencies of war, including deference to Germany, the power that guaranteed Iran's independence and territorial integrity. The Ottoman commitment to these goals was reaffirmed in mutual declarations and agreements with Germany throughout the war. Still, some German and Austro-Hungarian officials were suspicious about Turkish interest in Tabriz province. An influential theoretician of Turanism, Tekin Alp, took issue with the opinions that Turkey intended to seize any part of Iran. "No one could know better than the Turks what difficulties and disadvantages entails the rule over heterogeneous elements of the population." He believed that the interests of Iran and Turkey, facing the same dangers, were identical. "The existence of Turkey guarantees the existence of Persia, and vice versa, a strengthened Persia protects Turkey from Russian invasion." All the same, in this vision of the future relationship of Turkey and Iran, there was an implication of less than absolute equality. "The position of Persia versus the Turkish government," wrote Tekin Alp, "could resemble that of Bavaria toward Prussia, or Hungary toward Austria, i.e., Persia would internally be fully independent; outwardly, however, it would form one entity with Turkey, one body and soul."[45] In practice, Turkey adopted toward Iran a posture of Pan-Islamism, with its appeal to Muslim solidarity across sectarian lines. This policy, not quite in tune with Turanian-inspired dreams, was paying off with the generally favorable disposition of the Iranians. The *fetva* of the *Shaikh-ul-Islam* in Istanbul proclaiming the duty of every Muslim to join the jihad against the Entente powers was echoed in the pronouncements of the Shi'a 'ulama in the holy cities of Karbala and Najaf. While mollahs led prayers for the victory of Turkey and Germany, the same wishes were shared by the Democratic Party and a large part of the press. The behavior of Teheran elicited this comment from an American diplomat, referring to an Ottoman incursion: "Persia made only a formal protest and it is not impossible that she in reality connived at such a violation. There is little reason to doubt that her sympathies were antagonistic to Russia and Britain, and friendly to Turkey."[46]

Unlike Tabriz province, Eastern Transcaucasia, sheltered behind by distance and mountainous terrain, remained far from the zone of military operations for most of the war. Here attitudes were more complex, and reflected the changing fortunes of the Russo-Ottoman conflict. The first project for an independent state of Transcaucasian and Caucasian Muslims was conceived in the circles of the former Difai Party at the time of Enver's Sarikamish offensive. Aslan Khan Khoiskii, their emissary and the nephew of Fath 'Ali, secretly visited Enver Pasha in February 1915 to secure endorsement for the formation of a republic to consist of Eastern Transcaucasia and Daghestan. The project's chief significance was that it signaled preference for an independent statehood rather than union with Turkey.[47] There were no *mujahidin* from the Russian-held part of Azerbaijan fighting on the Ottoman side.

As the war in the Caucasus began to favor Russia, the Azeri elite gladly responded to the Tsardom's attempt at improving relations with the Transcaucasian Muslims. This new approach began in the fall of 1915 with the dismissal of Vorontsov-Dashkov, known for his anti-Muslim bias and for the 1915 massacre of the Ajars. His replacement was the grand duke Nicholas Nicholaevich, who among other gestures, granted the former revolutionary Räsulzadä a permit to publish the daily newspaper *Achiq söz* (Open word). First issued in October 1915, *Achiq söz* called itself a "Turkic newspaper," a description that met with no objection from the authorities, as the term *Tiurkskii* had already gained circulation in Russia. In his inaugural editorial, Räsulzadä included a statement of what he considered the Azerbaijani identity at the time:

> With regard to language we are Turks, Turkism is our nationality. With regard to religion we are Muslims. Every religion creates among its followers a particular civilization, and this civilization generates some form of internationalism. As Muslims and Turks we are a part of the International of Islam.[48]

Otherwise, *Achiq söz* gave its support to Russia's war effort and official Tsarist patriotism.

The improved atmosphere in relations between tsardom and the Azeri community coincided with the recovery of oil prices, a welcome development for Baku oil producers, who had witnessed a steep decline in prices at the outset of the war because of the threat to the Black Sea shipping. The threat receded with the Russian successes on the Caucasus front, and the year 1916 brought another series of impressive Russian victories. Baku's inhabitants grew accustomed to long columns of Ottoman prisoners of war marching through the city to the detention camp on the offshore island of Nargin. In a display of psychological adaptation, Azeri religious leaders held prayers of thanksgiving on the occasion of the Russian seizure of Erzerum. It was obvious that the war was going against Turkey on the Caucasus front, and Ottoman fortunes were not destined for restoration until the Russian Revolution of 1917 created an entirely new situation, both behind the front line and on the front itself. Even so, Turkey's recovered initiative would not be apparent in the first phase of the Russian upheaval, which began with the overthrow of the tsardom in March of that year.

Parties and Programs in 1917

In 1917's new era of freedom, political life, unlike in 1905, immediately burst into the open, and of the nascent Azeri organizations, political parties commanded the largest measure of popular support. Each stood for one of the ideological currents that were to shape the politics of Azerbaijan: nationalism, Pan-Islamism, and socialism.

At this point nationalism still meant, broadly, Turkism with a growing component of Azerbaijani identity. The main proponent of this ideology was Musavat, the largest political force that emerged in 1917. A different party from the handful of ex-Himmätists of the prewar years, the new Musavat evolved from the merger of the old Baku-based cadre with the Ganja Turkic Party of Federalists, an association that traced its roots to the Difai. The group's full name, which reflected its hybrid character, was the Turkic Party of Federalists—Musavat. In effect, the Musavat consisted of two distinct wings, the Left, or Baku wing, led by Räsulzadä and Hajinskii, and the Right, or Ganja wing, led by Nasib Ussubäkov (Yusufbäyli), Hasan Aghazadä, Rustambäkov, and the brothers Khasmammädov. The wings differed on social and economic issues, most notably that of land reform, but were held together by two overriding commitments. One was secular Turkic nationalism, the essence of Musavatism. A nation, as the party statement defined it, was:

> the community of language, religion, tradition, culture, literature, and law. The community of religion in itself does not constitute a nation, contrary to assumption of some of our contemporaries. From the standpoint of the above attributes the Turks are a nation.[49]

The other commitment was to the vision of Azerbaijan as an autonomous republic in association with a Russia restructured into a federation of free and equal states. The provisional party platform adopted in October 1917 stated:

> Each nationality possessed of a defined territory, i.e., constituting a majority in a given region, should be granted territorial autonomy. This principle in the view of our Party should be applied to such Turkic lands as Azerbaijan, Turkestan, Kirghizia, and Bashkiria. . . . Nationalities not inhabiting defined territories should be granted the right of cultural autonomy.[50]

The program of federalism marked a new stage of the Azeris' historical evolution-transition toward a nation-state. Their impulse to federalize was to remain a constant rather than a transitory trait, rooted as it was in doubts about the viability of a fully independent Azerbaijan.

Although the Musavat was the strongest of the native parties, the Azeri community was more differentiated politically than were Dashnakist-dominated Armenia or Menshevik-run Georgia, and the main point of division was the question of autonomy. An entirely new political organization, the conservative *Ittihad* (Union) Party was fundamentally Pan-Islamic, rejecting the idea of Turkism (or any form of nationalism) as disruptive to the 'umma, and was always critical of the notion of Azerbaijanism. Likewise, it opposed tendencies toward separation from Russia, and called for the unity of all Russia's Muslims within one organization that would represent them as a religious community. The Ittihad advocated a democratic and decentralized Russian republic, under which Muslims would attain "freedom from European capitalism and imperialism." This formula indicated an attempt to combine Islamic traditionalism with some traits of social radicalism, a blend that at times caused the Ittihad to take positions close to the far left. While the party was not adept at the polls, its influence among the population was stronger than voting results indicated. It was the only group with an appeal to the core of the peasantry, even though its leaders were professionals. The head of the party was Karabäy Karabäkov, a former Social Democrat who developed close links to the Young Turks but during the war became known as loyal to the tsardom. The Ittihad saw its main enemy in the Musavat, and antagonism between the two groups, one symbolizing commitment to change, the other attachment to tradition, was so deep that it appeared as a major feature of Azeri domestic politics, in a pattern typical of a Muslim society in transition.[51]

At the moment of the tsardom's downfall, Azeri socialism was represented by *Ädälät* (Justice), an organization of immigrants from Iran. These immigrants formed not only the most numerous part of the Baku oil workers but, with the experience of the revolution in Tabriz behind them, had shed the old fear of joining strikes and turned into the most radical element in the Muslim proletariat.

Founded in Baku in 1916 by a group that included Asadullah Gafarzadä, Agha Baba Yusifzadä, and the youthful Javadzadä Khalkali, who was later to be famous as Jafar Pishevari, Ädälät saw itself as a successor to the former *Ejtima-i Amiyyun* of the 1905 period.[52] By contrast, there had been no continuation of the Himmät, and those Russian Azeri veterans of the years 1905–1907 who remained faithful to socialism became fully integrated into the RSDWP. A handful of the old-timers met to debate whether to revive the Himmät at all or to call instead on Muslim workers to join the ranks of the Russian Social Democrats. Having concluded that the Muslims would be unlikely to enter a Russian organization, they eventually opted for a native identity. On March 3, 1917, they resumed the party's activity through the adoption of a resolution that took into account "the psychology of the Muslim masses as well as the fact that the Himmät had its own history."[53] The Himmätists might well have felt their hand forced by the existence in Baku of the Ädälät, and of another organization of Muslim workers, *Birlik* (Unity), which represented the Volga Tatars. Both the Ädälät and Birlik looked to their Russian Azerbaijani comrades for guidance or assistance, and in the future they would in all but name affiliate themselves with the Himmät.

The head of the new Himmät's provisional committee was Narimanov and its members were Äzizbäkov, Buniatzadä, M. N. Israfilbäkov, and Hamid Sultanov. The latter two were new faces in this company, with no past in the old Himmät but with close ties to the Bolshevik wing of the RSDWP.

The reborn Himmät, though far more strongly Marxist than ten years earlier, failed to recapture its following. It faced a formidable contender for the allegiance of the masses in the Musavat, the party that attracted a large segment of native workers in Baku. Furthermore, the Himmät, having so far managed to steer clear of the Bolshevik-Menshevik strife, could no longer escape the consequences of polarization within the Russian Social Democracy. The Transcaucasian chapter of the RSDWP, after a brief reunification, split irrevocably in June 1917. The Azeri socialists saw themselves forced to take sides, with the result that the Himmät broke up in a manner paralleling the alignment among their Russian comrades. The Baku Himmätists, following Narimanov, declared themselves pro-Bolshevik, whereas the provincial chapters tended to side with the Mensheviks, who were dominant throughout the rest of the region, notably in Georgia. In Tiflis, Ibrahim Abilov, Samad Aghamalioghli, Ahmäd Pepinov, and Haidar Karayev formed the nucleus of the Himmät's Menshevik wing.

The division among the Himmätists was neither as deep-seated nor as permanent as was the case of the RSDWP. As though in tacit recognition that the quarrel was not of their making, the two factions maintained contact with each other and in the course of the next three years reunited twice. During most of this period, the Bolshevik Himmät went through the motions of carrying on routine political work, showing limited vitality even though its leaders were often active in the Russian party. Unlike the Menshevik Himmätists, they refrained from running for elections to representative bodies and were absent from the Baku Soviet. In the November 1917 elections to the Constituent Assembly, the Himmätist-Mensheviks received 84,000 votes, compared to 615,000 for the Musavat, 66,000 for the Ittihad, and 159,000 for the Muslim Socialist Bloc, a native equivalent of the Russian Social-Revolutionaries.[54]

The shock waves of the tsardom's overthrow reached immediately across the Araxes, putting an end to Russian-imposed order. "Tabriz, which six years before had fallen under the pressure of the Tsar's aggression and imperialism, and had been oppressed by that regime's agents . . . now suddenly felt itself free," reminisced Kasravi. "The same soldiers and Cossacks who only yesterday were the tools of the Tsardom, today extended their hands to the liberals and kept saying: 'Come, let's be brothers, come, let's shake hands.'"[55]

The new situation brought prominence to a leading member of the Democratic Party in Azerbaijan, the Majlis deputy Shaikh Muhammad Khiabani. He was a well-educated cleric with the experience of a sojourn in Russia. Acting quickly to establish his party as the ruling group in the province, one of his first moves was to summon the conference of the Democrats' regional chapters. The meeting resolved to begin publication of a Persian-language newspaper, *Tajaddod* (Renewal), and to adopt a minor but significant change in the group's name from the "Democratic Party *in* Azerbaijan" to the "Democratic Party *of* Azerbaijan." This change was immediately understood to hint at loosening ties with Teheran. In addition, the Party addressed a series of demands to the central government, calling for the appointment of a provincial governor trusted by the local population, the creation of provincial councils as provided by the constitution, land distribution, a convening of the National Assembly, equitable parliamentary representation, and an increase in the budgetary allocation for Azerbaijan. These demands displayed an unmistakably autonomist-decentralizing disposition, and sounded like echoes from north of the border. In their desire for closer integration with Iran, a minority faction of the Democrats, led by Kasravi, who opposed the name change and the thrust of the demands from the government, found themselves expelled from the party.[56]

The Tabriz Democrats extended their activities to Baku by setting up a party chapter there, which early in 1918 began to publish a newspaper, *Azerbaijan*. Because by this time the term *Azerbaijan* was rapidly gaining currency as the name for the future state of the Transcaucasian Muslims, the newspaper deemed it appropriate to emphasize the difference by using as subtitle the words "Inseparable part of Iran."[57]

Transcaucasian Federation and the Baku Commune

In Baku, the controversy over the nature of the association with Russia was becoming academic as Russia sank into chaos and disintegration. Upon Lenin's dispersal of the Constituent Assembly on January 5, 1918, the Azeri parties lent their support to the Georgian Mensheviks' initiative to establish a supreme authority over Transcaucasia in the form of the regional *Seim* (Diet). The convocation of the Seim on

February 10, 1918, was a prelude to the legal separation of Transcaucasia from Russia, an act on which the Ottoman State insisted as the condition for ceasing hostilities on the Caucasus front. In the vacuum that resulted from the Russian army's collapse, Turkey became the uncontested military power in the region, and among the local Muslims a pro-Ottoman orientation resurfaced. Its strongest proponent was the anti-nationalist Ittihad, which was ready to substitute Turkey for Russia as the partner in the union. As for the Musavatists, the prospect of a Transcaucasian state offered the immediate fulfillment of their federalist aspirations, yet their position remained circumspect. A Russian anti-Bolshevik author quotes a confidential statement by Ussubäkov that offers an insight into the thinking of the Azeri leadership at this juncture. In the words of Ussubäkov, a Transcaucasian state was hardly an ideal for the Musavatists. Now that disintegration of the Russian army had created in Tabriz a situation resembling that in Baku or Ganja, Pan-Azerbaijani sentiments were again on the rise. The Musavatists had set their sights on the creation of a greater Azerbaijan consisting of the Russian and Iranian parts of the country with addition of Daghestan. Upon entering the Seim, they had reluctantly accepted the current line dividing the two Azerbaijans but maintained the hope of erasing it one day. The Musavatist leader expressed no enthusiasm for the alternative of union with Turkey, because Transcaucasia, owing to a hundred years of Russian rule, was more advanced than the Ottoman State. "Turkey, however," stated Ussubäkov, "recognizes that fact and has let us known that it would be accommodating."[58]

After much hesitation and numerous delays, on April 22 the Seim proclaimed the independence of the Transcaucasian Federation, which united Georgia, Armenia, and Azerbaijan. The Federation's government was formed under the Georgian Menshevik Akakii Chkhenkeli, but otherwise each of the national groups pursued its own political concerns.[59]

A vital part of Azerbaijani territory remained outside the Federation's control because of the Bolshevik seizure of power in Baku. The seizure came in the aftermath of another eruption of ethnic violence. Just as Turkey was poised to become the dominant power in the region, the Baku Dashnakist forces, which included many of the refugees from Anatolia, staged a sudden and unprovoked massacre of the city's Muslims. The debacle lasted from March 31 until April 2 and resulted in at least 3,000 fatalities, many of whom were Iranians.[60] Armenian historians do not offer an explanation for the political calculations behind this move, which was bound to entail terrible retribution, and they hint rather at an uncontrollable emotional outburst.[61] Such an interpretation would confirm the view of the weakness of the Armenian leadership, which had just concluded an agreement with the Muslims on neutrality in their coming confrontation with the Bolsheviks, and they proved to be unable to restrain the rank and file. Likewise, it would confirm the lack of coordination with the Armenian efforts at putting together the Transcaucasian Federation.

The immediate beneficiary of the Baku March Days were the Bolsheviks, who seized the opportunity to institute in the city a dictatorship of the proletariat under the name of the Baku Commune. The local *Sovnarkom* (Council of People's Commissars) was headed by a prominent Armenian Bolshevik, Stepan Shaumian, who proclaimed its undivided loyalty and subordination to Soviet Russia.[62] In the Azeri mind, the Baku Commune became the bitter symbol of the Bolshevik-Armenian collusion born out of the March Days bloodbath.

Short-lived as the Commune turned out to be—in all, less than four months (April 13 to July 25)—it survived the Transcaucasian Federation, which fell apart after five weeks of internal strife and external pressures from Turkey and Germany. At the last moment before the Federation's break-up, the Azerbaijani leaders, as if to salvage some measure of reassurance for the uncertain future, proposed a dualistic state in partnership with the Georgians, by far the less antagonistic of their Christian neighbors. When the Georgians rejected the proposal, the Federation dissolved on May 26.

FOUR

Nation-State and Regional Autonomy: Independent Azerbaijan and Azadistan

Independent Azerbaijan in the Ottoman Shadow

Upon the dissolution of the Transcaucasian Federation, Muslim representation in the defunct Seim constituted itself into the Azerbaijani National Council. A brief debate followed, during which the possibility of entering into federation with Turkey was raised, but it ended when the word came that the Ottomans declined.[1] That day, May 28, 1918, the Council proclaimed that a new state was born. The proclamation, which was couched in terms of the ideas linking national self-determination to democracy, read as follows:

1. Azerbaijan is a fully sovereign state; it consists of the southern and eastern parts of Transcaucasia under the authority of the Azerbaijani people.

2. It is resolved that the form of government of the independent Azerbaijani state be a democratic republic.

3. The Azerbaijani Democratic Republic is determined to establish friendly relations with all, especially with the neighboring nations and states.

4. The Azerbaijani Democratic Republic guarantees to all its citizens within its borders full civil and political rights, regardless of ethnic origin, religion, class, profession, or gender.

5. The Azerbaijani Democratic Republic encourages the free development of all nationalities inhabiting its territory.

6. Until the Azerbaijani Constituent Assembly is convened, the supreme authority over Azerbaijan is vested in a universally elected National Council and the provisional government responsible to this Council.[2]

Although the proclamation restricted its claim to the territory north of the Araxes, the use of the name *Azerbaijan* would soon bring objections from Iran. In Teheran, suspicions were aroused that the Republic of Azerbaijan served as an Ottoman device for detaching the Tabriz province from Iran. Likewise, the national revolutionary *Jangali* movement in Gilan, while welcoming the independence of every Muslim land as a "source of joy," asked in its newspaper if the choice of the name Azerbaijan implied the new republic's desire to join Iran. If so, they said, it should be stated clearly, otherwise Iranians would be opposed to calling that republic Azerbaijan.[3] Consequently, to allay Iranian fears, the Azerbaijani government would accommodatingly use the term *Caucasian Azerbaijan* in its documents for circulation abroad.

Following the proclamation of independence, the next step in organizing the first republic in the Muslim world was to select a prime minister. To no one's surprise, the choice fell on Khan Khoiskii, who began his work by sending telegrams notifying foreign governments of the establishment of the Azerbaijani Republic with the interim capital in Ganja.

The Democratic Republic lasted twenty-three months, and its lifespan falls into three distinct phases. First was the period of the Ottoman tutelage. On June 4, all three successor states to the Transcaucasian Federation signed in Batum separate treaties of peace and friendship with the Ottoman State. Unlike Armenia, which was reduced to barely four thousand square miles , or Georgia, which was forced to relinquish two of its districts, there was much substance to the term *friendship* in describing the Azerbaijani-Ottoman settlement. Not only did Azerbaijan retain all its territory, but under Article IV of the treaty it received the promise of Ottoman military assistance for restoration of security and order, an obvious reference to the recovery of Baku and to the suppression of the Armenian guerrillas active in Nagorno-Karabagh.[4] Yet the treaty stopped short of recognizing Azerbaijan as an independent state, and it soon became apparent that Soviet rule of Baku was not the only limitation to Azerbaijani sovereignty; indeed these limitations were imposed not only by the foe but also by the friend.

The failure to recognize Azerbaijan's independence reflected the general thrust of the Ottoman policy in the region, where Turkey had become the supreme power and was eager to throw its weight. Among the consequences of the collapse of the Russian Caucasus Front was the resurgence of Turanian designs, now that the Ottoman troops were facing denuded enemy positions. In the spring and summer of 1918, as in 1914, these designs were predicated on achieving two immediate and interlinked goals, which at last seemed to be within the realm of possibility: the conquest of Baku and the extension of an Ottoman military presence over both Azerbaijans. After this stage, even more ambitious moves on the road to Turan might be undertaken: the penetration of Transcaspia and Turkestan. These conquests in turn would allow Pan-Islamic revolts against the British in Afghanistan, Southern Iran, and India.

For the new Caucasian offensive, Enver Pasha had nine infantry divisions, totaling some 55,000 to 60,000 soldiers and several thousand irregulars. This well-equipped task force, although made up of battle-tested units, of which some had been diverted from the route to the hard-pressed Palestinian front, was scarcely sufficient for the grandiose mission assigned to it. No less than troops, Enver needed commanders whom he could fully trust to understand and carry out his grand design. Typically, he resorted to making use of close relatives. He gave Halil Pasha command of the Eastern Army Group and recalled his twenty-eight-year-old half-brother, Nuri Pasha, from Tripolitania, where he had gained experience organizing the Arab tribes against the Italians. Nuri's new assignment was the command of the Army of Islam, a special force to be created in the territory of Azerbaijan north of Araxes. By the end of May, Nuri Pasha left via Ottoman-held Tabriz for Ganja, where he hurriedly began to build the Army of Islam. This motley Ottoman-Azerbaijani-Daghestani force was to be the chief instrument of Enver Pasha's policies in Transcaucasia. It absorbed most of the nascent Muslim National Corps and bands of Azeri irregulars. Altogether, 16,000 to 18,000 troops were under Nuri's command. Ottomans accounted for one third, and the balance largely were militia-men who lacked proper training or significant battle experience.[5]

Ostensibly, this was an entirely irregular unit outside Ottoman jurisdiction, as the Istanbul regime wished to avoid complications with Soviet Russia, and even more with its German ally, for breaking the provisions of the treaty of Brest-Litovsk. Nuri Pasha received his instructions to liberate the Muslims in Baku from Bolshevik rule "in accordance with the request of the independent Islamic government of Azerbaijan" by June 2—that is, before the signing of the Azerbaijani-

Ottoman pact.[6] The population greeted the Ottomans warmly and feelings of Muslim solidarity ran high, but relations between the Ottoman commanders and Azerbaijani statesmen soon ran into difficulties. Nuri Pasha, through his political adviser Ahmäd Aghayev, let it be known that Ottoman sympathies lay with the conservative and Pan-Islamist elements, rather than with the left or those who might be inclined toward an "Azerbaijan first" policy. A crisis arose in mid-June, when Nuri expressed his disapproval of the Khan Khoiskii cabinet, on grounds that it included leftists and Azerbaijani nationalists such as Mammad Jafarov. In protest against Ottoman meddling to the benefit of the right-wingers, the Himmätists withdrew from the National Council, followed by the deputies from the Muslim Socialist Bloc. The rump legislature concurred with the opinion of its speaker, Räsulzadä, that "unless we find some legal way out, there will be the danger of the black reaction taking over," and on June 17 a compromise went into effect. Khan Khoiskii presented his second cabinet, which was acceptable to Nuri.[7]

At the same time, the National Council, which the Ottomans viewed merely as a by-product of the Russian Revolution, fulfilled another of Nuri's wishes by transferring its powers to the Council of Ministers, pending the convocation of the Azerbaijani Constituent Assembly. There followed a series of other measures associated with the Ottoman pressure: land reform was suspended, the labor unions were suppressed, and socialist activities banned. In general, the policies under Ottoman military rule were perceived as eroding the achievements of the Russian revolution, and its ultimate aim was seen as *Ilhaq*, some form of unification rather than federation with Turkey. The Ottoman authorities removed a few political figures from the Azerbaijani scene, among them Räsulzadä, by inviting them for prolonged visits to Turkey.

Ottoman interference strengthened the tendencies toward Azerbaijani nationalism within the political elite. Azerbaijan's relations with Turkey would henceforth be tainted with uneasiness bordering on distrust, and Pan-Turkism would gradually be reduced from a political program to a cultural doctrine.

Because the Ottomans envisioned close, if still undefined, links between both Azerbaijans and Turkey, they were intent on discouraging assertiveness of Azerbaijani nationalism in the north and of regional particularism south of the Araxes. Their moves in Tabriz paralleled those they made across the Russo-Iranian border, with differences arising from local conditions.

South of the frontier, the mass of the population suffered heavily from military operations, and like in the north, tensions were quick to develop between the Ottomans and, the political elite. Instead of having to deal with the elected legislature and the parliamentary cabinet, the Ottomans had to contend with Khiabani and his party. The Democrats were known to have been well-disposed toward Turkey and Germany during the war years, yet as Khiabani recalled, he told the Ottoman representatives in Tabriz that his party "considered Azerbaijan an integral part of Iran when they tried annexionist propaganda."[8]

Although he was careful not to unduly antagonize the Ottomans, within less than a month Khiabani, along with Nubari and Badamchi, found himself on the way to exile in Urmia and then Kars. The cause of Khiabani's removal from Tabriz was not only the frictions with the occupiers but also the intrigues of the *Vali'ahd* Muhammad Hasan Mirza, a source of his lasting bitterness with the central government. The Ottomans not only left the Iranian head of the province undisturbed but got him to appoint their candidate as the governor of Tabriz. In recognition, Halil Pasha awarded the viceroy an Ottoman decoration.[9]

The Democratic Party's activities were banned, and the field was left open to the only political organization that was officially allowed and strongly promoted—the pro-Ottoman and Pan-Islamic Union of Islam (*Ittihad al-Islam*). A namesake and rough equivalent of the *Ittihad* from north of the Araxes, the organization was led by Yusuf Ziya and Mirza Agha Biluri. Its press organ was *Azarabadegan*, published in Ottoman Turkish by Mirza Taqi Khan Raf'at, a close confidant of Khiabani and a leading literary figure of Azerbaijan, known for his advocacy of the adoption of modern spirit and form into native literature through links with Turkey. The newspaper emphasized the historically Turkic character of Azerbaijan and downplayed the significance of the Shi'ite-Sunni split.[10]

The Ottomans failed to occupy all of Iranian Azerbaijan, especially its Caspian coast. In the spring of 1918 the inland town of Hamadan was in the hands of the British Expeditionary Force of General Lionel C. Dunsterville, who subsequently seized the Caspian ports of Enzeli and Rasht. Here the British clashed with the guerrillas of Kuchuk Khan, the leader of the Jangali insurrection. The immediate concern of the British was to prevent the Baku oil fields from falling into hands of the Central Powers. As the Army of Islam and Ottoman forces closed in on Baku, the Baku Commune was overthrown by non-Communist parties, largely over the issue of whether to call the British for help or to surrender to the Ottomans. Without delay, the new government of the city, the *Tsentrokaspiy* Dictatorship, which was dominated by the Russian Social-Revolutionaries, approached Dunsterville, and his units began to arrive in Baku by sea immediately after the first abortive Ottoman assault on August 5. The under-strength British troops remained in Baku until September 15, when they withdrew the way they had come.[11] The departing ships also took as many Armenian civilians as they could carry. In the interval between the British departure and the Ottoman entry the revenge for the March Days in the Armenian sections of the city was ferocious, and conservative estimates put the number of the lives lost between 9,000 and 10,000.[12]

With the seizure of Baku, the Ottomans reached the high-water mark in their pursuit of the Turanian dream, having almost all of Azerbaijan, north and south of the Araxes, under their control. Whatever the Ottoman designs in the Azerbaijani question—German reports mention the protectorate over Eastern Transcaucasia that would gradually absorb Tabriz province—they were not given the time to progress beyond the embryonic stage.[13] In practice, the Ottoman policy limited itself to discouraging emergence of forceful political leadership espousing local particularism, a troublesome proclivity for the long-range prospects of Turanism. Turkey's moment of glory in both Azerbaijans came when the Ottoman State was nearing the final stages of its war fatigue, which could not escape the attention of its potential partners, the political elites on both sides of the Araxes. The food situation of Turkey was so extreme that the immediate concern of Ottoman commanders was to ship home as much grain as possible rather than to chase the dream of Turan, a practice that was bound to generate resentment among the otherwise friendly local populations. Moreover, Turkey's military condition was turning rapidly from bad to disastrous, even as the Istanbul newspapers filled their pages with reports of the conquests in the Caucasus. The Allies were advancing in Syria and the Balkans, and, most ominous of all, the Germans continued their retreat on the Western Front. These hard facts began to have their effect on the Ottoman position on Azerbaijan. Formal recognition of

Azerbaijan and Armenia by Turkey was agreed upon in the German-Ottoman Protocol of September 23, as was the reconfirmation of the territorial integrity of Iran. The Germans even undertook to secure Soviet consent to recognize the two Transcaucasian republics. When the Ottomans took Baku they proclaimed to have done so on behalf of the Azerbaijani government, and Nuri Pasha forthwith invited Khan Khoiskii to transfer his offices from Ganja to the recovered capital of the Republic. The Ottoman general was now careful to avoid appearances of interfering in Azerbaijani affairs, and he routinely referred all but military matters to local authorities.

While Young Turkish leaders still spoke of setting up independent and friendly states in the zone between Turkey and Russia, the Ottoman State itself was on the verge of total collapse. On September 30, Bulgaria surrendered to the Allies and with this link to Austro-Hungary and Germany severed, Turkey's continuation of the war became impossible. The CUP government fell on October 9, and the new cabinet of Ahmet Izzet Pasha signed an armistice with the Allies before the end of the month at Mudros. Under the provisions of this agreement, the Ottoman forces were required to leave Transcaucasia and northern Iran, while the Allies were to occupy Baku and take control of the Transcaucasian railways. No mention of the Transcaucasian republics was included in the agreement.

There followed a flurry of activity, in the hope of salvaging anything for the future cause of Turan. In Baku, Nuri Pasha authorized his soldiers to enter the Azerbaijani army. With the inducement of promotion and higher pay, hundreds took advantage of this opportunity to continue their careers, and former Ottoman servicemen became an important element in the Azerbaijani military.[14] Likewise, a number of the Ottomans managed to remain in military service south of the Araxes, and Khiabani, who with the end of the war had returned to Tabriz, accepted their presence. A characteristic incident demonstrates that he drew a line between Ottoman expansionism and Turkism as an expression of ethnic and linguistic identity. On the departure of the Ottoman garrison from Tabriz, the Democrats resumed their activities, and one of their first acts was an attempt to purge those members of the party who had collaborated too closely with the occupier. A meeting of the Democrats voted to expel Mirza Taqi Khan for having published his pro-Ottoman newspaper and, even worse, for praising Halil Pasha in a Turkish poem. In the same spirit of backlash, it was resolved that the party meetings should be conducted in Persian, a decision that indicated how sensitive and divisive the language issue had suddenly grown.

Khiabani, however, served notice of his disapproval of Persianizing tendencies: after his return from exile, he chose Mirza Taqi Khan as a close associate, and kept delivering his speeches in Azeri.[15] The practice of addressing the public in their native language paid off handsomely with the unstoppable growth of his popularity and political influence in Tabriz.

The British Presence and the Consolidation of the Republic

As the Ottoman armies started home, the British filled the vacuum. Once again, both Azerbaijans fell under the tutelage of an outside power. Britain was in every respect more distant than Turkey and showed scant interest in furthering Azerbaijan's future unity. The British intention was to maintain their presence in Iran indefinitely, and they viewed that country as one entity, especially as the Russian sphere of influence had become a matter of lesser relevance. At the same time the British considered their venture into Transcaucasia as a temporary expedient arising from the turmoil of the Russian Civil War. Yet some of the Britons who had served in India favored creation of a large Shi'ite Muslim state that would buffer British possessions from both Bolshevik Russia and Sunni Turkey. One such Briton was General W. M. Thomson, who had succeeded Dunsterville as the commander of the British North Persian Force.[16]

Even though he arrived in Baku on November 17, purportedly to restore Transcaucasia to non-Bolshevik Russia, and on his landing ordered the Azerbaijani flag be removed from the pier, Thomson was not eager to hand power to the Baku Russian *Kadet* Party, who could claim the backing of only a small, nonnative fraction of the local population. Nor would he agree with the Russians' contention that Azerbaijan was merely a figment of the imagination of a handful of political adventurers; the Khoiskii government, he pointed out, remained the only effective civilian authority throughout the country.

Thomson also found himself taking the side of the Azeris in their territorial dispute with the Armenians. There was no single stretch of the frontier that both governments could accept as permanent, but the focal points of contention were Nakhichevan, Zangezur, and, above all, Nagorno-Karabagh. Economically gravitating to Eastern Transcaucasia, Nagorno-Karabagh, was also situated within the strategic corridor extending through Nakhichevan toward Turkey. Depending on who controlled it, Nagorno-Karabagh could either be could be a link or a barrier in the communications between Azerbaijan and Anatolia. Upon the Ottoman withdrawal, General Andranik made an attempt to extend Armenian rule over this disputed territory, but on December 1 Thomson asked him to cease his military operations. Furthermore, as of mid-January 1919, the British general put Nagorno-Karabagh together with the neighboring Zangezur uezd under provisional Azerbaijani administration. Armenian reactions became even more heated when Thomson confirmed the nomination of Khosrow Sultanov as governor of the two areas. Thomson's comment was that the British occupation was not an opportunity for revenge. His personal inclination was toward a solution through population exchange: "Transplanting will be necessary but not on a large scale. For example, the Armenian enclave in Karabagh cannot remain, nor can the hostile Mussulman sit round the SW of Erivan as at present."[17]

For all the protests that greeted him, Sultanov succeeded over the next several months in getting the Armenian Assembly in Nagorno-Karabagh to formally accept Azerbaijani rule, an act that recognized the realities of geography, economy, and transportation that linked this ethnic enclave with Azerbaijan rather than with Armenia beyond the mountains. This major breakthrough remained subject to some conditions restricting the size and deplacement of Azerbaijani garrisons in peacetime.[18]

The British, whose long-range objectives in Transcaucasia were anything but clear to themselves, assumed the role of a supervisory power over Azerbaijan. They kept garrisons in some towns, above all in Baku, where they proclaimed martial law. They controlled the railways, especially the Baku-Batum line, over which oil exports, this time to satisfy British needs, again began to flow. Their involvement extended into certain key branches of the civilian administration—the issuing of currency, food supply, and labor relations through their mediating of disputes in the oil fields and railways. On the other hand, unlike the Ottomans, they refrained from interfering in the politics of the Azerbaijani state. Indirectly, the British presence had a positive impact on Azerbaijan in two important ways: it provided a sense of security from outside threats such as the White General Denikin's attempts to reimpose Russian rule and the Armenian territorial claims. Second, it stimulated the growth of national institutions along the lines of Western-style liberal democracy.[19]

The Azerbaijani leaders did not go along with the position of Ahmäd bäy Aghayev, who in November 1918 voiced an opinion that might well have expressed the feelings of many of his countrymen: Azerbaijan was not able to survive as an independent state and had to lean either on Turkey or Russia. Since the Ottoman State had collapsed, there remained no alternative but reconciliation with the Russians, whose civilization, in any case, he said, was higher than that of the Ottomans.[20] What Ahmäd bäy proposed was, in effect, a dramatic volte-face, and such a maneuver was performed with remarkable dispatch, even thought the target was different from his recommendations.

The Azerbaijani elite showed its political acumen by playing to the democratic sensitivities of the British. The day before Thomson's force landed in Baku, the National Council reconvened after its forced hibernation and passed a law on the elections to the Constituent Assembly. No date was set for voting, and the elections were never held, but the National Council at once reconstituted itself into a broad based legislature. Assuming, significantly, the name "Parliament," the body enlarged itself by co-opting new members and representatives of national minorities.

The Azerbaijani Parliament was to consist of 120 deputies, 96 of whom had agreed to join by the time of its inaugural session on December 7, 1918 (the remaining 24 deputies were Armenians who boycotted the Assembly). The Musavat was represented by 38 deputies, the Ittihad by 13, the Socialists—including the deputies of the Muslim Socialist Bloc—and the Menshevik Himmät by 13, the *Ahrar* (Liberal) Party by 5, Independents by 8, the Dashnaktsutiun by 6, Armenians who did not join the boycott by 5, and other national minorities by 5.[21] Although it was the largest political force, the Musavat held less than half the seats in the Parliament, and the formation of a government was possible only with participation of other parties. Coalition cabinets that dissolved in governmental crises became a feature of Azerbaijani politics. There were five cabinets in two years of independence, all but the last put together without ministers from the Ittihad, the party that acquired the status of quasi-permanent opposition. The first three were headed by Khan Khoiskii (established May 28, 1918, June 17, 1918, and April 5, 1919); the other two were headed by Ussubäkov (April 5, 1919; December 29, 1919).[22] The instability of the executive enhanced the importance of the Parliament, which became the focus of Azerbaijani political life. The high number of plenary sessions (105) and legislative proposals (203) are yardsticks of parliamentary activity. The office of the president of the Parliament, held by Topchibashev, was recognized as head of state.

The Parliament was opened by Räsulzadä, who stated that "our separation from Russia is not an act of hostility toward Russia. We have not felt hurt by the Russian people, who have suffered more than us from despotism."[23] In the new era of democracy, the Musavat Party would be guided by the principles of nationalism and federalism. The meaning of nationalism was now embodied in the recognition that the Azeris, while part of a larger family of Turkic peoples, constituted a nation of their own. As for the second principle, federalism, it was a constant element in the Musavat's programs and policy declarations, as a prescription for attaining a small nation's security, but the question with whom to federalize seemed to be left open.[24] Transcaucasian federalism did not appear to be a realistic prospect until the neighboring nations sorted out their quarrels. Later, in the postindependence years, Musavat would be criticized for its implicit readiness to federalize with most diverse partners—not only the Transcaucasian neighbors but also Iran, Turkey, and even Russia, White or Red. For the moment, behind the shield of the Pax Britannica, the Baku coalition regime was able to concentrate on the task of government, with notable successes in some fields.

The Azerbaijani Republic offered a textbook example of a colonial country unexpectedly catapulted into independence. Lacking the experience of indigenous statehood, its leaders resorted to adaptation of the preindependence administrative machinery. The crucial difficulty in building the framework of the new state was not in revamping institutional structures but in the shortage of human resources to staff them. As qualified Azeris were able to fill only some of the positions in the government bureaucracy, crash programs were launched to train candidates for all kinds of jobs down to the level of railway workers, telegraph operators, and typists. At the middle and lower levels, Russian civil servants kept their posts; they were even allowed to conduct official business in Russian, although all state employees were given a two-year deadline for learning the native language.[25]

With the intelligentsia running the country, the old dream of national education began to materialize. Although linguistic Russification was stopped, there was still no consensus on what constituted the native literary language. The echoes of the *Azarijilar*-Ottomanizers debate still resounded, and, remarkably, the latter group's views prevailed among the framers of the Musavat's new program. Adopted at the party's Second Congress in December 1919, the program stated that teaching of the "Ottoman dialect" would be obligatory in Azerbaijan's high schools, a reflection of the current revaluation of Pan-Turkism: political separateness but cultural closeness.[26] Teaching of a Turkic language was introduced to all schools at any level, and the history of Turkic peoples replaced the study of Russian history. In many primary schools Russian was eliminated as the language of instruction, but the lack of personnel slowed the Turkification of secondary education. A special board was in charge of preparing textbooks, largely through translations, and recruitment in Turkey partly alleviated the shortage of teachers. Simultaneously, newly established teachers' seminaries were training Azeris, and the government sent more than a hundred young people to study in Turkey and Europe. In the Republic's second year, Azerbaijan gained its first center of higher education with the opening of the Baku University on September 1, 1919. This institution, headed by the Russian scientist V. I. Razumovskii, was transferred from Tiflis, where it had been conceived as the University of Transcaucasia. Its language of instruction was Russian, and the university consisted of two departments—medical and historical-philological. Among the educational reforms, projects for Latinization of the alphabet were under consideration.[27]

Azerbaijan lacked not only the tradition of an indigenous statehood but also that of military service, from which Russia's Muslims had been exempt. In the unsettled condition of Transcaucasia, the creation of a national army became a matter of urgency, all the more so because the Azeris remained at an obvious disadvantage to the well-trained and battle-tested forces of their Christian neighbors. The transformation of the Muslim National Corps into a regular, combat-worthy force began in earnest only after the coming of the Ottomans, who helped train Azeri officers and specialists. Under the parliamentary regime the Ministry of War was led by Samad bäy Mahmandiarov, formerly a general of artillery in the Russian army. His principal assistants were generals 'Ali Shikhlinskii and Suleyman Sulkiewicz, the latter a Lithuanian "Tatar," who had led the German-installed administration of the Crimea and then joined the Azerbaijani army as its chief of staff.

The officer corps included Ottomans as well as Russians and Georgians of the former Tsarist army. The Russians, rather than the Ottomans, set the tone for the Azerbaijani military. The organizational structure and regulations were all copied from the Russian model under Nicholas II.

Combining former irregulars, new draftees, and a sprinkling of Azeris who had experienced military service under tsardom, the Azerbaijani army reached a strength of some 35,000. Organized into two infantry divisions and one cavalry division, the army also included two artillery brigades, officer- and specialist-training schools, and auxiliary services. There were plans to expand the armed forces to 50,000, with equipment to be purchased from Italy.[28]

The combat-worthiness of the army remained unproven, except in small-scale operations against Russian settlers in the Mugan Steppe or Armenian insurgents in Nagorno-Karabagh. General Mahmandiarov continued to remind the Parliament that it takes a long time and much effort to forge an effective army, and he once shocked the deputies by saying that the entire Azerbaijani army would be needed to stand up to one Russian battalion.[29] The young republic footed a heavy bill for its defense establishment: estimated expenditures for 1919 amounted to one-fourth of the state budget, a large proportion in a disrupted economy.[30]

Economically, Azerbaijan fared better than neighboring Georgia and Armenia, and even Narimanov reported in Moscow that the Baku "food situation is good. Products are plentiful. Manufactured goods come from Persia. . . . Entry and exit across the border is free. . . . There is in effect a freedom-of-press law on the English model."[31] Through the British-controlled State Bank, the Republic was successful in organizing its finances, and as oil shipments resumed through the Baku-Batum pipeline, prospects appeared for commercial contacts with Europe. "It can be said," stated a British report, "that at present opportunities exist for trade because the country is wealthy and yet is starved of all manufactured goods."[32] All the same, the oil-based economy that had grown as an appendage of Russia's suffered a deep crisis when the Russian Civil War severed Azerbaijan's traditional markets. Under the independent republic the oil exports fell precipitously to some 30 percent of the preceding years' averages. Whatever quantities of oil could be sold went to buyers in Transcaucasia and northern Iran or through Batum to the British forces and their allies. In reviewing Azerbaijan's economic condition, an official government publication stressed that regardless of the amount of oil Europe might purchase, the Republic's finances would not be restored to normal "as long as the Russian markets remain closed to us."[33]

Despite the low volume of exports, which was compounded by the postwar drop in world oil prices, the government was committed to preventing drastic cuts in oil production; high unemployment would have been politically dangerous. The oil companies received subsidies to cover wages and operating costs, with the result that by early 1920 an entire year's production of oil filled every storage tank available, and there were plans to pump the oil into the sea. These subsidies, together with the upkeep of the army, bureaucracy, and education system, were met by heavy deficit financing. Estimates of government expenditures for 1919 were 1,085 million rubles, while revenues were only slightly more than half this amount. Inevitably, the inflationary pressures were considerable.[34] Despite efforts to contain it, unemployment crept up, and by May 1919 there were some 10,000 idle workers in Baku and its environs. The discontent of the city's proletariat manifested itself in strikes, and there was some resurgence of Bolshevik influence, though chiefly among the nonnative element.

Difficult as the economic problems appeared, there were grounds for guarded optimism. Azerbaijan's oil wealth alone could in the long run provide the country with a sound economic foundation for independent existence. One day, it was hoped, with the end of civil war in Russia, bright prospects would emerge for a free and prosperous Azerbaijan. Such prospects hinged, however, on two questions: which side would win the struggle in Russia, and, even more crucial, what would be the attitude of the victor toward an Azerbaijan that had cut itself loose from Russia?

Diplomacy and Special Relationships

In August 1919, Great Britain, which did not have "strong enough interests to warrant more than a brief continuance of this thankless responsibility," completed the withdrawal of its troops from Transcaucasia and left a token force in Batum.[35] For Azerbaijan, the phase of full independence began. Ironically, the absence of an outside power's tutelage also spelled the twilight of the Democratic Republic. The danger no longer came from Denikin, who in the second half of 1919 was too weak to threaten Transcaucasia. Now an even darker cloud loomed on the horizon: the Red Army pushed relentlessly south in pursuit of the Whites. There were no grounds for assuming that the Reds would stop at Azerbaijan's frontier, and against this peril Baku sought frantically for assurances. Attempts to create a common front of Transcaucasian states did not progress beyond the Azerbaijani-Georgian mutual-defense pact, from which Armenia abstained. The Azerbaijani delegation at the Versailles Conference tried strenuously to elicit some support from the Entente leaders. As a result, they merely received de facto diplomatic recognition in January 1920 and vague promises of arms deliveries. In the end, it was vis-à-vis the historically special-relationship countries, Iran and Turkey, that Azerbaijani foreign policy retained some freedom of maneuver. The most significant initiative of the Democratic Republic's diplomacy took place in relations with Iran, even though the very beginning seemed to bode ill. In Versailles, the Teheran government presented its claims to the "cities and provinces wrested from Persia after the Russian war," and these included the entire Azerbaijani Republic as well as part of Daghestan.[36] As a nonbelligerent in the World War, Iran was refused admission to the Conference, and the memorandum of its chief delegate 'Ali Qulu Khan was greeted with ridicule by Western diplomats. Topchibashov, the chief Azerbaijani representative at the conference, remarked in his report to Baku that the Iranian delegation itself did not expect that its demands would be met in Versailles. He added a note on what was, in his view, the deeper meaning of Iranian intentions: "They keep telling us that we should unite with them; they want it strongly and talk about and talk about our intelligentsia, which does not exist among them."[37]

Still, the claims from Teheran did not prevent a remarkable improvement in the relations with Iran, proof of the vitality of the ties between the two countries. The Azerbaijani vice-minister of foreign affairs, Adil Ziyatkhanov, took up residence in Teheran as the Republic's representative, and from Iran a mission under Sayyid Zia al-Din Tabatabai, a rising star of Iranian politics, traveled to Baku to negotiate agreements on tariffs, postal service, and commerce. Meanwhile the talks on the desirability of confederation of the Azerbaijani Republic and Iran were conducted. For both sides the idea held the prospect of fulfilling major aspirations: Iran would recover the territories lost to Russia, and Baku would draw closer to Tabriz. The rapprochement found further stimulation in the signing of the Anglo-Iranian Agreement of August 9, 1919. The agreement, which provided for assigning

British advisors to key agencies of the central government in return for a £2 million loan, was seen as virtually turning Iran into a protectorate. While many Iranians voiced their patriotic indignation, the Baku Azeris saw London's new involvement in Iran as a way to slip back under the British shield, all the more so because an appendix to the treaty stated that Britain would cooperate in "the rectification of the frontier of Persia at the points where it is agreed upon by the parties to be justifiable."[38]

A joint Iranian-Azerbaijani commission met in Paris between October 29 and November 1 and produced a document that the Iranian foreign minister, Nasr al-Din Dovleh, subsequently handed to the British government. The memorandum, which restated the separation of Caucasian Azerbaijan from Russia in whatever form and its full independence, defined the future relationship with Iran:

> Article III. Azerbaijani Democratic Republic establishes political-economic link with its neighbor, the Empire of Persia, in the form of confederation, whose principles, form, and the means of implementation will be elaborated and discussed jointly by the Persian and Azerbaijani governments, and will be submitted for approval by the Parliaments of both countries. But henceforth, the foreign relations of both countries will be unified.
>
> Article IV. With the view to attain the goals indicated above (Article I, and II), the Azerbaijani Republic desires the support of Great Britain for the recognition and maintenance of its independence, for the assurances against any attempt at its integrity, as well as for the development of political, economic, and military strength, the support similar to that accorded to Persia.[39]

For the Baku regime, the most essential element of this plan was the assumption that Britain would offer Azerbaijan and Iran the same degree of protection. By the same token, the Azeris implied that they might be less interested in joining a weak Iran without the inducement of its link to Britain. As for the British, they saw here the game-playing of Nasr al-Din, who:

> wishes with our assistance and under our patronage, to bring the whole of the Republic of Azerbaijan, including Baku, into the Persian orbit. He has contrived to get an obscurely worded declaration out of some Azerbaijani delegates in Paris and it would

be interesting to know with whom he has been intriguing. For the Azerbaijani delegates are of varied political complexion.[40]

In his confidential comments, Foreign Secretary Lord Curzon laid out what were, in essence, the British interests at stake in Azerbaijan:

> If our control in Persia is to be a really thorough one, there might be considerable advantage to us eventually in extending it in some form to both shores of the Caspian including Baku, . . . but any move in this direction at present would of course mean an immediate and irreparable breach with Denikin or with any Russia of the future, even a Bolshevik Russia. It is one thing to sympathize with the aspirations of the parts of the Russian Empire that have declared for independence, but quite another to facilitate the acquisition of the former Russian territory by a neighboring Oriental Power. Nor can I readily believe that there is any genuine or popular desire in Baku for incorporation in the Persian Empire. . . . I can hardly imagine any country caring to come under Persian control and maladministration.[41]

This back-door attempt at regaining British protection was undermined further by the spread of protests against the Anglo-Iranian Agreement. As a result, the Majlis refused to agree to its ratification. The setback did not, however, seriously damage the steady growth of contacts between the Azerbaijani Republic and its southern neighbor, a process that culminated in the signing of a treaty of friendship and commerce in March 1920. A confidential memorandum for the Baku cabinet by a former Russian diplomat, V. F. Maevskii, recommended the rapid expansion of these contacts as a matter of importance on the following grounds:

> The population of Northern Persia is akin to that of Azerbaijan; it has always gravitated toward this country, and will gravitate even more with the growth of close economic ties. . . . We have the right to assume that Azerbaijan will have the dominant role in the mutual relations; it should not, by resorting to injudicious policies, deprive itself of brilliant prospects which the future has for it in store.[42]

On the other hand, the rapprochement of Baku with the Teheran regime of Vusuq ul-Dovleh, which had signed the Anglo-Iranian Agreement, and the Republic's desperately pro-British orientation produced inimical repercussions in Tabriz. Here the agreement was received with disfavor by all classes, but especially among the bazaar merchants who feared that the issue at stake was the scheme to divert the trade routes to British-held Baghdad. The city became the focus of the protest activities against the "colonial" Anglo-Iranian compact, a movement spearheaded by Khiabani's Democrats, who, in addition to their traditional distrust of Teheran, developed hostility toward Baku.[43]

Even more complex were Azerbaijan's relations with Turkey, a reflection of historical realities as well as of the condition of that country in the aftermath of the Great War. Occupied in parts by foreign troops, the Ottoman state was split between the Allied-backed regime of Sultan Mehmet VI and the resistance movement, whose leader from the summer of 1919 was the war hero Mustafa Kemal Pasha. Baku's official contacts were with the sultan's government in Istanbul, where the Azerbaijani diplomatic mission resided; yet the facts of geography and politics drew Azerbaijan into a web of intricate and uneasy relations with the rebels, who in their nascent nationalism called themselves Turks rather than Ottomans, and whose power base centered on eastern and central Anatolia. Additional complications stemmed from the division within the Turkish anti-imperialist forces in Turkey between the Kemal-led Nationalists and the loyalists of the fallen CUP regime. The Young Turks, anxious for restoration of their power, were the silent rivals of Kemal, and he prudently kept them from gaining control of his movement. At his insistence the participants in the September 1919 Nationalist Congress in Sivaş took an oath renouncing the CUP and its policies. The rift between the two groups, while subdued in Anatolia, was more pronounced in Transcaucasia.[44]

The Turkish factor in Azerbaijan did not vanish with the retreat of the Ottoman troops after the Mudros armistice. While some 3,000 former Ottoman military personnel and schoolteachers who had entered Azerbaijani service were the most visible sign of the Turkish presence, pro-Turkish sympathies surged again when Kemal began his liberation war against the Allies. Strong as it was, the Turkish influence in Azerbaijan initially tilted toward the Young Turks. In the last days of the Great War, Enver Pasha sought to use Baku as a base from which to launch his campaign for reconquering Turkey but failed even to reach Azerbaijan. The same intention had motivated Nuri Pasha in his attempt to place the Ottoman forces under Azerbaijani jurisdiction following the Mudros armistice. The Young Turks saw possible advantages from cooperation with Soviet Russia in the struggle against Western imperialism, and Kemal shared this view. Both Kemalists and Young Turks sought contacts with the Bolsheviks, and one of the most suitable venues for this purpose seemed to be Azerbaijan. The first of the prominent Turks to appear in Azerbaijan after the war was the familiar figure of Nuri, who had escaped British detention in Batum and established in the fall of 1919 the semi-official Representation of the People of Turkey. When the Representation approached the Baku regime for financial aid to the Turkish struggle, it met with an evasive answer because of fear of alienating the British. More auspicious were the Turks' contacts with the Bolshevik underground in Baku, which led to promises of financial support.[45]

Another channel of communications between Turkey and the Bolsheviks was opened through the efforts of Halil Pasha. Having joined the Nationalists, this prominent Young Turk was sent on a secret mission to Transcaucasia to arrange for military assistance from Soviet Russia. In December 1919 he made his way to Azerbaijan, where he began his personal diplomacy by establishing contacts with the Bolshevik Regional Committee and at the same time with the Baku government. Halil's immediate concern was to secure the corridor linking Anatolia with Azerbaijan for the future flow of Soviet aid, and to this end he joined forces with the volunteers resisting Armenian rule over Nakhichevan.[46]

The Turks, both in Transcaucasia and Anatolia, showed little faith in Azerbaijan's prospects for retaining its independence. Mustafa Kemal himself predicted that the weak Transcaucasian states would eventually return to Russian rule, a view shared by the rival Sultan's regime: "Intelligent opinion here considers the independent aspirations of small peoples of Caucasus illusioned and impracticable," wrote a diplomat from Istanbul.[47] Jointly with Kazim Pasha Karabekir, the commander of the Fifteenth Army Corps who was in charge of Turkish policies in the eastern frontier regions, Kemal Pasha defined strategic objectives for Transcaucasia: the interests of Turkey's struggle for independence required suppression of Armenia, the replacement of the Azerbaijani regime by a pro-Soviet one, and neutrality of Georgia—the only of the three republics that could be left intact. In this manner Azerbaijan would serve as a bridge linking Soviet Russia and embattled Anatolia, instead of being a barrier between the two. When the Allied powers extended on January 12, 1920, their recognition to the Transcaucasian republics, Kemal saw it as an imperialist plot to erect a fence separating free Turkey from a friendly Russia, with the possibility of igniting disastrous consequences for the Nationalists. He wrote that it was imperative to start preparations for breaking the

> Caucasian barrier . . . to contact the new governments of the Caucasus, particularly those of Islamic Azerbaijan and Daghestan, in order to ascertain what is their position with regard to the designs of the Entente powers. Should the Caucasian nations decide to act as a barrier against us, we will agree with the Bolsheviks on a coordinated offensive against them.[48]

This Turkish position signaled an abrupt reversal of the political tradition that had allowed the Azeris to see Turkey as a natural supporter of their emancipation. As for Pan-Islamism, Pan-Turkism, and especially Turanism as elements of Turkey's foreign policy, Kemal rejected them outright, unlike the Young Turks, who upheld them even after 1918. In his view, these programs were not only incompatible with Turkey's need for friendship with Russia, but, more essentially, they conflicted with his "Turkey first" brand of nationalism, differing from the Ottoman-imperial sense of obligations to other Turkic peoples.

Of the two special-relationship neighboring Muslim countries, Turkey's record was less propitious than Iran's for the aspirations of the Azerbaijani nation-state. By contrast, the association with Iran offered a prospect, vague as it was, for the best attainable outcome: external security and the link with Tabriz. Yet Iran was weak and comparatively passivist, while Turkey was activist and embarked on a new war. In Azerbaijan the Turkish liberation struggle gained a large number of sympathizers, from a broad spectrum of the public. Their numbers included Pan-Islamists of the Ittihad, who believed that the Young Turks would eventually replace the Kemalists; the leftists, who perceived in the Turkish struggle the beginning of the worldwide anti-imperialist upheaval; and those of diverse political persuasions, who generally disapproved of "parochial" Azeri nationalism. "The sympathies of the population are Turkish rather than, as might be expected, Persian," noted an American report.[49]

The Native Communists and the Twilight of Independence

The harsh reality was that while the Russian Civil War prevented the recovery of the Azerbaijani economy, independence was based on the war's stalemate. Presumably, whichever side won the war would begin the process of the ingathering of lost territories. During October and November 1919, the turning point in the Russian conflict occurred when the Volunteer Army's drive on Moscow collapsed like a pierced balloon. In a dramatic reversal of their fortunes, the White troops began a headlong flight southward, and it was increasingly obvious that the winners would be the Reds. Such circumstances were bound to improve the prospects of the Azeri far left.

Numerically weak, the Bolshevik Himmät nonetheless assumed a singular weight as the only native group with which Soviet Russia would likely discuss arrangements for Azerbaijan's future. The Himmät of 1919 differed in some ways from what it had been two years earlier. The Narimanov-led Old Guard that had backed the Baku Commune had dispersed after the fall, its members taking refuge in Russia. The very experience of the Commune, which began with a massacre of the Muslims and ended with the massacre of the Armenians, induced the Himmätists to question the validity of Russian centralism and its disregard for national distinctions. As for the new crop of native Communists at home, they were mostly in their twenties, and their leaders were such men as Haidar Karayev, Mirza Daud Huseynov, and Fattah Musavi. They accepted as their goal the power of the Soviets in Azerbaijan, deeming it both desirable and inevitable, but they did not relish the prospect of the Himmät's absorption into the Russian party, and they insisted on autonomy within the Soviet system.

The Baku Himmätists generally found support among their comrades in Russia, some of whom had gained a voice in shaping Soviet policies toward the Muslims. By far the most influential of them was Narimanov, whom Stalin appointed in June 1919 first as head of the Near East Section of the People's Commissariat for Foreign Affairs (*Narkomindel*) and then as Deputy Commissar of the Commissariat for Nationalities Affairs (*Narkomnats*). In these capacities he became known as an advocate of carrying the revolution to the Muslim East: "We fully agreed with Comrade Stalin in our views of the eastern question. . . . The social revolution in Europe, and especially in England, will come with the economic crisis and its source will be in Asia. For this reason the attention of our foreign policy and of the Party's Central Committee should be turned toward the East, especially toward the Muslim East." The natural base for carrying the revolution in this direction was Azerbaijan, "the connecting link between Turkey and Persia," and he called for the Sovietization of his homeland with the help of Russian bayonets. At the same time he criticized non-Azeri Communists' lack of consideration for "traditions, national-historical outlook, the patterns of communal life, spiritual issues, and psychology."[50] Narimanov believed that Russia should proclaim an independent Soviet Azerbaijan, a significant step ahead of autonomy that corresponded with his concern to attract Muslims abroad. By contrast with his view, the young Himmätists in Baku seemed to regard Azerbaijan as a part of the Russian Revolution only.

Still, the two groups cooperated, and the Moscow-based Himmätists helped to bring the case of Azerbaijan and its indigenous Communist organization for review at the highest level. On July 19, 1919, the Politburo in Moscow adopted a resolution bearing a ponderous title: "On Recognizing the Himmät Party as the Autonomous Communist Party with the Rights of an Oblast' Committee and on Recognizing Azerbaijan as an Independent Soviet Republic." The language of the resolution is remarkable for its contradictions intertwined with caveats, itself an indication of Moscow's discomfort with the underlying issue:

> It is recognized that the Central Committee in principle has no objections to the proposal of the Himmät Party, it being understood that the definitive solution of the case will be submitted for the approval of the Transcaucasian Committee of the RCP(B). Comrade Stalin will be informed about its decision, which will be binding if no objections are raised by him. The same applies to the recognition of an independent Azerbaijan.[51]

The party of an independent country would be merely autonomous, and its status would be no higher than that of a district organization. The apparent meaning of Azerbaijani independence was statehood, patterned after that of the Soviet Ukraine or Byelorussia, an important concession in itself. Still, the willingness to tolerate the existence of an autonomous Himmät ran contrary to the principle of centralism, which precluded a federal structure of the party. Most contradictory of all, the decision on the question of Azerbaijan, that distant corner of the former empire, was relegated to the Transcaucasian Regional Committee (*Kraikom*), known for its opposition to the Himmätist aspirations. Remarkably, even this decision was to be approved by Stalin, the only Bolshevik leader with some knowledge of political conditions of the region. The Politburo resolution sounded as though it meant to accommodate the centralizers, autonomists, and independence-minded alike, but in the end its actions amounted to a washing of its hands.

There followed debates between the Himmätist leaders and the Kraikom in Tiflis. One side stood for the autonomy of their party and, by extension, of their country. The other side defended orthodox Bolshevik centralism. Behind the dispute loomed the fundamental question: would Sovietization turn Azerbaijan merely into a province of Russia, or would it offer a measure of identity within the Soviet system? The Himmätists stuck to their guns, and instead of preparing, as the Kraikom wished, for the merger with the RCP(B), they put forward an alternative smacking of the heresy that was to be spread later by the "Tatar" Communist Mir Sultan Galiev. There would be separate parties for Muslims and all others; the Himmät would have an exclusively Azeri membership; the Ädälät would continue in its present status as an organization of immigrants from Iran. During the confrontation with the Kraikom, the Ädälät in every way supported the Himmätists' position, an indication of cultural and ethnic solidarity as well as organizational links. Many of the immigrants' party cells were enmeshed with the Himmät, and a prominent Himmätist, Dadash Buniatzadä, served as the chairman of the Ädälät's Central Committee.[52]

The final word on the controversy came from Moscow—that is, with the endorsement of Stalin—in early January 1920: there was to be one Communist organization for all nationalities inhabiting Azerbaijan. The name Himmät was to be dropped, as were any references to its Muslim or Turkic character. The organization was to be called the Communist Party of Azerbaijan (CPAz), a name carrying more territorial than national connotations. Although the imposed solution was closer to Kraikom's position, the Himmätists no longer raised protests. They could have derived some feeling of compensation from the fact that the Constituent Congress of the CPAz, which met semi-clandestinely in Baku on February 11, 1920, had an overwhelmingly Muslim majority. The Himmät's representation from Baku equalled that of the

RCP(B), that is, thirty representatives each. Another thirty came from the Ädälät, and an additional sixty from the Communist cells outside the city, which were mostly Himmätist.

Reflecting the strength of the native element, the forty-three-member Central Committee consisted chiefly of Azeris, with Huseynov as chairman. The Congress concluded with a manifesto calling for the "overthrow of the rule of bays, khans, and nationalists," and the preparations for the seizure of power were stepped up.[53]

In their propaganda, the Communists played on the doubts, fears, and disillusionments that took hold of the public: if good relations with Russia were indispensible for the existence of Azerbaijan, could they materialize under any other rule but that of the Soviets? The change of regime in Baku would lead to resumption of the exports of oil—now pumped into the sea—thus ending at once the economic crisis. Soviet power would not, however, mean the loss of Azerbaijani statehood, but rather a cutting loose from the Western powers, which were far away and not concerned with the fate of Azerbaijan. "If England had sincerely wished to make other peoples independent, why, one could ask, did it destroy the independence of the Turkish state and now is trying to strangle the people of Turkey?"[54] The Communists were eager to capitalize on Pan-Islamic and Pan-Turkish sentiments that were surging among the population with the echoes of the Turkish war of liberation. The most straightforward tone in this Communist propaganda campaign sounded in the open letter of Narimanov to the Prime Minister Ussubäkov: "For Soviet Russia the union with Georgia or Armenia is not a matter of particular importance," he reminded his old time acquaintance, "—but Baku—that is the very life of Soviet Russia."[55]

The Azerbaijani Communists experienced some upsurge in their following, and a Soviet source puts the party membership at 4,000 by late April 1920, an increase of 1,000 since the beginning of the year, but the growth occurred mainly in Baku.[56] The realities of Azerbaijan's situation were far more persuasive than any of the Communists' propaganda: with the victorious Red Army approaching the Azerbaijani border, absorption by Soviet Russia was seen as imminent. In fact, on March 17 Lenin issued a directive that "it is extremely, extremely important for us to take Baku," and he soon appointed an official to take charge of the Baku oil, A. P. Serebrovskii. A special high-powered body, the Caucasian Bureau (*Kavbiuro*), under Ordzhonikidze and his deputy, Sergei Kirov, was set up on April 8 to coordinate the military and political aspects of the conquest.[57]

By now, dissension had come to the open within the Baku coalition regime. Likewise, the rift in the ranks of the Musavat between the two wings reemerged more sharply than ever before. The spokesman for the left, Interior Minister Mammad H. Hajinskii, urged a "placate Russia" policy, and he gained at least tacit support of Räsulzadä against the tougher-minded foreign minister, Khan Khoiskii. During March and early April the Eleventh Red Army occupied Daghestan and menaced the Azerbaijani frontier. This alone portended the twilight of independence. Other events followed in quick succession. On March 23 an Armenian uprising broke out in Nagorno-Karabagh, and the Azerbaijani high command promptly committed most of the army against the insurgents defending the frontier with Russia. On April 1 the cabinet of Ussubäkov, having just lost the support of the Socialist Parliamentary Group, resigned.

The fall of the government seemed to present an opportunity for Hajinskii, who within a period of three weeks tried to put together a new cabinet with the participation of Communists. He had the backing of Halil Pasha, because the Turkish general saw in him a friend of Turkey, an enemy of Britain, and a man able to deal amicably with the Bolsheviks. As the crisis deepened, various groups of émigré Turks, including the Turkish Communist Party, in existence from March 1920, coordinated their efforts to influence the events to the benefit of the Ankara regime. A Turkish conclave, with notable participants such as Halil Pasha and Fuad Sabit, resolved that the pro-British government in Baku should be overthrown as soon as possible and be replaced by one capable of cooperating with the Bolsheviks. At the same time, the Turks registered their misgivings about possible repercussions from the armed conquest: the Red Army should not enter Baku unless the Turkish Communist Party requested it.[58]

As for Hajinskii's prospective partners, they were set on seizing power by themselves, while the Red Army would wait across the border ready to march in. In the spirit of the Turkish comrades' advice, a delegation of the CPAz asked the Eleventh Army command that Red Army troops should not enter Azerbaijan earlier than twenty-four hours after the uprising had started.

The downfall of the Democratic Republic turned out to be an anticlimax to the months of mounting tensions. On April 22 Hajinskii told the stunned Parliament of the failure of his mission to form the government with the Communists. Many high officials understood that the time had come to catch the next train to Tiflis. Others, such as Rustambäkov, talked about the dictatorship of the Musavat—or more exactly of the party's right wing—an unthinkable prospect without the backing of the army. Still others arranged for a governmental delegation under Pepinov to meet with Ordzhonikidze and the Kavbiuro and offer immediate oil deliveries. They were arrested during the negotiations in Piatigorsk when the denouement took place the in Azerbaijani capital.

Having mobilized its poorly armed fighting squads, the CPAz fixed the date of the coup for April 27. Shortly after midnight of this fateful day, telephones began to ring in Baku with reports that four armored trains had crossed the border at Yalama station and that General Shikhlinskii had failed to carry his orders to blow up the railway bridges. The news came as a surprise to the Azeri Communists, as it became clear that the Red Army had disregarded the twenty-four hours waiting time, depriving the native Communists of even the token claim of having seized power by their own effort. Years later, the commander of the armored train, M. G. Efremov, would admit that the overriding consideration for the haste in moving on to Baku had been the need to prevent the destruction of the oil fields.[59]

In the morning, the Central Committee of the CPAz issued a proclamation that the "treacherous, criminal, counterrevolutionary government of the Musavat Party was overthrown and that the only lawful authority" had now become the Provisional Azerbaijani Military-Revolutionary Committee (*Azrevkom*) consisting of Huseynov, Musabäkov, Buniatzadä, Alimov, and Karayev, with Narimanov as chairman.[60] A solidly Azeri membership, except that the Azrevkom was politically subordinated to the Kavbiuro.

With the Red Army about to enter Baku and the Democratic Republic doomed, the Azrevkom was nonetheless concerned about the formalities of the transfer of power. Its representatives held talks with the delegation of the Parliament on an arrangement that would give the Communist coup some legitimacy and also provide for a modus vivendi with the Azeri intelligentsia.

On its part, the ruling elite of the Democratic Republic, having exhausted diplomatic means for salvaging the independence, gave no indication of considering the armed defense against the Red Army. This invasion was seen in Baku as a process of in-gathering, the inescapable restitution of the Russian-ruled multinational empire from one of its periods of troubles. All the same, many in the Baku regime were anxious to derive the best deal from what appeared as historical inevitability.

The outcome of the negotiations amounted to a compact, an early example of similar deals and settlements that would be struck throughout the non-Russian regions of the former empire. This statement was a reply to the ultimatum that Hamid Sultanov handed to the Parliament demanding the surrender of all its powers within twelve hours.

1. Full independence of Azerbaijan under Soviet power will be maintained.

2. The government formed by the Communist Party of Azerbaijan will have provisional authority.

3. The final system of government in Azerbaijan will be determined, without any outside pressure, by the supreme legislative organ of Azerbaijan, the Soviet of Azerbaijani Workers, Peasants, and Soldiers.

4. All functionaries of the government agencies will retain their posts and only those holding positions of responsibility will be replaced.

5. The newly formed provisional Communist government guarantees the life and property of the members of the present government and parliament.

6. This government will take measures to prevent the entry of the Red Army under battle conditions.

7. The new government will resist, using strong measures and all the means at its disposal, all outside forces, from whatever quarter, aiming at the suppression of Azerbaijani independence.[61]

Some parts of the parliamentary declaration were of a face-saving character to facilitate the surrender; other provisions concerned the safety of the outgoing regime's personnel. The Parliament accepted the terms, and with its act of abdication the experiment in an independent Azerbaijani nation-state came to an end, one hour before the deadline of the Communist ultimatum.

The Tabriz Revolt of 1920

At the time when the independent Baku regime was inexorably sliding to its doom, in Tabriz the Democrats were making strides toward the self-assertion of the other part of Azerbaijan. After eight months of preparations—i.e., as Khiabani admitted, since the beginning of the protest movement against the Anglo-Iranian Agreement and the Vosuq ul Dovleh cabinet—on April 9, 1920, the Democrats carried out a revolt against the Teheran government. The immediate cause was friction with Swedish-officered police force sent from Teheran. In the words of the proclamation, the purpose of the uprising was to protest

> reactionary tendencies which manifested themselves in a series of anticonstitutional acts committed by the local authorities. . . . The liberals of Tabriz declare that their entire program consists of achieving full satisfaction as to the government's respect of the liberal regime of the country and the loyal observance on its part of the constitutional laws that define its character.[62]

Power over the city passed into the hands of the Public Committee (*Heyet-i-Ejtimai*), local police and gendarmerie accepted its authority, and the new ruling body began its work replacing the Teheran-appointed officials with the Democrats.

The rebels, who made clear their partiality for the republican form of government, gave a new name to the province, Azadistan (Land of Freedom). The choice of the name was interpreted not only as a rebuff to Teheran but also as a rebuff to the Baku regime and a way of keeping a safe distance from it. Kasravi explained the origin of this name, not without a characteristic tone of bias:

> After the break up of the Russian empire, there emerged in Baku and its environs a small Turkic-speaking Caucasian republic which called itself the Republic of Azerbaijan. In the old books, the name of this region was "Arran," but the name has long fallen into disuse. The hope and ambition of that republic was to unite one day with Azerbaijan and for this reason it chose the name of Azerbaijan for itself and its territory. The (Iranian) Azerbaijanis who had no desire for such unification, nor a wish to turn away from Iran, felt much annoyed with that appropriation of the name. But as this name had become accepted, many would say: it would be better if we assumed a different name for our province. In such a manner the name "Azadistan" was coined.[63]

Another Iranian Azerbaijani author, 'Ali Azari, offers a simpler explanation for the name Azadistan: it commemorated the sacrifices that Azerbaijan had suffered in the struggles during the Constitutional Revolution.[64]

Before long, on May 1, a British political officer from Qazvin, Major P. J. Edmonds, paid a visit to Khiabani. He described the ruler of Tabriz as "a man of about forty, of slight build, with black beard thin below the corners of the mouth, pallid complexion, slightly discoloured teeth, wearing gold-rimmed spectacles, and a small white turban," who "spoke with restraint deliberately and with no hesitation as one who knew exactly what he wanted." Khiabani assured his guest that there was nothing separatist or anti-British in their movement. On the contrary, the uprising was to secure the enforcement of that constitution which, they could not forget, had been won for Persia by the British Legation. Nonetheless, Edmonds carried away the impression that "they aim either at Bolshevism or the independence of Azerbaijan. They are said to have a list of fifteen persons to put in charge of government departments."[65] Among them were the names of Khiabani's close associates Badamchi, Ismail Amir Khizi, and the Turcophile Mirza Taqi.

The British officer, concerned about preserving the integrity of Iran, approached Kasravi, who was known for his disagreements with Khiabani, and suggested he form a movement to overthrow the Democrats' rule. Kasravi declined, giving three reasons:

> First, because my followers are mostly merchants and unable to fight; second, we dispersed our group the first day of Khiabani's rebellion, a good thing for us; third, since Khiabani has risen up in the name of Azerbaijan, we do not want to fight against him in this rebellion.[66]

All the same, he prudently left Tabriz, breaking off once for all with Khiabani.

Since 1917 Khiabani had been peppering some of his speeches with friendly references to the Russian Revolution; he had no use for Pan-Azerbaijani solidarity with the imperialist-backed Musavatists, whose government had been doomed in any case by the time of the Tabriz uprising, and he viewed the April 28 coup in Baku sympathetically, as a victory for the former Himmätists hoping for trade and diplomatic links with the Narimanov regime. He also maintained cor-

dial relations with the enigmatic German consul in Tabriz, Kurt Wustrow, a convert to Communism who used his office for promoting pro-
Soviet activities. But the May 18 landing of the Red Army forces in
Enzeli in support of Kuchuk Khan made it clear to him that the position of Azadistan had been endangered. When the Bolshevik forces
turned toward Zinjan, as if with the intention to enter Azerbaijan, the
Tabriz Democrats, whose social base was bazaar merchants and arti-
sans, denounced the Enzeli landing. Khiabani, reacting as an indignant
Iranian patriot, declared that no foreigners, whether they were British
or Russian, had a right to intervene in the internal affairs of Iran. "Iran
must be made free by Iranians."[67] He warned that should the Bolsheviks attempt to annex any part of Iranian territory, Azerbaijan would
fight against them to the end. To drive his point home, he banned activities of the Ädälät. The reports from the Tabriz branch of the Ädälät
intercepted by British intelligence in the summer of 1920 complain of
persecutions at the hands of the Democrats, who were acting at the
instigation of the British. Otherwise, the Ädälät expressed confidence
in popular support for the Bolsheviks when the invasion of Azerbaijan
was launched.[68]

Khiabani also put Wustrow under strict supervision, an arrangement that ended with the German's death on June 3, either through
assassination or, as the official version of the Azadistan authorities had
it, through suicide. At this juncture, the name Azadistan went into the
officially prescribed use, possibly indicating that Khiabani was now
anxious to distance himself from Bolshevik-ruled Baku. In the same
spirit, he refused to cooperate with Kuchuk Khan, who had allied himself with the Communists.

Khiabani created his government along the lines Major Edmonds
had expected. He called it the National Government (*Melli Hokumat*),
and on the day of its formation, June 24, among crowds singing "La
Marseillaise," symbolically moved his office to *'Ali Kapu*, the residence
of the viceroy of Azerbaijan. His cabinet mainly included members of
the merchant class, in addition to some intellectuals. The key positions
were held by the following persons: Khiabani was in charge of finances;
Abul Qasim Fiyuzat, of education; Muhammad Huseyn Savfat, administration of the Waqfs; and Muzzafar A'lam Sardar, defense.[69]

As the threat of the Bolshevik invasion receded, Khiabani's main
preoccupation was, apart from price control, the establishment of the
native language schools system with teachers brought from north of

the Araxes or Turkey. "A nation cannot retain its freedom without education," was one of his favorite sayings. Likewise he promoted the Azeri literary revival, with a symbol no less eloquent than the planned resumption of publication of the *Molla Nasr al-Din*. It was to be based in Tabriz, and its publisher was to be Jalal Mammäd Quluzadä, who had recently become a resident of the city. Of the natives involved in this revival, the most accomplished continued to be Mirza Taqi Khan. A historian of Iranian Azerbaijani literature, Sakina Berengian, lists a number of other writers linked to the Khiabani movement who took part in this rebirth and also quotes alarmist Persian voices on the progress of literary Turkification in Azerbaijan, which were calling on the Teheran government to counteract the process.[70]

Still the Bolshevik presence across the Araxes did not allow itself to be forgotten. Increasingly, Azadistan was becoming a refuge for Azeris fleeing from the violent suppression of their resistance north of the Araxes. Among the refugees was an infantry regiment that had taken part in the Ganja uprising.

The end of Azadistan came not at the hands of the foreigners but through the action of the central government to restore its authority in the provinces. The new prime minister, Mushir al-Dovleh, who in June replaced Vusuq al-Dovleh, was a man whose Iranian patriotism was beyond question, and Khiabani could no longer claim that his rebellion was in opposition to imperialism. Yet he refused to recognize Teheran's appointed governor Muhbar al-Sultaneh and provoked accusations that he was a separatist at heart. Khiabani justified his refusal on the ground that the central government, even though not a British stooge, was undemocratic:

> In our country the state consists of the grand vizier who, having gathered around himself five–ten men, rules over the nation with no participation of the people. . . . Our goal is that the people themselves should choose the grand vizier and ministers. We do not need a new governor.[71]

A stand-off followed. Finally, when the Azadistan militia forces were out of Tabriz, Muhbar al-Sultaneh ordered Iranian Cossacks to enter the city. On September 4, 1920, they dispersed the Democrats and killed Khiabani in the process.

A controversial historical figure, Khiabani's life and work have been subject to diverse interpretations:

He was both a philosopher and a politician and was well at home in the world of ideas. He was a full-fledged intellectual with an established citizenship in the kingdom of the mind, yet he combined with this status its opposite: he was a politician. He played on the feelings of men to get from them what he wanted by planning popular appeals and stirring crowds to action. As a practical politician he manipulated means to serve ends, getting everything he could, taking a compromise if he could get no more.[72]

Generally, Soviet historiography tended to see him as aiming at regional autonomy in the context of the widespread centrifugal movements elsewhere in Iran, notably in Gilan and Khorasan, and as a proponent of federal restructuring of the state on ethnic lines. On the other hand, Iranian authors are prone to regard him as an Iranian patriot above all committed to upholding independence, freedom, and integrity of Iran. Neither school of thought dotted all its "i"s and crossed all its "t"s, and each left a wide margin for doubt. Both emphasized Khiabani's hostility to British imperialism, although this was not the main concern of his life.

The controversiality of Khiabani has deeper roots not only in his personality or even in the complex circumstances of the time and place. It reflects a larger and unsolved dilemma of Iranian Azerbaijan: a province or a nation? In the light of this dilemma, the Soviet and Iranian views of Khiabani do not necessarily appear as mutually exclusive.

There were divergent currents among the Tabriz Democrats, various shades of Turkism on one side and Persian assimilationists on the other, while Khiabani held to the middle of the road. He stood, in principle, for the territorial integrity of Iran. At the same time, he was adamant about preserving the distinct identity of Azerbaijan. Iran, in his view, should remain a structure that assured the rights of provinces against the center, a fatherland of fatherlands, a historical, religious, and cultural entity, but not an ethnolinguistic one. Like Akhundzadä before him, he used the term *vatan* for both Azerbaijan and Iran. The task of his movement was to work for democratization of Iran in the vital interest of Azerbaijan. "Today the government of Tabriz [is] in the hands of the Democrats. This democratic government starting from Tabriz will spread to the smallest town of Iran. Slowly, we will attain this lofty goal. All power and authority will be shaped by our outlook."[73] Should Teheran be stubbornly opposed to accept such an evolution, there was in the experiment of Azadistan an implicit threat of further loosening the ties to the central government, although such prospects were hardly auspicious in the conditions of 1920.[74]

The Battle of Azerbaijan

Within a month of the fall of Baku, the Soviet thrust beyond the frontiers of the Azerbaijani republic, into Iran, Georgia, and Armenia, lost its momentum, and this realization contributed to the restiveness of the Azeris as they recovered from the demoralizing shock of conquest. The opposition was neither unified nor well organized, even though there emerged two centers of anti-Soviet political activity: the Committee for the Salvation of Azerbaijan, formed by the refugees in Tiflis under Khan Khoiskii, and the Azerbaijani Independence Organization, of the young Musavatists, led by Mirza Bala Mammadzadä, Abd-ul Vahab Yurdsever, and Jäfär Jabbarli. The mainspring of the resistance to Soviet rule was the growing disaffection with the brutal application of the practices of War Communism.

> About senseless cruelties of drunk sailors, soldiers, and *Chekists*; about robberies, humiliations, mockeries of the fundamental human rights; about raping of women and similar countless criminal acts; about carefully concealed horrors of the *Cheka* cells—the eyewitnesses would be recounting later. . . . Every day, every hour there were searches, illegal and willful confiscations.[75]

The spirit of discontent also infected the Azerbaijani troops, who had not been notable for their excessive devotion to the fallen regime. The military was angered by the restructuring of the Azerbaijani forces on the pattern of the Red Army, an undertaking that would entail dismissal of officers and breaking up of units. An attempt by Red Army officers to replace Colonel Mirza Qajar, the commander of a division stationed in Ganja, sparked the first and the most violent of the Azerbaijani uprisings. Thus, belatedly, began the true Battle of Azerbaijan.

The Ganja division, only eighteen-hundred strong, mutinied on the night of May 26. They quickly seized the Muslim sections of the city, and heavy fighting developed around the railroad station, where the Azeris unsuccessfully tried to dislodge the Russians. When a large number of Red Army reinforcements arrived by rail, most of Ganja was surrounded and cut off from the countryside. The Russians launched a series of attacks only to be repelled with heavy losses. In the end, however, their numerical strength and their devastating artillery fire prevailed. Before the fighting was over on May 31, about one thousand rebels perished; some died on the last day at the hands of local Armenians. Others managed to escape to the mountains. The retribution that followed was massive and ruthless. Hamid Sultanov was dispatched from Baku and ordered several hundred summary executions.[76] Throughout the army an immediate purge went into effect, and among its victims were all Azerbaijani generals, except for Shikhlinskii and Mahmandiarov, who were saved by the intervention of Narimanov. In addition, six colonels, three majors, and seven captains lost their lives. Most of them were among the group of seventy-nine men shot on the island of Nargin the day after the Ganja mutiny broke out. The estimate of the number of lives lost from April 1920 to August 1921 reaches 48,000.[77]

The Ganja uprising produced a sense of alarm in the Eleventh Army command, and a special order foresaw the possibility that "the disturbances rooted in national and religious prejudices (may) assume a massive character." If so, the troops were to withdraw to Baku as the base for a counteroffensive.[78] Another order tried to deal with the deeper causes of the popular discontent.

> It is absolutely inadmissible to requisition anything without paying in money. Do not give receipts, but pay at once in cash. Explain to every man that it is necessary to respect their religion, and to stop, for the time being, all agitation against their clergy; to respect their customs.[79]

In retrospect, the alarmist tone of these high command orders appears excessive, given the character and scope of the uprisings. The insurgency spread, but it never equalled the Ganja fighting in intensity. After Ganja had been thoroughly pacified, and the Red forces had been deployed for combat throughout Azerbaijan, a major uprising began in Karabagh. At its head stood Nuri Pasha, who, like most of the Pan-Islamists, became thoroughly disillusioned with the Bolsheviks. The rebels seized Shusha, where an Azerbaijani infantry regiment passed over to their side, but then came face to face with a Red Army cavalry division supported by an air squadron. Although the Reds were threatened by another uprising in Zakataly, they easily retook Shusha on June 15. Nuri's force disintegrated soon afterward, its remnants retreating across the Iranian frontier and into Khiabani's Azadistan.

In Zakataly, the direct cause for the revolt was the order of the local *revkom* to disarm the inhabitants, but there were signs that it was an upheaval inspired by religious motives. Its leader was a cleric, Hafiz Äfändiyev, who gathered a thousand villagers and an infantry battalion. After ten days the rebellion lost its momentum and the fighters dispersed. Some took refuge in the mountains between Georgia and Azerbaijan.[80] The Islamic character of these uprisings served as an excuse for arresting hundreds of the *Ittihadists* and for the banning of the party, despite its anti-nationalist and sometimes pro-Bolshevik record of the past years.

While harsh repression blunted the insurgency, its effectiveness also suffered from the weaknesses characteristically inherent in local rebellions of rural populations. The paucity of calls for the restoration of the independent republic was notable. The notion of a state was foreign, and an indigenous state was too much of a novelty to put down roots. In their limited scope, lack of coordination, and short duration, the anti-Soviet uprisings resembled the insurrectionary movements of the first half of the nineteenth century. Just as a hundred years before, these widely scattered local rebellions were quickly suppressed one after another. Even though the Russians could no longer take advantage of the Sunni-Shi'ite differences, they were able to muster detachments of native workers, thus infusing an element of civil war, this time of the city versus the countryside.

Still, the insurgency went on, if sporadically. A new series of popular uprisings began almost immediately after the September 1920 Baku Congress of the Peoples of the East. Of these, the most extensive broke out in Daghestan, where it threatened the Eleventh Army's communications with Russia. In this historic stronghold of Muslim resistance, fighting continued well into the spring of 1921 in the name of defense of the Shari'a. The struggle made its impact felt in Azerbaijan, most notably through example and encouragement. The Daghestani leaders, Said bey and Ali Khanov, found those who, primarily out of religious impulse, emulated them in Azerbaijan. In the Kuba uezd, a group of five thousand fighters was raised; in Karadanli and Karabulak, a guerrilla force under Jammad bäy was active; in Karadanli, another was led by Khan Shirvanskii. In November 1920 a large band headed by a certain Namaz seized mountain passes in the Dzegam

River valley, tying up Red Army forces for weeks. At the end of the year, the southern coastal area of Lenkoran was the scene of a major revolt that was put down only through a complex military operation that involved combined attacks from sea and land.[81]

With the conquest of Armenia on December 2, 1920, and Georgia on March 18, 1921, the Communists consolidated their hold over Azerbaijan, even though armed resistance smoldered until 1924 and underground organizations held on through the remainder of the decade.[82]

FIVE

Soviet National Consolidation and the Pahlavi Assimilation

Independent Soviet Azerbaijan and Territorial Settlements

The Sovietization of Azerbaijan is a highly important step in the development of Communism in the Near East. Just as Red Turkestan is acting as a revolutionary beacon for Chinese Turkestan, Tibet, Afghanistan, India, Bukhara, and Khiva, so Soviet Azerbaijan, with its old and experienced proletariat and its already unified Communist Party, will become the Red beacon for Persia, Arabia, and Turkey. . . . From Azerbaijan we could hurt the British in Persia, reach out to Arabia and lead the revolutionary movement in Turkey.[1]

These words of Sultan Galiev in the official organ of the Nark-momnats offered a good reflection of the thinking of Russia's Communists. There was a wave of revolutionary fervor spilling over from the seizure of Azerbaijan, and it left its mark on the Baku Congress of the Peoples of the East. A festive occasion celebrating a victory of the revolution and heralding its farther march into Asia, the Congress held its meetings in September 1920 in the interval between the local uprisings in the Azerbaijani countryside. Delegates came from thirty-eight countries, but the overwhelming majority were from Turkey or Iran, and most were nationalists rather than Communists.[2] Among the guests of honor was Enver Pasha, now a resident of Transcaucasia, from where he hoped to make his return to Turkey when the Kemalist movement failed. As it turned out, before the end of the next year he would move to Bukhara to take over the leadership of the anti-Soviet Muslim Basmachi insurgency, a sign that the revolutionary wave had already crested.

For the time being, Azerbaijan, the window for the revolution in the Muslim East, enjoyed the status of an independent Soviet state. In this capacity, the Baku *Sovnarkom* had the right to establish diplomatic relations with foreign countries, and the most important posting, in Ankara, was held by the former Menshevik Ibrahim Abilov. In addition, Soviet Azerbaijan maintained consulates in Kars, Trebizond, and Samsun. As Azerbaijan was no longer a barrier separating Turkey from Soviet Russia, Ankara's position toward Baku became more sympathetic. Mustafa Kemal, welcoming Abilov, sounded tones of encouragement for Azerbaijan's independence. Remarkably, he emphasized ethnic brotherhood and religious affinity:

> In this holy struggle, our nation is proud to serve the liberation of Islam, and the cause of the well-being for the oppressed of the world. Our nation is happy to hear it that this truth is confirmed by the representative of the brotherly Azerbaijan. The people of Rumelia and Anatolia know that the hearts of their Azeri brothers beat together with their own hearts. . . . They wish the Azeri-Turks not to fall again into captivity and not be deprived of their rights. As the sorrow of the Azeri-Turks is our own sorrow, and their joy is our joy, it makes us happy that their wishes have been fulfilled and that they live free and independent.[3]

According to Abilov, Pan-Turkish and Pan-Turanian instincts had not been successfully exorcised from the minds of the nationalists. Some of Kemal Pasha's ministers were clearly more outspoken and less concerned about diplomatic niceties. In one of his reports, Abilov wrote:

> Many Turks have still not given up their aggressive intentions and cultivate the hope for joining Azerbaijan to Turkey. For example at the small reception which I gave recently, the minister of post and telegraphs at the end of his Pan-Turkist speech, expressed his wish to see in the near future the deputies from Azerbaijan in the Ankara parliament.[4]

The rapprochement with Kemalist Turkey strengthened Azerbaijan's hand in reaching the outcome of the territorial disputes with Armenia. The most notable case was that of Nakhichevan, an area of intermittent fighting. The March 1921 Friendship Treaty of Moscow that normalized the relations between Soviet Russia and the Ankara regime acceded to the Turkish insistence on having a link with an Azerbaijani territory. One of the treaty's provisions held that Nakhichevan would not be included in Soviet Armenia but rather would be formed into an autonomous region under the jurisdiction of Azerbaijan, even though it was separated from that republic by a belt of Armenian territory. In the words of a historian of Armenia, "Soviet Russia sacrificed the Armenian question to cement the Turkish alliance."[5] The treaty of Kars of October 1921, which the Ankara government signed with the Soviet republics of Georgia, Azerbaijan, and Armenia, confirmed the stipulations reached earlier in Moscow. After the creation of the Soviet Union in 1922, Nakhichevan received the status of an Autonomous Soviet Republic, a part of the Azerbaijani SSR (Soviet Socialist Republic).

The case of Nagorno-Karabagh, a region smaller in population and territory, proved to be even more complex, its solution more elusive. One of the first acts of the Azrevkom in May 1920 was to send an ultimatum demanding the withdrawal of Armenian forces from Nagorno-Karabagh and Zangezur, with which the Erivan government promptly complied. Several months later, by December 2, local Communists took over power in Armenia, although their hold was still very weak. With the intention to prop up the position of the Armenian comrades, Narimanov, on behalf of the CPAz, came out with his famous statement of December 1, 1920:

> Soviet Azerbaijan . . . declares that from now on no territorial questions could become the cause for spilling of blood between the two people who for centuries lived as neighbors: the Muslims and Armenians. The laboring peasantry of Nagorno-Karabagh is given the full right for self-determination; all military operations in the Zangezur region are to end forthwith and the forces of the Soviet to withdraw.[6]

Narimanov's declaration only opened a new chapter in Nagorno-Karabagh's politics of intractability. In essence, the arguments raised for retaining the status quo stressed geographic and economic integration of Nagorno-Karabagh with Azerbaijan, while those for the unification with Armenia emphasized the fact of the indisputably Armenian composition of its population. The compromise solution appeared to be the creation of an autonomous administrative unit within the Azerbaijani Soviet Republic. The Kavbiuro, with the participation of

Stalin, still far from the pinnacle of his power, decided in principle on this course of action in July 1921. It took another two years of complex and controversial maneuvering before the Kavbiuro arrived at concrete recommendations. On July 7, 1923, the decree of the Azerbaijani Executive Committee of the Soviets created the Nagorno-Karabagh Autonomous Oblast.' The new unit covered 2,600 square miles, or 5.1 percent of the Republic's territory, and had its capital in the town of Khankend, later renamed Stepanakert. The territorial arrangements resulted in a geographical chessboard pattern, which boded ill for the prospects of stable intercommunal harmony.[7]

Useful as the independence of Azerbaijan might have appeared for the relations with the nations of the East, Moscow was not prepared to tolerate too much of it for too long. Almost immediately after the Baku Congress, on September 30, 1920, the Azerbaijani Sovnarkom signed a series of treaties with Soviet Russia, whereby it ceded to RSFSR its authority over the Commissariats of War, Supply, Finance, and Transportation, as well as all organs of internal and external trade. Still, this step did not amount to immediate and direct incorporation of Azerbaijan into the structure of the Soviet Russian state. After the conquest of Armenia (December 1920), and Georgia (February 1921), there followed an intermediary stage of the consolidation of Transcaucasia into one unit. This Soviet variation on the 1918 idea of the regional federation was guided by economic considerations: the need to unify the whole region before the final incorporation. The operation was carried out by the Kavbiuro, which had to contend with opposition from the CPAz's old guard, led by Narimanov. Meanwhile, the former young Himmätists fully endorsed the dismantling of Soviet Azerbaijani independence. In a letter recently made public, Narimanov wrote with unmistakable bitterness:

> Members of the Central Committee, Karaev—in 1918 a Menshevik—and M. D. Huseynov—in 1918 a Musavatist—elaborated on the idea that we do not need any independence, that we should unite with Soviet Russia. . . . Huseynov not so long ago cursed me that I, as a Communist, by calling in 1918 the Azerbaijani masses to join the workers of Russia had been selling the nation's interests. Now, in 1920, he tries to show me as a nationalist.[8]

In its final form, the Transcaucasian Soviet Federative Socialist Republic (*Zakfederatsia*) came to being in December 1922. Its constitution provided that the supreme bodies of the Federation had the power of deciding on a general budget, regulating internal commerce, and establishing the principles of utilization of land and natural resources, as well as the general principles of law, judicial organization, education, health protection, and labor conditions in Transcaucasia.[9] Of the personnel changes that came with the formation of the Zakfederatsia, the most significant was the removal of Narimanov from Transcaucasia. In a typical "kick upstairs," he was transferred to Moscow in January 1923, where he assumed the largely ceremonial position of one of the four Chairs of the Central Executive Committee of the newly created USSR. The Zakfederatsia became one of the Soviet Union's constituent republics.

Still, Narimanov stuck to his critical views of the regional union of culturally diverse peoples: "I am convinced in what follows," he wrote in a letter, "as long as the literacy ratio in Armenia and Georgia is close to 50 percent, and in Azerbaijan barely some 3 percent, we can not think of a normal work in the Federation. Some may wish to delude themselves, but I do not."[10] He died in his glorified exile in Moscow in 1925.

The National Contract and the Korenizatsiia in Its Heyday

In the Bolshevik councils there was much hesitation about what should be the Soviet policy on the nationality question in general, and the uncertainty was even greater about that policy toward the Muslim in particular. Yet amidst sharp turns and tactical zigzagging, the general line became discernible: promotion of the millät over the 'umma identity, of the secular, rather than the Islamic foundations of communal life, and of fragmentation rather than of the Muslim unity.

Two major considerations tipped the scale toward this long-term approach. First was the recognition that the transition from a religion-based community to socialist society would not be feasible in any foreseeable future. In the distinctly Eurocentric view of the Bolsheviks, nationality was an unavoidable stage in historical development, even though it was an intermediate stage that would not, hopefully, last very long. A second consideration of a less theoretical nature was the "surrogate proletariat" syndrome.[11] The working class in most of Russia's Muslim regions was either nonexistent or, as in Azerbaijan, weak in numbers and even weaker in class consciousness. On the other hand, the intelligentsia, it could be assumed, would be won over to the Soviet cause more easily than the Muslim masses, on whose apathy and backwardness the Bolsheviks commented without excessive inhibition. Moreover, the intelligentsia, enlightenment-minded and populist, had before 1917 begun to promote distinct literary languages on national bases, and these trends seemed to suit the Bolshevik grand strategy goals.

The chief Soviet agency in charge of formulating, elaborating, and implementing nationality policy was the Narkomnats, a preserve of Stalin's personal influence. Under his aegis, during the civil war specialized bodies were established to deal with Muslim affairs. The Muslim Commissariats (*Muskoms*) and Bureaus (*Musbiuros*) tended to be organized on principles of territoriality, i.e, concerned themselves with particular regions or provinces, and agitated against the all-Muslim movement in Russia. Whenever possible, members of the native intelligentsia would be encouraged to join the work of these bodies. In such a way the intelligentsia began to trickle into the ranks of the Soviet regime. Stalin further expanded the process after the civil war.

In Azerbaijan, the April 27 surrender agreement offered the ground for accommodating the intelligentsia, notably in its article promising that government employees, except for those in positions of highest responsibility, would retain their posts. At this juncture, the Stalin-supervised nationality policy displayed flexibility and rejected rigid application of class warfare in the non-Russian regions. A case in point was the treatment of Räsulzadä at the hands of Stalin, who in the fall of 1920 was on an inspection tour of Azerbaijan. He rushed to the jail where the *Osobyi Otdel* (Special Section) kept the Musavatist leader and had him released. In repaying his personal debt of gratitude to the man who had been helpful to him in dangerous moments of the 1905 revolution, Stalin acted also in step with his opening to the intelligentsia. Years later, Räsulzadä recollected this encounter as follows:

> "Well," said Stalin, "you are a small nation, unable to go on ruling by yourself, and have to come to terms with some other big state."
>
> I replied, "In this case, we would again make a deal with you as our big neighbor, but not in Narimanov's way."
>
> Stalin smiled. "Did Narimanov make a deal with us or we with Narimanov?"[12]

For all his generosity, Stalin chose not to leave Räsulzadä in

Azerbaijan, where the Soviet regime had not yet jelled. Instead, he took him along to Moscow and appointed him to a position in the Narkomnats. Two years later Mammäd Amin succeeded in escaping abroad.

Meanwhile, the Musavat Party was allowed to exist, to be sure, in the form of its left wing, to the exclusion of the rightists, whose surviving leaders resided abroad. In 1923 the Musavatists, after growing harassment by the Cheka, found themselves under pressure to dissolve the party altogether on the ground that its work had become superfluous after the recently proclaimed Soviet nationality program. On August 14 newspapers printed a declaration on the Musavat's voluntary dissolution, stating that "the decisions accepted by the Twelfth Congress of the RKP on the nationality question offer now real assurances for equal rights of the nationalities within the confines off the USSR; furthermore, the task of liberation of the peoples of the East has obtained now a stronger base."[13] The Soviet policy toward non-Russians had by now evolved toward what was in effect a contract. Some of its parts were implicit, and some were spelled out at the Twelfth Party Congress in April 1923. In return for the acceptance of and cooperation with the Soviet regime, the nationalities received the guarantees of the right to develop their distinct cultures, to use freely and develop their languages, and to train and employ native cadres in their republics. The legacy of the Russian rule of the past, with its imperialism, chauvinism, and Russification, was to be explicitly rejected. In essence, the contract promised the completion of the process of national consolidation within the Soviet federal structure. As for Azerbaijan, while it no longer possessed its shaky independence, it had autonomy, the initial goal of the national movement, and autonomy presumed the existence and growth of the native bureaucracy.

The most visible aspect of the Soviet nation-making activity, after 1923, was the *korenizatsiia* (indigenization) policy, which amounted to more than simply promoting the natives into high positions in the Party and government. The korenizatsiia also called for the full equality of non-Russian languages with Russian and attempted to reconcile the nationalities to the Soviet rule. It sought to legitimize an urban-based revolution in a predominantly agricultural and multiethnic state by encouraging the development of distinct national identities.[14] In the words of Stalin, who gave the report on the nationality problem to the Twelfth Party Congress:

The first means is to adopt all measures to make the Soviet regime understood and loved in the republics, to make the Soviet regime not only Russian but international. For this it is necessary that not only the schools, but all institutions and all bodies, both Party and Soviet, should step by step be made national in character, that they should be conducted in the language that is understood by the masses, that they should function in conditions that correspond to the manner of life of the given nation. Only on this condition will we be able to convert the Soviet regime from a Russian into an international one, understood by and near and dear to the labouring masses in all the republics, particularly those which are economically and culturally backward.[15]

Inasmuch as the korenizatsiia offered the promise of overcoming backwardness or underdevelopment, it met the fundamental aspirations of the Muslim intelligentsia halfway. Many nationalistically inclined members of this social group gave a guarded endorsement to the Soviet experiment as attempt at modernization. In Azerbaijan, while former Musavatists were being sent by the hundreds to prison camps in the Solovki Islands, one of the first large contingents in the population of the emerging Gulag Archipelago, or continued their political activity underground, others were given positions in the rapidly expanding Soviet bureaucracy and cultural-educational establishment. By the end of the decade the secret police (GPU) estimated that only 10 to 15 percent of the intelligentsia remained consistently hostile to the regime, with the balance either loyal or, for the most part, hesitant.[16] In the korenizatsiia climate they resumed the time-honored pursuits of the jadidist-enlightenment character, such as the elimination of illiteracy, increasing the number of schools, the growth of communication media, the promotion of women's rights, and the development of a literary language based on native vernacular, purified of Ottomanisms—a process paralleling what was currently under way in Kemalist Turkey. The theaters flourished, and several literary-artistic associations sprung up, as did the feminist Bayramov club.[17]

The reverberations of the cultural revival north of the border reached across the Araxes. In the 1920s Baku theater and musical companies regularly visited Tabriz, Rasht, and Urmia; they performed the plays of Soviet Azeri playwrights or operettas of Uzeir Hajibäyli.[18] In

Tabriz, the symbol of the ties between the two parts became the publication of *Molla Nasr al-Din*.

These efforts that clearly aimed at broadening the base for national identity soon brought into focus the typically Azerbaijani contraposition: Baku versus the rest of the country. At the early stage of the korenizatsiia, Eyyub Khanbudagov, a former head of Azerbaijani *Cheka*, who had since become a national Communist, called for a sharp increase of the native element among the Baku proletariat, still ethnically to large extent a foreign body. Otherwise, he warned, there could follow unexpected consequences. The Russian and other nonnative workers who could not be made to leave Azerbaijan should be required to learn the language of the country. Khanbudagov was especially insistent on this point. His proposals met with angry rejections from most of the Party leadership, and he soon saw the decline in his political fortunes.[19] Later, as the proportion of Azeri laborers grew in a majority with the influx of labor under the industrialization drive, the requirement that all residents study Azeri went into force. Yet its application became notorious for perfunctory ways, and very few of those who took the required instruction would ever master the language.

Somewhat more successful was the aspect of the korenizatsiia that became known as the Turkification of higher learning. An Education Commissariat directive called for making Azeri the language of instruction on the university level, a goal that assumed that the nonnative instructors would master this idiom and that all the students would understand it. Turkification was carried on by increasing the proportion of Azeris in the university, until, by 1930, they accounted for about 70 percent of students and about 75 percent of instructors.[20] This effort opened tensions in the academic community with the characteristic manifestations: "A Russian professor—complained publicly a nonnative instructor—should select among those of Turkic nationality a person equal to him . . . but because of objective conditions, students of that nationality represent rather low intellectual level." On the other hand, an official report said that "some students from the countryside are so nationalistically minded that they refuse to attend any courses in Russian language, even though they could understand it."[21]

A pivotal issue of the 1920s transformations, and a facet of educational progress, was the alphabet reform, with its wide political, cultural, and religious ramifications. The idea itself was as old as the native Enlightenment movement. Arabic script, particularly ill-suited to the phonetics of Turkic languages, made learning to read and write a difficult task. The first project for a thoroughgoing reform was Mirza Fathali Akhundzadä's proposal to replace the Arabic alphabet with the Latin one. Other projects followed, including those of Mammad Agha Shahtakhtinskii, the publisher of the newspaper *Sharg-i Rus* (1903–1904), devoted to the promotion of literary Azeri and alphabet reform. There were the recommendations of the 1906 Baku teachers' convention, and the three proposals that occurred during the existence of the independent republic. Only under the Soviet regime were circumstances right for a radical solution. Narimanov, whose revolutionary zeal extended to the question of Azeri orthography, appointed in 1922 an ardent advocate of the Latinization, Samäd Agha Aghamalioghli, the head of Commission for the Alphabet Reform. The same year, a newspaper, *Yeni Yol* (The new road), began its publication printed in Latin characters. The issue of the reform soon turned into a bitter controversy, and the Latinization was opposed not only by traditionalists defending the continuity of historical and literary heritage, but also by the revolutionary-minded followers of Sultan Galiev throughout the Soviet Union. In their eyes, the Arabic alphabet, by not marking the vowel sounds, kept alive the notion of one literary idiom for all Turkic peoples, because it allowed to slur over phonetic peculiarities of diverse dialects and languages. As for Moscow, it continued its usual policy of encouraging national differentiation among the Muslims. Lenin gave his blessing to Aghamalioghli, and the reform went ahead in successive stages. On June 27, 1924, Latin alphabet began to be used officially by the administration of the Azerbaijani SSR.[22]

When in February 1926, the First Soviet Turcology Congress met in Baku, the question of the new alphabet for all the Soviet Turkic nationalities dominated the proceedings. The recommendation of the Congress was that other Turco-Tatar republics should study the Azerbaijani experience for Latinization of their respective alphabets. With the introduction of the Latin-based alphabets, Soviet Turkic peoples speeded up radically the growth of their distinct literary languages, the basis for the formation of their national identities.

In the aftermath of the Turcology Congress, Aghamalioghli defined the issue of the reform in political terms of the struggle against the legacy of the Islamic past:

The Great October Revolution, which shook the whole world down to its foundations was bound to change the Turco-Tatar psychology with regard to the impact of petrified Islamic dogmas imposed centuries ago, and dead today. . . . . The progress of the new Turkic alphabet among the working masses of Azerbaijan, is an irrefutable proof of consciousness of those masses, once reputed to have been hopelessly narrow-minded. I have no doubt that the same will happen among the working masses of other republics, in Uzbekistan, Kazakhstan, Turkmenistan. One can hear that now they . . . do not wish anything more than to retain their old customs, to keep their own enslavement. But, I believe that this is a myth cultivated by reactionary elements. I believe that the Latin alphabet, as an instrument of change will be as much welcomed in those republics as it has been in Azerbaijan.[23]

The issue of Latinization soon transcended the purely Soviet-Turkic concern and aroused the interest of the Kemalist regime. This interest was additionally fueled by exiles from Azerbaijan who urged the Latinization of Turkish alphabet in the hope to stave off the isolation of their homeland from Turkey. The idea of the reform on these lines suited Kemal's desire to perpetuate the break with the Ottoman past. The young generation, brought up on the new alphabet, would be open only to the ideas expressed in the Latin script. Somewhat hurriedly, without intermediate stages, Turkey adopted the new alphabet in November 1928 and banned the use of the Arabic from the new year on, following a similar ban in Azerbaijan by less than half a year. The upshot of the alphabet reform was that Azerbaijan's links to Turkey appeared to have been retained, but a farther step was taken in the process of drifting apart from Iranian Azerbaijan, where the question of replacing the Arabic script could not be even openly discussed.

Meanwhile, in Soviet Azerbaijan the alphabet reform gave a new momentum to the drive against illiteracy, and the results were turning impressive. Literacy, 25.2 percent in 1926, grew to 31.4 percent in 1931, and to 50.9 percent in 1933. By this time, the law on compulsory education had taken effect.[24] The successes of the alphabet reform, seen as a part of korenizatsiia, contrasted with the coming revision of the Soviet nationality policy in the late 1920s and early 1930s. The center began to publicize complaints from Russians in the non-Russian republics about their forced assimilation. Also in Azerbaijan, the new Party head, Mir Jäfär Baghirov, publicly assured Russian university professors that their positions were not endangered by their lack of fluency in Azeri. Criticisms of the excesses of the nativization began to multiply, and Party spokesmen began to present a new view of nationality question. With the victory of the Socialist Revolution, the argument went, the Russian language stopped being a tool of oppression of non-Russians. Rather, it became a means of introducing non-Russian nationalities to the highly developed Russian culture, which had world importance.[25] Korenizatsiia was not an absolute value in itself, and its application should be slowed down.

From Native Secularism to Soviet Atheism

In the long run, secularism was the centerpiece of the Soviet policies toward the peoples whose primary identity remained Islamic, and in Azerbaijan its tradition predated the Bolshevik conquest, reaching back well into the mid-nineteenth century. Even more than the rationalism of Akhundzadä's hue, the native secularism drew upon the need for counteracting the effects of the sectarian split. The secular outlook of the national intelligentsia was an additional factor that facilitated the national contract and the subsequent modus vivendi with the Soviet regime. Initially, Soviet-sponsored secularism tended to be moderate and did not go beyond such measures of overall modernization, as gradual expropriation of the *waqfs* (charitable foundations), phasing out of the Muslim civil courts and *maktabs*, or banning the *Shahsey-Vahsey*. These processions, held on the day of tenth of Muharram, in commemoration of Imam Husain's martyrdom, were occasions for painful self-flagellation, and had long been criticized among the intelligentsia. Such sweeping statements as "Islam degrades human dignity" made by the fiery native crusader for atheism, Aghamalioghli, were still out of tune with the spirit of the time.

The all-out offensive against Islam began only toward the close of the 1920s upon the consolidation of Stalin's personal rule, but some encouragement came also from the forceful anti-Islamic drive currently under way in Kemalist Turkey. The signal was sounded in the spring of 1927 with the *Hujum* (Attack), a campaign for the emancipation of the Muslim women throughout the USSR. Hujum centered on discarding the veil, generally regarded as a symbol of enslavement and ignorance. The Hujum was repeated on International Women's Day, March 8, 1928, when Muslim women publicly removed their veils and burned them in a pile. By the next year, administrative measures were in effect. An Azerbaijani government ordinance banned veiled women from entering cinemas and theaters, a preparatory step for banning the veil altogether. In a manifestation of zealotry, some local authorities prohibited the use of the *zur* and the *tara*, musical instruments associated with religious ceremonies.

The main thrust was aimed at mosques. In the words of a Party publication,

> Only in the beginning of 1929 in the course of the (antireligious) campaign, some 400 mosques were closed. Among some uezds there was a form of competition: which would faster close more mosques or churches. There were cases of the *Komsomol* members beating up mollahs.[26]

The hapless mollahs, who symbolized the clerical obscurantism of the past, were rendered even more harmless by their acquisition of the reputation as police informers. This circumstance kept many faithful from attending services in the few remaining mosques.[27] In the end, the number of mosques in the burgeoning metropolitan area of Baku was dramatically reduced. Party and government officials who were guilty of signs of tolerance, or of insufficient ardor in the struggle against the religion, became victims of the purges of the mid-1930s. They were usually accused of Pan-Islamism, a reactionary ideology serving the interest of foreign powers.

What was the long-range effect of the brutal, persistent, and all-pervasive campaign against Islam? By its nature, Islam is not merely a religion but also a way of life. As a set of customs, traditions, and prohibitions, it survived, and the erosion of the Muslim ways was not much more advanced than elsewhere in the rapidly modernizing societies of the Middle East. On the one hand, the visible manifestations of Islamic identity, such as the observance of the Five Pillars of Islam (Profession of Faith, the *Hajj*, the month of Ramadan fast, and the five daily prayers) came into disuse, except for almsgiving. Likewise, polygamy, forbidden by law, disappeared entirely, and women's seclusion ended together with discarding the veil. Even so, Azerbaijani marriages were often arranged, men seldom married outside of the community, and women hardly ever did. Azeris maintain strong kinship loyalties, rarely emigrate, especially to non-Muslim republics, refuse to eat pork, and only slowly succumb to the attractions of alcohol.

As a religion, Islam clearly suffered from the repression and atmosphere of terror. Not only there was no observation of the Five Pillars, but it was deemed too risky to pass the knowledge of the tenets and rites of Islam to the younger generation, which grew up unable even to tell if they were Shi'ite or Sunni. Yet the widely circulating adage was: "Keep religion in your heart." These words echoed the age-old native response to religious persecution. *Taqiya*, known also as *Ketman*, is the practice of dissimulation, including apostasy under compulsion or threat, endorsed by a Quranic commentary: "If anyone is compelled and professes unbelief with his tongue, while his heart contradicts him, no blame falls upon him, because God takes His servants as their hearts believe." The heartland of the taqiya tradition was northern Iran, the historic battleground between Shi'ite and Sunni Islam, a hotbed of heresies and sectarian upheavals. Here, rulers frequently changed religious allegiance and subjects had to develop the art of adaptation through dissimulation. This trait allows one to understand better the make-up of the Azeri mind, with its seeming volatility, its ability for sudden reversal of attitudes, while retaining loyalty to fundamental values. Taqiya accounts also for the mystifying significance of political manifestations in Azerbaijani history, which often revealed little of underlying realities. The nineteenth-century observer of Iran, Joseph de Gobineau, who became intrigued with the impact of this sociopsychological phenomenon, noted also that there were various levels of taqiya, in response to the intensity of the threat:

> Nevertheless, occasions arise when silence no longer suffices, when it may pass for an avowal. Then one must not hesitate. Not only must one deny one's true opinion, but one is commanded to resort to all ruses in order to deceive one's adversary. One makes all the protestations of faith that can please him, one performs all the rites one recognizes to be the most vain, one falsifies one's own books, one exhausts all possible means of deceit . . . ketman fills the man who practices it with pride. Thanks to it, a believer raises himself to a permanent state of superiority over the man he deceives, be he a minister of state or a powerful king. . . . It is an unintelligent being that you make sport of; it is a dangerous beast that you disarm.[28]

While the practice of ketman became a necessity everywhere under the Communist rule, nowhere had it deeper historical roots than in Azerbaijan. As if under the ingrained impulse of dissimulation, the membership of the Godless Society shot up from a meager 3,000 in 1930 to 70,000 in 1931. Next to the *Komsomol*, the Godless Society were to be the cutting edge of the cultural revolution that aimed at instilling the scientific view of the universe and man.[29] Historians were busily discovering anti-Islamic and atheistic elements in the heritage of the Azeri thinkers of the past, and in this context there began what amounted to a virtual cult of Akhundzadä. Among his newly published writings was the philosophical treatise, the "Three Letters," in which the readers could find the passage describing a Akhundzadä's favorite historical hero as the master of the art of taqiya:

> Reluctantly, out of fear of his royal father, Ala Zikrihi al-Salam made an about-face, resorted to dissimulation, and began to write epistles in support of his father's views. In the end, Muhammad Buzorg Umid wiped anger from his heart and handed over to him the succession to the throne. As soon as his father passed away, Ala Zikrihi al-Salam began his wise reign that opened the new age and his reformation was accepted in all parts of the kingdom.[30]

Ala Zikrihi was the twelfth-century north Iranian ruler of Alam, but his example might have well served as the guidance in the twentieth century, not only for those under the Soviet rule but also for the people of his native land.

The Pahlavi Centralization and Iranian Azerbaijan

The thrust of the changes under the Soviet rule offered a stark contrast to the processes south of the Araxes, even though here also government-imposed transformations were under way. Of these, some were in response to challenges of the neighboring Soviet Union and Turkey; others were caused by changing conditions in Iran.

The 1920 fall of Baku immediately produced reverberations in Iran, and less than three weeks later a Soviet naval force under F. F. Raskolnikov arrived at Enzeli from the Azerbaijani capital. Ostensibly, its purpose was to seize the ships of the White Russians. In fact, its purpose was to give the support to the Jangalis of Gilan in their struggle against the Teheran government and what was left of the British presence. The Soviet expedition included a contingent of Ädälät members from Baku, and jointly with the Jangalis, on June 4, they proclaimed the creation of the Soviet Socialist Republic of Iran. A nine-seat revolutionary committee was established, with Kuchuk Khan as the leader. The real power was in the hands of the presidium consisting of the nationalist Kuchuk Khan, the Communists Ehsanullah, Javadzadä (Pishevari), who was interior commissar, and Abrahamov, who was the governor of Rasht.

By the end of June, the delegates of Ädälät from both Azerbaijans, Central Asia, and Gilan, convened in Enzeli. Having elected Lenin and Narimanov as the honorary chairmen, the meeting transformed itself into the First Congress of the Communist Party of Iran. Of the 48 participants almost all, except for a few Armenians, were Azeris, but they spoke for all of Iran as a unified and centralized state. The Party program, proposed by Sultanzadeh, included, however, the recognition of the right for self-determination for all nationalities within the framework of the unity of the country.[31]

The weakness and disintegration that engulfed Iran were the backdrop for emergence of a strong leader who undertook the task of pulling the country from its sorry condition. The man on the horseback was, appropriately, an officer of the Persian Cossack Brigade— Colonel Reza Khan, who had been born to a Turkic-speaking family in Mazanderan.

Reza Khan began his bidding for power in February 1921 with his march on Teheran, where he prevailed upon the weak Shah Ahmad to promote him to the command of the Army. At the same time, Reza Khan forced the shah to name his then-ally Sayyid Ziya Tabatabai as prime minister. The two men achieved the abrogation of the unpopular 1919 Agreement with Britain and, in an act of counterbalancing, concluded the treaty with Soviet Russia. This treaty, signed in February 1921, appeared far more advantageous to Iran in most of its provisions. It voided the treaties, conventions, and agreements between Iran and the Tsarist regime that infringed upon the rights of the Iranian people, with the exception for the Turkmanchai settlement, from which only the stipulation banning the Iranian flag shipping from the Caspian was removed. The treaty canceled Iran's debt and commercial concessions to Russia, but despite its anti-imperialist tenor, its Article Six gave Soviet Russia the right to bring troops into Iran under vaguely specified conditions, such as "policy of usurpation by a third party by means of armed intervention," "the desire to use Iranian territory as a base of operations against Russia," or "if a foreign Power should threaten the frontiers of Federal Russia, or those of its allies and if the Iranian Government should not be able to put a stop to such a menace after having been once called upon to do so by Russia."[32] After the British withdrawal from Iran, the Teheran government obtained with some difficulty the Soviet evacuation in September 1921. The Iranian troops marched into Gilan, defeated the Jangalis, and the head of Kuchuk Khan was put on display in Teheran. "With our own hands we killed the liberation movement in Iran,"[33] commented Narimanov, his eyes fixed at the Muslim world across the border.

Having suppressed the uprising in Gilan, Reza Khan fought a long series of regional and tribal rebellions, including a new Tabriz uprising of February 1, 1922, led by Major Abu'l Qasim Lahuti Khan, the commander of the local gendarmerie. Lahuti had been a participant of the Baku Congress of the Peoples of the East and was later to be known as a gifted poet. Reza Khan's attempt to control the gendarmerie, whose pay was long in the arrears, sparked the mutiny in which Lahuti's troops joined forces with Khiabani's survivors. The rebels arrested the governor of Tabriz and proclaimed the gendarmerie defenders of freedom and enemies of despotism; they hung out red flags and smashed the portraits of the shah, but otherwise made no appeal to feelings of Azerbaijani identity. The rebellion was easily put down by Reza Khan's Cossacks. Within a week, Lakhuti Khan fled across the Araxes to remain in the Soviet Union for the rest of his life, residing in Tajikistan rather than Azerbaijan.[34] Subsequently, Reza Khan dealt with the insurgency among the Kurds, Baluchis, Lurs, Turkmens, and the Shahseven tribesmen. By December 1925, his position was so strong that he induced the Majlis to depose the Qajar royal family and to crown him as the founder of the new dynasty. He assumed the name Pahlavi, which evoked the greatness of pre-Islamic Iran.

Once firmly established in power, Reza Shah launched his reforms. Although less thorough than Mustafa Kemal's, they were a sharp departure from Iranian political tradition. The crown had historically tolerated or even encouraged regional, tribal, and sectarian rivalries, exploiting these divisions for its own benefit. Reza Shah, by contrast, embarked upon the course of integration and centralization. Despite the oppression, brutality, and corruption that marred his reign, the Shah enjoyed a measure of support in the population, at least for some time, including those who saw him as an instrument of modernization and Iranian national consolidation.

The lessons of the recent past, with its centrifugal movements in the provinces and among the minorities, were disturbing enough, and a common thread in the intellectual discourse of the 1920s was the inherent danger in ethnic diversity to Iran's future. Of all the non-Persian regions Azerbaijan was seen as potentially the most troublesome and it commanded special attention in the leading journals, *Iranshahr*, *Farangistan* (Western world), and *Ayandeh* (Future). Characteristically, the articles dealing with Azerbaijan focused on its distant past, proved its unquestionably Iranian character before the advent of Turks and Mongols, and tended to disregard recent history. The thrust was nonetheless clear: if Azerbaijan had once been Iranian and not Turkic, it should be restored to its original character, and the overriding consideration had to be the national interest of Iran. Writers of diverse political persuasions shared this view, and natives of Azerbaijan were prominent among them. They all presented rationalization for the assimilation of ethnic, linguistic, and religious minorities in general and the Azeris in particular. While their arguments stressed the need to forge a viable, uniform, modern nation, their recommendations included official limitations on the use of the Azeri language. In *Ayandeh*, Mahmud Afshar went as far as to propose resettling a part of Azerbaijan's population in Persian-speaking provinces, with the view of discouraging Turkey from annexionist designs in the future. "Azerbaijan: The Issue of Life or Death for Iran" was the telling title of an essay by Tabriz-born Taqi Arani, who later would become the spiritual father of the Iranian far-left *Tudeh* Party. He called the replacement of *Turki* by Persian "a patriotic duty of all Iranians, especially of the Ministry of Education officials."[35]

Likewise, the idea of linguistic assimilation was espoused by a leading intellectual of Azarbaijan. Ahmad Kasravi, who has been described as the most controversial of modern Iranian thinkers, saw as his chief concern the transformation of a disunited Iran into what he hoped would be an integrated Iran at whatever the cost. He wrote his magisterial work, *Tarikh-i Hijdah Saleh-i Azarbaijan* (Eighteen years of history of Azarbaijan), to prove that the fate of Azerbaijan lay with the rest of Iran. He believed that Iran owed its backwardness to multidimensional disunity, and among the forces working for this condition were linguistic differences, which he considered as harmful as tribal loyalties. Kasravi's concern with the lack of linguistic unity began at the early stage of the constitutional movement, when the shah had attempted to fragment the reformist forces by playing up the differences between Persian- and Turkic-speaking liberals, and this concern grew stronger when the Ottomans tried to awaken separatist sentiments in Tabriz. In the mid 1920s, as Shah Reza was preparing for his assimilation campaign, Kasravi wrote a pamphlet titled *Zaban-i Azari ya zaban-i bastani Azarbaijan* (The Azari language; or, the ancient language of Azarbaijan), a venture into historical linguistics. Azari, the original language of Azarbaijan, had been closely related to Persian, and the influx of Turkic words began only with the Seljuk invasion. Therefore, the argument went, *Turki* was a foreign tongue imposed by conquerors, and the true national language of Azarbaijan was Azari, which survived only in geographical names and among inhabitants of a few remote villages. The belief in the intrinsically Iranian character of the Azeris, as well as in the need for national integration on the basis of Persian, was the essence of what became known as Kasravism (*Kasraviyya*).[36]

The steps that the Teheran regime took in the 1930s with the aim of Persianization of the Azeris and other minorities appeared to take a leaf from the writings of the reformist-minded intellectuals in the previous decade. In the quest of imposing national homogeneity on the country where half of the population consisted of ethnic minorities, the Pahlavi regime issued in quick succession bans on the use of Azeri on the premises of schools, in theatrical performances, religious ceremonies, and, finally, in the publication of books. Azeri was reduced to the status of a language that only could be spoken and hardly ever written. As the Persianization campaign gained momentum, it drew inspiration from the revivalist spirit of Zoroastrian national glories. There followed even more invasive official practices, such as changing Turkic-sounding geographic names and interference with giving children names other than Persian ones. While cultivating cordial relations with Kemalist Turkey, Reza Shah carried on a forceful de-Turkification campaign in Iran.

The cultural and educational contacts with the other Azerbaijan came abruptly to an end following the 1930 espionage scandal. Georgii Agabekov, a Soviet diplomat in Teheran, made detailed revelations of his enlistment of a large number of Iranian officials into a spy network. His disclosures also mentioned Soviet intentions to detach from Iran Kurdish- and Azerbaijani-populated regions.[37] Mindful of the Soviet threat and Azeri regionalism, the regime subdivided the bulk of Azer-

baijani territory into two provinces (*Ostans*) in 1937. The area south of
the Araxes was now organized into Eastern and Western Azerbaijan,
with capitals respectively in Rezaieh (formerly Urmia) and Tabriz.
Western Azerbaijan included a large Kurdish minority.

Economically, Azerbaijan under Reza Shah fared poorly. The
long period of interdependency with Russia showed its negative effects
once the old ties were disrupted in the 1930s. Germany became the
most important trading partner of Iran, and received 40 percent of
Iranian exports by 1940, while the Soviet Union's share had fallen to a
negligible 0.5 percent.[38] In addition to the painful decline of trade with
the northern neighbor, the Pahlavi regime's policy of centralizing commerce in the capital dealt a heavy blow to Tabriz. The city lost its commercial supremacy, and its most active inhabitants moved to Teheran,
weakening Azerbaijan as a political center. Likewise, the closing of the
outlets for labor migration across the Araxes drove Azeris to settle in
other parts of Iran. The plight of the Azerbaijani economy was aggravated further by the taxation policy of the centralized state, a system
devised by an American expert, the chief financial administrator of
Iran, Arthur Millspaugh. Under this system the provinces contributed
to the center far more than they received back. In one notorious
instance the budget allocations for Teheran were twenty times higher
than for Western Azerbaijan, with its population three time larger.[39]
The grounds for disaffection were extensive, and those Azeris who had
always opposed the efforts at excessive centralization of Iran saw their
misgivings vindicated. The condition of Azerbaijan bred separatist
and Communist sentiments that the regime, on its part, did its best to
stamp out with all the means the dictatorship had at its disposal.

Always susceptible to the shock waves from the north, Azerbaijan also experienced some side-effects of the mid-1930 Soviet purges
through the USSR's forced repatriation of Iranian citizens, most of
whom were Azeris. A diplomatic report described the background of
this repatriation:

> In the Caucasus, there have always lived large groups of Iranian
> passport holders, and the Russian Revolution or the anticapitalist
> repressions reduced their numbers only marginally. Despite all
> the difficulties that the Soviet regime had created, most of these
> immigrants did their best to adapt themselves to the new condi-
> tions of life. Only the recent measures that the Soviet authorities

applied to foreigners radically changed their condition. . . . In the current year [1938], the expulsions of Iranian citizens assumed drastic forms. Those who delay their departure are to have their property confiscated. There are cases of men being arrested and women with children sent across the border with only the most necessary belongings.[40]

In Iran, the *muhajirin* (immigrants), the term specifically referring to those arriving from the Soviet Union, met with suspicions of being contaminated by Communism. Whenever possible, the authorities tried to disperse them and prevented, rather than facilitated, their integration into local communities. For all their experience of harassment and deportation, many muhajirin came to cultivate the memories of the USSR as the land of greater opportunity and paradoxically would form a reservoir of pro-Soviet sympathies in Iranian Azerbaijan. In a number of cases, the assumption that they might be potentially Soviet agents would in time turn into a self-fulfilling prophecy.

The Great Purges and Azerbaijanism

North of the border, as the 1930s began, it was obvious that the new decade would be vastly different from the preceding one. Already the Azeris experienced the anti-Islamic campaign, collectivization in the countryside, industrialization in the cities, and the cultural revolution that cut the links to the non-Soviet world. There was the feeling in the air of an unending series of shocks, and their intensity mounted as the decade rolled on, to reach their climax in the late 1930s.

The symbol of the new epoch was Mir Jäfär Baghirov, who in 1933 became the First Secretary of the CPAz Central Committee and was to rule Azerbaijan for the next twenty years. "People of the older generation remember his heavy look from behind the horn-rimmed glasses, his deep, angry voice, his hands that seemed to be searching for lost pencils," wrote *Bakinskii Rabochii* in the Glasnost era.

In the manner of the Leader, he sported a moustache, but of more modest size. In general, he emphasized his modest habits in every way and urged the Party activists to act likewise. Even though he occupied with his family a palace in the center of the city, he always wore a very simple bluish-satin tunic.[41]

Baghirov reached his position through the ranks of the secret police, and during the years of his service in the Cheka and later OGPU, he established a close relationship with Lavrentei Beria, a classic example of the Soviet high-level patronage. As Beria rose through the Transcaucasian and Moscow power hierarchy, Baghirov followed him in his climb in Azerbaijan.[42] In an early stage in his career in the Cheka, Baghirov demonstrated his animosity to Narimanov, and after his coming to power soon followed the denunciation campaign of the long-dead leader, even though he had been close to Stalin. After being called "bourgeois nationalist," "deviationist," "deserter," "agent-provocateur," and anti-Communist, Narimanov subsequently became a non-person, his name unmentionable in any context, but the message was served to his companions and associates, the *Narimanovshchina*. They were politically paralyzed before even worse fates befell them.

The cataclysm of Stalin's purges spread to every corner of the huge state and shook the Soviet society to its foundation. Terror, by itself, was not a novelty under the Soviet regime, and even mass terror was not unknown, as had been the case in the collectivization drive. But in the past the terror tended to be selective, targeted only at parts of the population. The terror of the mid-1930s was an unlimited, pervasive exercise in social psychology, under which no one could feel safe. The machinery of mass repression, once set in motion, soon began to run by its own momentum. It devoured one group of victims after another, each new group more improbable than the last. Yet, on closer inspection, there was a method in this madness, and it was even clearer in the case of the Muslim regions.

Well in the midst of the show trials, but before the carnage had reached its culmination, the 1936 Stalin constitution brought essential administrative changes to the Soviet Union. Partly in recognition of the fact that the national differentiation of the Muslims had progressed, partly with the view to speed up the process even more, the Autonomous Republics of Kirghizia and Kazakhstan were upgraded to constituent republics of the USSR. The same status was bestowed upon Azerbaijan, Georgia, and Armenia, the three members of the Zakfederatsiia, which was now dissolved amongst hints that the idea of regional association smacked of the counterrevolutionary 1918 Transcaucasian Federation. This was the crowning act in the Stalinist policy of promoting local particularisms by splitting cultural, linguistic, or regional entities. From now on, only vertical relations with the center would be allowed, rather than horizontal links among the national republics, a prelude to the process of forging a new Soviet nation, and it would go hand in hand with Russification. In keeping with the thrust of these transformations, the adjective referring to the country's language and its inhabitants now became the rigorously observed term *Azerbaijani* rather than *Turkic* (*Tiurskii*). The purpose was clearly to expunge the identification with Turkic-speaking world.

The next year, the sinister 1937, of *Ezhovshchina* (the time of Ezhov), when the orgy of arrests, deportations, and executions reached its crescendo, the tenor of the accusations confirmed what was the regime's chief concern in Azerbaijan. Unlike in the non-Muslim republics, the charges less frequently invoked terrorism, conspiracies to seize power, sabotage, or espionage, and more often the victims were found guilty of criminal activities inspired by Pan-Turkism, Pan-Islamism, Musavatism, separatism, or bourgeois nationalism.[43] Such accusations were invariably directed at the Party leaders with the past in the ranks of Himmät, an organization with a record of political activity in the neighboring Muslim lands. The victims included both the companions of Narimanov and his opponents, the "young" Himmätists.

Nonsensical as these incriminations sounded, their message was not lost on the public. Many might even have rejoiced at the condemnation of Sultanov, who had drawn in blood the 1920 Ganja uprising. Likewise, not all would miss Karayev, Huseynov, Akhundov, Musabäkov, Äfändiyev, or Buniatzadä, who had spared no effort for the overthrow of the independent republic, but it was obvious that they were not the chief target of the carnage. If the founders of Soviet Azerbaijan and its exalted leaders could be destroyed in one sweep on the absurd charges, what could be in store for an average Azeri who had in fact identified himself with the Muslim world and had little, if any, attachment to the Soviet regime? Everybody was guilty and had reasons to expect the punishment. Even a book in the Arabic alphabet found at one's home would be enough ground for a denunciation.

Besides destroying the bulk of the CPAz leadership, the purges decimated its middle echelon. Above all, the non-Party intelligentsia were targets for repression. Baghirov gave special attention to the Writers Union, an association that lost through purges many of its members, among whom were such literary figures as Salman Mumtaz, Huseyn Javid, M. Mushfiq, S. M. Hanizadä, H. Sanlinin, Qurban Musayev, Taqi Shahbazi, and Ali Nazim. Some were denounced as

Pan-Turkists or Musavatists, others as German spies or Trotskyists. The repressions of the writers marked the final trampling of the compact between the Soviet regime and the Azeri intelligentsia. The policy of cooperation was replaced by physical annihilation. Of the 70,000 Azeri fatalities, those classified as the intelligentsia by profession, accounted for 29,000.[44] In comparative terms, the Great Terror of 1937, in Azerbaijan and Georgia, is described as "probably worse than in any other republic, barring the Ukraine."[45] Its chief victim, the intelligentsia, in effect ceased to exist as a social force with a sense of historical mission, ethos, and esprit de corps. They were replaced by a motley assemblage of university diploma holders, professionals, scholars, and artists. Those who survived the purges were broken-down, withdrawn from the life of action, or all too often grew into moral wrecks who eagerly denounced each other and humiliated themselves in endless adulation of Stalin and his shadow on the local scene, Baghirov. Many displayed probably a genuine affection for the man who easily could have each of them killed but had not done so. "For a few decades there spread out such offshoots of the bureaucratic-political culture as hierarchism, monopolism, cynicism, equalization, nihilism toward law, duplicity, and belief in the salutary effects of violence."[46] The intelligentsia's prestige sunk dramatically in the eyes of the population, all the more so because they had always to contend with their image as an alien body. Above all, there came the disabling effect of fear, a permanently encoded reflex in the mind of at least one generation, and to some degree in the generation to come.

If colonial rule is based on either adaptation of the old elites or creation of the new, the purges signified the choice of the second option. The bloodletting resulted in an abundance of vacancies, and these were quickly filled with the product of Soviet upbringing, the devoted—if provincial in outlook—newcomers to the ruling elite. They brought along the values and attitudes instilled in them: conformism, servility, obedience, and fear of creativity. These qualities were useful in the art of survival, but not for those who could assume the role of the guide and conscience of the community.

The purges turned out to be more than a bloody political and bureaucratic shake-up. They also were a cultural reorientation. Its essence was the ascendance of parochial, ethnic, and secular nationalism, hostile to any broader vision such as Turkism and indifferent to the mirage of Azerbaijani unity. This nationalism contained distorted echoes of the linguistic *Azarajiliq* and of Azerbaijanism of the 1918–1920 period, but it now appealed to the instincts of peasants uprooted by industrialization.

In a series of moves that might have appeared contradictory, the regime promoted both Azeri particularism and intensified Russification. This two-pronged operation was aimed to cut the links to the past and ensure Azerbaijan's integration into the Soviet system. In the midst of the purges, the Central Committee in Moscow passed a resolution that called for improvement in the quality of Russian-language instruction in non-Russian schools. Especially disturbing was the fact that in almost 3,000 non-Russian schools in Azerbaijan there were only 440 teachers of Russian. A crash teacher-training program was launched, but even so, there remained a shortfall of 30 percent.[47] All the same, the study of Russian became obligatory from the fifth grade of primary schools, and a thorough knowledge of the language became a prerequisite for success in Soviet society.

In step with these new cultural policies came the 1940 alphabet reform, the second in a little more than a decade. This time, Cyrillic was adopted as the official alphabet. The preparatory campaign went to the accompaniment of such arguments as those of the education commissar, M. Mammadov:

> The Russian alphabet has many advantages in comparison to the Latin. It is the alphabet of the great Russian people, who have raised the banner of the October Socialist Revolution—the Revolution opening a new epoch in the history of mankind. This is the alphabet of the great geniuses of mankind—Lenin and Stalin. The Russian alphabet is the script of the richest and most expressive language of the great classics of literature—Pushkin, Gogol, Tolstoi, Gorkii.[48]

Unlike in the 1920s there was no heated controversy. In fact, there was no debate on this reform. Instead, one only heard endless acclamations in public meetings.

Nationalism and Federalism in Exile

Even during the USSR's most liberal period—the early 1920s—when the regime offered a margin of flexibility to the intelligentsia, there still was no accommodation for uncontrolled non-Communist political activities, which only could be pursued by the émigrés. The main centers of political emigration were, quite naturally, Iran and Turkey. Yet these also were neighbors of the Soviet Union, which they could ill-afford to antagonize. Because their host countries were subject to Soviet pressure, the activities of Azeri exiles were bound to be affected, both in scope and character.

In Iran, the émigré community was under the unchallenged sway of the Musavat. During the 1920s, the party had concentrated its network of cells in Iranian Azarbaijan, notably in Tabriz, Rasht, Enzeli, Ardabil, Khoi, and Maku, but also in Teheran and Khorasan. In addition, there were Musavatist cells at most crossing points along the Soviet frontier. As a diplomat noted, "Persia gives shelter to the exiles from the Caucasus, and it is concerned about gaining their appreciation, but the government does not want to have on its territory any politically active Caucasian organization. To my assurance that the Musavatists at the moment any aggressive actions against the Soviets, I heard in reply that they were preparing such actions for the future."[49] Furthermore, the Musavatists were seen in Iran as Turcophiles, not well disposed toward Iran.

> Their contacts with such persons as Fevzi Pasha, the head of Turkish General Staff, who publicly spoke about the necessity of joining Iranian Azerbaijan to Turkey, are well known. To reach further back, the Musavatists during their short-lived rule in Baku, regardless of their ostensibly good relations with Persia, were always strongly pro-Turkish and prone to disparage Persia, which at that time was very weak. Consequently, some Musavatists saw themselves expelled from Persia and the police have somewhat harassed others. The example is Mammäd 'Ali Rasulzadä (brother of Mammäd Ämin) who wrote in an Istanbul newspaper a series of articles insulting Persia.[50]

Teheran may have been irritated by the presence of 1920-vintage Musavatist émigrés, but it also had to contend with a constant trickle of refugees crossing the Araxes frontier. The refugees' numbers grew during the collectivization campaign of the early 1930s and ultimately reached 15,000 persons.[51] Most of the leaders of the independent republic who managed to find their way out of the USSR had taken residence in Turkey. They tried to uphold the multiparty system, but only the Musavat had an organizational structure and a rank-and-file membership. Other "parties" consisted of individual leaders.

The presence of Räsulzadä strengthened the Azeris in Turkey, notably in terms of intellectual accomplishment. Within a short time of his arrival in 1922, he produced two books that were well received by the Turkish public: *Azerbaycan Cumhuriyeti* (The Azerbaijani republic) and *Asrimizin Siyavuşu* (Siyavush of our age), a literary divagation on the theme from the Persian national epic, *Shahnameh*. It focused on a legendary hero, Siyavush, in whose veins flowed both Persian and Turkic blood and who symbolized present-day Azerbaijan, a parable that suggested split personality.

In fact, publishing became the most visible and longest-lasting achievement of the Azeris in Turkey. The émigré press began with the Turkish language *Yeni Kafkasya* (The new Caucasia, 1923–1927), which purported to serve as the forum for all the nationalities of the region. Its replacement was the biweekly *Azeri-Türk*, which focused on Azerbaijani concerns. *Azeri-Türk* began to appear early in 1928 and closed down before the year was over, to be replaced the next year by two publications in the new Latin alphabet: the monthly *Odlu yurt* (The land of fire), and the weekly *Bildiriş* (Message). In September 1931, both publications were banned as a part of the crackdown on political activities of Soviet émigrés in Turkey. Only one press organ was allowed to continue publication: a scholarly journal, *Azerbaycan Yurt Bilgisi* (Studies of the Azerbaijani homeland). Despite its innocuous character, it was also banned after two years.[52]

The 1931 suppression of the émigré publications coincided with Räsulzadä's expulsion from Turkey, and some saw it all as the result of caving in to the Soviet pressure. In reality, the reason went deep into the complex relationship between Turkey and Azerbaijan, a love story with its ups and downs amidst stormy episodes. Tensions had been growing toward the end of the decade, and by 1930, they had reached a boiling point. In reply to Turkish criticism that the Musavat was neglecting the cause of Turkic unity, Räsulzadä published a pamphlet titled *O Pantiurkizme v sviazii s kavkazskoi problemoi* (Pan-Turkism with regard to the caucasian problem). Among the references to the experience of the 1918 Ottoman occupation, he firmly stated his view: Pan-Turkism was a cultural movement rather that a political program. Future unity with Turkey would be based on far-reaching decentralization; meanwhile the Azeris, mindful of their own identity, had to concentrate their efforts on relations with their Caucasian neighbors. But, as a Polish diplomatic report from Ankara observed, in the eyes of the Turkish regime, there was no "Azerbaijani question." There only was the problem of the Turkic peoples abroad:

> The émigrés, be they Circassians, Azerbaijanis, or Tatars who have acquired Turkish citizenship, are not considered by Turks as minorities but as Turks. They are subject to the ban on political activities, and the government circles cannot allow that a group of citizens recognized as Turks and not as a minority should pursue its own political goals. The Interior Minister Şükrü Kaya bey told me that the reason for the expulsion of Ämin bäy [Räsulzadä] and the ban for his return was not so much the intervention of the Soviets, because in his case the law of the freedom of press could have been stretched, but rather the fact that Ämin was engaged in . . . minority politics.[53]

The equal opportunity treatment that Turkey offered to the émigrés had an additional effect of discouraging them from participation in the work of non-Turkish associations.

> The more dynamic and intelligent human element from among the Azerbaijanis succeeded in integrating itself into the Turkish community and arranged somehow its existence. Fearing to jeopardize their means of livelihood, this element does not want in any way to take part in political activities. Only the less active individuals of the Azerbaijani émigrés maintain contact with our organization to receive permanent subsidy.[54]

Quite naturally for an exile community, Azeri émigrés were beset by quarrels, splits, and dissension, which often reflected personal ambitions rather than fundamental issues of politics. The earliest effort at overcoming the disunity was the creation of the Azerbaijani National Center in 1923, a coordinating body dominated by Musavat. The Center consisted of Räsulzadä, Väkilov, Khasmammädov, Shafibäkov, Rustambäkov, and Mirza-Bala of the Musavat, Yakub Mir-Mäkhtiyev of Ittihad, and the Socialist Muharramov. This list of prominent personalities from the independent republic did not, however, include its highest office-holder, Topchibashev. He was in Paris, leading the opposition struggle against the Center, and against Räsulzadä in particular. Mammäd Ämin's past relations with Stalin were never quite forgiven among the émigrés. Furthermore, within the Musavat leadership, rebellion against him was brewing with strong undertones of the old-time divisions of the left and right wings of the party. In 1928 the split burst into the open, and the right-wingers, with Khasmammädov and Rustambäkov at their head, seceded.

Apart from the intracommunal squabbling, the Azeri émigrés were absorbed by the question of alignments with other national groups in quest for the restoration of independence. The most natural step seemed to be the reanimation of Transcaucasian federalism. In June 1921, representatives of Georgia (Chkhenkeli), Azerbaijan (Topchibashev), Armenia (Agoronian), and the Republic of the Caucasian Mountaineers (Chermoy) signed a declaration on cooperation. Similar declarations followed in the years to come, but actual cooperation remained elusive.[55] The divisions within each émigré community were too deep. Moreover, the Armenians were unwilling to be involved in activities that could benefit Turkey while unduly weakening Russia.

An attempt to bring together not only the Transcaucasian but all the non-Russian émigré centers was the formation of the Prometheus, an organization launched in 1926 in Paris with the support of the Polish regime of Marshal Jozef Pilsudski, who once in power revived his old vision of splitting Russia on the nationality lines. The Promethean movement included Georgian, Azeri, Ukrainian, Crimean and Volga "Tatar," Turkmen, Caucasian Mountaineer, and even Karelian Finish sections, but it failed to attract the Armenians.[56] The Polish involvement consisted of a modest financial support—$1,000 per month—for the work among the Caucasian émigrés and efforts at synchronizing activities of diverse groups in the spirit of regional unity.

For the Azeris, notably Rasulzadä and his associates, the Polish connection was a welcome circumstance after the expulsion from Turkey. Ämin bäy took up residence in Warsaw, where he found a group of Azeri students and officers on contract with the Polish army. Here he found also his Polish wife. With the assistance of the Polish Ministry of Foreign Affairs, if not under its pressure, the 1934 Brussels Pact was hammered out, an agreement providing for the confederate, rather than federal, structure of the Caucasian state in the future. The pact received endorsement from the three Azeri émigré centers, Warsaw, Paris, and Istanbul, as well as from Georgians and Caucasian Mountaineers. It left the door open for the Armenian participation, and the invitation would eventually be accepted in 1940, when the Soviet Union had become the friend of Nazi Germany.

The spirit of the Brussels Pact together with the leadership of

Räsulzadä within the party found confirmation from the clandestine congress of Musavat that met in the Polish capital in 1936.

At the outbreak of World War II, Polish intelligence estimated the number of active members of the Musavat in Turkey and Iran at no more than 150.

> The number of its followers and sympathizers is larger, as only the Musavatists have conducted any visible political action for the Azerbaijani cause. . . . In Soviet Azerbaijan any manifestation of nationalism, any act hostile to Communism is termed Musavatist-inspired. It is therefore very difficult to determine the Musavatists' influence in Azerbaijan. It can be assumed that this influence is potentially very extensive, but in concretely organizational terms is very modest and in the condition of hibernation.[57]

As the war with the USSR approached, Germany showed an increasing interest in Azeri émigrés, and Berlin turned into a major center of their activities. In the second year of this war, German armies reached the Caucasus Mountains. By that time, they had accumulated a large mass of Azeri POWs. Short on manpower, the German Command of the Caucasus front began to draw upon them to fill the ranks of the Ost-Legionen, the troops consisting of the Oriental peoples of the USSR. The estimates for the figures of the Azeris who, not always voluntarily, joined the German forces, range from 25,000 to 35,000.[58] As much as other Soviet Muslims, the Germans found the Azeris to be more cooperative than the Russians or Armenians. All the same, they usually were not allowed to form units larger than battalions. On occasion, they were assigned to first line combat duty, but more often their tasks were behind the front, and included counter-guerrilla operations.[59] In this role, they fought against the Soviet partisans and also against the *Maquis* in France. These Azeri units also took part in suppressing the 1944 Polish uprising in Warsaw; a source of embarrassment for the political leaders of the German-uniformed Azeris, some of whom had served in the Polish army.

The attempts at the creation of an Azerbaijani political representation on the German side began in the spring of 1942, with the invitation of luminary émigrés, including Räsulzadä, to Berlin for exploratory talks. Ämin bäy found opportunities to meet the German-held POWs and was impressed by the level of education among the younger generation of his compatriots. When he asked them how many hundreds of university graduates would help to organize the Azerbaijani state of the future, the answer was: "Do not talk to us about hundreds but thousands. We are in the position to govern ourselves."[60] In his negotiations with the Germans, Ämin bäy insisted that the Reich as the first step should declare its unconditional commitment to the restoration of the Transcaucasian states. When his interlocutors acted evasively, he left Berlin, the soundest political decision he ever took. Eventually, he made his way to post-Kemalist Turkey, which extended him its hospitality for the rest of his life.

The Azerbaijani Majlis of National Unity came to existence in Berlin in November 1943, and its leaders did not see eye to eye with the old-time émigrés. For the most part, these were men whose outlook was shaped by Soviet upbringing, even though they were hostile to the USSR. The moving spirit of this group was the former Red Army officer, Fathali bäy Dudaginskii.[61] The Reich government kept withholding official recognition of the Majlis until March 1945, when Germany has as much as lost the war. Meanwhile, Moscow had prudently chosen to assign Azeri soldiers in the largest numbers possible for occupation duty in northern Iran, the region that once again passed under Russian domination.

SIX

Soviet Occupation and
the Autonomy of Iranian Azerbaijan

World War II and Iranian Azerbaijan

In the second year of World War II, the still-neutral Soviet Union informed Nazi Germany of its readiness for a compact on delineating the spheres of influence, provided that among other arrangements "the area south of Baku and Batum in the general direction of the Persian Gulf is recognized as the center of the Soviet aspirations."[1] As fate would have it, the USSR never reached a compact with Hitler: in June 1941 the USSR became the victim of German aggression, and its aspirations south of Baku had to be negotiated with Great Britain.

After the outbreak of the war, neutral Iran was a source of concern for the British. Reza Shah's regime barely concealed its pro-German sympathies, and in this regard the public largely shared the government's disposition, with German prestige growing higher as Allied defeats and setbacks mounted.

The German invasion of the Soviet Union brought another dimension to Iran's strategic significance: securing the flow of supplies to newfound ally Britain via land from the Persian Gulf, one of the few remaining routes available. Preventive action in Iran appeared to be in the interest of both powers, and the stakes were even higher for the USSR. But Britain took the initiative. "We welcomed the opportunity of joining hands with Russia," wrote Churchill, "and proposed to them a joint campaign."[2] The prime minister displayed foresight when, prior to the beginning of the campaign, he issued a directive that in all correspondence the name Iran should be replaced by the name Persia, since the confusion of Iran with Iraq could lead to mistakes with undesirable consequences.

As the Iranian government was slow to expel German agents and residents, a joint note of August 17—the "final word"—was sent to Iran invoking Article VI of the 1921 Soviet-Iranian Treaty. The invasion of Iran began on August 25. British operations were completed three days later, at the cost of 22 killed and 42 wounded. "Thus ended," remarked Churchill, "this brief and fruitful exercise of overwhelming force against a weak and ancient state."[3]

There are no exact figures of the casualties suffered by either side from the encounter of Soviet and Iranian forces; Soviet sources however, mention that the Red Army and Air Force dropped or delivered in northern Iran 15 million pamphlets containing the note to the Iranian government and the appeal by the Soviet Command to the Iranian people. Most of the pamphlets were in Azeri, others were in Persian or Armenian; some even were in French.[4]

The British and Soviet troops met in Teheran on September 16, and the same day, Reza Shah abdicated the throne in favor of his twenty-two-year-old son Muhammad Reza. The event marked the end of the two-decade-long Pahlavi dictatorship as the new Shah, on the Allies' advice, restored the constitutional monarchy and made guarantees of civil liberties. The deep and delicate questions about oil, Communism, and Iran's postwar future stayed in the background, but they were overlooked for the sake of the cooperation and goodwill between the Allies.

The status of Iran under the presence of foreign troops was defined by the Tripartite Treaty of Alliance of January 29, 1942, whose signatories were Britain, the USSR, and Iran. The two occupying powers "jointly and severally undertook to respect the territorial integrity, sovereignty, and political independence of Iran." Article V of the treaty stated that the Allied powers were to withdraw their forces from Iranian territory not later than six months after all hostilities between them and Germany as well as its associates had been suspended by the conclusion of an armistice or armistices or on the conclusion of peace between them, whichever date was earlier. Under this provision foreign troops could legally remain in Iran until six months after hostilities with Japan had ended. The spirit of the treaty was reaffirmed in the 1943 Teheran Declaration signed by Churchill, Roosevelt, and Stalin, which stated that they were "at one with the government of Iran in their desire for the maintenance of the independence, sovereignty, and territorial integrity of Iran."[5]

Although Iran had been divided, care was taken not to evoke echoes of earlier imperialist partitions. A British circular emphasized that there were no defined zones within which "we or the Russians have special rights or obligations, or outside of which we or they are precluded from stationing troops."[6] The term *zones* was to be avoided and was given no legal validity. Nonetheless there were clearly drawn lines beyond which one found the occupation forces instead of Iranian troops. In the north, the Iranians were forced to withdraw from the areas of Ushni, Haidarabad, Miandoab, Zinjan, Qazvin, Khurramabad, Babul, Zirab, Semnan, Shahrud, and Aliabad, and leave them to the Soviet troops. The core of this territory was Azerbaijan.

The number of troops in the Soviet-occupied part of Iran varied, but they usually ranged between 20,000 and 60,000. There was little to indicate that Soviet troops had been deployed in an aggressive manner, but the assumption among Western diplomats was that the political objective of these forces was to exert pressure not only on Iran but also on Turkey.[7]

The Red Army's occupation forces' ethnic composition raised more intriguing questions than did their troop strength or deployment patterns in Iranian Azerbaijan. "The Russian troops at Rezaieh are now mainly composed of *Turki*-speaking Azerbaijanis and many have their families with them," wrote a British diplomat.[8] Another British report from Tabriz noticed that there

> is now a clear policy of posting Soviet Azerbaijanis to both civil and military posts here in preference to personnel from other parts of the USSR. Most of the military officers in Tabriz are at present in that category and as pointed out in the last Diary, the Soviet Consulate General has been increased by a Muslim Vice-Consul, Hassan Hassanov. These Soviet Azerbaijanis, like . . . persons from Soviet Armenia, are the most fervent propagators of Russian expansionism.[9]

The presence of the Azeris in the Soviet occupation forces served as justification for bringing theater groups, opera, and ballet from Baku, whose Azeri-language performances were open to the public. Likewise, Soviet schools and a hospital were made accessible to the Iranian Azeris. The local unit of the Chief Administration for Political Propaganda of the Red Army (GUPP) mainly employed Azeris from the USSR, including Baku intellectuals, who among their other pursuits published the newspaper *Vatan Yolunda* (On the fatherland's road) in Azeri and in Arabic script. Its first editor-in-chief was the rising star of the Soviet Azerbaijani literature, Mirza Ibrahimov, who later would gain a reputation as an advocate of Pan-Azerbaijani sentiments.[10]

In 1944, after the opening of the House of the Soviet Culture in Tabriz, all pretenses of restraint in addressing the local population were abandoned. The House turned into the local center of cultural and intellectual propaganda and secured the participation of noted guests from Soviet Azerbaijan. Most of Baku's luminaries of the arts, literature, and scholarship visited Tabriz, and many remember it as a profound experience in the life of their generation.[11] Some, hopeful about the national contract, saw the prospects for Azerbaijan's reunification through the agency of the USSR, the way the Ukraine and Byelorussia had recently been reunited after the invasion of Poland in 1939.

Toward the end of the war, sensitive foreign observers noticed that the term *Greater Azerbaijan* kept cropping up in conversations and that, ominously, there was no reduction in the strength of Soviet garrisons after the Germans had retreated from the Caucasus front in early 1943. The Red Army occupation force retained its numbers even after the Persian Gulf ceased to serve as the supply route to the USSR with the opening of the Black Sea for Allied shipping in November 1944.

In the 1944 elections to Iran's Fourteenth Majlis, the Soviets applied pressure to secure parliamentary seats for candidates they trusted. Among them was Sayyid Jafar Pishevari, whose credentials ultimately were rejected on the grounds of irregularities resulting from Soviet interference, even though the mandates of other deputies from Azerbaijan elected under the same circumstances were accepted. Still, for the duration of the war, Soviet representatives tried to maintain low profiles and not interfere excessively in the Iranian administration. In the final analysis, outside meddling could be made easier or more difficult according to the dynamics of internal developments in Iran.

A major consequence of the overthrow of Reza Shah's dictatorship and the relaxation of political controls was the revival of political parties or the rise of new ones. Among the latter category was the far-Left Iran People's Party, commonly known as *Tudeh* (Masses), the closest approximation of a Communist organization. As Tudeh branched out into the provinces, Azerbaijan became a powerful center of its

influence. Here, the Leftist traditions were strong, the social and economic conditions favorable, and the Soviet occupation authorities
clearly well-disposed. The Azerbaijani branch of Tudeh was formed in
early 1942 through the merger of three radical clubs in Tabriz, of
which one was Armenian, another consisted of intellectuals, and the
third, of the *muhajirin*. Of the original five leaders of the local Tudeh,
Sadeq Padeghan, Ghulam Yahya Daneshiyan, 'Ali Shabustari, Mir
Rahim Velai, and Muhammad Biriya, all but the first had lived for
some time in the USSR. Shabustari and Biriya returned to Tabriz only
with the coming of Soviet troops in 1941.[12]

The Azerbaijani Tudeh soon developed differences with the
party's Central Committee. These differences reflected the perennial
tug-of-war between the center and periphery and between the integra-
tionists and decentralizers, but with the added dimension of an ethnic
distinctiveness that somewhat resembled the Himmätist-Bolshevik
controversy of 1919–1920. While the Central Committee preferred to
ignore as much as possible the problem of ethnicity, the Tabriz branch
of Tudeh called for establishing provincial councils as provided for by
the constitution and for the use of the native language in the local
courts and primary schools.

In the debates between the two groups, it soon became obvious
that the underlying issue was the meaning of nationhood. Were the
Azeris, who possessed a distinct language and inhabited a definite territory, a nationality (*melliyat*) with the implicit right to full autonomy,
and even self-determination, or, as the Teheran Tudeh leaders were
inclined to think, were they just a people (*mardum*), speaking not a
national (*melli*) language but a local dialect. By this reasoning, the
Azeris were not a distinct nation of their own but an integral part of the
Iranian nation. From the viewpoint of Teheran, Iran was one indivisi-
ble nation. From Tabriz, Iran was composed of diverse nationalities.
As historian L'Estrange-Fawcett observed, the Tudeh Party's leadership in its position toward Azerbaijan took a leaf from the writings of
Arani, who had died as a prisoner of Reza Shah's regime.[13] All the
same, the Tabriz Tudeh was anxious to avoid being perceived as
extremist on the nationality question. The provincial party conference
in January 1945 kept silent on the crucial language issue; it even
expelled Shabustari, the veteran of Khiabani movement and editor of
the bilingual Azeri-Persian newspaper, *Azarbaijan*, for having published excessively nationalistic contributions. Shabustari continued to

put out his newspaper, although no longer as the organ of Tudeh. He even established the Society of Azerbaijan, dedicated to the preservation of native language and culture.

Against this backdrop of division and theoretical confusion on the issue of national identity, the figure of Pishevari came to the fore. The American consul, Robert Rossow, described him as "a small man in his middle fifties, with steely gray hair and a small brush mustache under a sharp and slightly hooked nose." He also had a disarming smile and kindly eyes with deep crow's feet in the corners. But Rossow also perceived he was "not alien to suffering nor to the burdens of hard command."[14]

Pishevari had been a prominent figure in the Iranian Communist movement since World War I, with a record of work in the Ädälät, the Gilan Republic, where he served as the Interior Commissar, and in prolonged sojourns in Baku under the Soviets. He spent the decade from 1931 to 1941 in Iranian prisons, and after his release with the fall of Reza Shah, he stayed mostly in Teheran. One of the most prominent survivors of the early days of Communist activities, he refused to associate himself with the "young, inexperienced intellectuals" of the Tudeh leadership, whose educational background was Western European rather than Soviet. Instead, he founded in Teheran an independent Leftist newspaper, *Azhir*, which occasionally voiced criticism of the Tudeh as being insufficiently Marxist, or revolutionary, or of being too sectarian. He had now become able to turn the Fourteenth Majlis's rejection of his credentials to his advantage.[15]

The Democratic Party of Azerbaijan and the Seizure of Power

The political condition of Iranian Azerbaijan grew markedly dynamic while the war in Europe was winding down. There was an upsurge in the activities of the Tudeh Party and of the trade unions under its sway, with a resulting proliferation of strikes and labor disputes, all of which the Soviet media ascribed to the inspiring effect of the Red Army's victory over fascism. Other observers saw here manifestations of worsening economic conditions. As tensions in Azerbaijan mounted, Stalin announced at the Potsdam Conference that the USSR would keep its forces in Iran longer than it had originally said. Soviet troops would leave Iran within six months of the end of the war—but not the war with Germany. They would wait until six months after the end of the still-unconcluded war with Japan.

In the same month, August 1945, the militants of the Tudeh occupied several government buildings in Tabriz, and it seemed as though the party was bent on seizing power in the city and its environs. A manifesto was circulated demanding autonomy for Azerbaijan, recognition of Azeri as the official language in the region, and land reform.[16] The Iranian governor, Murtaza Bayat, was powerless to put down the disturbances because the Soviet forces prevented the gendarmerie and the army from leaving their barracks. After a few weeks, the situation appeared to calm down. The occupied buildings were vacated, and the governor again was allowed to exercise his authority.

This unexpected turn of the August events marked not so much the Tudeh's dress rehearsal for the seizure of power as it did an important shift in the Communists' overall course of action. The essence of this reorientation seems to have been Moscow's endorsement for the prospect of an Iran decentralized on the lines of ethnic and national minorities, the same way the Bolsheviks had once opted for splintering the Muslim community of Russia along the lines of nascent national identities. As a corollary, this policy was to be reflected in the structure of the Communist movement in Iran. Azerbaijan should loosen its links to Teheran, and local Communists, who would spearhead the movement for broad autonomy, should be free from their subordination to their Persian comrades in the Iranian capital.

In the midst of these developments of the summer of 1945, Pishevari suddenly began his efforts to establish a political party that was to supplant the Tudeh. "At that moment, there existed in Azerbaijan no political organization, other than the Tudeh Party," he recalled. "This party, after several years of activity, acquired a bad reputation and became ineffective. . . . So after long discussions which went on for three days among Shabustari, Sadeq Padeghani and myself, we decided to form a democratic party in Azerbaijan. First of all, I entrusted Sadeq Padhegani with the task of talking to the leaders of Tudeh and the labor unions in Azerbaijan, so as to prepare for their joining our movement."[17] Pishevari's recollections are short on details, but the conversations within these small groups were clearly fruitful.

The new party announced its birth on September 3 in a proclamation written by Pishevari and signed by seventy-six people. The organization called itself the Democratic Party of Azerbaijan (DPAz), a name that was of special concern for Pishevari. The term *democratic* was chosen not only to evoke memories of Khiabani's movement, whose survivors Pishevari was anxious to attract, but also to indicate that the party intended to have a broad social base that crossed class lines. Although the new party absorbed the regional chapter of Tudeh, there was no question of its simply continuing its activities under a different name. In fact, the DPAz was conceived as an alternative to some tenets and practices of Tudeh: specifically, it rejected sectarianism, implying that its ranks were open to all Azeris regardless of their class distinctions, unlike the Tudeh, which welcomed only the radically leftist elements.[18] This aspect of the party's character reflected current ideas of National or Patriotic Fronts in Eastern Europe, whereby attempts were made to forge as broad-based a political force as possible, but invariably under the hegemony of the Communists. Theoretical justifications were based on Stalin's pronouncements on national roads to socialism reflecting the specific conditions of a given country. In contrast to the position of Tudeh, the DPAz emphasized two new issues: the identity of the Azeris as a distinct nationality and the need for a far-reaching decentralization of Iran.

Likewise, in their background, the DPAz leaders differed from their opposite numbers in the Tudeh. A scholar who analyzed their biographies observed that of those about whom data could be gathered all but one were born in Iranian Azerbaijan and spoke Azeri; none had the record of endorsing Persianization; all were involved in the creation of the Communist Party of Iran; all took part in the Jangali uprising or the Khiabani movement, or both; only one, Biriya, was a founding member of the Tudeh, although others had at some time been associated with Tudeh but left before the autumn of 1945. Only Biriya had been a member of the local chapter of the Tudeh at the time of its dissolution.[19]

Developments began to follow one another in rapid succession, every few days bringing some important step toward completing the party's formation. On September 5, the newspaper *Azarbaijan* appeared as the organ of the DPAz, written now entirely in Azeri, with Pishevari as its editor-in-chief. Two days later, Biriya brought into the ranks of the party the Tabriz Workers' Union. Likewise, the Azerbaijani branch of the Tudeh joined in en masse without so much as consulting its central authorities in Teheran. The DPAz membership skyrocketed from 50 to 65,750.[20]

The DPAz's constituent congress met on October 2. It elected the Central Committee, and approved the program, which called for regional autonomy for Azerbaijan and for securing the right to national self-determination. Although the DPAz advertised its open-door attitude for all patriotic elements, and was willing to include landowners and clergy, it remained committed to the Bolshevik idea of democratic centralism.

Pishevari was not only the uncontested leader of the party but also the spokesman for its ideology and arcane tactics, a task that he performed primarily in his frequent articles in the newspaper *Azerbaijan*. He drew a line on what was the absolute minimum of the DPAz demands: education in the national language, the establishment of administrative and economic autonomy based on the constitution, and formation of the Provincial Council: "These issues are not subject to concessions on our part."[21] Others, by implication, could be negotiable.

Repeatedly he denied any inclination on the part of his movement toward separatism:

All the enemies of our party spread the word that we are working for the secession of Azerbaijan from Iran and for its incorporation into another state. We have proven that such rumors are baseless lies. Our strong interest is in the preservation of Iran's independence and integrity. Within Iran, Azerbaijan must enjoy its cultural and national rights.[22]

All the same, he would not refrain from hints at the possibility of Azerbaijan's drawing apart, should the central government persist in following a diametrically opposite political line. "Let the Teheran government know that it cannot remain at the crossroads. Azerbaijan is choosing its own road that will lead it to freedom and democracy. If Teheran chooses the road of the reaction, then after farewells, let it go on without Azerbaijan."[23]

The propaganda campaign for the twin goals of autonomy and reforms was intensifying, and from mid-November preparations for the seizure of power were under way. These included cutting telephone lines to Teheran and between the army garrisons in Azerbaijan. The DPAz began to distribute weapons to its members and select groups of workers and peasants using the stocks that the Red Army had taken from the Iranian forces in 1941. The Soviet troops generally maintained a discreet but unmistakenly helpful posture and on at least one occasion threatened to intervene on a large scale. When two Iranian battalions arrived from Teheran at Sharifabad threats of Soviet action caused the battalions to depart forthwith.

Some armed clashes occurred between the DPAz *fida'iyan* and the Iranian gendarmerie, and the atmosphere of intimidation against potentially hostile elements was widespread. Otherwise, the seizure of power by the Democrats ended with little bloodshed.

On November 20 the National Constituent Congress convened in a Tabriz movie theater. The same day, the assembly adopted the proclamation addressed to the Shah and the Majlis of Iran, as well as the governments of the United States, USSR, Great Britain, France, and China. The proclamation read as follows:

1. The People of Azerbaijan have been endowed by history with distinct national, linguistic, cultural, and traditional characteristics. These characteristics entitle Azerbaijan to freedom and autonomy, as promised to all nations by the Atlantic Charter.

2. The Nation (*Mellat*) of Azerbaijan has no desire to separate itself from Iran or to harm the territorial integrity of Iran, for it is aware of the close cultural, educational, and political ties that exist between itself and the other provinces, and it is proud of the great sacrifices it has made for the creation of modern Iran.

3. The Nation of Azerbaijan supports, with all its might, democracy, which in Iran takes a form of a constitutional government.

4. The Nation of Azerbaijan, like all citizens of Iran, will participate in the functioning of the central government by electing deputies to the Majlis and by paying taxes.

5. The Nation of Azerbaijan officially and openly declares that it has the right to form its own government, like other living nations, and to administer its internal and national affairs, respecting the integrity of Iran.

6. The Nation of Azerbaijan, having made great sacrifices for freedom, is determined to base its autonomy on the firm foundation of democracy. It therefore calls for a National Congress that will elect the ministers for the Autonomous Government of Azerbaijan.

7. The Nation of Azerbaijan has a special attachment to its national and mother language. It realizes that the imposition of another language on the people of Azerbaijan has hindered their

historical progress. This Congress therefore instructs its ministers to use the Azerbaijani language in schools and government offices as soon as possible.

8. This Congress, supported by 150,000 signatures, declares itself a constituent Assembly and appoints a Committee to administer Azerbaijan and implement the above resolutions until the convening of a National Majlis.[24]

In his address to the Congress, Pishevari once again denied that Azerbaijan held separatist goals, while upholding its need for self-government. He said the "Azerbaijani people will remain within the framework of Iran. But this does not mean that its native language, its traditions and customs should be destroyed. They will be secured by autonomy for Azerbaijan."[25] Although he spoke at length about the need for agrarian reforms, improvements in agricultural techniques, reconstruction of villages, and the opening of new schools, his declaration again included terminology such as "the nations inhabiting Iran," "national rights of Azerbaijan," and "the Azerbaijani nation" that were bound to raise objections in Teheran. These were expressions that directly contradicted the official doctrine of one Iranian nation (*mellat*).

British reactions to the developments in Azerbaijan acknowledged the effects of the larger issue of the center versus periphery and what followed from it, namely the need for administrative decentralization of Iran, though not nearly on the scale that the Soviets had in mind and not with the view toward further weakening of the Iranian state. "Whether the Persian Government can deal with this problem alone is, I fear, doubtful," wrote Ambassador Sir R. Bullard.

> I have no doubt at all that to treat the province of Azerbaijan as an isolated problem is to play in the hands of the Russians. . . . My proposal is to reduce the Azerbaijani question to its rightful proportions by treating it as one of local government not of autonomy, and that can best perhaps only be done by introducing into all provinces system of limited local government which is long overdue. . . . I do not think many who know the Persians from inside would agree that my plan would tend to disintegration. Persia is disintegrating all the time because of over-centralization which leads to complete stagnation in provinces. Generally speaking, Teheran takes no notice of provinces until one of them breaks out

into disorder. The trouble in Azerbaijan could never have obtained the present proportions without Russian instigation and help, but the province has genuine grievances which might well have caused a revolt sooner or later against the corrupt and inefficient officials sent from Teheran. All revenue of the country is sucked into Teheran.[26]

In another observation, the ambassador referred to the ethnic aspect of the problem and suggested that "to give reasonable satisfaction to minorities, the Persian government [should] pass immediately [a] law providing that *Turki*, Arabic, and Kurdish, respectively, which the minorities have always been perfectly free to talk and write, should be taught" as well.[27]

If Pishevari's movement capitalized on Azerbaijani resentments that had accumulated during the years of Reza Shah's attempts at Persianization, Teheran's reactions to efforts at upgrading the status of the Azeri language could only inflame these feelings. Historian Ervand Abrahamian, in a review of typical comments from the capital's newspapers, offers insight into the psychological dimension of the language issue on the Iranian side: "Whereas we are ashamed of Turkish as a disgraced stigma of the humiliation Iran suffered under the barbarian invaders, we are proud of Persian as our rich literary language that has contributed generously to world civilization." This statement appeared in the Teheran newspaper *Ettela'at* in an article entitled "Azerbaijan Is the Center of Iranian Patriotism." A series of articles in the same newspaper on "The Turkish Language of Azerbaijan" ended with a question that conveyed the flavor of the debate: "Who would exchange the cultured and world-famous literature of Ferdowsi, Sa'adi, and Hafiz for the uncouth and unknown babble of the Turkish plunderers?" Another newspaper (*Kushesh*) argued that "Persian must continue as the sole language of instruction throughout the public schools because Turkish was only an 'unfortunate deposit' left by the savage Mongols as they crossed Iran, plundering, destroying, and devastating the Middle East." Kasravi, the indefatigable crusader for Azerbaijan's integration with Iran, denounced the Tabriz Democrats for their claims that Azeris were a distinct nation and pointed to the crucial dangers to the unity of the state: "If similar claims are advanced by the other linguistic minorities—especially Armenians, Assyrians, Arabs, Gilanis, and Mazanderanis—nothing will be left of Iran."[28] This was one of Kasravi's last political pronouncements—he would soon be assassinated by a religious fanatic for heresy.

The shrillness of the press and parliament reached the highest pitch upon the declaration of autonomy. By contrast, the Tudeh declared its support for the people of Azerbaijan, who were the avant-garde of freedom in Iran. They blamed past governments in Teheran for not having established a sufficient number of schools in which the Azeris could learn Persian. Muhammad Mosaddeq, governor of Azerbaijan in the 1920s and now a senior statesman of impeccable credentials as an Iranian nationalist, stood out from the crowd when he admitted that Azerbaijan had grounds for disaffection. He suggested that one day Iran might be transformed into a federal state such as the United States or Switzerland, but that the status quo, in which one part of the country was under an autonomist regime and others were under the central government, was not acceptable.[29]

Another group of the population among whom the Soviet military authorities also encouraged autonomist aspirations were the Kurds. This group was numerically much smaller than the Azeris, but they also were less integrated into Iran. In November 1945 a handful of their notables came to Baku, where Baghirov harangued them into demanding their rights from Iran. Yet in his view Iranian Kurdistan should remain a part of Azerbaijan, and the 101-member National Majlis of Azerbaijan included five representatives from the Democratic Party of Kurdistan.

The Kurdish tribal chiefs tended to be noncommittal, fearing for their special position between the Iranian government and the tribes. Many of them would rather have fled than risk antagonizing Teheran. Increasingly, the Soviets came to rely on the townspeople of Mahabad and on the followers of the popular leader of the Kurdish Democratic Party, local judge Qazi Muhammad. The Kurdish Democrats made clear their unwillingness to live under the Azeri rule, and on January 22, 1946, they proclaimed an autonomous Kurdish government in Mahabad. Predictably, Mahabad became the magnet for Kurdish nationalists outside Iran, and soon it gave refuge to 3,000 seasoned fighters from Iraqi Kurdistan, led by Mustafa Barazani.[30]

Although both autonomous governments arose under Soviet tutelage, frictions between them grew, centering on territorial issues. The Kurds insisted that their frontier should be Lake Rezaieh, an arrangement that would cede them some Azeri-populated towns, notably Rezaieh and Shapur. The dispute was patched over by the Soviet-imposed Treaty of Friendship of April 23, 1946. The treaty's main provisions were: accreditation of official representatives in each other's territory; appointment of officials from the respective national-ities to government agencies in the areas where either of them held the majority; the formation of a joint economic committee; a military alliance in time of need; the commitment to secure the approval of the other's signatory in negotiations with Iran; and the mutual commit-ment to promote the cultural progress of each other's populations in their respective territories.[31] Otherwise, the territorial question was sidestepped at the insistence of the Soviets, who tended to be more sympathetic to the Azeri position. They also might have found the Mahabad regime was less affected by revolutionary zeal than was the government in Tabriz.

Autonomy and Experiments in Nation-Building

The elections to the Azerbaijani Majlis, which ended on Decem-ber 3, were based on universal suffrage, but candidates were required to be literate in Azeri and friendly to the aims of the Democrats. With the formation of the government of autonomous Azerbaijan, attempts to build the structure of a state within the state were officially launched a quarter of a century later than north of the border. The fundamental difference was that in 1918 Baku's autonomy was a stepping-stone toward independence. In 1945 the next step after Tabriz's autonomy would have to be absorption by the USSR.

The story of the Tabriz autonomous government presents in microcosm the rise and fall of a Communist regime allied with nation-alism, an account compressed to one year, its typical lights and shadows growing into fatal flaws magnified by the working of self-destructive mechanisms. As in many other cases, the inception of this Communist regime was accompanied by Soviet military presence, which offered firm if discreet assistance, and the seizure of power took place under national rather than purely revolutionary slogans.

For all the reservations, apprehensions, and suspicions of the ulti-mate Soviet goals, the Democrats' promise of changes met with some hope and goodwill among the population. The general perception, shared even by opponents of the DPAz, was that in terms of physical improvement—paving roads, building schools, and opening hospi-tals—Azerbaijan had achieved more in one year than it had during the twenty years of the Pahlavi regime. William O. Douglas, the American jurist, visited Azerbaijan in 1950 and assembled a list of changes and improvements that the inhabitants appreciatively remembered as coming to them from Pishevari:

1. The part of his program which most impressed the peasants was land reform. It had some communism in it. He confiscated the land of all absentee landlords and distributed it to the peasants. But he left untouched the land of resident landlords: a new law merely increased the tenants' share of crops.

2. Pishevari also gave a socialistic flavor to his program. His government nationalized the larger banks.

3. Second only to land reform in popular appeal was the law that made it a capital offense for a public official to take a bribe. Two top officials and a few lesser ones were hanged for this offense. The law had an electrifying effect. Merchants told me that they could keep their stores unlocked all night and be safe from robbers. . . .

4. Health clinics were created, some being itinerant and serving the villages from Tabriz.

5. The prices of basic commodities were rigidly controlled, hoarding of food was severely punished, a rationing system was adopted whereby everyone received the minimum requirements for living. Pishevari promised that the cost of living would be reduced per 40 percent; and it was.

6. A minimum-wage and maximum-hours-of-work law was established and collective bargaining between employees and employers was introduced.

7. A public works program was undertaken. The unemployed were put to work. [32]

In addition to measures that dealt primarily with day-to-day conditions of life, the regime launched a series of reforms that could be seen as setting Azerbaijan apart from the rest of Iran. Of all these actions the one most incongruous with the Democrats' declarations of support for the integrity and sovereignty of Iran was the creation of the Azerbaijani National Army. The justification was that an armed force was necessary to protect the achievements of the people of Azerbaijan from the enemies of progress. On the other hand, the Tabriz government refrained from setting up offices for foreign policy and diplomacy, thereby hoping to prove that it harbored no separatist designs.

The Azerbaijani Army came into existence on December 13, the day that the Tabriz Iranian Army Corps surrendered to the Pishevari regime. Under the terms of the surrender, all the weapons were to be delivered to the Democrats, and the officers who wished could join the Azerbaijani Army after taking the oath of loyalty. One hundred sixty officers availed themselves of this opportunity, at the price of gaining the status of deserters in the eyes of Iranian authorities.

The nucleus of the Azerbaijani Army were the fida'iyan squads. Now transforming themselves into regular forces, their organization was patterned on the Soviet model with its typical duality of command: each unit was under the supervision of a military commander and a propaganda/political officer. The positions of political officers were usually held by the muhajirin or even Soviet Azeris, as military cooperation between two Azerbaijans became close.

In addition to the former Iranian army officers, 350 muhajirin and 810 Iranian Azeris were promoted to the officer ranks during the first six months of the autonomist rule; many of these new officers were trained in crash courses at training camps beyond the Araxes. The troops were equipped only with light weapons, some Soviet-made, some seized from the Iranian Tabriz garrison, others from the Iranian forces disarmed by the Soviets in 1941. With the offer of relatively high pay, the army attracted volunteers from the poorer strata of the population. The introduction of the draft provided an additional source of manpower.[33]

Other reforms fell broadly into three categories: first, there was the indigenization of local government. Attempts were made to fill all levels of administrative positions with native personnel, preferably those who, in the eyes of the Democrats, were politically reliable. The quality of this personnel, according to reports of Western diplomats, was not inferior to that of the Persian Pahlavi regime officials, even though they lacked some of the latter's graces.

There followed attempts at a veritable cultural revolution that aimed to reverse the Pahlavi assimilationist policies and to assert an Azeri national identity. In line with the long-standing concern among the opponents of Persianization, the central issue was that of the native language. The process of cultural transformations based on upgrading Azeri had begun even before November 1945, but its official inauguration was the January 6, 1946, *Decree of the National Government on Language*. This document proclaimed that "from this day, the official language in Azerbaijan is Azeri." By this time, the native language had already been introduced into many primary schools and there had been hasty printing of textbooks transliterated from Baku Cyrillic editions. The process quickly gained momentum, and its highlights were such events as the opening of: the first Azerbaijani School of Fine Arts and Painting (January 19), the State Theater (March 23), the Azerbaijani Broadcasting Agency (July 4), and the State University (June 6). Beginning with the new school year in September 1946, instruction in all schools was to be offered in the native language.[34]

The driving spirit behind these impressive achievements was the education minister, Muhammad Biriya, one of the 1941 returnees from Soviet Azerbaijan. A gifted poet whose biography included a stint as a labor organizer in Tabriz, Biriya was an outspoken advocate of close relations with Baku. Rossow described him as "a dark cocky little man with a thin black mustache and slick black hair . . . [who] had risen to prominence in the Communist movement as head of the street-cleaners union in Tabriz." The American consul, who in his dislike of him would misspell his name as Beria, commented on a more sinister aspect of his diverse activities:

> To execute his campaign of terror he used a sort of goon squad known as the Society of Friends of the Soviet Azerbaijan. Recruitment to the Society was carried out by agents of the political police, and anyone who showed opposition or even reluctance was lucky to get off with only a pistol whipping or clubbing.[35]

The regime also began to enact a third category of reforms aimed at some degree of social change, but it clearly was not willing to antagonize those who were not yet hostile. Rather, it attempted to be circumspect and conciliatory toward the privileged classes. Pishevari resisted the pressures for a radical land reform, agreeing initially only to the reduction of rents. The February 19, 1946, law on the distribution of land dealt only with the state-owned *khaliseh* lands. In contradiction of its national-unity approach, the regime also used this reform against its political opponents. Another law passed the same day provided for the

confiscation of entire movable and immovable property of the persons described below:

a) those who, having left Azerbaijan and gone to Teheran and other places carry on propaganda against the freedom of Azerbaijan and the National Government;

b) those who, outside of Azerbaijan, are fighting against the freedom of Azerbaijan and the National Government, whether such persons are Azerbaijanis or not.[36]

The task of identifying those whose properties were to be confiscated was entrusted to the Ministry of the Interior. The struggle against the enemies of the regime—whether real, imaginary, or potential—did not remain limited to economic retaliation. More effective than Biriya's Society of Friends was the political police force. Modeled on the Soviet NKVD, its personnel consisted largely of the most reliable muhajirin. Soon, foreign observers began to notice the unmistakable features of Soviet life of the Stalinist epoch:

> A black cloud of fear descended on Azerbaijan: fear of the Democrats, and fear of the Soviet shadow which was all too near. Spies abounded. People were torn from their beds, never to return. Friend learned to distrust friend. Even the mollahs were afraid to speak out against the party in case their valuable property might be taken away from them.[37]

Contacts between the two Azerbaijans were both numerous and diverse, though as extensive or at the grass-root level as in the years before the Soviet period. Cultural exchanges, which were tilted in favor of Baku performing groups' visits to Tabriz, were intensified, as were the visits of official delegations. The Soviet presence heavily influenced the character of the cultural revolution, whose most prominent feature was government sponsorship of literature. The campaign for purification of the literary language, from Persian rather than Arabic elements, turned into an effort to make it identical with the Azeri of Baku, including the use of loan words from Russian. Such terms as *forma*, *tematika*, *dramaturgiya*, *gazeta*, *redaksiya*, as well as the purely Russian *obraz* (image), *zavod* (factory), *povest* (story), entered the language of Tabriz newspapers and magazines, the result of the editorial work of resident Soviet writers, journalists, and propaganda experts. The same writers who encouraged the themes of love for the homeland, the mother tongue, the glorious past of Azerbaijan, and its historical figures also promoted the adulation of the Soviet Union. Sakina

Berengian quotes typical titles of poems from the Tabriz press publications, among which were odes to the October Revolution, the victorious Red Army, May Day, and, most frequent of all, to Stalin and Lenin.[38] In a manner strikingly resembling Eastern Europe of the period, promotion of local nationalism went hand in hand with expressions of subservience to the USSR.

Likewise, a large number of specialists and advisors from beyond the Araxes, some of them Armenians, took positions in various agencies in Tabriz. On the other hand, the influx of Soviet newspapers, books, and other printed matter remained limited in scope: the reading public was not familiar with Cyrillic script. The switch from the Arabic alphabet, for which the Baku intellectuals had crusaded with such a vigor, was now exacting its toll. Aid from Soviet Azerbaijan to the Democrats focused on military and propaganda efforts, including deliveries of arms, ammunition, and radio-station equipment (originally an American lend-lease gift to the USSR). In addition, army personnel were trained on the spot or across the Araxes. In return, the Soviets took payment in grain, cattle, and other agricultural products. For all the growing ties, there was no open talk of the possibility of unification of the two Azerbaijans, though such speculations were rampant both in the country and abroad.

An intriguing question concerns the role of Baghirov in fostering these ties. The Soviet records that have been made available for archival research show that even relatively minor decisions on the contacts with Iranian Azerbaijan were being taken up at the highest levels of the Baku regime.[39] Some authors speculate that as a trusted satrap he enjoyed a margin of freedom of action within Moscow's goals in Iran and played a crucial part in launching the autonomist movement.[40] Unquestionably, Baghirov exercised his personal influence south of the border, yet within limits set by Moscow. At least two leading personalities in the Tabriz regime, Daneshyian and Kabiri, were known for their beliefs in the necessity to unite the two Azerbaijans, and they were in permanent contact with agents of Baghirov, possibly without knowledge of Pishevari. Indeed, the latter repeatedly intimated to Rossow that he lacked full control over some of his government officials and publicly was emphatic in his denials that unification had ever been contemplated. "At first, some vicious men were saying that we desired to join Iranian Azerbaijan to Soviet Azerbaijan, as if the Democrat Party had sold itself to the Soviet government. But we have proved that they were all liars. The facts have confirmed it and today the Red Army is leaving us."[41] He wrote these words in the aftermath of the settlements by which the big powers became involved in the case of Azerbaijan.

Azerbaijan in the World News

Taking a long view, the Democrats' greatest weakness turned out to be what had seemed their ultimate strength: a special relationship with the Soviet Union. The belief that if should things go wrong, the Soviet comrades would rush to pull the chestnuts from the fire engendered boldness and self-assurance that were helpful in the regime's initial successes.

Meanwhile, the name *Azerbaijan* was finding its way into the headlines of world newspapers. The case of the rebellious province of Iran assumed an international dimension as a concern of the great powers' diplomacy, indeed, as one of the first skirmishes of the unfolding Cold War—and it brought to the Middle East the active involvement of the United States. The treaty deadline for the withdrawal of Soviet troops came on March 2, 1946, but the occupiers showed no signs of departing. Moscow acknowledged the day by a communique stating that in view of unsettled conditions endangering the security of the USSR frontier, Soviet forces were compelled to remain in occupation of northern Iran. In fact, there was a sudden arrival of reinforcements. Rossow reported on any movements of the Soviet forces to the State Department, running up telegraph fees to the tune of $10,000 to $15,000 a month, a virtual subsidy to the autonomist regime that otherwise would not meet its bills. He wrote later:

> One may fairly say that the Cold War began on March 4, 1946. On that day fifteen Soviet armored brigades began to pour into the northern Iranian province of Azerbaijan and to deploy along the Turkish and Iraqi frontiers and toward central Iran. Simultaneously, another Soviet army of comparable size and composition moved south across Bulgaria to deploy along the European frontier of Turkey.[42]

In the view of the United States State Department, the problem of Azerbaijan played an important part in the Soviet strategy of penetration into the Middle East and Eastern Mediterranean. The Western, and notably American, reactions to the threats to Turkey's security were unequivocally firm, and there followed a U.N. Security Council debate about Azerbaijan. By the end of March, Moscow suddenly performed a volte-face by declaring that the Red Army would leave the territory of Iran within five or six weeks unless "unforeseen circumstances" intervened. Following this declaration came the announcement that in return for the withdrawal of Soviet forces, the Majlis would debate a proposal for the creation of a Soviet-dominated joint-stock oil company with a renewable fifty year lease. The agreement also called for negotiating the settlement between Teheran and Tabriz as an internal affair of Iran, in a spirit of goodwill toward the population of the province.

Moscow's plan to form a Soviet-Iranian oil company—in itself a colonial-type enterprise that would operate in the geologically unpromising territory of northern Iran—might have signaled to Pishevari an important attempt at extending its influence over a larger part of Iran. But because the Soviet forces had left the country, Pishevari's position was weakened. Clearly, Soviet support was a far cry from a carte blanche. Furthermore, the implication was that in pursuit of a larger goal, Moscow would be less willing to give full endorsement for the autonomist regime in Tabriz. Pishevari toned down the hints at going it alone, and, forgetting all past disagreements, he was anxious to have the backing of the Tudeh forces in Iran. In the spring of 1946 the power of the Iranian Left seemed to be dramatically increasing.

The decision to withdraw the Soviet forces resulted in two rounds of negotiations between the Tabriz regime and the central government, now under the premiership of an astute senior statesman, Qavam al-Saltaneh. The first round, which began on April 28, ended inconclusively, as the Teheran cabinet insisted on its prerogative to appoint the commanders of the provincial armed forces, the gendarmerie, and the governor-general of Azerbaijan. The Qavam government also made clear its position that the question of land distribution could be resolved only by the national Majlis, thus invalidating the distributions that had been carried out thus far.[43] Before the talks ended on May 9, the Soviet troops had left Iran. They needed the assistance from Western oil companies' emergency deliveries, however: the Red Army vehicles ran out of fuel on the way home.

Upon his return to Tabriz, Pishevari had reason for concern. In a public speech he warned the Teheran government that an attempt to seize military control over Azerbaijan would amount to breaking the agreement with the USSR. At the same time, Tabriz radio continued to assert that "we will not entrust our army to others, and in such a way we secure the freedom for all the nations of Iran. We remind them that they should follow the example of Azerbaijan and to act courageously for achieving their true freedom."[44]

The Qavam cabinet was not ready for confrontation; both sides desired a settlement, and the negotiations resumed, this time in Tabriz. To display its goodwill, the Teheran government appointed as the head of its delegation Vice-Premier and Propaganda Minister Mozafar Firuz, a man known for his pro-Soviet views. On June 13 an agreement was signed resolving the most controversial issues: selection of the governor-general, land distribution, taxes, armed forces, and parliamentary representation. The agreement, in itself a comprehensive statement of Azerbaijani autonomist aspirations vis-à-vis Teheran, consisted of the following main provisions:

1. The chief financial officer of the province will be appointed at the proposal of the Provincial Council with the approval of the central government.

2. The Provincial Council will make four nominations for the Provincial Governor-General, and the central government's Minister of Interior will appoint one of them.

3. In consideration of recent changes in Azerbaijan, the elective body under the name "National Majlis of Azerbaijan" will be recognized by the government as the Provincial Council of Azerbaijan.

4. The Azerbaijani army will be incorporated into the Iranian army with a commission arranging for details.

5. Seventy-five percent of revenues from Azerbaijan will be expended for the local needs, with the balance to be sent to the capital. The government agrees to assign twenty-five percent of custom revenues from Azerbaijan to the budget of the University of Tabriz.

6. With the use of Azerbaijani workers and specialists, the central government will extend the railroad from Mianeh to Tabriz.

7. Azerbaijani irregular forces, the fida'iyan, will be incorporated into the Iranian gendarmerie.

8. The central government does not raise objections to the land distribution carried out in Azerbaijan. The government will pay for private lands confiscated for the distribution. A special mixed

commission will decide on the final status of the confiscated lands.

9. Electoral laws will be revised to establish parliamentary representation on a proportional basis with enfranchisement of women.

10. For supervisory purposes, an administrative council will be established, consisting of the governor, heads of departments and of the board of the Provincial Council.

11. Both Persian and Azerbaijani Turkish will be recognized as official languages in the province. They will be taught in primary and secondary schools. [45]

In addition, the Tabriz regime presented a document of far-reaching ramifications that contained its demands on the armed forces: 160 officers who in 1945 had left the Iranian army were to be promoted by two ranks; 350 muhajirin, among them a number of generals and colonels, were to be kept at their present ranks; 810 officers of the Azerbaijani Army were to have their ranks recognized; the central government was to contribute fifteen million rials annually to the military budget of Azerbaijan; the Provincial Council was to have the right to nominate division commanders in Azerbaijan.[46] If accepted, these demands would virtually assure the permanent power of the DPAz regime and move it one step away from quasi-independence.

Although the outstanding issues of the army and land distribution left Qavam some room for further negotiations and maneuvering, the agreement was generally thought to have strengthened the hand of the DPAz and its closest ally, the Iranian Left, with whose fortunes the fate of the Tabriz government now became closely linked. It seemed to be the moment of triumph Pishevari himself, and it was made more dramatic because it came without the presence of Soviet troops. Upon signing the agreement, he declared the readiness to fight for establishing democracy throughout all of Iran. In the Majlis of Iran, if an increased Azerbaijani deputation joined forces with the Tudeh, it would constitute a powerful pressure group for influencing the government to take a leftist and pro-Soviet line.

For his part, Qavam quickly appointed the former Azerbaijani Minister of the Interior Salamollah Javid as governor-general. Then, as though in recognition of Iran's move to the Left, he co-opted the Tudeh by bringing some of its members into his cabinet. This calculated step

involved the party in the preservation of law and order and also stimulated dissension among its leaders.

The Autonomous Regime in the Face of Popular Discontent

The Tabriz government savored its successful negotiations and
looked with confidence at the prospects for the Iranian Left, as it had
Soviet backing and felt little incentive to heed the mounting disaffection among the population. The cultural revolution, for all its achievements, fell short of stemming the tide, and hostile dispositions gradually spread beyond what had been the initial nucleus of the opposition—the landowning class and wealthy merchants. In the towns, the
clergy became antagonized by the anti-Islamic tenor of the Democrats'
propaganda. In harmony with this forceful secularism was the barely
disguised anti-Iranian disposition of the regime. At the same time,
manifestations of subservience to the Soviet Union became increasingly obsequious. "The people realized bitterly that . . . [the Democrats]
were prepared to sell their country to Moscow—and to sell it cheaply
at that," noted a diplomatic report, "for, in spite of past discourage-
ment, oppression and disillusionment, the Azerbaijani remained a fer-
vent patriot, first Azerbaijani and second Persian."[47]

In the countryside, where religious fervor and the sense of identification with Iran were less in evidence, other factors produced discontent among the peasants, who initially had been the Democrats'
most solid supporters. In the spring, the regime ordered the conscrip-
tion of young men from country villages for security assignments
against the hostile Zulfiqari and Arasbaran tribes. As a result, vital
labor was lost at a crucial time, and many rural families were frequently reduced to starvation, while the young men got paid next to
nothing for their guard duties.

In addition, there was the grain collection program, which met
with popular resistance. Later, as the extent of the summer 1946 crop
failure became obvious, the authorities ordered the peasants to cede all
but one ton of their entire share. Meanwhile, shipments of grain to the
Soviet Union continued, and the party leaders were believed to be
enriching themselves.[48] When the central government launched its
counteroffensive, the Tabriz regime, its popular support eroded, was
taken off guard.

In Teheran, on October 17, Qavam handed his resignation to the
shah and immediately formed a new cabinet, this time without partic-

ipation of the Tudeh ministers. The reshuffling amounted to an eviction, and the Teheran government now took a sharp turn away from its policy of accommodating the Left. The next day, the Azerbaijani delegation negotiating the unresolved issues of the June 13 agreement returned to Tabriz with none of the concessions the DPAz had confidently expected. "Take it or leave it" was Qavam's new position. As a British report commented, the Democrats' "shaky structure had received its first shock from outside and a faint glimmer of hope arose among the Azerbaijanis that this might be the beginning of the end."[49]

Following this first show of firmness, Qavam, now assured of the Western powers' backing, announced that government troops would supervise the forthcoming elections to the Iranian Majlis in all constituencies, including Azerbaijan. The date of the voting was set for December 7.

Pishevari reacted in anger. He threatened the reactionaries with the extension of Azerbaijani freedom over all of Iran, with destruction of the "criminal and dilapidated" Teheran regime and its replacement by a "national government."[50] Radio Tabriz poured venom on the Qavam cabinet, and the Democrats busily tried to mobilize the support of the Iranian Left. The Tudeh Party warned that the Soviet Union could regard the dispatch of troops as endangering the security of its border, and under the terms of the 1921 treaty the Red Army might reappear on Iranian territory. As for Moscow, its position reflected the dilemma: on the one hand it desired the approval of the Majlis for the oil concession agreement, and the new elections thus were indispensable; on the other hand, it realized that the Democrats' regime would not survive the entry of troops from Teheran. The choice was either to support the cause of Azerbaijani autonomy or to sacrifice it for the sake of the oil concession, whatever its worth. In the end, the Soviet Union did not go beyond diplomatic warnings that it could not remain passive in the event of an attack on Azerbaijan, or that the arrival of Iranian forces would provoke disorder and insecurity in the region adjacent to its frontier.[51] These steps did nothing to save the Tabriz regime but only irritated Teheran. While Pishevari kept fulminating against Qavam, his more moderate colleagues, Salmollah and Shabustari, began talks with the Iranian government in search of a compromise. On the election supervision issue, no solution was acceptable for both sides, but the Democrats agreed to evacuate Zinjan, which was held by their fida'iyan. The town passed into the hands of government forces, and Teheran saw their welcome by the inhabitants as a good omen for the operation to dismantle the DPAz rule.

As the tense November days slowly wore on, the condition of the Tabriz regime resembled that of the Azerbaijani Republic on the eve of downfall in 1920, yet there was an essential difference. The Democrats' response to the growing hostility of the masses was to intensify the terror campaign; spies worked overtime, and wholesale arrests were frequent.

The mood of the population was affecting the armed forces, the half-hearted fida'iyan, and unwilling conscripts who were to stand up to the Iranian army. They were all the more disheartened that the war matériel that had come from the Soviet Union included only ammunition and light arms. The supplies were hardly adequate to fight the Iranian forces, which were armed with American-supplied planes and armored vehicles.

The Democrat leaders repeatedly addressed public meetings to whip up support for the resistance, but their efforts produced no visible effects. Yet when the Party began to distribute rifles and ammunition to anyone willing to fight for "the defense of freedom," the population eagerly seized them, with the intention of settling scores against the Democrats once circumstances allowed.

The last communication from Qavam to Tabriz ended with the words: "I hope that you will welcome these troops with full trust and that you will see to it that no difficulties should be created for them, so that the elections could take place as soon as possible. Then it will be possible to proceed with necessary reforms."[52]

On November 30 the Provincial Council of Azerbaijan held an extraordinary meeting to debate the message of Qavam. The outcome was the cable to Teheran protesting against dispatch of the troops as contrary to the June agreement. By this time, the central government forces were deploying for the offensive action at Gaflankuh Pass.

The Demise of the Autonomous Regime

On the eve of the first anniversary of the autonomous Azerbaijani government, there was nothing to suggest that it would be a joyful occasion. By now, all illusions of rescue at the hands of the Soviet Union had evaporated, and from the standpoint of Moscow's interest there could be no question of the tail wagging the dog. The first skirmishes at Gaflankuh on December 8 made obvious the overwhelming numerical and logistic superiority of Teheran's forces, and the outcome of the battle, should it come to pass, would not be in doubt. The Democrats' leadership sank into dejection, and its hidden cracks, primarily between the politicians and civil servants, burst into the open. Salamollah and Shabustari counseled immediate surrender. Shabustari had been an early fighter for Azeri identity, but now was among the first Democrats to lead the way back to Iran's fold. Most of the other leaders still talked about resistance. But the December 11 proclamation that called for a fight to the death bore the signatures of only Pishevari and Biriya.

The downfall of the regime was swift and unglorious, an intimation of how Communist power would collapse decades later in Eastern Europe. Seeing the hopelessness of the situation, Governor-General Salamollah cabled the notice of surrender. In Teheran the shah showed the communiqué to the Soviet ambassador, who had come with the warning of the grave consequences of the disturbances close to the frontier. There would be no fighting, the shah assured his visitor.[53]

The Central Committee of the DPAz acknowledged defeat in their December 12 declaration, affirming that the Party had always supported the sovereignty and independence of Iran. The issue was presented as the confrontation between excessive centralism and the desire for autonomy.

> We have proclaimed before the whole world that Azerbaijan should remain an integral part of Iran. But a group of traitors and reactionaries tried to falsify the meaning of the Azerbaijani movement in an attempt to carry out their designs. To deny the triumph to the enemies of our people, we agree to the supervision of the elections by the government forces.[54]

Addressing the troops entering Azerbaijan, General 'Ali Razmara proclaimed that they were restoring the soul of Iran to the nation, and henceforth the anniversary of the event would be celebrated by a military parade. By all accounts the population's enthusiastic welcome of the Iranian army was genuine. Among the elated throngs were many who barely a year ago had also enthusiastically greeted the rise of the Pishevari government; the change of heart was due not only to disenchantment with the Democrats but also to the uncontrollable violence being meted out at the sympathizers of the fallen regime. Rossow conservatively estimated 500 killed during the lawless interregnum that preceded the coming of the Iranian troops. Hundreds of others were tried and jailed, and scores were hanged. "For months afterward nearly every public square in Azerbaijan and northern Kurdistan sported rows of rebels swinging from crude gibbets."[55]

The only possibility of evading Iranian vengeance seemed to be emigration, and the USSR opened its frontiers to the refugees, many of whom, with time, would find themselves in Soviet prisons. The border crossings hummed with heavy traffic flowing in only one direction. Over the Julfa bridge 110 trucks carrying Iranian Azeris were observed, including officials, military personnel, the muhajirin, and the party leaders, among them Pishevari. The total number of refugees is estimated at 15,000.[56]

Western diplomats, who had expected the launching of a guerrilla movement with the use of the Soviet Azeris, had to contend with the puzzling question of why Moscow abandoned Iranian Azerbaijan. Staying put would have been far easier than swallowing Eastern European countries, a process that was then under way. There are many possible explanations, but they also are tenuous and contradictory. Was it proof of Soviet conciliatory intentions? Or of the effectiveness of the Western powers' firmness? Was it that Stalin allowed himself to be shamefully outsmarted by the wily Qavam, who in the end let the Majlis reject the agreement on the oil concession for the USSR? Was there at the root of it Moscow's conviction that a large part of Iran would inevitably fall into the Soviet orbit, and from this viewpoint the promotion of Azerbaijani autonomy would be a complicating factor? The dearth of convincing explanations leaves the field open for speculation. It is likely that in early 1946 Moscow faced a choice of lasting geopolitical consequence: should it push into Iran and the Middle East, an expansion certain to be contested by Britain and the United States, or should it seize the historic opportunity to establish itself firmly in Eastern and Central Europe, where the Soviets would not be opposed by the Western powers, but at the most by the local populations. There were not sufficient resources to move in both directions, and in the tradition of Russian geopolitical thinking, Central Europe took priority over the Middle East.[57]

SEVEN

The Two Azerbaijans and the Empires in Decline

Soviet Pan-Azerbaijanism After 1946

"Five months have elapsed since the Central Government's troops marched into the province to depose the Democrats, many of whom poured into the USSR along the 480-mile Azerbaijani-Soviet border," wrote a U.S. intelligence report.

> Within this time the enthusiasm with which the population welcomed the return of Iranian authority changed to widespread dissatisfaction over government maladministration and army corruption. Since the fall of Azerbaijan, the army has conducted a virtual military occupation of the province which is still under Martial Law. It filled the jails not only with political prisoners but also with persons who resisted its venal practices. The execution of collaborationists unable to buy their freedom, although temporarily suspended during the recent Majlis elections, has now been renewed.[1]

Another American source, William O. Douglas, known for his concern about the threat of communism in Asia, tells of the return of the absentee landlords ("the most callous I have known") on the heels of the army and of the landlords' demand not only for the current rentals but also those not paid under Pishevari. This extortion, combined with crop failures, a series of severe winters, and the loss of the grain and cattle that the escaping Democrats took with them, produced near-starvation and inevitable social restiveness. Douglas relates the story of an angry crowd in front of a jail shouting in the faces of the gendarmes, "Pishevari! We want Pishevari!"

In his words,

> Pishevari's program was so popular—especially land reform, severe punishment of public officials who took bribes, and price control—that if there had been a free election in Azerbaijan during the summer of 1950, Pishevari would have been restored to power by the vote of 90 percent of the people. And yet not a thousand people in Azerbaijan out of three million are Communists.[2]

Douglas's reporting failed to add: "had Pishevari been alive."

After crossing the bridge over the Araxes in December 1946, Pishevari, along with other leaders of his regime, took up residence in Baku. From the start, this exile was marked by bitter resentment against the Soviet hosts for their unwillingness to rescue the autonomous Azerbaijan, its fate resembling Pishevari's experience of the fall of the Gilan Republic a quarter of a century before. Alongside their Soviet compatriots, the refugees emphasized their otherness, including retention of their Iranian identity. Even after many years, few of them would yield to the pressures of life and seek Soviet citizenship.

Seasoned political operative that he was, Pishevari nonetheless not only failed to show signs of toeing the Moscow-set party line, he continued to quarrel with Baghirov in front of witnesses. Stories abound of angry clashes between the two men. The common thread seemed to be that Baghirov, while disparaging the Iranian Azeris (whose character had not yet been shaped by the Soviet mold), tended to see the two Azerbaijans as parts of one Soviet whole of the future. For his part, Pishevari insisted that the Azeris were one of the nations of Iran struggling against the oppression of the Shah. One story relates that during an especially stormy altercation Baghirov yelled rudely: "Sit down, you ass," and, taking off his glasses, wiped his forehead in a gesture that seemed to express his wish to wipe Pishevari off the face of the earth.[3]

A few days after this (early July 1947), the Democrats' community in Baku was stunned by the news that Pishevari had became a fatality in the collision of his MVD (Ministry of Internal Affairs)-supplied car with a military vehicle. On his hospital bed he kept repeating the word *treason*, and in his last statement he said: "I stayed eleven years in solitary confinement in Iran. Neither Reza Shah nor Qavam could destroy me. Now, those people got me for their own ends."[4] Although Pishevari's death was pronounced an unfortunate accident, his name soon ceased to be mentioned publicly in any context, and he joined the cortege of prominent Azeris who turned into nonpersons. The same fate befell his close surviving companions, some of whom found themselves in prison before the end of 1947. Among these the most remarkable case was that of Biriya. This firebrand revolutionary and erstwhile enthusiast of the Soviet Union had not been beaten to death by an angry crowd in December 1946, as Rossow's account had it, but rather had succeeded in escaping across the Araxes a few months later, only to become a victim of the purge that followed Pishevari's death. Charges against him included the accusation, which he did not deny, that he had recently tried to obtain a return visa to Iran without permission of the MVD. Of his thirty-three years of exile in the USSR, Biriya spent twenty-two in Soviet jails. As for the rank and file refugees, they were dispersed among *kolkhozes*, and a special directive ordered to conduct intensive agitational work in their midst.[5]

The purge of the Democrats' leadership did not signal Moscow's intention to discard the issue of Azerbaijan as an instrument of Soviet foreign policy. If anything the reverse was true, and Pishevari and his companions might well have been an impediment to this policy. In fact, after Pishevari's death a large-scale radio propaganda campaign beamed to Iranian Azerbaijan was launched in December 1947 from a mobile station in Transcaucasia (known as Azerbaijani Democratic Station or Radio Azerbaijan). Broadcasting in Azeri, Persian, and Kurdish, the ostensibly clandestine character of the station allowed it to use more extreme and seditious language than official Soviet broadcasts, thereby relieving Moscow of responsibility for the programs' content. Instead of broadcasting news and commentaries about the USSR, Radio Azerbaijan specifically targeted Azeri and Persian listeners with programs whose particular concerns included domestic conditions of Iranian Azerbaijan, professions of hatred for the Shah, threats to traitors, and calls for the overthrow of the government. As it was during Pishevari's regime, the term *Azerbaijani nation* (millät) was used, sometimes in the context of an implicit claim for sovereignty: "The Azerbaijani nation wants peace. We want to get rid of the Teheran invaders and American spies. . . . The Azerbaijani nation will never allow its territory to be turned into an arena of war for aggressive aims." Azerbaijan was never called a part or province of Iran but always "our motherland," "our country," or "our nation." For programs in Azeri, the phrase "foreign oppression" clearly meant Iranian rule, and Iranians could summarily and without class distinction be called invaders. Occasionally this propaganda campaign was not above crude attempts at whipping up Azeri chauvinism:

> The patience of the Azerbaijani people is exhausted. Five million Azerbaijanis who speak a different language, who are by all standards superior to the Iranians, will not continue to live as slaves under the Iranian reactionaries' yoke. The Azerbaijani people would rather die honorably than live in disgrace under the Iranian yoke.

Yet somewhat contradictorily, the old tendency to deliberately obscure the line between Iranian and Azerbaijani identity would also resurface. Whenever a broadcast addressed itself to Iran as a whole, emphasis was on the unity of Iran's peoples in their struggle against imperialism and reaction. Indeed, Azerbaijan was to be the leading force in the liberation of all of Iran, and the "Iranian brothers" were called to follow the Azeris in their struggle.[6]

The radio propaganda across the border went hand in hand with encouragement for Pan-Azerbaijani sentiments among the intellectual community in Baku, its ranks swollen now by refugees from Tabriz. A focal point of the agitation for the unity of Azerbaijan became the Writers Union, which among its members counted many with experience of wartime service in Tabriz, some of it on the editorial staff of *Vatan Yolunda*. The feelings of closeness of the two Azerbaijans gave birth to the "literature of longing," a current devoted to the subject of the separation expressed largely in poetry. The following lines by the Soviet poet Kamran Mahdi conveys its typical symbolism: "The Araxes, nurturing with sorrow/Flows on, cutting like lightning/True, the Araxes divides a nation/But the earth underneath is one."[7]

One of the outstanding traits of this literary current was the encouragement it received from the Soviet authorities in the form of honors and awards. Upon his return from Tabriz, a leading Azeri poet, Suleyman Rustam, published a collection of poems, *Iki sahil* (Two shores), which were the personal impressions of a Soviet Azeri in the Iranian Azerbaijan during the war years. As a token of the regime's special endorsement, it received the Soviet State Prize for 1947, and his epic poem *Tabrizda qish* (Winter in Tabriz) won another seal of official approval, gaining recognition as one of the outstanding poetic works of 1949 by the Moscow journal *Ogonyok*. Memories of the other Azerbaijan were also the theme of the poetic cycle *Tabrizda* (In Tabriz) by

Mammad Rahim, as well as of the short stories and a play, *Ot ichinda* (In the fire, 1951), by Anvär Mammädkhanli.

In addition, two major novels with themes of Tabriz, both having strong undertones of Pan-Azerbaijanism, were translated into Russian, a sure sign of commendation on the all-Union level. *Dumanli Tabriz* (The fog of Tabriz) by Mammäd Said Ordubadi dealt with the 1909 uprising and focused on the heroic figure of Sattar Khan. Written in 1934, the book was heavily reworked for its Russian-language version. *Gäläjäk gün* (The coming day) by Mirza Ibrahimov, which drew on the author's experiences in Tabriz, was also revised before it appeared in Russian in 1950, to be recognized as one of the greatest Soviet literary works on the theme of national liberation.[8]

South of the border, after several years of intensive Soviet propaganda, an opportunity arose for the Azeris to express their feelings under the new Iranian government. Muhammad Mosaddeq rose to power by virtue of his opposition to foreign influence in Iran, especially his long campaign for nationalization of the Anglo-Iranian Oil Company. Having become prime minister in April 1951, Mosaddeq carried out the nationalization, precipitating a prolonged political crisis in which Iran was pitted against the Western powers, and the shah became so weakened that he fled the country briefly in August 1953. Mussadegh was successful in generating support for his uncompromising stance across ethnic lines. Among his staunchest backers were Teheran's numerous Azeri bazaar merchants who had taken their money out of Pishevari's reach. The merchants' disposition was generally shared in Tabriz, where Mussadegh was remembered for his moderate position on Azerbaijan's grievances in 1945. Whatever their resentment over the post-1946 repressions, the Azeris did not display any spirit of rebellion, let alone separatism, when the central government under Mosaddeq relaxed its controls over the provinces. For the Iranian Azeris, fond as their memories of Pishevari might have been, the issue of separatism as a weapon in a confrontation with Teheran must have appeared as playing with fire. The lesson of 1945–1946, with the prospect of Communist oppression and possible incorporation into the USSR, was not lost on them.

In the end the question of a divided Azerbaijan depended, as usual, on the state of Soviet-Iranian relations. During the remainder of the Stalinist period, these relations fared poorly. Trade was negligible, and the Tudeh Party had become outlawed after an assassination attempt on the shah in February 1949. The sense of a threat from the USSR had driven Pahlavi Iran toward closing ranks with the United States. Only under the post-Stalin Soviet regime, with its campaign of peaceful coexistence, was some relaxation of tensions achieved. It was then that negotiations were concluded on the final delineation of the frontier as well as on sharing the water resources of the Araxes and Atrak rivers. Still, relations did not improve materially, partly because Iran joined the American-supported Baghdad Pact in 1955 and signed a bilateral defense treaty with the United States, and partly because the Soviets refused to renounce Articles V and VI of the 1921 treaty.

The turning point came in 1962, when Iran declared it would not permit foreign rocket installations on its territory. From then until the end of the Pahlavi regime, relations between Moscow and Teheran were marked by good political ties and even better economic cooperation. The Soviet Union lent its support for Iran's industrialization through more than a hundred joint projects, which among other effects contributed to marring the beauty of the Iranian landscape. With each side clear in its expectations, the relationship was conducted in a calculated, businesslike spirit.[9]

Meanwhile, disagreements between the Democrats and the Tudeh continued well after Mosaddeq's downfall in 1953. If anything, these were more intensified by the declining fortunes of first the former, then the latter group. DPAz stuck to its position as mouthpiece for Azerbaijani particularism, while the Tudeh stood for Iranian centralism on the basis of the orthodox theory of class warfare. Not until 1960, in much-changed international circumstances, did the two parties agree to bury their differences and to unite the DPAz with the Tudeh. The new program of the party nonetheless recognized the validity of the Azerbaijani group's guiding principles:

> Iran is a multinational state, yet many factors help to bring together various peoples living in Iran: their common history during many centuries; their common contribution to the creation of a rich culture; and their common struggle against imperialism. Since the Tudeh party desires the unity of all peoples of Iran, and believes that this unity can be secured only on the basis of equality and the right of nations to self-determination, it rec-

ognizes clearly the national, social, and cultural rights of all the nations living in Iran.[10]

In the new political climate the issue of Azerbaijan faded from the radio waves and public pronouncements as the two declining empires cultivated their friendship—or at least its facade. The spirit of Soviet-sponsored Pan-Azerbaijanism went into hibernation, though not so completely as in the 1930s. Not only was the genie out of the bottle but efforts to put it back were not overly strenuous. For all its good relations with Teheran, Moscow allowed some low-profile manifestations of Pan-Azerbaijanism on the local level of Baku, and in scholarship rather than literature. Historians could use such expressions as the "bleeding wound of Turkmanchai," "liberation from the hateful yoke of Iranian oppression," and "Iranian oriental despotism." In the words of one author, the Tabriz uprising of 1909 was

> on the one hand a revolution of the Iranian people for their deliverance from the oppression of the despotic regime of the Shah, and on the other, an attempt at gaining freedom for Southern Azerbaijan, at emancipating it from Iranian rule, and at creating an independent Azerbaijan, which would eventually bring about the abolition of the Turkmanchai frontier.[11]

In the same vein, the cult of historical figures who were important for both Azerbaijans was promoted, especially of those safely remote in the distant past, such as Shah Ismail I, founder of the Safavid dynasty, Fath 'Ali Khan of Kuba, or Sattar Khan, who was glorified in *Dumanli Tabriz*. By contrast, little was said about the more controversial figures of Khiabani or Pishevari, and almost nothing about the leaders of the Musavatist republic.

These disclosures of Pan-Azerbaijani spirit after 1960 were not intended for a mass audience and remained generally absent from large-circulation newspapers, popular magazines, and Russian-language media. In its desire to maintain a relationship of correctness with the Pahlavi regime, Moscow would give only the most limited imprimatur to the advocacy of the ideas of Azerbaijani unity, but it kept this card ready for play at a later date.

For all these flickers of the spirit of "longing," contacts across the Araxes frontier atrophied, with the Iron Curtain deepening the cultural estrangement. Moreover, the two parts became subjected to vigorous integrationist efforts on the part of their respective central governments.

Politics of Accelerated Assimilation: South and North of the Border

Upon the demise of the autonomist regime in Tabriz, the laws and decrees on the use of Azeri in the administration, schools, and cultural institutions were summarily abrogated. In a display of loyalty to Iran, crowds burned native-language books. The university and theaters were closed down, Azeri radio programs were halted, Persian again was declared the only official language. The old Persianization drive seemed to have returned with a vengeance. To secure the Persian language's firm hold, plans were announced to reopen the university, to train badly needed language teachers, to begin teaching the language from kindergarten on, and to repair school buildings and open libraries. Yet the central government lacked the resources to set up Persian-language schools, as well as the personnel with which to staff them, and Teheran newspapers reported at the end of 1949 that classes in the state schools were still taught in *Turki*.[12]

During the years that followed, Azeri was successfully eliminated from classrooms and banned from the university, which reopened in 1949. Those who attended schools at the time recall paying fines or being slapped on their hands for talking in the native language. Some were forbidden by their parents to speak Azeri on the theory that knowledge of the language could corrupt a proper Persian accent. Azeri was thus reduced to the status of a spoken idiom with a stigma of social inferiority attached to those who used it. To insist that Azerbaijan had its own national language was politically dangerous, and a writer arrested by the secret police was forced to deny in front of television cameras that such a language existed.[13]

Restrictions on the use of Azeri did not extend to the exclusion of natives of Azerbaijan from the Iranian power elite, in which they had held prominent and, in past centuries, sometimes dominant positions. Nonetheless, under the Pahlavis their numbers declined to a level disproportionately lower than their share in Iran's population. As the figures of an American scholar show, while half the population in the early 1960s spoke languages other than Persian, only 17 percent of the elite had knowledge of any of them (other than Arabic). Furthermore, although almost a quarter of the population spoke Turkic, the sampling showed that only one out of eight members of the elite knew any variation of these languages. Such figures indicate the extent to which the "Teheran elite is divorced from vast sectors of their nation," the result of a centralization policy under which "local, regional, tribal, or ethnic bases of political power are of little consequence in the game of politics now played in Teheran. . . . No longer do the outlying centers play the roles they did in the past."[14]

All the same, the ban on publishing in Azeri was neither airtight nor uninterrupted, particularly in poetry and folk literature. In 1954 Muhammad Huseyn Shahriyari succeeded in publishing the first part of his *Haidar Babaya Salam* (Greetings to Haidar Baba), a poetic expression of an Azeri's attachment to his language, customs, homeland, and, not least, his sense of ethnic identity. Republished in Soviet Azerbaijan and Turkey, it was recognized as one of the major poetic works of the year in any Turkic language.[15] A few other books on Azerbaijan's folklore and language saw publication following *Haidar Baba*, some in Persian.

Another period of relaxation came in the mid-1960s, when the growth of electronic communications unexpectedly strengthened a sense of ethnicity among the rural population. The proliferation of radio sets relieved villagers of their sense of isolation and also enabled them to view themselves not just as Iranians but as Azeris, Kurds, Baluchis, or Turkmens. As if recognizing this phenomenon, radio stations in Tabriz and Rezaieh began to broadcast in Azeri, and even the Voice of Iran introduced a special Azerbaijani program, mostly of folk music. Likewise, limited possibilities appeared for the publication of books by Azeri authors, among them Samad Bahrangi, Behruz Daghani, and 'Ali Reza Nabdel (Ohtay), although more books were published abroad than at home. Some books, such as 'Ali Tabrizli's *Adabiyyat va melliyyat* (Literature and nationality) and Nabdel's, *Azarbaijan va masala-yi melli* (Azerbaijan and the national question), were written in the manner of Soviet dissidents, "for the drawer," as it were, awaiting more propitious circumstances for publication. Both writers, despite their hostility to what they called "Persian chauvinism," wrote in Persian, by now the uncontested literary idiom of Azerbaijan. As for newspapers, their publication in Azeri was banned entirely, although some twenty titles—mostly in Persian but also in English and other Western languages—were published between 1947 and 1978.[16]

With the rapid industrialization of the 1970s, the demand for specialists and managers led to the expansion of higher education, including the University of Tabriz, from which ten thousand persons graduated in 1975 alone, a fact that strengthened the native educated class of Azerbaijan.[17] By this time Azeri began to be used in some university classrooms.

The books of Nabdel and Tabrizli dealt with the fundamental issue of Azerbaijan's relation to Iran, each reflecting a major current of thought among opposition-minded Azeri intellectuals of the 1960s. The two positions sharply contradicted one another, but both authors agreed at least on one point: the irrelevance of the argument on the ancient language of Azerbaijan for the present day. In the words of Nabdel: "Chauvinists try to make most of the fact that the population of Azerbaijan had spoken Persian, let's say eight hundred years ago, and they imagine that having proved this fact (which does not need proofs, it is so easy to accept), they have already solved the crucial problem of our time."[18] A radical Leftist, Nabdel condemned Pahlavi policies for being based on "ideas of Persian chauvinism and Aryan racism," but he also was critical of Pishevari's Democrats for their nationalist leanings, a divisive factor in the class war throughout Iran. To raise the issue of Azeri national grievances amid the struggle against the shah's regime would be untimely.

Tabrizli, reputedly a Pan-Turkist, viewed the history of Iran as a battleground of Turks against Persians. Still he upheld his Iranian identity and argued that the Iranian nation was a supraethnic entity consisting of diverse groups, each with its own distinct language, and one of these was the Azeris. Yet they had become strangers in their homeland of Iran, uncertain even under what name they should be known: as Turks, Azeris, Azeri Turks, or Azerbaijanis? The right name ought simply to be Turks. In confronting Pahlavi oppression, Tabrizli called for spreading the written native word among the population, training teachers to serve in future schools and colleges, and, above all, enlisting the help of other Turkic peoples of the world.[19]

The 1960s, while providing some relaxation of restrictions on Azeri intellectuals, witnessed further intensification of the government's Persianization effort at the grass-roots level. One part of the reform program was the Literacy Corps, an organization consisting of Persian-speaking draftees fulfilling their military service as village teachers whose mission was to combat illiteracy among the rural population. The establishment of the corps was opposed by the clergy, who found in state personnel a rival for their influence in the countryside. A special focus of the Literacy Corps' efforts was non-Persian regions, and it became an effective instrument of Persianization in Azerbaijan and Kurdistan. In 1975–1976 the corps used 38 percent of its entire staff to run the schools in Azerbaijan. The number of pupils in these schools exceeded 100,000, with more than 20,000 adults attending courses for illiterates. Although the scale of the effort resembled the Soviet regime's campaign north of the border in the 1920s, results were more modest. Within a twenty-year period from 1956 to 1976, literacy in Iranian Azerbaijan grew by 27 percent, even though 65 percent of the population remained illiterate, and 70 percent did not know Persian.[20]

As the Soviet scholar Trubetskoi observed, two divergent trends existed in the historical development of Iran: one, the consolidation of minorities; the other, an all-Iranian consolidation, with the latter appearing to be stronger. "The integration of various ethnic groups, a process helped by quick economic and cultural development, is taking place on the basis of the ruling nationality. Its language has become the lingua franca in contacts among other groups, and its knowledge is spreading rapidly in the course of the literacy campaign."[21]

The suppression of Azeri identity in Iran had certain parallels, albeit different in scope and character, in the Soviet Union. Ominous signals appeared in 1950 with the condemnation of Shamil's role in history in a scholarly publication whose title termed him "The Henchman of Sultan's Turkey and British Colonizers." Next, after the epic *Dede Korkut*, reputedly the "*Iliad* of Turkic peoples," was officially denounced as reactionary, Baghirov stepped in in a big way. In February 1953 he published in the Moscow journal *Kommunist* the article "The elder brother in the family of Soviet peoples," a strikingly sycophantic statement on the relationship of Soviet nationalities to Russia. "The peoples of our country regard the great Russian people with an attitude of special respect and gratitude. The peoples of the Soviet Union cannot think of strengthening the friendship of peoples without the development, without the guidance of all Soviet peoples by the love, deep respect, gratitude, and unbounded devotion to the elder brother, the great Russian people, who have the primary and guiding role in the construction of communism."

He asserted that the peoples living on the Caspian coast prayed "for nothing so much as the coming of the Muscovites as quickly as possible to deliver them from the yoke of Persian monarchy."[22] The annexation by Russia had indeed brought immediate economic gains to the non-Russian peoples, but even more beneficial for them was the radiation of Russian culture, literature, and language. Baghirov, who had recently driven the Baku scholar Haidar Huseynov to suicide, pointedly reproached Soviet historians for insufficiently elaborating examples of friendship between the peoples.

In his *Kommunist* article, Baghirov also attempted to distance himself from his mentor Beria. The latter, in late 1952 or early 1953, played the nationality card in maneuvering to become Stalin's successor by casting himself as the champion of the non-Russian cadres against great-power chauvinism. Within a month after the article appeared Stalin was dead, and a few months later came the fall of Beria. Prominent among the long list of crimes of which he was accused was his work in 1919 for the "Musavatist" regime's counterintelligence service, even though this had been his assignment from the Bolshevik underground.[23] Beria's demise in Moscow abruptly ended the Baghirov era in Azerbaijan. In July 1953 he was expelled from the Party and deprived of his posts; unlike Beria, however, he was not arrested.

Baghirov's stance on the nationalities issue helps to explain why, after his removal from office, he was allowed to stay alive in freedom and comfort for a relatively long period. Instead of sharing Beria's fate, Baghirov was appointed to a managerial position in Kuybishev, where, as he said, contemplating the errors of his ways, he studied the writings of Lenin.[24] Only three years after his political downfall, on April 12–26, 1956, Baghirov stood trial in Baku. Although he admitted the crimes with which he was charged and did not ask for leniency, he declared that he had never been an enemy of the Party or his country. He was found guilty, sentenced to death, and promptly executed. Six weeks later, the local press reported the trial and published a list of Baghirov's victims. In a manner revealing of the character of that stage of de-Stalinization, the list included mainly the names of highly placed persons. The message that the killings of dignitaries by a dignitary had become reprehensible, but still more so than dignitaries' killings of people from ordinary walks of life, was understood as an implicit reminder of the limits of change.[25] Yet it was also apparent that the mass terror had been discarded, and viewed in perspective of history, this fact alone marked the beginning of the regime's slow decline. At the time, however, this prospect was hardly visible. As an experiment in social psychology Stalinism seemed to have been eminently effective: a new Soviet man had been created through encoding Pavlovian reflexes of fear, an almost biological phenomenon. Mass terror, it could be argued, was no longer necessary, the more so because it made it difficult for the ruling group to enjoy its privileges. Should the need arise one day to resort to terror for the survival of the regime, there were no legal, political, or practical impediments for its restoration. All the same, a multicultural, polyglot formation lends itself with difficulty to sharp turns of policy, and the first cracks to be seen appeared in structure of the imperial edifice.

The nationalities issue that Beria had revived at high levels of Soviet politics reappeared among the non-Russian elites, who cautiously began mounting claims for the restoration of korenizatsiia in personnel appointments. Likewise, Khrushchev, as he went about consolidating his power, recognized publicly in 1954 the need to decentralize the economy and to devolve some rights to the republics. At the 1956 Twentieth Party Congress he emphatically endorsed *rastsvet* (flourishing), the policy of equality for Soviet nationalities, and refrained from singling out Russian language and culture. In Azerbaijan, where the Baghirov trial had become the quasi-official signal for de-Stalinization, there was an air of expectation for a reawakening of the spirit of the 1920s, which had been comparatively favorable to national aspirations. The litmus test for this gradual thaw was a revaluation of Shamil as a leader of a progressive struggle. Indeed, under an expanded freedom of expression some topics ceased to be taboo. Among the most conspicuous was the figure of Narimanov, his memory not only exonerated but in fact elevated to a personality cult as a father figure of the Soviet Azerbaijani nation. A giant statue of him would be erected on the hill overlooking Baku, his outstretched hand pointing north, and his quotation invoking friendship with Russia was carved in stone. Along with the rehabilitation of Baghirov's victims came that of the history of the Himmät. Other issues could be dealt with only partly—for instance, Pishevari's activities in Iran but not his exile in Baku and even less the circumstances of his death. And it was still obligatory to criticize the history of the Democratic Republic, invariably referred to as "Musavatist," for its nationalism, its bourgeois-landowning class contents, or its subservience to Western imperialism; but once these conditions were met, some factual information could be put into print.

By the end of 1956, with the Communist world shaken by unrest in Poland and an uprising in Hungary, Khrushchev slowed down and then reversed much of his new policy. In Azerbaijan a clear signal of the regime's changed position on the sensitive nationality questions appeared with the case of Bahtiar Vahabzadä's famous poem *Gulistan*. Written in 1958 and dedicated to the "radiant memories of Sattar Khan, Khiabani, and Pishevari," the poem's theme was the division of Azerbaijan. The edition of the local newspaper in Sheki that printed the poem was withdrawn from circulation, and the outstanding Azeri poet officially disgraced.[26]

Gradually the emphasis shifted from *rastsvet* to promoting the eventual *sliyanie*, or fusion of the Soviet nationalities, the supreme fulfillment of a Communist ideal. In step with this change of course, the issue of linguistic Russification reemerged.

A new law rescinded the obligatory study of the native language in Russian schools of the non-Russian republics, leaving to parents the choice of sending their children to schools with either Russian or the native language of instruction. Since many parents believed that attending a Russian school would enhance their children's future careers, the new law served to degrade the non-Russian languages to second-class status. When the Azerbaijani SSR did not implement the law, there followed a purge of the republican Party leadership. In June 1959 First Secretary Imam Mustafayev was ousted on the grounds of "having caused bewilderment in the completely clear language question."[27] Once again the official view of the past put stress on the friendship of the Soviet nationalities with Russia. In the 1960s, amid celebrations held to mark the 150th anniversary of Azerbaijan's conquest by Russia (officially referred to as unification, *prisoedinenie*), historians were directed to elaborate on the progressive consequences of annexation, notably for the economy, cultural development, and education. For the most part, these exercises turned out to be simply more sophisticated versions of the themes marked in Baghirov's last advisory.

Khrushchev, having passed into history as the man who had ended the mass terror, showed in his later years his other face, not only through intensifying the assimilation of non-Russians but also through a renewal of the antireligious campaign, in harmony with the spirit of *sliyanie*. Accusations of tolerance for Islamic traditions proved to be an additional factor in the purge of Mustafayev and his companions. Some mosques that had survived under Stalin were now closed down, and in the end only two remained open in Baku (out of sixteen throughout Azerbaijan).[28] There followed an intensification of the scientific criticism of Islam, but with such language as "a primitive and fanatic religion," "a chaotic mixture of Christian, Jewish, and pagan doctrines" whose founder was "a member of the feudal classes of Mecca, with the object of providing a religious pretext for plundering expeditions organized by the Arab aristocracy," and "a foreign religion imposed on the peoples of Central Asia and Transcaucasia by fire and sword."[29] Soviet statistics proudly registered the fact that between 1948 and 1976 ninety-six anti-Islamic books and pamphlets were published in Azerbaijan, and about 15,000 antireligious lectures were delivered each year.[30]

The White Revolution in Iran and the Crisis of Colonialism North of the Araxes

On the other side of the frontier, after the overthrow of the Mosaddeq government carried out with American help, Shah Muhammad Reza chose to consolidate his power through coercion, a policy in which he outdid his father. Martial law remained in force until 1957, and even after it ended formally, the Shah continued to exercise strict political controls and enforced censorship. In addition to building up the army and gendarmerie, he created an extensive security organization, SAVAK, which from 1957 on became the key element of his rule.

Gradually the shah diversified his policies by blending repressions with reforms. In 1963 he proclaimed his Royal or White Revolution, an ambitious and comprehensive blueprint for change that was to accelerate dramatically Iran's modernization. Central among the White Revolution's nineteen programs were land reform, nationalization of forests and pastures, enfranchisement of women, educational and administrative reforms, and the creation of the Health Corps and Literacy Corps. Politically, the revolution sought to undermine the economic position of those forces that traditionally threatened strong royal power—the landed aristocracy and, even more, the Shi'ite clergy. Although none of the programs contained so much as a reference to non-Persian minorities, the formation of the Literacy Corps had a direct impact on these groups, and land reform profoundly affected Azerbaijan, primarily an agricultural region. The breakup of large estates and the redistribution of land to peasants on ten-year credit terms helped create a more modern agricultural structure. More than a quarter-million Azerbaijani peasants—about 25 percent of those benefiting from the land reform program—acquired plots of land. Still, agrarian reform fell short of solving the twin problem of land shortage and rural overpopulation, and Azerbaijan, like other parts of Iran, got caught up in the accelerating migration from the countryside to the cities. Within twenty years the urban population grew from 23 percent, or 755,000, in 1956 to 30.3 percent, or 1,753,000, in 1976.[31]

While the White Revolution brought a series of essential if incomplete transformations to Iran, the impact of the unplanned Oil Revolution was even more profound. Oil revenues, which had risen only moderately for a number of years, suddenly quadrupled in the mid-1970s, reaching almost $20 billion in 1975–1976, and the national income grew at the rate of 30 percent. This torrential influx of money would prove to be a dislocating circumstance for Iran, a country barely beginning its transition from a traditional society to modernity—or, in the words of a skeptical foreign commentator, "where 60 percent of the population was illiterate and the people's outlook has still to be adapted to the industrial era."[32]

For the time being, however, optimistic expectations predicted that the standard of living would rise to that of Europe by the end of the decade, and that before the end of the century Iran would be one of the world's leading industrial powers. Among hundreds of industrial projects, some of the major ones—an oil refinery, a motor vehicle assembly plant, and a machine tool factory—were built in Tabriz. The impressive industrial growth of Azerbaijan, especially in its eastern *ostan*, increased economic development of the peripheries, which lagged behind Iran's central regions. Yet despite conditions comparable to those north of the Araxes, Iranian Azeris resorted to migration, with Teheran as their favorite destination—clearly a more congenial place for them than Soviet Azeris found in the Russian cities. In only five years, from 1971 to 1976, 601,200 people above the age of five migrated from East Azerbaijan to Teheran, with another 113,600 arriving from West Azerbaijan. Estimates of the Azeri-speaking population in the Iranian capital reached 1.5 to 2 million. These mass migrations of the Azeris from their homeland help explain why their total numbers could never be reliably determined, even though it is generally agreed that they exceed by a substantial margin the number of inhabitants of the Azerbaijani SSR.

Azerbaijan's proportion of the population of Iran, 17.1 percent in 1956, declined over twenty years to 15.4 percent.[33] With some limitations, Azerbaijan shared in the unprecedented prosperity of the Iranian oil boom, dubious though its foundations were. During the same period, its Soviet neighbor was beginning to endure unquestionable economic stagnation and then decline.

As decade after decade of the Soviet epoch wore on, the golden age of Baku oil receded into memory, a result of the steady depletion of the old fields through overexploitation and even more—underinvestment in exploration efforts. After World War II the center of Soviet oil extraction shifted from the Caspian coast to the Volga basin and the Ural Mountains. Then, in the 1960s, development of the Siberian oil fields began, mainly in the Tiumen region, inaugurating a new era in the Soviet oil industry that brought the USSR to first place among the world's producers. For Azerbaijan, the shift had cascading effects and their impact was exponential. By the 1980s Baku's oil output would dwindle to a meager 3 percent of the Soviet total. Even though the republic still provided most (70 percent) of the USSR's oil and gas-producing equipment, some of the equipment used in Baku dated back to the days of the Nobel Brothers Company. In contrast to the rapid economic expansion in the prewar decades, Azerbaijan during the 1950–1978 period now had the lowest rate of industrial growth among all Soviet republics. With the oil industry's decline, central planning authorities cut the once substantial influx of investment capital and technical assistance. Reduced investments accounted for the low growth in productivity: four-fifths of the USSR average. Real incomes lagged even more behind the growth of the Soviet Union's average, with per capita in Azerbaijan only two-thirds of the USSR's in 1975. The pace of socioeconomic transformations diminished so that, most notably, the number of laborers leaving the agricultural sector slowed down; by 1970 about two-fifths of the work force was still engaged in agriculture and related occupations.

Although the region as a whole remained underprivileged in relation to Russia and the western republics of the Soviet Union, deteriorating economic conditions once again revealed the Transcaucasian dichotomy between Azerbaijan on one side and Armenia and Georgia on the other. Between 1960 and 1978 per capita income grew in Azerbaijani SSR at the rate of 3 percent while figures for Georgia and Armenia were almost twice as high (5.5 percent) and those for the USSR were 6.3 percent. Part of the explanation for this difference is that under the system of centrally disbursed investment funds, Azerbaijan received 61 percent of the Union republics' average against 78 percent for Armenia and 64 percent for Georgia. Correspondingly, the standard of living in the two latter republics were 10 to 15 percent below the USSR median, but the figure for Azerbaijan was as much as one-third below. In this respect, Armenia and Georgia ranked with the western republics of the USSR while Azerbaijan was closer to the impoverished Central Asia.[34] Another reason for this imbalance was the pattern of trade within the region, as pointed out by a Baku economist: "Azerbaijan annually exports 135 million rubles' worth of wool to Georgia and Armenia, while finished products would bring ten to fifteen times that to the national income."[35]

By all available evidence, Azerbaijan, unlike Armenia and Georgia, contributed more to the rest of the USSR than it received in return. The reason for this, in the view of a Western economist, appears to have been a product mix based on oil and cotton, which suffered from arbitrary pricing. Also, Azerbaijan was affected by the "random incidence of the turnover tax allocations."[36]

An Azerbaijani view, stated only as a benefit of the glasnost climate, was more specific and pointed to correlation between central planning and colonial exploitation:

> Our republic has a yearly trade deficit of 2.5 billion rubles. If one considers the fact that the republic is a supplier of such raw materials as cotton, oil, grapes, etc., then it is loosing 8 to 10 billion rubles on a yearly basis. Take cotton. Cotton growers receive 500–700 rubles per ton of cotton. Considering that goods made from one ton of cotton bring a profit of 12,000 to 13,000 rubles, the picture becomes clear.[37]

Comparisons with Azerbaijan's non-Soviet neighbors, risky and unreliable statistical exercises as they are, indicate that in 1977 Iran's GNP was $2,160 per capita while estimates for the Azerbaijani SSR are $1,825, or 11 percent less. Even though Iran's GNP grew at a remarkably fast pace in the 1970s, some indicators still show its relative backwardness in comparison with Soviet Azerbaijan—notably in urbanization, literacy ratio, education, and health care.[38]

Western writings in the post-Stalinist and pre-perestroika period inclined toward a view that the Soviet Middle East benefited from its association with a large centralized economy, at a cost to the USSR as a whole: "The Soviet ideological commitment to creating a native proletariat and combating backwardness in the national republics caused a diversion of capital to these areas, which, on strictly economic grounds, would have provided a higher return elsewhere."[39] This view, expressed by Alec Nove and J. A. Newth in 1967, was generally upheld in a later study by Alastair McAuley, even though it noted that by 1975 the standard of living of the Soviet Muslim population as a whole had declined further, from four-fifths to three-quarters of the non-Muslim republics. All the same, this standard was termed as approximately twice as high as that of the neighboring nations of the Middle East, taking into account the benefits of the educational system and health service.[40] Such views tended to overlook specific conditions of Azerbaijan, notably the causes for the decline of the oil industry. It could be argued that the absence of a national government made it easier to deplete this natural wealth, through both the republic's defenselessness against unfair pricing and its lack of alternative industries. The example of the non-Soviet countries of the Middle East demonstrates that it was their emancipation from foreign control that enabled the proper use of oil wealth for national interest. As for the less debatable fact of unprofitable diversion of Soviet capital, the reality was that Moscow failed to reinvest enough money in sustaining Azerbaijani oil production. Apparently, Russia had reached the point beyond which colonialism brought more liabilities than assets.

The economic stagnation of Azerbaijan was aggravated by population growth. Even though this growth was the slowest among all Muslim republics of the Soviet Union, in thirty years the Azeris saw their numbers almost double from 3.5 million in 1959 to 6.8 million in 1989. Labor migrations were not a practical solution from the twin pressures of overpopulation and economic underdevelopment because of the Azeris' unwillingness to leave their homeland, in contrast to their compatriots in Iran. For the Soviet Azeris, migration meant transplantation into the alien, non-Muslim cultural environment of the Soviet Union's labor-short regions.[41] The inevitable effect was chronic underemployment, then blatant and rising unemployment.

As the twilight of the great age of Baku oil was setting in, the incentives that had attracted immigrants to Azerbaijan were no longer present, and the reverse process began—a slow but steady exodus, noticeable since 1959, of the Russian and Armenian populations. For the Armenians, an additional cause for out-migration was, in the words of a demographer, the "historical antipathy between members of the two groups, which has crystallized in recent years to encourage mutual avoidance and resettlement."[42] Figures for large-scale resettlements date back to 1948, when some 50,000 Azeris were deported from Armenia to the Mugan Steppe to make room for the expected repatriation of the Armenians from the diaspora.[43] From 1970 to 1979 the Armenian population of Azerbaijan in turn decreased by 82,000, and the Russian figure dropped by 75,000. By 1979 the proportion of Azeris rose to over three-fourths of the republic's population, with half of them urbanized; almost a quarter lived in Baku. While Azeris could see these figures as firm indications of national homogenization and proof that time was working for them, others might have concluded that Azerbaijan was less a land of opportunity than it used to be.[44]

The undercurrent of ethnic tensions at times assumed a political cast. On April 24, 1965, for the fiftieth anniversary of Armenia's sufferings in World War I, a crowd of 100,000 gathered in the streets of Erivan calling for the restoration of the "territories," a term that referred to Eastern Anatolia as well as to Nagorno-Karabagh and Nakhichevan. Before the day was over there were violent clashes with the militia. Another form of mobilizing the community for a national cause was petitioning for the transfer of Nagorno-Karabagh to the Armenian SSR. In 1966 an appeal with forty-five thousand signatures was submitted to Moscow and, likewise, a letter signed by tens of thousands was sent to the Twenty-seventh Party Congress. The standard reply was that accommodating Armenian demands would create a precedent for other territorial disputes in the USSR. Nonetheless, the agitation succeeded in launching the Armenian dissident movement, one of the first of its kind in the USSR.[45]

The Coming of the Aliyev Era

The Brezhnev regime, generally loath to rock the boat in matters of the Republican Party cadres, eventually saw the need for decisive intervention in Transcaucasia. In Moscow's eyes, a bad situation was made worse by Transcaucasia's pervasive traditions of nepotism, favoritism, and corruption with its countless links to the underground economy. By the end of the 1960s, the Center decided to promote from outside the entrenched networks new party leaders in all Transcaucasian republics. Eduard Shevardnadze was the choice for Georgia, Karen Demirchiyan for Armenia, and for Azerbaijan Haidar Aliyev, a native of Nakhichevan and a career KGB officer with a degree in history, who in July 1969 replaced Veli Akhundov as First Secretary of the CPAz. Among the strong men in twentieth-century Azerbaijan, Aliyev's impact has lasted longer than that of his predecessors.

To no one's surprise, he began his rule with a purge of highly placed officials. Within his first five years about 80 percent of the *nomenklatura*—the power elite consisting of government ministers, members of the CPAz Politburo, Central Committee secretaries, heads of Central Committee departments, secretaries of district committees, and industrial managers—were replaced by new appointees. To prevent a rebirth of networks, frequent cadre rotation became the norm. Aliyev's political style has been described as "a combination of toughness mixed with public criticism, energetic prosecution of wrongdoing tempered with moralism and calls for discipline," an example that Andropov would adopt in the transition period that followed Brezhnev.[46] The Azeri party boss seemed to be proving that despite adverse conditions and structural weakness in the economy, essential improvement through proper cadre policies, discipline, and legality was not only possible, it could actually reverse the trend.

By 1974 Azerbaijan had risen to fourth position among union republics in industrial labor productivity and national income growth, ranking sixth in overall industrial productivity. The most obvious source of Aliyev's success was his cadre policy, but this policy became also an application of korenizatsiia, with the result of consolidating the native nomenklatura and upgrading it through an infusion of the element of technocracy. Of his thirty-five chief clients and protégés almost all were Azeris.[47] He showed no inclination to use Slavic candidates for filling important vacancies, and the second secretary, invariably of Russian nationality, was appointed by Moscow. Otherwise Aliyev, whose personal ambitions aimed for higher posts at the all-Union level, trod carefully in matters of national sentiment. On the one hand, he sponsored such symbolic acts as bringing to Azerbaijan the remains of writer Javid Huseyn, a victim of Stalin's purges, and on the other, in his speeches he called for strengthening the spirit of sblizhenie.

Paradoxically, neither the consolidation of the native power elite nor the outflow of the Russian population provided protection against the impact of Russian language and culture. The 1960s and 1970s brought into sharp relief the interrelationship of three trends that shaped the cultural landscape of Azerbaijan. One was the rapid growth of urbanization, especially of the native population of Baku. Second, the population with a college-level education, a pool of reserves for the slowly reviving intelligentsia, rose to 150,000, while the proportion of white-collar employees reached 20.1 percent.[48] These increases came hand in hand with the growth of bilingualism, the third trend. Although outright assimilation—in which Azeris declared Russian as their first language—remained statistically negligible, the proportion of those who were fluent in both their native and another language, almost invariably Russian, nearly doubled to 30 percent between 1970 and 1979.[49] These statistics, however, do not answer the question of which was the prevailing spoken language and which the literary. Indeed, the term *bilingualism* covered a large though indeterminate part of the better educated, urban population, who, in declaring Azeri as their primary language, would use it mainly as the spoken idiom. In this respect the trend resembled conditions in Iranian Azerbaijan, although with a vast difference in the degree of assimilation. Among the younger generation of the Baku intelligentsia, the majority felt more comfortable writing in Russian than in Azeri, which they believed was less suitable for the expression of complex thinking. "Let's say it frankly," wrote a concerned Vahabzada,

> The Azerbaijanis attending the Russian schools are often unable to express their thoughts in the native language. . . . In Azerbaijani schools, the teaching of Russian begins in the first grade, that is, before the children have thorough knowledge of the native language, without the feeling for its nature and beauty.[50]

Still, in defense of bilingualism, the same author pointed out that Azeri recruits from the countryside suffered discrimination in military service because of their lack of fluency in Russian.

In the Circle of the Khomeini Revolution

For all the palliatives that Aliyev energetically applied, the elements of a structural crisis persisted in Soviet Azerbaijan during the 1970s: there seemed to be no remedy for the depletion of oil resources and no cure for the problems caused by overpopulation, particularly unemployment; living standards were low, housing and health services poor. Among the mass of the population, cultural alienation from the ruling nation continued, and intercommunal tensions were simmering.

Yet stability, which increasingly meant stagnation, remained the order of the day throughout the USSR and was strengthened by a reluctance to rock the boat for fear of unforeseeable consequences. This condition largely continued under the tenures of Brezhnev's immediate successors, Yuri Andropov and Konstantin Chernenko. The first challenge to the status quo came not through internal contradictions in the Soviet system but with the reverberations of revolution on the other side of the Araxes.

A new period of historical acceleration began south of the Iranian border with another upheaval in a vastly different setting, a crisis that was coming to a head at a faster pace than in the north. As in decades past, Tabriz became a major center of ferment, and here a series of violent riots of mass proportion broke out against the Pahlavi regime in February 1978. The disturbances, killing scores and wounding hundreds, further intimated the cultural dimension of the unfolding crisis: the targets of the mob violence were symbols of Pahlavi-era "Westoxication" frowned upon by the clerical opposition—liquor stores, movie theaters, international banks, and hair-dressing salons.[51] In Azerbaijan, some supporters of the clergy might have also protested against the Pahlavis' nationalist, non-Islamic Persianization practices.

During the spring and summer the waves of strikes, riots, and mass demonstrations against the shah spread through Iran's major cities. The clerical establishment's long-standing opposition toward the shah fused with popular discontent over the effects of the boom that had disproportionately benefited the rich. The spirit of the opposition infected the middle classes, then the workers. Corruption, economic inequities, inflation, poverty, and alienation among the uprooted masses of peasants migrating to the cities all fueled the erupting political protest. Strikes in the oil fields began to take their toll, paralyzing sectors of the economy. In September martial law went into effect in Teheran and was quickly extended to all of Iran's major cities. The effort was in vain. By the end of the year the Pahlavi monarchy was doomed, and in early January 1979 Shah Muhammad Reza departed from Iran for an "extended vacation," leaving room for the triumphal return of his archenemy, Ayatollah Ruhullah Khomeini, from exile on February 1. Two months later followed the official proclamation of the Islamic Republic of Iran.

The Iranian revolution was neither a military coup nor the result of a devious conspiracy, nor even a desperate outbreak of mass anger. Rather, it was a self-sustaining process that extended over many months and relentlessly gained momentum as it spread to all levels of the population. No longer focused on particular grievances, it turned rather into an all-out systemic crisis, a unison statement of non possumus. To stem the tide, the regime alternated between repressions and concessions, undermining its position further with each sharp turn, exhausting its strength, its credibility, its room to maneuver, and, in the end, its will to survive.

Proof that an oppressive regime could be overthrown by a population refusing to accept its sufferings any longer portended a world-wide series of popular upheavals for long overdue changes, and these extended to reasserting historical roots and cultural identities. Inexplicably, in essence a similar mechanism of revolutionary crisis would soon reemerge in the seemingly distant and unrelated Poland of the Solidarity period, where even the slogan "Let Poland be Poland" had a familiar ring. The Polish pattern would be repeated in other parts of Eastern Europe and, in the long run, no state would be more affected by the sweeping floods of change than the Soviet Union itself. For the time being, however, Moscow chose to ignore the writing on the wall and saw in the Iranian revolution only its specific character of an Islamic fundamentalist rising against the Western-oriented elite.

Closer to the mark might well have been the prominent clergyman of Iranian Azerbaijan, Ayatollah Qazim Shari'atmadari, who in a radio address heard across the Soviet border pointed to the many-sided significance of this revolution, though he spoke in a propagandistic style: "The triumphant struggle of the Muslim people of Iran is a turning point in the history of the world struggle and the best model to follow by the oppressed Muslim peoples of the world."[52]

The Iranian revolution's first and most obvious impact on Soviet Azerbaijan was the penetration of ideas across the iron curtain of the Araxes. Of all the Muslim peoples in the USSR, the Azeris, as the largest group of Shi'ites, were potentially the most receptive to the message of Khomeinism, now beamed to them in their language from a radio station in Tabriz. The result was the stimulation of an Islamic reawakening, a process already under way in the late 1970s when, according to Soviet sources, approximately one thousand clandestine houses of prayer were in use and some three hundred holy places of pilgrimages were designated. These could be viewed as breaking the ground for the opening of hundreds of mosques throughout the country in the next decade. Although few observers agreed on the depth and extent of this reawakening, Soviet surveys indicated that statistically the level of religiosity was highest in southern districts and around Baku, i.e., in the solidly Shi'ia parts of the country.[53] The head of the Azerbaijani KGB, General Yusifzadä, deemed it fit to denounce in *Bakinskii Rabochii* "the infiltration of foreign agents through our borders as well as the antisocial activity of the sectarian underground and of the reactionary Muslim clergy."[54]

The reawakening's emotional impact was further strengthened by shock waves from the Soviet invasion of Afghanistan and the successful resistance carried out under religious Islamic slogans. Characteristically, signs of the Islamic resurgence appeared to embarrass the secular-minded intelligentsia, who were unwilling to acknowledge the phenomenon, let alone to analyze it. In the words of an underground publication, "A part of the Azerbaijani intelligentsia, answering today the question: Does Muslim fundamentalism exist in our republic? says *no* with the hastiness beyond which is the fear to expose something that is indisputably ugly and shameful."[55]

While the example of the Iranian revolution was reanimating benumbed religious sentiments, the prevailing Soviet view was that by its very nature this clergy-led upheaval amounted to only a transitory phenomenon, a prelude to further transformations no longer driven by puritanical fervor. The Soviets assumed that, among the factors likely to influence these transformations, the tendency of the peoples of Iran to assert their ethnic and national identities would come to the fore as it had in the 1940s.[56] But none of these expectations materialized before the December 1979 invasion of Afghanistan opened a new period of Soviet-Iranian unease. Tensions mounted still higher when the Moscow-allied Iraqi regime of Saddam Hussein attacked Iran in September 1980, starting one of the longest wars in modern history. Iran found itself strategically encircled, a condition only worsened by its ongoing hostage crisis with the United States. While the order of the day was to close ranks rather than to manifest centrifugal aspirations, Azerbaijan would again remind the government in Teheran that it could be a continuing concern.

Tabriz, the Rebellious

With the monarchy overthrown, the new regime lifted the ban on the use of the native language in Azerbaijan. This was one of many assurances that the peoples of Iran would enjoy the right to govern their local and internal affairs. The revolutionary Islamic regime as a matter of principle was averse to fostering ethnic or national divisions and promoted the idea of one Muslim community, a departure from the "one Iranian nation" of the Pahlavi period, although the emphasis was still on "oneness."

All the same, the period immediately following the shah's demise witnessed a release of long-suppressed Azeri energies through the proliferation of native-language newspapers and magazines, the publication of books, and a rise of cultural and literary associations in Tabriz as well as in Teheran.[57] Political organizations took the form of Azerbaijani chapters of Iranian parties such as the *Mujahidin*, the Fida'iyan, and the ruling People's Party of Iran. Most Azeri—in character, if not in name—was the Republican Party of the Muslim People's Party of Iran (*Khalq*, for short) whose local branch used the name Azerbaijani Muslim Struggle Group. This party's proclamations called for autonomous rights for the people of Azerbaijan within the framework of sovereign Iran and enjoyed the blessing of Ayatollah Shari'atmadari.[58] A prominent theologian of Qum, he had been the unofficial spokesman of the Azeri clergy and, under the monarchy, had represented a moderate wing of the clerical opposition. His differences with Khomeini were widely known and touched on the crucial question of church-state relations: should the clergy, as Khomeini believed, be the supreme guide and arbiter of the state or, in the spirit of Shi'a doctrine that true power belongs only to the Invisible Imam, should they concentrate on upholding the *Shari'ah*? Following the victory of the revolution, Shari'atmadari did not receive a government post, but nonetheless he enjoyed wide and growing influence among the population of Azerbaijan.

Historically the most rebellion-prone region of Iran, Azerbaijan lived up to its reputation when, less than a year after the revolution's triumph, it became the first to challenge the authority of the post-Pahlavi regime. The simmering confrontation with the central government came to the fore over the issue of a new constitution for Iran, which was to be the embodiment of Khomeini's vision of an Islamic government under which the 'ulama would exercise supreme control. The project met with opposition from the country's liberal and secular-minded elements as well as from the non-Persian minorities, who feared overcentralization of power in Teheran. In July 1979 a solidarity conference of the peoples of Iran took place with representatives from the Kurds, Azeris, Turkmens, and Arabs. Organized under the auspices of the National Front, an opposition group to the Khomeini regime, the conference requested that the new constitution include provisions guaranteeing autonomous rights for minorities.[59] The question of restructuring the state on federal-national lines was openly put forward and was condemned by the Khomeini regime as foreign-inspired separatism.

As opposition groups were suppressed one after another during the fall of 1979, sometimes with the assistance of club-wielding Hizbollahs, Shari'atmadari continued his public criticism of the draft of the constitution. He cited as contrary to the sovereignty of the people, as well as to Shi'ite doctrine, Khomeini's idea of bestowing extensive powers on the Spiritual Vice-Regency, *Velayat-i Faqih*. Not only did Shari'atmadari oppose direct participation of the clergy in political life, but he also took exception to the revolution's various excesses, such as executions or public whippings, purges of university faculty, and the seizing of hostages at the United States Embassy.

Echoing familiar sentiments of distrust of centralized government, Shari'atmadari's criticism was instrumental in the successful boycott of the December 2 referendum on the constitution in Azerbaijan (80 percent of voters abstained), Kurdistan, and Baluchistan. Elsewhere throughout Iran the constitution received overwhelming approval, a measure of the differences between the center and the ethnic peripheries.

Four days after the referendum, demonstrators angered by an attack on Shari'atmadari's house in Qum took to the streets in Tabriz, beginning another rebellion against Teheran. The crowds seized public buildings and the television station, from which they broadcast resolutions adopted at mass meetings. The demands in these resolutions focused on such issues as changing Article 110 of the constitution; the appointment of governors of Azerbaijan and of civil as well as military personnel only with the approval of Ayatollah Shari'atmadari; removal of nonlocal guards from Tabriz; and abolition of censorship of mass communications in the local media. A radio broadcast hailed Shari'atmadari as leader of the world's Shi'ites, and some proclamations even went so far as to use the title "Azerbaijani Islamic Republic."[60]

Even though military units in Tabriz endorsed the uprising, the central government was not deterred from acting decisively to regain control. On orders from Teheran, the Revolutionary Guards took the radio station by force. A governmental delegation under Finance Minister Bani Sadr, dispatched to negotiate with the rebels, succeeded in organizing a large pro-Khomeini demonstration, further weakening Shari'atmadari's hold on the city. Although on December 13 an estimated 700,000 of his supporters marched through the streets of Tabriz, it was increasingly apparent that the octogenarian ayatollah was more a symbol than a leader in the crisis.

In accord with his disapproval of the clergy's involvement in politics, Shari'atmadari distanced himself from day-to-day developments. After a new series of bloody clashes with Khomeini's followers in early January 1980, he called on his supporters to end all violence. As Shari'atmadari washed his hands of the crisis, the absence of sustaining power became visible. The *Khalq* Party, accused of harboring pro-Soviet, separatist, Maoist, and American-inspired tendencies, suspended its activities. By mid-January order had returned to Tabriz following the execution of nine rebels on the grounds of, among other charges, having worked for the republic's autonomy.[61]

This last of a long series of Tabriz uprisings displayed the usual mixture of regional Azerbaijani grievances with all-Iranian concerns. The most spontaneous—but also shortest-lived—of the Azerbaijani rebellions, it suffered not only from a lack of leadership but also from uncertainty as to its goals and direction. As for Shari'atmadari, this clerical challenger to Khomeinism was accused in 1982 of contacts with the U.S. Secret Service and with SAVAK. Stripped of his honorific title *Marj'a Taqlid* (Source of emulation), he was removed from public life and put under house arrest, where he died in 1985.

The government promised to consider Azerbaijani grievances, including the consolidation of the two ostans into one province. But because of Iran's deteriorating international situation, circumstances were no longer conducive to new concessions for regionalism. Instead, previously existing concessions were whittled down. Some Azeri publications and associations came under the suspicion of being Soviet-inspired, both because of their calls for autonomy and because of their contacts with Baku from whence they brought films, performing artists, or school textbooks to be transliterated into Arabic-script editions. After the outbreak of the Iran-Iraq and Soviet-Afghanistan wars, the government resorted to suppressing activities that could be viewed as pro-Soviet. Members of the revived Tudeh Party, who became the first targets of repression, were imprisoned, driven underground, or else joined the ranks of the new post-1979 Iranian emigration. Similar treatment was dealt the former Democrats, some of whom had returned to Tabriz, where they attempted to recreate their old party. The most notable case was that of Biriya, who soon after his return was arrested and subsequently died in an Iranian prison. Citing their pro-Soviet disposition, the government began to suppress Azeri-language publications, in the process also shutting down those that could be suspected of inclination toward Pan-Turkism or anti-Communist Azerbaijani nationalism. One by one, magazines such as *Azarbaijan sesi, Inqilab yolunda, Dede Korkut, Gunash, Ulkar, Odlar yurdu,* and *Mollah Nasr al-Din* were suspended; by 1984 only the venerable literary review *Varliq,* published in Teheran rather than in Tabriz, remained in existence. Article 15 of the constitution, guaranteeing freedom of publication and education in the native languages of the peoples of Iran, was reinterpreted to mean that classes of the Azeri language and literature could be taught in Azeri, but other instruction was to be in Persian.

There followed, in effect, a resurgence of assimilationist policies drawing their justification from the sense of danger to Iran from the enemy outside. "The 1979 intervention of Soviet troops in Afghanistan and the civil war that went on there for the next ten years reinforced the internal unity of Iran. These events gave a new impetus to the integration of South Azerbaijan with Teheran," observed a Baku historian.[62] Still, Persianization did not proceed on the scale of the Pahlavi period, nor did it provoke a comparable resentment. Indeed, the Azeris were known to take pride in being strongly represented at the upper echelons of the Khomeini regime.

If Tabriz was the symbol of Islam triumphant, Baku wished to remain the symbol of national identity. Aliyev, now a rising star on the horizon of all-Union politics, began to emphasize in his speeches that the Soviet regime had from its first days promoted the national aspirations of Muslim peoples. Going a step further, at the Seventh Congress of Azerbaijani Writers in 1981, he called for "strengthening literary links with Southern Azerbaijan, developing broad contacts within all sectors of cultural and intellectual creativity in imparting to our comrades of the pen the rich aesthetic-artistic experience we have accumulated."[63]

On other occasions he repeated the call for a rapprochement between the North and the South, and the *Times* of London reported that he had told foreign diplomats of his hope for the unity of both Azerbaijans in the future.[64] Not long later, in the fall of 1982, he left the Baku scene for Moscow to become one of the most influential members of the Politburo, the highest position an Azeri in the USSR ever held. By this time in Baku, the two Azerbaijans were frequently referred to as one fatherland. The frontier dividing one people, an "open wound," was destined to disappear (even though it was never said through what means). The Turkmanchai Treaty acquired an ugly connotation as a monument to historical injustice.

While such statements were not entirely novel, the thrust and scope of their circulation were. Significantly, the statements were no longer restricted to scholarly works and periodicals but were allowed in the intermediate-range media-literary journals, weekly magazines, and theatrical performances. Revived Soviet Pan-Azerbaijani agitation, although pushed one notch higher, was still kept out of daily newspapers, especially those in Russian, indicating the absence of the highest degree of official endorsement. Moscow, playing an intricate game against Teheran, was not willing to commit itself to any long-term course of action.

In Baku, as if through an unspoken agreement between rulers and ruled, the "one Azerbaijan" campaign served as a substitute for dissident movements that began to grow in Armenia and Georgia. For their part, those who articulated the emerging phenomenon of independent public opinion welcomed this less-than-total encouragement for the vision of unity across the border. Whatever the permissible measure for promoting this vision, it would benefit Azeri national self-assertion, and any rapprochement between the two parts of this divided land would be a reinforcement of Azeri identity in the face of either Persianization or Russification.

Iranian reactions to the "one Azerbaijan" campaign were primarily restatements of views reaching all the way back to Kasravi:

> The territory of present-day Azerbaijan has been historically different from Albania and Arran; the name Azerbaijan for the land north of the Araxes was given by the Ottoman invaders and taken over by the Bolsheviks; the language spoken in Azerbaijan is not the original language of the Iranian population; Azerbaijan has always been part and parcel of Iranian national movements; and talk about the problem of Azerbaijan is merely a product of imperialist intrigues.[65]

EIGHT

Decolonization and Its Crises

Territorial Dispute and Political Reawakening

Gorbachev's accession to power in 1985 brought an abrupt end to the "one Azerbaijan" campaign, an unnecessary irritant in Moscow's relations with Iran. Even more disconcerting for the Azerbaijani nomenklatura were the multiplying signs of a decline in Aliyev's fortunes under Gorbachev. He was forced to resign from his Politburo post in the fall of 1987, but the Party apparatus in Azerbaijan consisting of his appointees could barely conceal its distrust of the new policies from Moscow. The reverberations of Aliyev's downfall were a contributing factor to the coming Azerbaijani upheaval.

As Gorbachev's perestroika gained momentum, it brought into focus the structural crisis of an overextended empire. The typical premises for decolonization were clearly in evidence: diminished returns from the conquered lands, economic stagnation combined with the pressures of rapid population growth, and the consolidation of native elites with their rising expectations for a greater share of power, a problem compounded by the specifically Soviet condition of bureaucratic overcentralization. The nationality question, although not among the initial concerns of perestroika, turned out to be the weakest link in the chain holding the Soviet system together. Not unlike the end of colonial rule in India, Palestine, Cyprus, or Angola, ethnic tensions exploded in outbreaks of intercommunal violence—first against the Russians in the Baltic republics and Kazakhstan, then on the largest scale in the strife among the native communities of Transcaucasia.

The old Azeri-Armenian conflict, hidden for almost seventy years of Soviet rule, erupted again with a fury during February 1988, when the Armenian SSR formally raised its claims to Nagorno-Karabagh, apparently on the assumption that the structure of the Union had weakened enough to attempt a change in the status quo. When Moscow once again rejected the oblast' Soviet's petition for unification with the Armenian Republic, a series of mass protests began in Erivan involving street demonstrations, industrial strikes, and school boycotts. Similar events unfolded in other Armenian cities as well as in Nagorno-Karabagh. These demonstrations led to outbreaks of ethnic violence in both republics, the most notorious of which were the riots in the Azerbaijani city of Sumgait, where scores of Armenian residents were killed or wounded.[1]

In an effort to reduce tensions and restore order, Moscow resorted to various extraordinary measures. A package of economic aid was put together for Nagorno-Karabagh, and numerous high-ranking officials were dismissed, including the first secretaries of the Party in both republics. In a show of force, Soviet troops were brought into the area, and the oblast' was de facto put under direct rule of Moscow through the appointment of a special committee headed by a Russian official, Arkadii Vol'skii. Among the Azeris, the revival of ethnic conflict produced a political awakening comparable to the effects of the "Tatar-Armenian War" of 1905–1907. Although the economic, social, and political environment was vastly different, Armenian entrepreneurs were no longer ruining their Azeri competitors, nor was there a clash of interests between the Armenian labor aristocracy and unskilled Muslim workers—yet the dynamics of social mobilization around ethnic strife remained strikingly similar. Once again, the Armenian challenge emerged, and it called for a response. Armenia's territorial claims were understood to be merely the opening move of a strategy in pursuit of a Greater Armenia. For Nagorno-Karabagh, the natural hinterland was not the Armenian Republic beyond the mountains but other parts of Azerbaijan to which Armenian rule would have to be extended to secure the viability of its hold over the oblast.' The dispute was turning into a mire of intractable contradictions: geography versus demography, the inviolability of frontiers versus national self-determination.

On the opposite side, where the underlying concern was steady growth of the oblast' Azeri minority, the Armenian national movement received a powerful stimulus under slogans that cast the struggle for unification with Nagorno-Karabagh as another chapter in the fight against the centuries-old Turkic-Muslim danger.[2]

As in past flare-ups, the conflict of the late 1980s made it painful-ly clear to the Azeris how well the Armenians were organized and how extensive was the support they enjoyed: hundreds of thousands of peo-ple joined mammoth demonstrations in the streets of Erivan and main-tained perfect order and discipline despite the huge crowds; above all, Armenian supporters were able to synchronize their efforts not only in Nagorno-Karabagh and Erivan but also among major émigré centers worldwide—in Moscow as well as in Beirut, Los Angeles, and Boston. In contrast with these impressive feats, initial Azeri rallies protesting Armenian actions ran the risk of turning into outbreaks of destructive mob violence, as happened in Sumgait. These killings, at the very onset of what was shaping up as a prolonged conflict, caused reverberations hostile to Azerbaijan throughout many countries, especially in the West.

As the crisis unfolded, it soon became obvious that the Commu-nist Party of Azerbaijan was ill-equipped to speak for national interests in the face of the Armenian challenge. In early 1988 the Party was still reeling from Aliyev's downfall, with the customary house-cleaning and reshuffling of upper-echelon personnel. Quite apart from the post-Aliyev shake-up, the Party as a bureaucratic organization engrossed in routine activities proved to be of limited relevance to what suddenly became the community's most pressing concern, the Nagorno-Karabagh issue and all its ramifications. Meetings of the Party's Central Commit-tee in late April still focused primarily on Azerbaijan's chronically bad economic conditions and called only for more effective Party supervi-sion of economic activity and an improvement in social services. This passivity cost First Secretary Kamran Baghirov his job, which the fol-lowing month passed to Abdurrahman Väzirov, formerly the Soviet ambassador to Pakistan. He saw as his first task the reinvigoration of the Party apparatus through yet another bureaucratic reorganization.[3]

As the official power structure failed to provide adequate leader-ship in the national emergency, grass-roots initiatives in diverse forms sprouted up, beginning with ad hoc relief committees, collection of funds, and distribution of leaflets and samizdat publications. In Baku huge crowds filling the square in front of the Stalinist-era House of the Soviets, once an area for official parades, soon became a familiar sight. Above the crowds fluttered the flags of the "Musavatist" republic, but also occasionally those of Iran and Turkey. From a stony podium once built for the regime's dignitaries, new men from their own ranks now addressed the crowds. Among these speakers was the charismatic figure of Näimät Panakhov, a "slender young man of twenty-seven, a factory worker with eight years of schooling, dubbed the Lech Walesa of Azerbaijan."[4]

As the ethnic violence spread, Baku was soon inundated by waves of refugees—Azeris from Armenia, Nagorno-Karabagh, or the border areas of the two republics, where a condition resembling a state of war became the norm. The official number of refugees, most of them expelled from Armenia in retaliation for similar Azerbaijani actions, reached 165,000 by the end of 1988, but some estimates put the actual figure at least 50,000 higher. In any case, the upshot was a sudden surge in the population exchange process between the two republics.[5]

This influx into Baku changed the character of the city, once a cosmopolitan and reasonably prosperous urban center. The plight of these homeless, hungry, and desperate refugees, with bleak prospects for the future, especially in a country where chronic unemployment already hovered around 25 percent, stimulated some voluntary action groups to become more political and to merge into larger associations. According to one survey, Azerbaijani's "informal" organizations, i.e., those with no legally recognized status, numbered close to forty at the end of 1988.[6] Of this number only a very few had been in existence prior to the outbreak of the ethnic conflict.

Among the better known of these organizations were *Dirchalish* (Regeneration), with its newspaper of the same name; the Committee of People's Aid for Karabagh, with its magazine *Azärbaijan*; the People's Front of the Kizilbashi, with its publication *Khalgin sesi* (The voice of the people); *Yurd* (Homeland); *Birlik* (Unity); *Yeni Musavat* (New Musavat); and some others. The floodgates of glasnost were finally open in Azerbaijan, which by comparison with most other Soviet republics had until then been behind in organized political dissent. In the press, official as well as underground, a wide array of subjects, until recently forbidden or almost unmentionable, became topics of discussion. The catalog of prominent themes of the Azeri media under glasnost was at first more notable for what it omitted than for what it included, and the most cautiously handled topics were the relations between the two Azerbaijans. "There is not a country about which we know less than the Southern part of our fatherland," remarked a samizdat author, alluding to official restraints as well as self-censorship.[7] The publication of Vahabzadä's *Gulistan* poem was an exception to the rule, as were references to the Turkmanchai Treaty. Otherwise, the press, even legal and official, devoted abundant space to such topics as reevaluation of the 1918–1920 "Musavatist" republic and the Musavat Party, often in tones so favorable as to border on idealization; presentation of the extent of Stalin's crimes and their impact on Azerbaijan; reviving memories of personalities of the past, especially the opponents of Communism; and the harmful effect of several alphabet reforms on the continuity of the heritage of the national culture.

Increasingly, voices were raised warning of the dangers of linguistic and cultural Russification. The environmental crisis that was rapidly destroying the Caspian Sea's ecology and depletion of the region's natural resources, particularly oil, which was keeping Azerbaijan from joining the ranks of prosperous Middle Eastern nations, at long last became a subject of public debate. Likewise, the disastrous pricing policy set by the Center, chronic unemployment, and various shortcomings of educational or health services began to be openly scrutinized. With growing public recognition of the need for closer ties with neighboring Muslim nations, Pan-Turkism was no longer a dirty word, even though it was still qualified as a cultural movement, and hints appeared about the future of the USSR as a Slavic-Turkic bloc. To be sure, there was also no dearth of anti-Armenian pronouncements, which in the twilight of totalitarianism seemed to be even more acceptable to the authorities than other topics.[8]

As the Nagorno-Karabagh dispute began to generate echoes in faraway places, the issue took on a new dimension in Azeri eyes. They saw that although the Armenian side had started the confrontation, the outside world for the most part showed an anti-Azeri disposition. Even Gorbachev, while rejecting Armenian demands for a change in the status quo, appeared to do so in such a way as to indicate his sympathy and understanding, perhaps leaving the door open for future reconsideration. The decision to remove Nagorno-Karabagh from Azerbaijani jurisdiction to that of the central government, and the appointment of the Vol'skii Committee, reinforced such apprehensions. Moreover, dissident groups in Russia, as well as in the "blue-eyed" republics of the Baltic coast, Byelorussia, and the Ukraine, appeared at first unequivocal in their support for the Armenian position. This included the man symbolizing the best of Russia, Andrei Sakharov, who became a crusader for the unification of Nagorno-Karabagh with Armenia. It also became apparent that the shock of the bloodshed in Sumgait would not be matched by concern for the suffering of the Azeris. The Azeri press took notice of the fact that the Soviet public did not react to the deportations of more than 200,000 Azerbaijanis from Armenia. Instead, Moscow's newspapers, the USSR's Supreme Soviet Deputies, and the Ministry of Transportation only expressed their indignation with the interruption of goods delivered to Armenia via Azerbaijani railways.[9] The natural Azeri reaction was resentment over what they perceived to be the common front of those with a Christian-European background. This front extended into the Western media, including the American, and in the Azeris' view victimized them without giving so much as perfunctory consideration to their view.

> In the eyes of foreign and Soviet public opinion, the Azeri people are often looked upon as a collection of bloodthirsty cutthroats, to whom you do not feed bread but give them a chance to rip open the belly of a pregnant woman, or to tear to pieces a small child for the sake of satisfying their aesthetic or gastronomic needs. They are depicted as being without kith or kin, but rather in the grip of the ideas of Khomeinism, and Cannibalism. A crushing victory, is it not?[10]

The People's Front of Azerbaijan: The Search for an Alternative

As resentment toward Christian-European attitudes grew, the effect was to reinforce fears of a conservative-Islamic backlash, which a samizdat publication described as follows:

> The Azerbaijani nation, humiliated in its national feelings, could turn sharply toward the Muslim religion. . . . The traditional internationalist leanings of the Azerbaijani people may be substituted by aspirations toward a religious consolidation with Muslim peoples and nationalities. This in turn will generate favorable climate for the spreading of the ideals of the "Islamic revolution." . . . As a natural reaction, the aspirations of the Azerbaijanis to unite with their brothers living in Armenia and other republics and in Azerbaijan (Iran) will be developed and strengthened.[11]

There is an undertone of regret in these predictions of an Islamic revival, as the publication had clearly emanated from the milieu of the secular intelligentsia, which came to make its own bid for political leadership of the Azerbaijani community.

Within several months of the February clashes over Nagorno-Karabagh, the largest non-Communist organization, the People's Front of Azerbaijan (PFA), began to coalesce. The PFA traces its origins to an initiative by seven research workers in the Azerbaijani Academy of Sciences—Araz Alizadä, Leyla Iunusova, Hikmät Hajizadä, Tofiq Gasymov, Salamov, Isa Gambar, and Aydin Balayev. They had set up an association to promote perestroika in the academic community but decided eventually to address the public at large.[12] The full name of the organization was patterned on similar "fronts" in the Baltic republics, and included the words "for the Support of Perestroika." Its declarations took pains to emphasize their loyalty to the constitutions of the Azerbaijani SSR and of the Soviet Union.

The first step toward launching the PFA was an August 1988 manifesto by the Provisional Initiating Center, a body that was also preparing a draft of its program in laborious consultations with specialists holding seminars. It took almost a year for the constituent conference of the PFA to convene in June 1989, at which time the program and bylaws were adopted. Grass-roots sentiment had run well ahead of the leaders' deliberations, for by this time some two hundred of the PFA's cells in Baku enterprises were already in existence. Its strongest support came from the ranks of students, about 70 percent of whom considered themselves to be PFA sympathizers.[13]Although the PFA sponsored various actions linked to the Nagorno-Karabagh dispute—not only mass protest rallies but also strikes and a very effective boycott of the rail transit to Armenia—its program did not contain direct references to this conflict, only an oblique comment that the "government of the Republic should be able to exercise its sovereign right to interrupt transportation and other forms of activity on its territory which threaten the interests of the Republic."[14]

This document, which contained the most comprehensive statement of national aspirations of Azerbaijan emerging from Russian totalitarian rule, focused generally on what appeared to be issues of fundamental significance for the community, ranging from economic reforms to the environment to religious freedom.

Rather gingerly, the program took up the issue of relations between the two Azerbaijans. Among the PFA's chief goals was the abolition of all political barriers to the development of cultural and economic links with Iranian Azerbaijan, but care was taken not to question the stability of the Araxes frontier.

While recognizing the indisputable nature of the borders between the USSR and Iran, the People's Front supports the restoration of ethnic unity of Azerbaijanis living on both sides of the border. The Azeri people should be recognized as a united whole. Economic, cultural, and social ties between our divided nation should be restored. All obstacles to the creation of direct human contacts (visits to relatives and friends) should be abolished.[15]

The motive for unity also emerged indirectly among the demands for economic reforms. The borders of Azerbaijan should be contact points, not barriers. Rather than perpetuating estrangement, they should aid cooperation, and the first step should be to abolish the frontier zones. Cautiously broaching the issue of links between the two Azerbaijans, the PFA served notice of a change: that concern for relations between the two Azerbaijans had passed from the hands of the Soviet regime pursuing its own foreign policy schemes to the non-Communist national movement.

In dealing with the question of national identity, the PFA's program linked it to the heritage of Islam and its role in the future:

> The PFA supports the inalienable observance of one of the most basic human rights—the right to freedom of conscience. All religious monuments should be restored and handed back to believers. . . . The PFA aims to spread a new attitude toward the Islamic religion and culture. It is essential that religious beliefs and traditions that are respected by billions of people throughout the world no longer be subjected to the ignorant attacks of Philistines. The PFA supports decisive steps toward the development of understanding and cooperation with the world of Islam.[16]

Along with the cause of freedom of religion, the PFA took up the issue of reinstating the national symbols of Azerbaijan, their own name for the nation (Azeri Turks), native surnames, and geographical names.

The strain of eclecticism in the PFA's declarations reflected its open door attitude of accepting the followers of all political trends, including the Communists. The PFA explicitly rejected the principles of centralism, strict discipline, and political accountability, all of which smacked of Bolshevik practices. It permitted the struggle of ideas within its ranks, which consequently led to factionalism. Likewise, regional chapters of the PFA were free to draw up their own programs and to decide on their own course of action. Despite, or on account of, this all-embracing quality, the PFA rapidly became the country's main center of political influence, rivaling and soon overshadowing the Communist Party. In fact, Party chief Väzirov felt compelled in the fall of 1989 to conclude a series of agreements with PFA leaders.

In return for ending the wave of protest strikes that made idle many thousands of workers, including the general strike of September 4, and for calling off the embargo on the rail transit to Armenia in retaliation for the Armenians' cutting of the transit to Nakhichevan, the regime agreed to a number of concessions. Apart from such steps as lifting the curfew, drafting legislation on the economic independence of the Azerbaijani SSR and on free elections, or legalizing the People's Front, the most notable concession of all called for a special session of the Azerbaijani Supreme Soviet to vote on the new Sovereignty Law.

This law, written in consideration of the PFA's objectives and passed on September 25, 1989, accepted the jurisdiction of the USSR's laws only "when they do not violate the sovereign rights of the Azerbaijani SSR."[17] It reaffirmed Azerbaijani sovereignty over Nagorno-Karabagh and Nakhichevan and stipulated that the frontiers of the Azerbaijani Republic could not be changed without approval of the Azerbaijani nation. The law included a provision for the right to secede from the USSR, after a referendum among the entire population of the Republic. Even though the Azerbaijani Sovereignty Law remained a safe step short of an outright declaration of independence, the Presidium of the Supreme Soviet in Moscow pronounced it invalid on grounds that it contradicted the USSR constitution "which charges the Supreme Soviet with guaranteeing the uniformity of legislative norms throughout the USSR." From the standpoint of the Nagorno-Karabagh dispute, this rejection was seen as yet another token of support for Armenia.[18]

The fall of 1989 seemed the moment of triumph for the PFA, which could regard itself as one of the most powerful movements of its kind in any of the Soviet republics. As if in recognition of the PFA's strength, in November Moscow returned direct control over Nagorno-Karabagh to Azerbaijan. Yet one of the PFA's intellectual spokespersons, Leyla Iunusova, noticed that it faced at least two dangers, clearly as a result of its extraordinarily rapid growth. First was the fear of infiltration by members of the Communist Party apparatus, who might try to deflect the Front toward a more accommodating line. The other and perhaps more ominous danger loomed in the "lumpenized" masses, apparently a reference to the refugees from the countryside and the victims of the economic crisis. These masses "could crush all the democratic elements, and the results of this outburst would be difficult to predict."[19] Between these conciliatory and extremist currents lay the uncomfortable place of the intelligentsia, traditionally the leading force of the national movement. By this time, however, a large part of this group had become Russian-speaking, a circumstance that blunted their claim to leadership. It could be added that this was also a group whose members were less averse to migrating out of Azerbaijan, showed little attachment to Muslim ways, and looked for inspiration to the outside world, usually either to the Russian democracy or to Turkey. In effect, the underlying issue was the age-old and deepening divide between the intelligentsia, urban, and educated elements on one side and the bulk of tradition-bound, mainly rural, and often Shi'ite population on the other. At the end of 1989 there was a danger that "Azerbaijan [was] once again is at the crossroads, and the Mensheviks as before were in the minority."[20] The two-nations-within-one syndrome again reared its head at a historical turning point, and the hypothetical issue of Azerbaijani unity appeared as an additional potentially divisive factor. While traditionalist Islamic elements seemed favorably disposed to this possibility, a good part of the intelligentsia viewed with horror the prospect of an Azerbaijan submerged one day in an Iran ruled by fanatical and ignorant mollahs.

The PFA was effectively split into three wings that came to be known as liberal, national-liberationist, and Islamic-fundamentalist. Some activists could not find a place for themselves in any of these and left the ranks of the Front. The Islamic wing also drifted apart, and what remained of the PFA was, in the words of an early historian of the movement, "a part of the liberal wing united with the national-liberation wing on the basis of the national-democratic platform."[21]

Baku's January Days

A new phase of the Azerbaijani crisis began in the last days of 1989 when local chapters of the PFA in Nakhichevan organized protest demonstrations along the Araxes frontier. Grievances focused on the seizure of valuable farmland for the buffer zone and on the ban on Soviet Azeris to maintain contacts with relatives or to visit grave sites across the border, but calls were also heard for the unification of both Azerbaijans. Crowds took to dismantling frontier installations with no opposition from Soviet guards. Images of joyful people clipping barbed wire or burning frontier posts were broadcast on television networks around the world, recalling recent scenes at the Berlin Wall. Groups of visitors freely crossed the border in both directions, and the town of Lenkoran came under the authority of the local PFA chapter.

At once, differences surfaced in the perception of what was happening at the border, revealing divisions within the PFA. The radical wing saw the opening of the frontier as a result of popular upheaval, a step in the direction of the two Azerbaijans drawing together. This view was shared by a group of academicians who, recognizing the historical significance of events on the frontier, signed an appeal to the Moscow Politburo and the Presidium of the Supreme Soviet of the USSR. The appeal drew a parallel between the division of Azerbaijan to that of Vietnam in the past and of Korea in the present. "Azerbaijan was artificially split into two parts after the Russo-Iranian wars of the early nineteenth century, a fact that found its reflection in the tragic, for our nation, Turkmanchai Treaty of 1828." The academicians called for an "essential relaxation of the frontier regime in existence between the two parts of our fatherland."[22]

As for the moderates among the PFA's leadership, they showed little enthusiasm for the border demonstrations and tended to view them as a product of devious political provocation. They argued that the border installations had in fact been dismantled a week before with the help of the troops, and not because of the demonstrators' demands.[23] The Soviet press, however, was quick to seize on the slogans heard from the crowds to insist that Islamic fundamentalism had raised its head and that it aimed to change the frontier of the USSR to benefit Iran. Such an interpretation sat well with those in the intelligentsia for whom Iran epitomized religious fanaticism and obscurantism, and this description extended to Iranian Azerbaijan. Some in this secular wing of the Front expressed relief at the fact that many of the visitors to the South returned home disappointed with what they had seen on the other side.

There arose a special sensitivity over accusations and even mere suggestions of fundamentalism, as these could serve as a way to discredit Azeri national aspirations in the eyes of Soviet and Western opinion. To counteract the thrust of such allegations, some moderates in the PFA's leadership went so far as to question the existence of Islam in the country: "In the strictest sense, there are no Muslims in Azerbaijan. Most Azeris do not even know what's inside the Qu'ran. Religion has been so profoundly suppressed in our republic, that it has been nearly forgotten," wrote Tofiq Gasymov, in an article published in the West.[24] Another writer refuting the presence of fundamentalism in Azerbaijan explained how such "black legends" were being created: "For example, when in Baku a series of meetings were held at which the policy of national discrimination toward the Azeri population of Iran was discussed, when the ideas of the unity of North and South Azerbaijan were put forward and the disturbed Iranian side made diplomatic enquiries, the Moscow press accused the participants of these meetings of a 'pro-Khomeini' disposition."[25]

Disagreements within the PFA's leadership grew so intense at the turn of the year that the Executive Committee became paralyzed and was virtually absent from the political arena. All the same, within the ranks the balance of power was shifting toward the group that included E'tibar Mammadov, Rahim Gaziyev, and Abulfaz Aliyev and opposed excessive moderation in its political tactics. In further contrast to the moderates, they proclaimed themselves in favor of an undefined "Eastern" rather than Western democracy. But even these comparative radicals seemed too conciliatory for Panakhov, who broke with the PFA and disappeared for almost two years from the Baku scene, taking refuge in Iran and Turkey.[26]

E'tibar Mammadov's group gained a majority in the Executive Committee at the Third Conference of the PFA, held January 6–7, 1990, in the tense atmosphere that descended upon Baku during the troubling events at the border. Iunusova, Zardusht Alizadä, and some other moderates left the committee and subsequently formed the Azerbaijani Social Democratic Party.

Yet there were other strains in the unfolding drama, and within less than two weeks of the border events a new wave of ethnic violence erupted. On January 10 the Supreme Soviet of Armenia voted to include Nagorno-Karabagh in the republic's budget and to grant the residents of the oblast' the right to vote in Armenia's elections. At the same time, news came that some villages of the Shaumian and Khanlar regions were attacked by Armenian fighting squads. The angry reaction of the PFA was to set up the National Council, to be in charge of preparations to fight against the Armenians. In Baku, on January 13, mobs broke away from a PFA rally and used typed lists of addresses to attack local Armenian residents. These acts of killing and pillaging in the better-off sections of the city were attributed primarily to young, embittered drifters who were refugees from Armenia. Witnesses described Interior Ministry soldiers as standing by passively, possible evidence that the regime condoned the anti-Armenian excesses to create a pretext for the crackdown. Suspicions that authorities had been involved in fomenting the violence were rampant, and in light of the lessons of history would have been aroused in any event.

The PFA's position regarding the pogroms provided a measure of its disunity. Many reports agreed that PFA leaders and activists sometimes risked their own lives to protect the Armenians. Special vigilante patrols helped them in the evacuation from the city, which took the time-honored escape route via the Caspian Sea to the eastern coast port of Krasnovodsk. Yet there were also reports that other elements of the Front remained passive and that some of its members were inciting or even committing acts of violence.[27] In fact, the failure of the PFA to forestall the pogroms reinforced the perception that its influence was in decline.

By January 16 the surviving Armenians and also part of the Russian population had left the city and the violence largely subsided, but Soviet troops kept concentrating around Baku, apparently aiming to save the power of the regime. To prevent them from entering the city, the PFA barricaded the access routes. After the razing of frontier installations and the eruption of ethnic violence, the Azerbaijani crisis headed into a new stage—collision with the military might of the Soviet Union. The culminating phase of the January upheaval began at midnight on the nineteenth with the expected assault on Baku. A task force consisting of land, naval, and airborne troops, as well as the *Spetsnaz* (Special Assignment) elite troops of the KGB and MVD, entered Baku from three sides. The tanks easily broke through the makeshift barricades and clashes took place, the bloodiest of them in the vicinity of the Salyany army barracks.[28] There were reports of numerous instances of indiscriminate shooting by the troops. The official death count would repeatedly be revised upward, while rumors put the toll into the thousands. Eventually, the number of killed civilians was reliably established at 168, the wounded at 715, and more than 400 persons remained unaccounted for. Twenty-eight servicemen were killed and more than eighty were wounded, many at the hands of their own companions as a result of poorly coordinated actions by the high command.[29]

The decree on emergency rule banned all public meetings and imposed a curfew. On January 20, Väzirov, a man with scant personal appeal, had to resign, and the Party leadership passed to Ayaz Mutalibov, a fifty-one-year-old engineer with a fatherly appearance and a worried look to his face. The Party's stalwart number two man, the ethnic Russian Viktor Polianichko, remained at his post.

The same day Gorbachev, in a televised address, accused the Party and state authorities of Azerbaijan and Armenia for having caved in to the pressures of nationalist groups. He put more blame on the side of Azerbaijan, where the "actions of extremist forces assumed increasingly an openly anti-state, anti-constitution, and anti-people character."[30]

The shock of the military crackdown compelled the Azerbaijani Communist regime to take a stand bordering on open confrontation with the USSR. In a January 22 speech, Elmira Kafarova, president of the republic's Supreme Soviet, sounded previously unheard tones from Baku in addressing Moscow.

> The army criminals, having lost all humanity, crushed even ambulance vehicles under their tanks and killed doctors who were trying to help the wounded. The military tried to hide the real number of casualties by removing the bodies by helicopter, dumping them in the sea and burning them. The intervention was being justified by the disorders which had taken place in Baku on January 13–15. To this day it has not been elucidated who were the real organizers [of the massacres].[31]

A resolution by the Azerbaijani Supreme Soviet, with Kafarova's signature, demanded the withdrawal of troops and the lifting of Moscow's imposed state of emergency. Should the "Union organs" fail to give a positive response, the statement threatened, "we propose to continue the work of the extraordinary session, and to begin discussion on the question of maintaining Azerbaijan's relationship with the USSR."[32] However, neither this nor similar protests crossed the line of irrevocability. Unlike Lithuania, Azerbaijan did not act on its veiled threats of secession. The only notable exception to its pattern of restraint was a proclamation by the Nakhichevan Autonomous SSR on secession from the Soviet Union, broadcast in a few languages on January 20. It was ignored on all sides, as were the statements of Kafarova in the end.

The tragic events of January 1990 seemed to offer a ray of hope for the issue that had been the prime impetus for the convulsions shaking Azerbaijan since early 1988. The Nagorno-Karabagh conflict, overshadowed by other national problems, at last became the subject of direct negotiations between the Azeris and Armenians on the level of their respective national movements. In February the delegates of the PFA and the Armenian National Movement began direct talks in Riga, through the good offices of the "informal" Baltic Council. Yet the switch from killings to embraces—not unheard of in Transcaucasia—failed to materialize this time. Behind the failure of the talks loomed a perception of the PFA's weakness. An Armenian delegate in Riga described this view later on:

> We learned that the Azerbaijani People's Front as a political organization does not exist. The PFA includes all political forces, from intellectuals fighting against totalitarianism . . . to mobs involved in ransacking Armenian homes. . . . By their own account, their organization, unlike the Armenian National Movement, is unable to assume responsibility for the whole of Azerbaijan. . . . We asked them about Pan-Turanism and about the degree to which they wanted to be united with Turkey. "We are separate people," they said, smiling. "If we secede from the Soviet Union, why would we want to be united with Turkey, or worse, Iran?"[33]

As with other national issues, the solution to the ethnic strife remained in suspension.

In the West, events in Baku received wide media coverage, and for a few days Azerbaijan became a household word. The tone of the reporting from Moscow-stationed correspondents or Moscow-supplied information tended to be unfriendly to the Azeris, as though they might be on the verge of beginning a new round of massacres against the Armenians. Reaction from Western governments was hardly less injudicious nor based on better intelligence. The United States State Department expressed guarded approval of the Soviet military intervention in Baku on grounds that it was saving lives endangered by the ethnic strife. Western statements usually made no reference to the much larger number of Azeri lives lost through the action of Soviet troops. The effect was to further enlarge the pool of anti-Western resentment.[34]

Worldwide echoes of Baku's January Days nowhere resounded stronger than in Iran and Turkey. There were some striking similarities in both countries' reactions to the Azerbaijani crisis but also remarkable differences in their perception of events. The two governments' first instinct was to maintain distance from their neighbor's domestic upheaval. Turkish President Turgut Özal, then visiting the United States, declared offhandedly that the Azeris "are Shi'ites, we are Sunnis," and therefore of more concern to Iran than to Turkey. Later, he would insist that this remark was misinterpreted; nonetheless, he repeated that "these are internal affairs of the Soviet Union. It is impossible for us to interfere."[35] Özal's opposite number in Iran, Rafsanjani, in the words of one newspaper commentary, "has been remarkably silent on the issue," apparently regarding a recent economic agreement with the Soviet Union as "too important to sacrifice on the altar of ideological purity."[36] But ideological zealots in Iran refused to toe the government's pragmatic line and were outspoken in their views of events in Baku. Ayatollah Ahmad Jannati announced plans to send Shi'a clerics to proselytize in Soviet Azerbaijan, a task to be combined with translating the works of Khomeini into Azeri. Another ayatollah, 'Ali Khamenei, saw an outburst of Islamic zeal in Azerbaijan and warned that it would be "a big blunder to think that ethnic and national motives are behind this move." A widely publicized speech by a Majlis deputy pointed to "America's dirty hands and ugly face" behind the crisis. "The United States directly and indirectly . . . is raising ethnic issues such as Azeri-Armenian differences" as well as "instilling such ideas as the unification of Northern and Southern Azerbaijan."[37]

Turkish reactions, by contrast, emphasized what appeared to be anathema to Iranian officials—the ethnic and national character of the Azerbaijani upheaval. Large-circulation newspapers in Ankara and Istanbul declared their sympathy and moral support for the "indestructible ties between Azerbaijan and Turkey based on common race, language, and culture." But these same newspapers generally endorsed the government's cautious stance and elaborated on the thinking among the ruling establishment on Azerbaijan: considerations of realism required maintaining good relations with the USSR; the possibility of the reunification of the two Azerbaijans risked

upsetting the regional balance of power. "Turkey," said a press commentary, "should not allow itself to fall in the trap arising from the situation in the Caucasus."[38]

In its concern for correct relations with the Soviet Union, the
Ankara government found itself under pressure to take a more supportive stand toward the Azeris, not so much from the media but from
the public. This pressure included mass demonstrations of solidarity in
Eastern Anatolia, where a large part of the population was of Azeri
descent. A typical theme in these rallies, in harmony with voices heard
in Iran and Azerbaijan, was indignation at applying different standards toward Muslims and others. Moscow used strong-arm tactics in
Azerbaijan while handling Lithuania with kid gloves. Likewise, Armenia was spared the onslaught while Muslims had to pay the price in
blood. And Western countries were conspicuously silent in the face of
this violence. "Have the Crusades returned?" exclaimed Iranian radio.

As developments in the Soviet Union and the Middle East gained
momentum amid signs of the disintegration of the old order, Ankara's
caution and reserve appeared out of tune with the spirit of the time. By
mid-1990 Özal found it appropriate to send to Baku no less prominent
a Turkish representative than his wife, whose task it was to mend
fences with the Azeri public. Her visit marked also an impressive
expansion of economic and cultural exchanges between Azerbaijan
and Turkey. Özal himself was to die in 1993 of exhaustion, a condition
aggravated by a weight problem and heart bypasses, from a trip to
enlist international support for Azerbaijan in defense against Armenian attacks.

Of all the outside reactions to the Azerbaijani crisis, those south
of the border were particularly telling. Because information was
remarkably scant, one account by an anonymous but well-informed
writer who had traveled from Baku across the Araxes soon after January 1990 stood out. In his words, the Soviet Azeris who had made their
way to Tabriz with the slogan "Araxes is another Berlin Wall" collid-
ed there with a wall of passivity from their Iranian brothers. "The
excitement and sympathy remained confined to the frontier zone settlements with their family ties to the North. Further to the South, the
vision of Azerbaijani unity did not absorb people's minds. . . . Clearly,
the South was not comparable to West Germany—strong and prosperous, ready to receive people from the other side of the Wall."[39]
Nonetheless, the question of unity was a subject of interest among

Tabriz intellectuals: "The problem is here, in Iran," said one of them. "Azerbaijan should first of all regain its position in the chessboard of Iranian politics, and then we will be able to extend our hand to our brothers in the Soviet Union. . . . The Azeris have lost their cultural identity . . . and are no longer able to form a solid bloc to influence Iranian politics." If the malaise in the South came from a sense of "cultural humiliation," in the North the issue was revolt against religious and economic oppression by colonial rule, even though the cultural and linguistic autonomy allowed the survival of national identity. Six million Northerners consider themselves to be "Azeris only," and this deepens the rift between them and their brothers, who are "Iranian first."[40]

Nomenklatura Versus the Intelligentsia: The 1990 Elections

After Baku's January Days, the pace of the PFA's decline appeared to quicken, a process helped by the fact that hundreds of its activists were under arrest, including E'tibar Mammadov, head of the Executive Committee. At the same time, the Communist Party, which in the fall of 1989 had seemed moribund, suddenly began to revive, "as a phoenix rising from the ashes of burnt membership cards." In the long run neither the Front's decline nor the Party's revival were to signify a long-term trend, but for a time both offered temptations for quick political solutions. For the CPAz, the favorable circumstances were not only the weakness of the Front but also the reassuring presence of troops and the continuation of martial law. Even so, the regime did not feel itself recovered enough to hold elections as scheduled in March. The balloting was postponed until September 2, and then again until September 30.

The opposition forces grouped together into the Democratic Bloc, an electoral alliance consisting of some fifty non-Communist associations, among them the PFA, the *Yeni Musavat* Party, the Democratic Union of Azerbaijani Intelligentsia, the Karabagh Relief Committee, the January Twentieth Group, the Council of Elders, and various refugee organizations. These diverse groups produced an electoral platform with three fundamental planks: political and economic sovereignty for Azerbaijan, human rights, and economic and political pluralism. The Front's own electoral program included a point calling for increased contacts with Iran to secure ethnocultural closeness with the other part of Azerbaijan.[41]

The election campaign was conducted under continuing martial law, a situation that generated complaints against the military author-ities. The gravest charges concerned the murder of two candidates of the Democratic Bloc by unknown perpetrators.

The possibility of challenging the Communist Party existed—for the first time since 1918—but election day passed in an atmosphere of remarkable apathy. "Many inhabitants of Baku preferred television sets to ballot boxes—quorum has not been reached in practically any of the electoral precincts in central Baku, apparently not only because of bad weather," noted a journalistic report.[42]

Violations of the election law that occurred on balloting day received coverage even in the official press. About a thousand com-plaints were lodged, not only by the opposition but some also by the Communist Party. A group of observers from Leningrad declared on their return from Baku: "These were not elections, but a caricature thereof." PFA leaders told American observers that they had consid-ered boycotting the elections but in the end had decided that half a loaf is better than none as the opposition did obtain some representation in parliament and a legitimized status in political life.[43]

Results from the first round delivered a heavy blow to the Demo-cratic Bloc, which received only 26 out of 350 mandates—less than 10 percent—with no candidate from the PFA's leadership elected to the Supreme Soviet. In the Baku metropolitan area, where the opposition was best organized, voter participation hovered around 50 percent.[44] In the provinces, where influence of the local Party bosses was stronger, the turnout was much higher, averaging 81 percent for the whole of Azerbaijan. "In Central Asia and Transcaucasia the vestiges of a feudal system adapted themselves with astonishing harmony to the Stalinist model of socialism, and the power has not simply been put in the hands of bureaucracy, but the bureaucracy itself has become enmeshed with the networks of family and kinship bonds," commented one Moscow magazine on the Azerbaijani elections.[45]

An extreme example of provincial voters' attitudes was the election of Haidar Aliyev, who in his retirement had become an outspoken critic of Gorbachev and his policies. Running unopposed in his electoral dis-trict in Nakhichevan, he received 95 percent of the votes. His spectacular success at the polls produced a spate of newspaper speculations in the "Aliyev is back" mode, although the commentators were not clear if the comeback was to be counted on the scale of the Soviet Union or of the Azerbaijani SSR.[46] Given the general climate of national assertiveness, an Azeri scoring an electoral success in an obscure corner of the border-land could not conceivably become an alternative to the Russian, Gorbachev. His true power base had to be his native land, and he emerged from the elections with personal rule over the most sensitive part of the Azerbaijani republic, a strategically located enclave surrounded—except for a several-mile stretch of the frontier bordering Turkey—by a hostile Armenia and a suspicious Iran. The only open land route between Nakhichevan and Azerbaijan led through Iranian territory and bypassed Armenia, but the Teheran government threatened to close it whenever Baku allowed Iranian Azerbaijan to voice its claims.

The outcome of the Azerbaijani parliamentary elections was seen as a striking contrast to the results in Georgia and Armenia, where the local Communist parties met with sound defeats and power passed into the hands of nationalist governments, led by Zviad Gamsakhurdia and Levon Ter-Petrosyan, respectively, aiming at independence. Once again the Transcaucasian dichotomy revealed itself in what seemed to be differing patterns of political development. The Azerbaijani regime's declarations upholding the Soviet Union appeared as a sharp reversal of historical alignments in a region where the Christian element formed the mainstay of Russian rule.

The September 1990 elections also confirmed a persistent trait of Azerbaijani politics over the last century: the rift quite typical for a Muslim society in transition anywhere, including Turkey and Iran, that reflected the division between the modern-oriented and tradition-minded elements. In giving its support for the Communists, the village and small-town population displayed its instinctive fear of sudden changes as much as its distrust of the big city intelligentsia. For the latter group, numerically stronger than ever before, the 1990 elections results, with all the mitigating circumstances, appeared to be a continuation of the historical limited-confidence vote. By contrast, the Communist Party offered the "silent majority," who were anything but politically naive, the prospect of slow modifications in the status quo, a less uncertain alternative. Moreover, the nomenklatura, cultivating its new image of benevolence, tolerance, and folksy populism, seemed more appealing to provincial voters than the intellectuals from the PFA's leadership.

The Politics of Unreality and the Declaration of Independence

With its apparently impressive success in the electoral process, the regime at first adopted a self-congratulatory mood. Yet the general evolution of the Soviet system did not quite confirm the assumption that *plus ça change, plus c'est le même chose*, and success took on a hollow ring when scored against an increasingly obvious trend. For its part, the opposition appeared as a poorly equipped army of irregulars that was losing most of the battles, while the war was turning its way. As if in tacit admission of this truth, the Democratic Bloc was granted a larger parliamentary role than its number of seats warranted, and one of the PFA's prominent figures, Tamerlan Karayev, became deputy speaker of the legislature. The Supreme Soviet of Azerbaijan passed a few laws deferring to, or trying to capitalize on, national sentiments. Some were symbolic, such as recognizing May 28 as a national holiday commemorating the proclamation of independence in 1918, adopting the tricolor flag of the Democratic Republic for the Soviet Azerbaijani SSR, or renaming Baku State University after Mammad Amin Rasulzadä.

More essential was the regime's willingness to accommodate the thrust of the long public debate on the new alphabet reform. While there was a consensus that Cyrillic should be rejected as a symbol of Stalinist-imposed Russification and a barrier that had cut off the Azeris from the world outside the Soviet Union, the question remained: should Azerbaijan restore the Latin alphabet of the 1920s with the prospect of easier contacts with Turkey and the West, or should it return to Arabic script, a change that would help in drawing closer to the Azeris in Iran, while also helping Azerbaijan to recover the continuity of its historical and literary heritage? The latter option would have had the best chance of acceptance on the condition that a comprehensive primary education system be established for the Azeris in Iran. But the possibility of using the written Azeri language in Iran remained so limited that "it was not worth the sacrifice" to bring back the Arabic script with all its shortcomings. In January 1993 Azerbaijan adopted its fourth alphabet in less than seventy years, a Latin version more simplified than that of the 1920s. The reason for the simplifications was the requirements of the computer age.[47]

In the twilight of the Soviet epoch, the political stirrings within the nomenklatura became increasingly noticeable, and from the utterances of high officials they could be summarized as follows: Azerbaijan is evolving toward independence, but this process should not lead to a collision with the Soviet Union. Russia has played a positive role in Azerbaijani history and still offers huge markets for Azerbaijan's economy. Yet Prime Minister Hasan Hasanov, Mutalibov's adversary within the ruling elite, registered publicly a set of grievances that went beyond the customary complaints in the quest for more elbowroom from the Center:

> We delegated to the Center the responsibility for securing equal development of all the Union republics, but in return we have suffered inequity at the distribution of profits, with the result that every year we have been losing 15 to 20 percent of our national income, our standard of living has been reduced to one of the lowest in the Union, we have hundreds of thousands of unemployed and a devastated environment. We delegated to the Center our foreign trade, but our hard currency account consists only of pitiful crumbs, of no use for reviving the economy. We delegated to the Center our foreign policy, but have been subject to the information blockade, and our voice is not heard even under glasnost, either in the international community or in the United Nations, or inside the USSR itself.[48]

The regime displayed its ambitions in the field of foreign relations, and contacts with both Turkey and Iran expanded impressively, starting with official visits followed by commercial and cultural exchanges. In its special relationship with these two neighbors, Baku seemed to prefer Turkey, a country for which both the nomenklatura and the intelligentsia felt the additional affinity of secularism. Thus emboldened, Turkey proceeded to establish its visibility in Azerbaijan in a big way, ranging from financial credits to supplying Latin alphabet typewriters, to television programs that began to affect the way Azeri was spoken. This cultural expansion provoked the first murmurs of criticism at excessive Turkification. For all the signs of Azerbaijan's drift away from control by Moscow, "separatism" continued to be used as a word of condemnation in official pronouncements.

On August 19, 1991, the day of the Moscow coup, President Mutalibov was on an official visit to Iran. A report from an Iranian radio broadcast indicated that, during a stopover in Tabriz, he had spoken approvingly about Gorbachev's confusing disappearance from the scene. He was quoted as having termed these events as the "natural consequences of the policies that had brought chaos during the past several years. . . . We welcome the developments in the Soviet Union."[49]

Upon his return to Baku, the official Azerinform agency hastily issued a denial that President Mutalibov had ever expressed his approval for the attempted seizure of power.[50] In Moscow the coup was unraveling, and the Azerbaijani Communist leader acted with dispatch and skill. Appreciating that it was Boris Yeltsin who had emerged as the victor, he sent a cable with warmest congratulations. Meanwhile, in the streets of Baku the People's Front held daily demonstrations protesting Mutalibov's endorsement of the coup. In a show of firmness, the government used force to disperse the crowds and temporarily arrested some of the PFA leaders.

The aura of unreality thickened further when Elmira Kafarova of Baku's January Days fame assured the Union parliament in Moscow that the leadership of Azerbaijan had always been supportive of the constitutional organs, while in Nakhichevan Haidar Aliyev called for the wholesale removal of the top echelon of the Communist Party of Azerbaijan because of their cooperation with the Moscow junta. By now Aliyev had already left the ranks of the Party and, confirming signs of the nomenklatura's disintegration, he busily agitated for putting an end to the Communist monopoly of power. He adamantly opposed holding presidential elections with Mutalibov as the only candidate and used his powers as head of the Nakhichevan ASSR Soviet to ban the balloting on the Autonomous Republic's territory. He indignantly denied rumors that his intention was to take Nakhichevan out of the Azerbaijani republic, even though he would later conduct negotiations with Armenia, Iran, and Turkey; indeed, from Turkey, with whose leaders he had established close ties, Aliyev would obtain a one-hundred-million dollar loan to prop up the viability of the Nakhichevan enclave.[51]

The collapse of the August coup was the signal that released the pent-up demand for a new series of changes, and one Union republic after another issued decrees dissolving their Communist parties. The CPAz, which only recently had recovered its fortunes after withstanding the challenge of the People's Front, now entered the stage of self-liquidation for no pressing reason except to follow suit. The first act was to ban the Party from the Supreme Court, the KGB, Procuracy, and the Ministries of Internal Affairs and Justice.[52]

In Nakhichevan, where Aliyev was anxious to be one step ahead, the legislature of the Autonomous Republic proceeded at once to dissolve the local Communist Party organization and to nationalize its property. The next day, a decree on the state's takeover of the Party's property was issued in Baku, and on August 30 the Supreme Soviet convened an extraordinary session. Its purpose was to vote on the independence of the Azerbaijani republic, its name no longer to be preceded by the adjectives "Soviet" and "Socialist." The following resolution was adopted:

> Whereas the Supreme Soviet of the Azerbaijani Republic, guided by the highest interests of the Azerbaijani people and expressing its will; Noting that in the years 1918–1920 the existence of the Azerbaijani Republic was recognized by the international community; Basing its action on the Constitution of the Azerbaijani Republic and the constitutional laws on the Azerbaijani Republic's sovereignty and economic independence; Reaffirming its responsibility for the destiny and freedom of the Azerbaijani people; Confirming, in accordance with international acts, fundamental freedoms and human rights for all the citizens of the Azerbaijani Republic, regardless of nationality and religious beliefs; Striving to remove threats to sovereignty and territorial integrity of the Azerbaijani Republic; Accepting all international pacts, conventions, and other acts that are not contrary to the interests of the Azerbaijani Republic and its people; Desiring to secure friendly relations in the future with all the republics that were part of the USSR; Declaring its readiness to establish lawful relations with the states belonging to the international community; Expecting that the independence of the Azerbaijani Republic will be recognized by the United Nations Organization and members of the international community in accordance with the principles of the charter of the United Nations Organization and other legal acts and conventions; The Azerbaijani Republic proclaims restoration of its state independence.

The declaration included popular references to the 1918–1920 republic, the historical legitimization of the new independence, and human rights. There was an appeal to the opposition forces for unity in the face of danger from Armenia. It signaled Azerbaijan's eagerness for international contacts and recognition, but at the same time it indicated its closeness to the heritage of the USSR. The meaning of independence was still not entirely clear, as the declaration did not spell out the secession, and Mutalibov until the last moment went on castigating unnamed separatists. In parliament the declaration passed unanimously, with the opposition taken off guard but unable and unwilling to cast votes against it.

Azerbaijan at once joined the State Council, the provisional governing body for what was left of the USSR. Along with the republics of Central Asia, the Azerbaijani regime formed a bloc committed to upholding as much of the old Union bonds as was feasible. As the nomenklatura was seemingly falling apart, Mutalibov kept reminding everyone of the dangers from Armenian nationalists, whose aim was to divide the Azeri people. It was in this light that the attacks on him should be seen, he persistently declared.

"It is hard to find anyone in the streets of this Caspian capital who takes these astonishing developments at face value," the *New York Times* correspondent reported from Baku. "But even the cynics—who are plentiful—admired the audacious showmanship of a leadership performing for its political life." A case in point might be the assertion by an aide to Mutalibov that "only after the failure of the coup makers . . . could his boss afford to admit that he is a genuine anti-Communist. The aide confided that Mr. Mutalibov is a secret Muslim." The correspondent's own observation was that "even among those who disparage the Communist Party, Mr. Mutalibov appears to enjoy substantial popularity."[53]

Before the eyes of a skeptical public, events continued to unfold with dizzying speed. The presidential elections were held on September 8, with Mutalibov running unopposed. The only other candidate, Zardusht Alizadä of the Social Democratic Party, had dropped out of the race to avoid giving the elections an appearance of pluralistic legitimacy. According to the Central Electoral Commission, Mutalibov received over 98.5 percent of the votes cast, with 85.7 percent of the electorate taking part in the balloting. These figures meant that opposition's call for a boycott of the elections went unheeded, although the People's Front estimated that in Baku 66 percent of the electorate failed to show up at the polls.[54]

The last formalities of discarding the shibboleths of a long-outlived ideology went most smoothly of all. On September 14, in the shortest session of congress ever held by the Communist Party of Azerbaijan, it was resolved to disband the organization. Congress requested the president of the Republic to help former Party functionaries find new employment. The obvious reference was the transfer of apparatchiks to government positions, a process already well under way for some time, with Mutalibov as the prime case in point.

Like the leaders of most of the former Soviet republics, with the notable exceptions of the Baltics, Georgia, and Armenia, Mutalibov sought to adapt the old ruling elite to the post-Soviet situation by means of a perfunctory facelift. Behind this transparent attempt loomed the assumption that the public would maintain the inertia to which it had been conditioned for so long as it pondered the unanswerable question: in reality, was it going to be business as usual?

Before long, the hollowness of a questionable electoral victory under unusual circumstances revealed itself once again. A helicopter carrying senior government officials was shot down over Karabagh, precipitating the first political crisis in Baku under independence. Admitting his regime's doubtful legitimacy, Mutalibov agreed in late November 1991 to form a fifty-person National Council (*Milli Majlis*) with equal representation by the nomenklatura and the opposition. Essentially, the Majlis displaced the Supreme Soviet as the locus of power, though the Soviet remained in existence. In fact, acting impulsively, the Soviet annulled the autonomous status of Nagorno-Karabagh, and the Armenians responded by declaring an independent Nagorno-Karabagh Republic on December 6.[55]

For all his political dexterity, Mutalibov continued to lose ground with typical missteps. As one example, he committed Azerbaijan to join the Commonwealth of Independent States (CIS) without securing prior endorsement at home. But his true nemesis became the Nagorno-Karabagh conflict, the catalyst for the rise of the national movement, which was now becoming a time bomb. Not only was a lasting solution nowhere in sight, but the Azerbaijani position was clearly worsening.

As in 1918, the Azeris were coming to realize that their lack of military experience was among the most insidious effects of Russian rule. Not that they had been exempt from compulsory service altogether, as they were under the tsardom, but they usually had to discharge this duty of Soviet citizens in construction battalions. This indication of Moscow's distrust did not apply to the Armenians, who with their better training, equipment, and field commanders usually got the upper hand when fighting.

As the situation in Nagorno-Karabagh deteriorated, Mutalibov proved to be unbelievably sluggish in organizing a national army. Four defense ministers in five months coped with all manner of shortages, lacking trained reserves, arms, uniforms, and native officers, and last but not least, a sense of military discipline. Almost half a year after its inception, the army was reported to consist of only five hundred soldiers.[56] Mutalibov was suspected of sabotaging the formation of a national armed forces for fear that, in typical Middle Eastern fashion, they would be more involved in politics than in defense of the country. He ordered the disbanding of units under the opposition's influence, with the result that these political groups then proceeded to set up their own militias. Meanwhile, reverses suffered by Azerbaijani forces in Nagorno-Karabagh grew increasingly painful. In February 1992 Armenian forces launched an offensive at Shusha and Lachin aimed at opening a road link to Armenia. At the beginning of this operation, the massacre at the town of Khojali took place, completing the ethnic cleansing of the oblast' from the Azeri minority. Grisly images of hundreds of dead bodies, many of them women and children whom the army had abandoned to the tender mercies of the attackers, produced in the public a shock that the Mutalibov regime could no longer survive.[57]

On March 5 the parliament gathered for an extraordinary session, while outside the building the PFA held a mass meeting. After two days of intense maneuvering and bitter recriminations, Mutalibov resigned. The legislators treated him with generosity, allowing him the use of his dacha and apartment and giving him a pension as well as nine bodyguards. For all the political passions, the Azeris maintained their tradition of moderation and restraint, and there was no trace in the air of the vindictiveness that sparked a civil war next door in Georgia.[58]

Provisionally, the presidency passed into the hands of Yaqub Mammadov, pending new elections for the office. After Armenian forces took Shusha, Mutalibov attempted a coup to restore his fortunes. On May 14 the Supreme Soviet reinstated him in the office and canceled the elections. The PFA responded with a massive assault on the Soviet's building. Mutalibov fled, and the Supreme Soviet dissolved itself, transferring its powers to the Majlis. Yaqub Mammadov stepped down as interim president in favor of Isa Gambar.[59]

The voting took place as originally scheduled, within three months, on June 7. Despite all the signs of his political comeback, Haidar Aliyev was out of the running because of the age limit set at sixty-five years, so the fragmented and demoralized nomenklatura did not put up a candidate. The front runner in the polls was the ascetic-looking Abulfaz Elchibäy, the chairman of the PFA, a fifty-three-year-old Arabic scholar and former dissident who had spent two years in a Soviet jail. He won not by a Soviet-style landslide but with a comfortable majority of 59 percent, trailed by Nizami Suleymanov, a candidate regarded as a technocrat.[60]

EPILOGUE

The Azerbaijani Republic's situation after shedding its facelifted nomenklatura's rule was typical for a post-colonial society that arrived at independence more through self-liquidation of an empire rather than by the prolonged struggle of its liberation movement. The usual characteristics were all in place: 47,000 troops of the Russian Fourth Army were stationed at various points in the country; interdependence upon the imperial economy meant that the country lacked economic self-sufficiency; there was a sizable settler population in the cities; and disputes over state borders and intercommunal strife were turning into full-fledged warfare.[1] Over this situation presided the newly emerging power elite, who lacked sufficient political or administrative experience and were dependent on assistance from the ancien régime's personnel.

Abulfaz Elchibäy, an intellectual who soon became a target of criticism for being naive and ineffective, could all the same articulate more clearly than any other public figure in Azerbaijan the community's historically ingrained aspirations and concerns. These were emancipation from Russia's all-pervasive grip, drawing closer to Turkey and establishing firm ties with their ethnic brothers across the Araxes frontier, the best assurance of national survival. Moreover, he sought to act upon these goals, only to find that they exacted a heavy price and could be mutually exclusive.

He wasted no time in withdrawing Azerbaijan from the CIS, a step that prompted Russia to retaliate by raising import duties on industrial products from Azerbaijan to 65 percent, causing many Russian enterprises to cancel their contracts in Azerbaijan. The economic dislocation deepened when Moscow authorities began to suppress petty traders who traditionally sold Azerbaijan products in Russia's markets. At the same time, demands for Russia to start pulling its troops out of Azerbaijan made it easier for Moscow to allow the use of mercenaries and equipment on the Armenian side in the Nagorno-Karabagh conflict, which was turning from bad to disastrous for the Azeris.[2]

Elchibäy's policy of rapprochement with Turkey, meant as a partial substitute for the long Russian presence, was pursued in an atmosphere of resuscitated Pan-Turkish sentiments. But these sometimes went against the grain of Azerbaijanism, which had put down sufficiently deep roots. When the country's language was officially redesignated as Turkish, it led to protests, the extent of which surprised the People's Front regime. Meanwhile, efforts to limit the use of the Russian language met with silent opposition in that segment of the intelligentsia whose preferred language of expression it had become.

On the Turkish side there was a growing realization of the burdens that involvement in Azerbaijan could put on Turkey's limited resources. And signals from the United States were discouraging. A Congressional Resolution on February 17, 1993, banning all except humanitarian aid to Azerbaijan in retaliation for the blockade of Armenia, seemed to put the U.S. government on one side of the conflict. Most importantly, Turkish policymakers became apprehensive of the prospect of Turkey's being on a collision course with Russia's effort to recover its former empire. Following the death of Turgut Özal, Turkey indicated its readiness to disengage and to return to the mold of the Kemalist foreign policy toward Azerbaijan—especially since Russian declarations, including those by high-ranking members of the military, made it clear that Moscow regarded Near Abroad, the territory of the former USSR, as its zone of strategic interest.

The Baku regime was also discovering that its friendship with Turkey hindered close ties with the other part of Azerbaijan, and relations with Iran developed in a troublesome way. Even before his coming to power, Elchibäy had been making statements about the two Azerbaijans in the following vein: "As an independent state rises in the north of Azerbaijan, it will make it easier for freedom to grow in the South," and the Iranian capital greeted his presidency with barely concealed hostility.[3] By contrast, Elchibäy's most formidable rival, Haidar Aliyev, was gaining a reputation as a man with whom the Islamic Republic of Iran could deal. For his part, Aliyev cultivated cordial relations between Nakhichevan and Teheran; on his visits to Iran he claimed credit for opening some two hundred new mosques in his province. An experienced politician, he could appreciate the potentialities of the religious revival, and he performed a highly publicized pilgrimage to the tomb of Imam Reza in Mashhad.[4]

Teheran's position toward Baku had its motivation primarily in an understanding of national rather than religious-ideological interest, and both the pragmatic and clerical factions took a common view. For those who wonder why concern over Tabriz should be more serious because of the independent Baku regime than because of the Soviet Union, the explanation was that behind Baku stood Turkey—and behind Turkey loomed the United States, even though the U.S. had taken a recent stand against the Azerbaijani Republic in its conflict with Armenia. On the Nagorno-Karabagh issue, Iran itself formally assumed a neutral position but left an impression of being inclined toward the Christian- and Western-oriented but staunchly anti-Turkish-Armenia, a cause for much indignation in Baku. Iranian clerics, meanwhile, quietly set about helping to restore religious life north of the Araxes, a task in which they faced no challenge from secular Turkey. With money from Iran, mosques were built or restored, and future 'ulama were invited by the hundreds to study in Iran.

Inevitably, an essential factor in Azerbaijan's relations to the outside world was the oil industry, the country's chief national wealth and a special concern of the Elchibäy regime. As had been the case in 1918, it appeared that, under the proper supervision of the national government, the oil industry could potentially be a solid foundation for the country's independence. Although the old fields were exhausted owing to Soviet methods of overexploitation, Azerbaijan still had huge untapped offshore oil deposits, whose costs of exploitation would be higher. On barely 7 percent of Azerbaijan's part of the Caspian Sea, reserves of more than five hundred million tons were recently identified, and estimates of potential resources have reached a billion tons.[5]

For all these rosy prospects, the most pressing issue at present has been a lack of funds to cover the costs of advanced technology—the main cause for the oil industry's decline in Azerbaijan. The situation had deteriorated so badly that the expenditures to extract the oil exceeded the income from it, and some two hundred wells remained out of commission for lack of repair funds. As an influx of foreign capital appeared vital for the very survival of Azerbaijan's oil industry, the new regime acted quickly—some critics on the right and left said too quickly—to secure funds from Western sources. In September 1992 a deal was signed with a consortium that included American, British, and Norwegian companies to develop the huge Azeri oil field. Preliminary agreements on other oil fields were concluded as well, and plans were made for laying a pipeline from the Caspian Sea to the Mediterranean coast of Turkey.[6]

Even though long-term economic prospects looked encouraging, the immediate reality facing Azerbaijan was the Armenian war and its costs and burdens, including a mass of refugees whose numbers grew to nearly one million. A people without a tradition of militarism were finding out that warfare was an attribute of statehood, and the army a key national institution. The army's poor performance was still blamed on the Soviet practice of denying military training to the Muslims, certainly a valid explanation. Yet those inclined to introspection could also see the effects of an identity crisis reaching beyond the two-nations-within-one syndrome. The notion of an indigenous state was a novelty among the people for whom the state was a foreign implantation to be confronted in the spirit of taqiya, while "nation" was still too complex and confusing an idea in the name of which to wage a protracted and difficult war. Was the war fought in the name of the Azerbaijani nation in which regional and kinship loyalties often overshadowed other ties? Or was it a religious war, whose true character had to remain taboo and from which the Muslim neighbors abstained or could even be suspected of assisting the enemy. As in the case of his Communist predecessor, the Nagorno-Karabagh war proved to be Elchibäy's supreme test.

The winter of 1993 brought a new Armenian offensive, resulting in the loss of almost all the region of Agderinsk, the last villages in the Lachin corridor, and all the region of Kelbajar. The political fallout of these setbacks was bound to be devastating. The government charged Colonel Suret Huseynov, who had withdrawn his troops from Karabagh to Ganja, with responsibility for some reverses on the front line. The thirty-four-year-old officer, formerly a textile factory manager, enjoyed widespread popularity among the troops, and when relieved of his duties, he refused to relinquish his command. In the standoff that followed, Ganja, the "second city," became the pole of attraction for the wide array of PFA opponents, who planned to reactivate the Supreme Soviet there.

In Ganja was also stationed the 104th Russian Airborne Division, and to prevent Huseynov's collusion with the Russian military the Baku government demanded its immediate evacuation from Azerbai-

jani territory. By June 4 the Russian troops had left, and the government felt encouraged to disarm Huseynov's brigade. The attempt mis-
fired, with some seventy lives lost, and Huseynov, in turn, felt free to
launch a rebellion, sending his troops on the march to Baku. There he
found support from not only those disaffected with the People's Front
but also a population overwhelmed and made passive by economic
hardships and the burdens of the Karabagh war. Put off balance by the
rebellion, the PFA regime showed itself ready for concessions. While
rebel troops moved leisurely toward the capital, the government frantically negotiated with Huseynov. Accommodatingly, three government ministers and Prime Minister Panah Huseynov were all dismissed, and Haidar Aliyev was brought back into the limelight to
replace Isa Gambar as speaker of the National Council (*Milli Majlis*).

Suret Huseynov remained unshakable in his insistence on
Elchibäy's resignation, and on June 18 the president left the capital "to
prevent fratricidal bloodshed," taking refuge in his native village in
Nakhichevan. Nevertheless, he refused to give up his office. In Baku
Huseynov took over as prime minister and Haidar Aliyev became the
acting head of state.[7] The latter consolidated his position in the August
29 referendum on no confidence in Elchibäy, and then in the presidential election of October 3, which formally gave him the highest office in
the republic.

The June 1993 coup reflected the wider pattern of a return to
power by former Soviet leaders throughout most of the republics of the
defunct USSR. Together with the comeback of the native nomenklatura, it was seen as the restoration of Russia's dominant influence in
this strategically vital region. The dispirited Azerbaijani public accepted the new regime's explanation that Russia was their only hope for
solving the Nagorno-Karabagh conflict. One of Aliyev's first steps as
president was to bring Azerbaijan back into the CIS, without, however, inviting Russian troops.

As much as a success for Russia, the overthrow of the Elchibäy
regime was perceived as a blow to Turkey, which proved to be unable
or unwilling to control the causes of the coup, to prevent it from happening, and to defend its position in Azerbaijan.[8] From the perspective
of history, the coup appeared as another failed test for the pro-Turkish
orientation in Azerbaijani politics. Not only did it evoke memories of
past disillusionments but it amounted to a setback for the social forces
that stood behind this orientation. In Turkey itself the coup provoked

a tempest of recriminations in the press and stirred heated controversy among politicians, who engaged in the usual finger-pointing for letting down a friend, Elchibäy. In the end the view prevailed that, while Turkey was in no position to challenge Russia, efforts should be made to salvage whatever could be done to continue a Turkish presence in Azerbaijan. By extension, June's events were also understood to be a blow to Western interests centered on exploiting Azerbaijan's oil resources. Another of the post-Elchibäy regime's first moves was to postpone the signing of the earlier oil agreements, which had been scheduled to be concluded in June 1993, and to order that these be renegotiated.

While the "winner" of the June coup—in terms of political influence—was clearly Russia, and the apparent loser Turkey, the runner-up appeared to be Iran. Teheran welcomed the change of regime in Baku, not only because this alleviated its concern about Iranian Azerbaijan but also because it improved Iran's prospects for a greater Iranian presence north of the Araxes. This presence, easily noticeable in the aftermath of the coup, is based on support from those who are apt to call themselves Muslims first and then Azeris, Azeri Turks, or Azerbaijanis. In the end, however, Azerbaijani's foreign policy orientations reflect the divisions within that society.

The first year of Aliyev saw no essential changes in the Karabagh war, but the highlight of this period became the conclusion of the oil deal. After protracted and difficult negotiations, the agreement hailed as "the contract of the century" was signed on September 20, 1994, in Baku. The deal, covering thirty years and valued at more than seven billion dollars, was concluded with an enlarged consortium of foreign companies—four American (Amoco, Unocal, Pennzoil, McDermott), one British (British Petroleum), Norwegian (Statoil), Turkish (TPAO), and Russian (Lukoil). The deal provided for laying down the pipeline within fifty-four months, but no decision had been reached as to its routing.[9] As an alternative to its construction in Turkey there was the possibility of passing the line through Russian territory. Likewise, the inclusion of a Russian company in the consortium was understood as a sop to mollify Moscow's objections that might stem from the fear of Western influences creeping into Azerbaijan. If so, the maneuver was less than entirely successful. Moscow hardly concealed its displeasure with the oil contract, and the reservations focused on the legal issue: the Caspian is not a sea in the generally accepted sense, but rather an inland body of water, and therefore should be subject to joint exploitation effort instead of demarcation into exclusive zones of the coastal states.

Within less than two weeks of the contract's signing Azerbaijan experienced a new political crisis of the post-Soviet period. The power-sharing arrangement between Haidar Aliyev and Surat Huseynov was uneasy from the start, and the underlying tensions came into the open when Aliyev, after signing the oil agreement, was away from the country for the U.N. General Assembly. Early in October two ranking officials linked to him were assassinated in Baku. Upon his return, October 4, came the announcement that a military coup had been attempted with its center in Ganja. Aliyev proclaimed emergency rule for sixty days, and dismissed Huseynov from premiership, even though the latter denied any involvement in the coup.[10] Neither he nor the alleged participants were to be punished, but they prudently disappeared from Azerbaijan. A mass meeting in Baku demonstrated popular support for the president, all the more so that he came now to be seen as the champion of Azerbaijani national interests from depredations by Russia. In what appeared as closing of the circle, Haidar Aliyev reestablished his uncontested power over Azerbaijan.

CONCLUSIONS

Early in the nineteenth century, long before the British occupation of Egypt in 1882 and the French seizure of Syria and Lebanon in 1920, Russia became the first European power to establish direct rule over part of the Middle East—Transcaucasia. As was typical in colonial conquest, the frontiers of the newly seized territory were drawn arbitrarily and in haste, chiefly to suit Russia's strategic needs. But for Azerbaijan the advent of the colonial age meant, above all, division of the land and its people. The two Azerbaijans were put on different tracks of historical development, with one part exposed to the influences of Europe, mainly through the prism of Russia. The post-conquest transformations were gradual and limited, yet in the long run the economy and society north of the Araxes drifted apart from those in the south.

Slower to change was the element of group identity. At the beginning of the twentieth century, Iranians traveling to Baku still felt themselves to be among Iranians, and conversely, such men as Rasulzadä, Narimanov, or Ahmäd Aghayev espoused Iran's causes as their own. As late as 1919, Iran formally presented its claims to Azerbaijan beyond the Turkmanchai line and, on a more realistic plane, negotiated on the confederation. Only in the 1920s did the Teheran government begin to view links between the two Azerbaijans as a threat to its new vision of a nationally homogeneous Persianized state.

As in any form of colonialism, Russian rule had both its dark and bright sides, but among its effects one stands out: north of the Araxes the sense of a distinct, language-based Azeri-Turkic nationality germinated, a process assisted by the rise of the intelligentsia, modern communications, and educational progress. A confluence of circumstances catapulted the incipient nationalism, still more Turkic than Azeri, into the creation an independent nation-state in 1918. Until the present day, the Democratic Republic has been the high watermark in the pursuit of Azeri national aspirations, even though in 1918 independence went beyond the national movement's goals of an autonomous statehood. The Soviet regime's policies of the 1920s—the national contract with the korenizatsiia, the alphabet reform, and secularism—continued and broadened the Azeris' development into a nation. At the height of Stalin's rule, Azerbaijanism, a particularistic strain of Azeri group identity that had been purged of its Turkism and Islamic heritage, was imposed with a brutality typical of the time.

While the political evolution north of the border was swift, with a new stage commencing almost every decade during some periods, the other Azerbaijan continued as part and parcel of Iran. Here the traditional educated class and those who were upwardly mobile acted as a force for linguistic assimilation, unlike the intelligentsia across the Araxes line. The aspirations of Tabriz did not exceed an assertion of regionalism, a largely reactive proposition to Teheran's centralization policies. Yet there was an element of ethnicity in this regionalism, and despite being well integrated into Iran, Azerbaijan was the country's most rebellious province: during the twentieth century Tabriz rose up against Teheran in four revolts. When the Teheran regime was perceived to be servile to a foreign power, as in the time of the Khiabani uprising, provincial rebellion fused with the sense of Iranian patriotism. The two were by no means mutually exclusive.

The autonomist regimes of Khiabani and Pishevari proved to be the highest expressions of Iranian Azerbaijani regionalist aspirations, with the latter having an Azeri, language-based nationalist tinge. But whatever the separatist strains of either regime, these remained concealed and never openly admitted, even if they might occasionally be hinted at as part of a political maneuver. Clearly, preaching secession from Iran was viewed as politically unproductive. There was little question that the inhabitants of Russian/Soviet Azerbaijan had come to consider themselves Azeris first, while those of Iranian Azerbaijan remained Iranians first.

Even more striking than the absence of definite separatist impulses in the Iranian part was the relative inaction on the issue of reunification of a country split by a foreign power. Concrete moves toward this end have been conceivable only through the agency of an outside power—Russia, Turkey, or even Britain, each of whom at one time brought the two Azerbaijans under the umbrella of its military occupation. The Turkish military presence on both sides of the Araxes in 1918 occurred at a moment when the Ottoman State was on its deathbed, hardly a propitious time for embarking on some grand design, or even for formulating expansionist policy goals. And Britain, in 1919–1920 already winding down its worldwide commitments, was not only uninterested in but opposed to reunification under its auspices. By far the longest-lasting involvement was with Russia, indirectly after the Turkmanchai Treaty and directly during two prolonged periods of occupation, from 1911 to 1917 and from 1941 to 1946. But even during those periods, Russia/the Soviet Union refrained from moves aimed at detaching Azerbaijan from Iran. Rather, Russia preferred to enmesh the two Azerbaijans in a web of ties and contacts. Under pressure, Russia would withdraw its troops beyond the Araxes, in the apparent belief that what is postponed is not necessarily lost.

The international aspect of Azerbaijan's division created a delicate balance of power in one corner of the turbulent Middle East, a situation resembling that of nineteenth-century East Central Europe, where maintenance of a partitioned Poland ensured lasting peace among Russia, Austro-Hungary, and Germany.

In the absence of any support from the outside, the indigenous movement for reunification appeared subdued. An outright call for the unity of this divided land has never been part of a political program or been made through official declarations; even public figures who might have favored this goal proved to be noncommittal in their utterances. On closer examination, however, the undercurrent of Pan-Azerbaijani sentiments now appears to be broad-based and long-lasting, fed by transborder commerce and migrations, involvement in the Iranian Constitutional Revolution, the joint work of Himmät and Ädälät, the Pishevari episode, the post-1946 "literature of longing," and the People's Front declarations. Characteristically, manifestations of these sentiments were strongest in times of upheavals—wars and revolutions that threatened the status quo—and became more dormant during periods of stability.

The status quo has been rooted in the long-established regional balance of power, yet even such long relationships are not immutable.

In the past, if Azerbaijani unity was considered at all, it was usually regarded as the vehicle for extending Russian/Soviet power at Iran's expense. Pishevari's regime was viewed almost entirely in this light, even though he did not indicate Pan-Azerbaijani aspirations.

There have been three hypothetical possibilities for reunifying Azerbaijan, according to opinions held in the early stages of glasnost: Soviet conquest of the South, Iranian conquest of the North, or for both Azerbaijans to become independent and then reunite as one state. Inasmuch as none of these possibilities was likely to occur, it was concluded that the vision of one Azerbaijan might well be abandoned. At best, the Azeris on both sides of the border should try to get to know each other.

Under more recent conditions unfolding with the decline and fall of the Soviet Union, this last assumption no longer seems unquestionably valid, and herein lies a new dimension of the historical issue. It has become apparent that more than three possibilities exist for the two Azerbaijans to draw closer together. Contemporary Europe offers numerous examples of peoples with the same language and cultural heritage maintaining close links across state boundaries with no claims at irredentism, for example: Germany, Switzerland, and Austria; France, Belgium, and Switzerland; Holland and Belgium. Even closer to Azerbaijan are the examples of the Albanians and Moldovans, the latter a people who only two generations ago had been split away from the fully formed Romanian nation-state, both of whom show no hurry to reunite following the downfall of the USSR. But then all these peoples live free from danger to their language and ethnicity.

In their quest for national self-preservation the Azeris north of the Araxes are bound to look for reinforcement through a closer connection with their compatriots south of the border. Few may act from a Pan-Turkish impulse, and some with a view to escape their big Turkish brother's embrace, while still others may wish to return to their historical and spiritual homeland, Iran. Probably the strongest reason for rapprochement will be the desire for protection from the reviving Russian threat.

Whatever their motivation, the formerly Soviet Azeris' concern with the other Azerbaijan is no longer the vehicle of Russian expansionism. Yet, while many Azeris on both sides of the frontier have expressed a desire for greater contacts, hardly any voices are heard calling for a merger. They recognize that the process of historical differentiation has gone too far. "We share much of common history, we speak the same language, but we live worlds apart" is the lesson they can draw from their meetings across the border. Indeed, the faint glimmer of a debate on the reunification provokes fear or becomes a divisive factor within the community. Clearly, in their debates, the formerly Soviet Azeris must confront the issues that have led to convulsions in the ranks of the People's Front. If Azerbaijan leaves Russia, or Russia leaves Azerbaijan, what next?

As Russia showed signs of retreating from Transcaucasia, a power vacuum developed that was bound to be filled one way or another. A sad commentary on the effects of the Soviet period is that, while after the downfall of the tsardom the natural solution was Transcaucasian federalism, this prospect now seems inconceivable after the demise of Communism, at least until after the ethnic conflicts run their course. The obvious candidates for filling this vacuum were those Middle Eastern neighbors with whom Azerbaijan has had a special relationship—Turkey and Iran. Both have indicated a certain initial caution, even reluctance, to be involved. For Iran, any significant steps to bring the two Azerbaijans closer would endanger the long Persianization effort. The very notion of eventually incorporating six million well-educated, Turkic-speaking people into Iran would obviously change the character of the centralized Iranian state, which has been the handiwork of the Pahlavi dynasty. For its part, Turkey has feared being distracted from its goal of integration with Europe and being driven into risky and costly ventures deep in Asia. All the same, both Iran and Turkey have found themselves drawn into ex-Soviet Azerbaijan, and each has a following attracted by differing appeals.

With a head start among the pro-Western, secular-minded intelligentsia, Turkey's appeal has become further enhanced by its expansion of cultural and economic links. The country has long had an attraction as a bridge to Western modernity, and in the short term nothing has drawn the Azeris more closely to Turkey than the Armenian threat. In turn, Teheran could not remain indifferent to the prospect of Turkish involvement in Baku, if for no other reason than its concern for maintaining a firm hold over Tabriz. Moreover, the solid Shi'ite following north of the Araxes grows as the Islamic revival progresses.

In another restoration of the broken thread of history, Azerbaijan, as it returns to its Middle Eastern environment, becomes again the arena for a contest between Iran and Turkey. Until only recently, these regional powers had themselves lived in the overpowering shadow of Russia, and it was Russia again that resolved the problem by coming back to Transcaucasia within two years of the end of the USSR. The power vacuum proved to be temporary, and the people of Azerbaijan accepted with resignation and some relief the possibility of a Pax Russica as the best solution available.

By 1993 the trend of events increasingly showed that Russia was on its way to reaffirming its grip on the Near Abroad countries. An empire does not die easily, especially if it sits astride the geopolitical center of the world's land mass and the relationship of forces evokes the image of a shark among sardines. But while the pendulum swings back, it does not return to the same point. The conditions that brought the Soviet Union toward decolonization still obtain, and former nomenklatura rulers reappear on the scene, but in a changed and unfamiliar setting.

In the past, when the process of imperial restoration from the time of troubles was under way in the years from 1917 to 1923, the empire did come back, but in a different form and at the price of national consolidation of its subject peoples. While Soviet colonialism was totalitarian, resurging Russian neoimperialism is of a different quality. More than ever, Moscow's concern is to secure strategic and economic advantages without incurring undue burdens. In practice, this approach amounts to leaving a wide and expanding margin for trade, investments, and travel while perhaps allowing an even larger berth for cultural and spiritual life. Rather than reverting to characteristic Soviet form of all-pervading controls, the new Russian imperialism harks back to the age of the tsardom at the time of the conquests: neither province nor colony, but with the status of a weak satellite. Nineteenth-century Azeri literature shows just how limited the impact of the Russian presence was on the life of the community as a whole: indeed, writers of the time barely acknowledge the fact.

Thus Russia's disinterest in filling the empty spaces on the margins (and its inability to do so, in any case) is likely to lead to a resumption of the Turkish-Iranian contest. The Islamic revival, a natural reaction to Soviet-imposed decades of irreligiosity, will probably remain an important trait of Azerbaijani life over the long term, with support for it coming not from secular Turkey but from Iran. Likewise, in asserting their national identity, the Azeris may well find that the most promising avenue toward rapprochement with their compatriots across the border is through Iran rather than against Iran, assuming that Teheran has no grounds for its fear of a revival of Pan-Turkish expansionism.

On the other hand, there remains the historical task of emancipating a large part of the Azeri community from Russian and Soviet cultural domination; while this influence had once lifted the Azeris from their tradition-bound pattern of existence, in the end it imposed on them another kind of stagnation and isolation from the non-Russian world. Here the role of Turkey will in all likelihood be paramount.

Over the centuries, the leading theme of Azerbaijan's history has been the syndrome of Siyavush, a hero with a split personality about whom Rasulzadä wrote with a point in mind. Will the Azeris, both north and south of the Araxes, be able to revive another historical role for their country, a land where the Iranian and Turkic civilizations have blended in creative harmony?

Whatever the future holds, the Azeris, in their dealings with the outside world, are apt to take guidance from their ancient political heritage: moderation and compromise. This is the heritage rooted in the realities of their country's geography and history, the realities of the quintessential borderland, between different continents, religions, and ethnic groups. In such configurations extremism lacks a fertile ground, and its avoidance has been understood as the essence of the community's survival.

ABBREVIATIONS

The following abbreviations are used in the notes and the bibliography:

AIS	Azärbayjan Inja Sanati
AKAK	Akty sobrannye Kavkazskuiu Arkheograficheskuiu Kommissieiu
ANAzSSR	Akademiia Nauk Azerbaidzhanskoi Sotsialisticheskoi Sovetskoi Respubliki
ANAzSSR, Isvestiia, Ser. Ob. N.	Seriia Obshchestvennykh Nauk
ANAzSSR, Ser. Lit. Iaz.,	Seriia Literatury, Iazyka i Isskustva
ANSSSR	Akademiia Nauk Soiuza Sotsialisticheskikh Sovetskikh Respubliki
AR	Asiatic Review
Azerbaijan TsGAPPODAzR	Tsentral'nyi Gosudarstvennyi Arkhiv Politicheskikh Partiii Obshchestvennykh Dvizhenii Azerbaidzhanskoi Respubliki
CCAC	The Caucasus and Central Asian Chronicle
CAS	Central Asian Survey
CMRS	Cahiers du monde russe at sovietique
IJMES	International Journal of Middle East Studies
MEJ	Middle East Journal
OM	Oriente Moderno
Poland. AANMSZ	Archiwum Akt Nowych, Ministerstwo Spraw Zagranicznych

RMM	Revue du monde musulmane
TTK Belleten	Türk Tarih Kurumu, Belleten
UK FO	United Kingdom, Foreign Office
WI	Welt des Islams

Azerbaijani Cyrillic characters

Azerbaijani Cyrillic	Latin equivalent	Azerbaijani Cyrillic	Latin equivalent
Аa	a	Өө	ö
Вб	b	Пп	p
Вв	v	Рp	r
Гг	g	Сc	s
Гɾ	gh	Тт	t
Дд	d	Уy	u
Ee	ye*, e†	Уv	ü
Әә	ä	Фф	f
Жж	zh	Хx	kh
Зз	z	Һһ	h
Ии	i	Цц	ts
Йй/Јј	y‡	Чч	ch
Кķ	k	Чч	j
Кҝ	q	Шш	sh
Лл	l	Ыы	ï
Мм	m	Ээ	ë
Нн	n	Юю	yu
Оo	o	Яя	ya

* initially.   † elsewhere.   ‡ J replaced Й in 1959.

NOTES

CHAPTER 1

1. For a Soviet overview of Azerbaijan's history before the eighteenth century, see Akademiia Nauk AzSSR, *Istoriia Azerbaidzhana* 1 (Baku, 1958). For monographic works related to particular periods, see V. Bartol'd, *Mesto prikaspiiskikh oblastei v istorii musul'manskogo mira* (Baku, 1925); Ziya Buniatov, *Azerbaidzhan v VII-IX vekakh* (Baku: Elm, 1965); A. S. Sumbatzade, *Azerbaidzhantsy—etnogenez i formirovanie naroda* (Baku: Elm, 1990); *Voprosy istorii kavkazskoi Albanii,* Igrar Aliyev, ed. (Baku, 1962); F. Sumer, "Azerbaycanin turkleşmesine umumi bir bakiş," *TTK, Belleten* 21 (1957): 429–47; Peter B. Golden, "The Turkic Peoples and Caucasia," in *Transcaucasia: Nationalism and Social Change,* Ronald G. Suny, ed. (Ann Arbor: University of Michigan Press, 1983), 45–68. *Istoricheskaia geografiia Azerbaidzhana*, Ziya Buniatov, ed. (Baku: Elm, 1987).

2. On the khanates, see G. Leviatov, *Ocherki po istorii Azerbaidzhana XVIII veka* (Baku, 1948); Gasi Abdullaev, *Azerbaidzhan v XVIII veke i vzaimootnosheniia s Rossiei* (Baku, 1956), 86–111; Petrushevskii, *Ocherki po istorii feodal'nykh otnoshenii v Azerbaidzhane i Armenii v XVI-nachale XIX veka* (Moscow-Leningrad: Izd-vo ANSSSR, 1949).

3. Abdullaev, *Vzaimootnosheniia* 182–281, and Abdullaev, *Iz istorii Severo-Vostochnogo Azerbaidzhana v 60–80 gg. XVIII veka* (Baku: Izd-vo ANAzSSR, 1958), 36–136.

4. On the Russian expansion south of the Caucasus, see Muriel Atkin, *Russia and Iran, 1780–1828* (Minneapolis: Univerity of Minnesota Press, 1980). Firuz Kazemzadeh, "Russian Penetration of the Caucasus" in *Russian Imperialism from Ivan the Great to the Revolution,* T. Hunczak, ed. (New Brunswick: Rutgers Univerity Press, 1974), 239–63; A. V. Fadeev, *Rossia i Kavkaz v pervoi tretii XIX veka* (Moscow: Izd-vo ANSSSR, 1958) 5; Az.SSR, EA, *Jänubi Azärbajan tarikhinin ocherki* (Baku: Elm, 1985).

6. For a recent discussion of this Russo-Iranian war, see Atkin, *Russia and Iran,* 99–122; see also J. F. Baddeley, *The Russian Conquest of the Caucasus* (London, 1908). Butkov, *Materialy dlia novoi istorii Kavkaza* (St. Petersburg, 1869).

7. For the full text of the treaty, see *AKAK* 6:377; for a Soviet view, see A. S. Sumbatzade and G. Mekhtiev, *Prisoedinenie Azerbaidzhana k Rosii i ego progressivnye posledstviia v oblastii ekonomiki i kul'tury* (Baku, 1955), 38–39.

8. For official documents on Azeri attitudes in this war, see *AKAK* 6:651, part 2.

9. A. M. Ismailov, "Ob uchastii Azerbaidzhantsev v riadakh russkikh voisk v russko-iranskikh i russko-turetskikh voinakh pervoi tretii XIX veka," *ANAzSSR Trudy* 4 (1954): 5–20; for a non-Soviet, Russian discussion, see V. Potto, *Pervye dobrovol'tsy Karabaga* (Tiflis, 1902).

10. Fasa'i Hasan, *History of Persia Under Qajar Rule,* trans. by Heribert Busse (New York: Columbia University Press, 1972), 172.

11. Avery, *Modern Iran* (New York: Praeger, 1956), 39.

12. For the current Azeri view of the Russo-Iranian treaties, see M. Aleskerov, "Mezhdunarodnaia protivopravnost' giulistanskogo i tiurkman-chaiskogo dogovorov," *Khazar* 1 (1990): 133–34.

13. On the nineteenth-century changes in land tenure in Iran, see A. Lambton, "Rural Development and Land Reform in Iran," in *The Economic History of Iran, 1800–1914,* Charles Issawi, ed. (Chicago: University of Chicago Press, 1971), 52-55.

14. Mirza Kazim b. Topchibashev, *Bab i Babidy* (St. Petersburg, 1865). For recent works on the Babid movement, see A. Amanat, *Resurrection and Renewal: The Making of the Babid Movement in Iran, 1844–1850* (Ithaca: Cornell University Press, 1989); Mangol Bayat, *Mysticism and Dissent: Socio-Religious Thought in Qajar Iran* (Syracuse: Cornell University Press, 1982); M. Momen, "The Social Basis of Babi Upheavals in Iran, 1848–53," *IJMES* 15 (1983): 159–83.

15. Sykes, *History of Persia,* 237.

16. L. Berezin, *Puteshestvie po Severnoi Persii* (Kazan, 1852), 58. For a selection of sources on the Tabriz trade in the nineteenth century, see Issawi, *The Economic History of Iran.*

17. George Curzon, *Persia and the Persian Question* 4 (London: Longmans, 1892), 593–644.

18. Earl of Ronaldshay, *The Life of Lord Curzon* (London: E. Benn, 1927), 147.

19. *Obozreniie rossiiskikh vladenii za Kavkazom v statisticheskom, topograficheskom i finansovom otnosheniakh* 4 (St. Petersburg, 1836), 361.

20. Ludwik Widerszal, *Sprawy kaukaskie w polityce europejskiej* (Warsaw, 1934), estimates the number of Muslim emigrants in the years 1863–1864

at 220,000. For the population statistics in various years, see Kavkazskii Statisticheskii Komitet, *Sbornik svedenii o Kavkaze* (Tiflis, 1871).

21. George Bournoutian, "The Ethnic Composition and the Socioconomic Condition of Eastern Armenia in the First Half of the Nineteenth Century," in Suny, *Transcaucasia,* 79; see also Bournoutian, *Eastern Armenia in the Last Decades of Persian Rule, 1807–1828: A Political and Socio-Economic Study of the Khanate of Erivan on the Eve of the Russian Conquest* (Malibu, Calif.: Undena Publications, 1982), p. 76.

22. *Obozrenie rossiiskikh vladenii.* Appendix, pages unnumbered.

23. ANSSSR, Institut Istorii, *Kolonial'naia politika rossiiskogo tsarizma v Azerbaidzhane v 20kh-60 gg XIX veka* 2 (Moscow: Izd-vo ANSSSR, 1937), 21.

24. For a monographic work on the waves of the nineteenth-century Armenian immigration into Transcaucasia, see G. Koutcharian, *Der Siedlungsraum der Armenier unter dem Einfluss der historisch-politischen Ereignisse seit dem Berliner Kongress 1878* (Berlin, 1899). For a Russian view of this immigration, see N. I. Shairov, *Novaia ugroza russkomu delu v Zakavkaz'e* (St. Petersburg, 1911).

25. *AKAK* 5, Appendix, 986.

26. M. K. Rozhkova, *Ekonomicheskaia politika tsarskogo pravitel'stva na Srednem Vostoke vo vtoroi chetverti XIX veka i russkaia burzhuaziia* (Moscow, 1949), 94; see also *Obozrenie rossiiskikh vladenii,* 12, for Kankrin's idea of turning Transcaucasia into "a new East India."

27. Alexandre Bennigsen, "Une temoignage française sur Chamil et les guerres du Caucase," *CMRS* 6 (1966): 32.

28. For critical reports on the work of the military government, see *AKAK* 7:411–13; for a detailed discussion, see A. S. Mil'man, *Politicheskii stroi Azerbaidzhana x XIX-nachale XX veka* (Baku: Azarnashr, 1966), 67–75.

29. For the discussion on the two schools of thought on the administration of Transcaucasia, see *Kolonial'naia politika* 1, 8.

30. Mil'man, *Politicheskii stroi,* 112–23.

31. For the official acts defining the powers of the Viceroyalty, see *AKAK* 10:1–2. For a discussion of Vorontsov's policies in Transcaucasia, see L. H. Rhinelander, "Viceroy Vorontsov's Administration of the Caucasus," in Suny, *Transcaucasia,* 87–108.

32. I. Gasanov, "K istorii podgotovki reskripta 6 dekabria 1846 goda," *ANAzSSR Trudy* 4 (1954): 25–26. For the text of the Rescript, see *Kolonial'naia politika* 2, 105–7.

33. On reorganization of territorial administration, see Mil'man, *Politicheskii stroi* 133.

34. Ibid., 156.

35. *Kavkazskii Kalendar na 1887* (Tiflis, 1886), 220.

36. B. Ischanian, *Nationaler Bestand berufmassige Gruppierung und Gliederung der kaukasischen Volker* (Berlin, 1914), 52–54.

37. Rozhkova, *Ekonomicheskaia politika,* 94.

38. For a Soviet discussion of the nineteenth-century industrialization of Azerbaijan, see A. S. Sumbatzade, *Promyshlennost' Azerbaidzhana v XIX veke* (Baku, 1964); A. S. Sumbatzade, "K voprosu o kharakteristike razvitiia promyshlennogo kapitalizma vo vtoroi polovine XIX veka" in *ANAz.SSSR, 10 let Akademii Nauk Az. SSR* (Baku, 1957), 623–34.

39. Ts. Agaian, *Krest'ianskaia reforma v Azerbaidzhane* (Baku, 1958); see also A. S. Sumbatzade, *Sel'skoe khoziaistvo Azerbaidzhana v XIX veke* (Baku, 1958), 151–54.

40. Ischanian, *Nationaler Bestand,* 53. For a recent discussion of the nineteenth-century urbanization, see D. I. Ismail-zade, *Naselenie gorodov Zakavkazskogo Kraia v XIX-nachale XX v. Istoriko-demograficheskii analiz* (Moscow: Nauka, 1991).

41. *Kaspiy,* 212 (1899).

42. On the origins of the Baku oil industry, see R. W. Tolf, *The Russian Rockefellers: The Saga of the Nobel Family and the Russian Oil Industry* (Stanford University Press: 1976), 50–108; K. A. Pazhitnov, *Ocherki po istorii bakinskoi neftevydobyvaiushchei promyshlennosti* (Moscow, 1940); S. M. Lisichkin, *Ocherki po istorii razvitiia otechestvennoi neftianoi promyshlennosti* (Moscow, 1954). For a monographic article on the change of the lease system, see M. Ismailov, "Azerbaijan neft sanesinda ijaradarlig sisteminin läghv edilmäsina dair," *ANAzSSR Trudy* 2 (1952): 75–104; John McKay, "Entrepreneurship and the Emergence of the Russian Petroleum Industry, 1813–1881," in Uselding ed., *Research in Economic History: A Research Annual* 8 (Greenwich, 1983). Marat Ibragimov, *Nettianaia promyshlenost' Azerbiadzhana v period imperializma* (Baku: Elm, 1984).

43. On the depletion of the Baku oil, see Daniel Yergin, *The Prize: The Epic Quest for Oil, Money, and Power* (New York: Simon & Schuster, 1991), 132.

44. *Baku po perepisi 22 oktiabria 1903 goda* (Baku, 1905) 30.

45. *The Near East,* August 3, 1920, 199.

46. On the urban growth of Baku, see Audrey Altstadt, *The Azerbaijani Turks: Power and Identity Under Russian Rule* (Stanford: Hoover Institution, 1992), 20–49. See also Ronald G. Suny, *The Baku Commune, 1917–1918: Class and Nationality in the Russian Revolution* (Princeton: Princeton University Press, 1972); I. V. Strigunov, "Baki proletariatinin täshäkkülü mäsäläsinä dair," *ANAzSSR Trudy* 10 (1955): 42–77.

47. Hasan Taqizadeh, "The Background of the Constitutional Movement in Azerbaijan," *MEJ* 14 (1960): 462.

48. Strigunov, "Baki proletariat," 53. On the labor migrations from Iranian Azerbaijan, see also N. K. Belova, *"Ob otkhodnichestvie iz severnogo Irana v kontse XIX veka,"* *Voprosy istorii* 10 (1956): 110–22; Audrey Altstadt, "Muslim Workers and the Labor Movement in Pre-War Baku," in S. M. Akural, *Turkic*

Culture: Continuity and Change (Indiana University Press: 1987), 83–91; Cosroe Chaqueri, *The Soviet Socialist Republic of Iran, 1920–21: Birth of the Trauma* (Pittsburgh: University of Pittsburgh Press, 1994), 24–26.

49. Ahmet Agaoğlu, *Iran ve inkilabi* (Ankara, 1941), 97.

50. G. Pichkian, "Kapitalisticheskie razvitie neftianoi promyshlennosti v Azerbadzhane," *Zakavkazskii Kommunisticheskii Universitet, Istoriia klassovoi bor'by v Zakavkazii* (Tiflis, 1930), 108–10; K. A. Pazhitnov, *Ocherki po istorii bakinskoi neftedobyvaiushchei promyshlennosti* (Moscow-Leningrad: Gospodt-tekhizdat, 1940). For a collection of sources, see ANSSSR, Institut Istorii, *Monopolisticheskii kapital v neftianoi promyshlennosti Rossii, 1883–1914. Dokumenty i materialy* (Moscow-Leningrad, 1961).

51. Dilara Seidzade, *Iz istorii azerbaidzhanskoi burzhuazii v nachale XX veka* (Baku, 1978), 23–38; Sumbatzade, *Promyshlennost'*, 461–64.

52. Altstadt, *Azerbaijani Turks*, 33; on Baku's trade with Iran, see M. A. Musayev, *XIX äsrin sonlarinda Baki shährinin tijaräti (1883–1900 illär)* (Baku: Elm, 1972).

53. For a recent monograph on Taghiyev, see M. Ibragimov, *Predprinimatel'neria deitel'nost' G. Z. Tagieva* (Baku: Elm, 1991); for a contemporary account see A. Novikov, "Zapiski gorodskogo golovy," *Obrazovanie* 9:2 (1904): 126–27. On Taghiyev's activity in Iran, Taqizadeh, "The Background," 461.

CHAPTER 2

1. On the "Russo-Tatar" schools and their students, see N. A. Tairzade, "Chislennost' i sostav uchashchikhsia russkikh uchebnykh zavedenii Azerbaidzhana v 40–50gg XIX veka," *ANAzSSR, Izvestiia, Ser. Ob. N.* 1 (1964), 43–56; on the Gori seminary, A. G. Teregulov, "V Goriiskoi Uchitel'noi Seminarii," *ANAzSSR, Izvestiia* 8 (1945), 69–84.

2. For a detailed analysis of Akhundzadä's plays, see H. W. Brands, *Aserbaidschanische Volksleben und modernistische Tendenz in den Schauspielen Mirza Fathali Ahundundzades* (The Hague: Mouton, 1958); A. Sultanli, *Azärbayjan dramturqiyasinin inkishafi tarihindan* (Baku, 1964).

3. Mirza Fathali Akhundov, *Äsärläri* 2 (Baku, 1961), 44. For a comprehensive discussion of his views on the alphabet reform, see Ingeborg Baldauf, *Schriftreform und Schriftwechsel bei den Muslimischen Russland und Sowjetturken (1850–1937): Ein Symptom ideen-geschichtlicher und kulturpolitischen Entwicklungen* (Budapest: Akademiai Kiado, 1993), 53–96; A. S. Levend, *Türk dilinde gelişme safhalarī* (Ankara, 1949), 171; "Popytki zakavkazskikh muzul'man reformirovat' svoiu azbuku," *Mir Islama* 2 (1913): 831–44; R. Tansel, "Arap harflerinin islahi ve degiştirilmesi hakkinda ilk teşebbüslar ve neticeleri," *TTK Belleten* 46 (1953): 224–49.

4. Akhundov, *Äsärläri* 2, 45–6.

5. On Akhundzadä's influence on Persian thought and literature, see F.

Adamiyat, *Andishaha-Mirza Fath 'Ali Akhunzadeh* (Teheran, 1349); Hamid Algar, *Mirza Malkum Khan: A Study in the History of Iranian Modernism* (Berkeley: University of California Press, 1973), 264–68; A. M. Aghakhi, "O vliianii M. F. Akhundova na razvitie obshchestvennoi mys'li v Irane," *ANAzSSR, Izvestiia, Ser. Ob. N.* 10 (1962), 75–85; H. Mammadzadä, *Mirza Fatali Akhundov va sharg* (Baku: Elm, 1979).

6. Akhundov, *Äsärläri* 2, 233. For a recent discussion of the rise of the Azeri Enlightenment, see E. M. Auch, "Zur Enstehung der aserbaidschanischen Aufklärungsbewegung im 19. Jahrhundert," *Asien, Afrika, Latein Amerika, Sonderheft* 3 (1991): 75–86.

7. For a survey of the nineteenth-century Azeri theater, see G. Mamadli, *Azärbaijan teatrinin salnamäsi (1850–1920)* (Baku, 1975); H. Israfilov, *Azärbaijan dramaturqiyasinin inkishaf problemläri (1890–1920-ji illär)* (Baku: Elm, 1988).

8. *Äkinchi* 14 (1876).

9. On Zardabi, see Z. B. Geiushev, *Mirovozzrenie G. B. Zardabi* (Baku, 1962); see also H. Baykara, *Azerbaycanda yenileşme hareketi* (Ankara, 1966), 132–37; G. Guseinov, *Iz istorii obshchestvennoi i filosofskoi mys'li v Azerbaidzhane* (Baku, 1958), 296–304. On Akinchi's language, see A. H. Orujov, "Äkinchi gazetenin dili haqqinda," *ANAzSSR, Doklady* 2:7 (1947): 410–18.

10. For a Soviet study of Aghayev, see A. Mirahmädov, "Ahmäd bäy Aghayev," *Fikrin Karvani* (Baku, 1984), 80–96. For a Turkish nationalist view, see Akçuraoğlu, "Türkchülük," 419–34.

11. *Nouvelle revue* (Paris 1893) 389.

12. *Nouvelle revue* (Paris 1893) 393.

13. For a monograph on Pan-Islamism see T. Z. Tunaya, *Islamcilik cereyani* (Istanbul, 1962). For a Soviet discussion of its history in Russia, see A. Arsharuni, Kh. Gabidullin, *Ocherki panislamizma i pantiurkizma v Rossii* (Moscow, 1931).

14. Nikki Keddie, *An Islamic Response to Imperialism: Political and Religious Writings of Sayyid Jamal ad-din "al-Afghani": A Political Biography* (Berkeley: California University Press, 1972).

15. Taqizadeh, "The Background," 457.

16. On the educational activity in Tabriz at the turn of the century, see AzSSR, EA, *Jänubi Azärbaijan Tarikhinin Ocherki (1828–1917)* (Baku: Elm, 1985), 207–18; Taqizadeh, "The Background," 462–63; Mangol Bayat, *Iran's First Revolution. Shi'ism and the Constitutional Revolution of 1905–1909* (New York: Oxford University Press, 1991), 98–99.

17. For a monographic work on Gasprinskii, see Mehmet Saray, *Gasprali Ismail bey, (1851–1914)* (Ankara, Türk Kültürünün Araştirma Enstitüsü, 1987). For a recent collection of studies on Gasprinskii, see *Türk Kültürü* 337:8 (special issue) (1991), 29. See also Allan Fisher, *The Crimean Tatars* (Stanford:

Stanford University Press, 1978), 100–6. Serge Zenkovky, *Pan-Turkism and Islam in Russia* (Cambridge: Harvard University Press, 1960), 24–36.

18. On the nineteenth-century post-Äkinchi press, see Alexandre Bennigsen and Chantal Lemercier-Quelquejay, *La presse et les mouvements nationaux chez les musulmans de Russie avant 1920* (Paris: Mouton, 1960), 27–30; D. Hajibeyli, "The Origins of the National Press in Azerbayjan," *AR* 25:88 (1930): 758–67.

19. *Käshkül* 22 (1891).

20. On Huseynzadä, see R. Kamaloghlu, "Turk dünyasinin boyuk ideologu," *Azärbaijan:* March 23, 1991; Yusuf Akchuraoghlu (Akçuraoglu), "Türkchülük," *Turk yili* (1928): 412–19. For a Soviet view, see Äziz Mirähmadov, "Alibäy Huseynzadä," *Fikrin karvani* 63–79.

21. Ziya Gökalp, *The Principles of Turkism* (Leiden, 1968), 5–6; U. Heyd, *Foundations of Turkish Natonalism: The Life and Teachings of Ziya Gökalp* (London, 1950), 107–8; E. B. Sapolyo, *Ziya Gökalp, Ittihad ve Terakki ve meşrutiyet tarihi* (Istanbul, 1943).

22. *Hayat* (Baku), June 7, 1905.

23. For a recent monograph on Azeri liberalism, see D. B. Seidzade, *Azerbaidzhanskie deputaty v Gosudarstvennoi Dume Rossii* (Baku: Azerb. Gos. Izd-vo, 1991). Consult also the same author's *Iz istorii azerbaidzhaskoi burzhuazii,* 46–62.

24. Mammad Ämin Räsulzadä, "Vospominaniia o I. V. Staline," *Vostochnyi Ekspress* 1 (Moscow: 1993): 42; on the rise of Himmät, see also Sultan Majid Äfandiyev, "Himmätin yaranmasi," *Azärbaijan elmi savhasi* 1:2 (1932), 83–89.

25. For the most recent biography of Narimanov, see T. Akhmedov, *Nariman Narimanov* (Baku: Iazichy, 1988). For a post-Soviet critical evaluation of Narimanov, see Aydin Balayev, "Plennik idei ili politicheskii slepets," *Azarbayjan* June 20, 1991.

26. For a survey of Himmät's history, see Tadeusz Swietochowski, "The Himmät Party: Socialism and the Nationality Question in Russian Azerbaijan, 1904–1920," *CMRS* 19 (1978): 119–42.

CHAPTER 3

1. U.S. National Archives, RG 256, *Special Memorandum* "The Nationality Problem in the Caucasus," Inquiry Doc. 770, 9.

2. Altstadt, *The Azerbaijani Turks,* 43.

3. On tsardom's confrontation with Armenian nationalism, see C. J. Walker, *Armenia: The Survival of a Nation* (New York: St. Martin's Press, 1980), 69–72; S. Atamian, *The Armenian Community: The Historical Development of a Social and Ideological Conflict* (New York: Philosophical Library, 1959), 114–15.

4. For accounts of the fighting, see L. Villari, *The Fire and Sword in the Caucasus* (London, 1906); J. D. Henry, *Baku: An Eventful History* (London,

1905); Walker, *Armenia, 73–81*. For an Azeri view, see M. S. Ordubadi, *Ganli Illar* (Baku: Karabagh Yardim Komitäsi, 1991).

5. Atamian, *The Armenian Community*, 116. For a similar view expressed in a contemporary report, see *Armenia* 2 (1906): 30–31.

6. For the data on the victims, see Richard Hovannisian, *Armenia on the Road to Independence, 1918* (Berkeley: California University Press, 1969), 264; E. Aknouni, *Political Persecutions: Armenian Prisoners of the Caucasus* (New York, 1911), 30.

7. Kasravi, A., *Tarikh-i mashruteh-yi Iran*, 146. The manuscript of the annotated translation was kindly made available to me by Evan Siegal.

8. On the rise of the Difai, see N. Keykurun, *Azerbaycan istiklal mücadelesinin hatiralari* (Istanbul, 1964), 10–15; Altstadt, *Azerbaijani Turks* 67–8; V. A. Lerner, "K voprosu o deiatel'nosti v Azerbaidzhane burzhuazno-natsionalisticheskoi organizatsii 'Difai'," *ANAzSSR, Doklady* 35:1 (1979): 92–97.

9. U. Hajibakov, "Otkrytoe pis'mo kavkazskim musul'manam," reprinted in *Khazar* 1 (1990): 8.

10. For recent monographs of the Iranian constitutional revolution, see M. Bayat, *Iran's First Revolution: Shi'ism and the Constitutional Revolution of 1905–1909* (New York: Oxford Univerity Press, 1991); Ervand Abrahamian, *Iran Between Two Revolutions* (Princeton: Princeton University Press, 1982), 50–92; for a detailed survey, see A. Kasravi, *Tarikh-i mashruteh-yi Iran*.

11. Taqizadeh, "The Background," 463.

12. On the rise of the socialist movement in Iranian Azerbaijan, see T. A. Ibrahimov, *Iran Kommunist Partiyasinin yaranmasi* (Baku, 1963), 78; S. Ravasani, *Soujetrepublik Gilan: Die sozialdemokratische Bewegung in Iran seit Ende des 19Jh. bis 1922* (Berlin, n.d.), 134–36; A. U. Martirosov, "Novye materialy o sotsial-demokraticheskom dvizhenii v Irane v 1905–1911 godakh," *Narody Azii i Afriki* 2 (1973): 116–22.

13. Mammäd Jäfär, *Azärbayjanda romantizm* (Baku: Izd-vo ANAzSSR, 1966), 141. For a detailed discussion of the links between Russian Azerbaijan and Iran in the period, see AzSSR, EA, *Jänubi Azärbaijan ocherki*, 112–87; see also Bayat, *Iran's First Revolution* 84–105.

14. Kasravi, *Tarikh-i mashruteh-yi Iran*, 194.

15. Kasravi, *Tarikh-i mashruta-yi Iran*, 194–95. For monographic works on the impact of Mollah Nasr al-din on the Iranian public, see V. Kliashtorna, "Zhurnal Molla Nasraddin i persidskaia politicheskaia satira perioda revoliutsii 1905–1911 godov," ANSSR, Institut Vostokovedeniia, *Kratkie soobshcheniia* 27:10 (1958): 31–41; M. Alizade, "Pervaia russkaia revoliutsiia i persidskaia demokraticheskaia literatura," *Az. GU, Uchenye zapiski* 10 (1955): 119–71.

16. For a recent monograph on Sattar Khan and the Tabriz uprising, see

N. Hasanov, *Oyanmish Tabriz va Sattarkhan* (Baku: Az. Dov. Nashr, 1986); see also A. S. Sumbatzadä ed., *Qorkämli ingilabchi Sattar Khan* (Baku, 1972); for an eyewitness account, see I. Amir-Khizi, *Qiam-i Azarbayjan va Sattar Khan* (Tabriz, 1960); M. R. Afriyat ed., *Sardar milli Sattar Khan* (1968).

17. E. G. Browne, *The Persian Revolution, 1905–1909* (London: Cambridge University Press, 1914), 250; on the threats of separatism, see also Abrahamian, *Iran Between Two Revolutions,* 91; on Ottoman involvement under Abdulhamid, see Kasravi, *Tarikh-i mashruteh-yi Iran,* 424–26; on Ottoman involvement under the Young Turks, see Ishtiaq Ahmad, *Anglo-Iranian Relations, 1905–1919* (Bombay: Aligarh University, 1974), 78–79; on Iranian émigré activities in Turkey, see "Une source pour l'histoire de la revolution iranienne de 1905–1911 et de la communaute iranienne d'Istanboul," *Toplumbilim* 1 (1992): 54–79.

18. C. Chaqueri, "The Role and Impact of Armenian Intellectuals in Iranian Politics, 1905–1911," *Armenian Review* 2 (Summer 1988): 9.

19. For a contemporary account of the participation of the Transcaucasians in Tabriz fighting see V. Tria, *Kavkazskie sotsialdemokraty v persidskoi revoliutsii* (Paris: Izd-vo Sotsialdemokrat, 1910); Bor-Ramenskii, "K voprosu o roli bol'shevikov Zakavkaz'ia v iranskoi revoliutsii 1905–1911 godov," *Istorik-marksist* 11 (1940): 84–99.

20. E. G. Browne, *The Press and Poetry of Modern Persia* (Cambridge, 1914): 52.

21. On Räsulzadä's activities in the Iranian Revolution, see F. Adamiyat, *Fekr-i demokrasi-yi ejtima'i dar nahzat-i mashrutiyat-i Iran,* Tehran (n.d.), 155–285. Abrahamian, *Iran Between,* 105. For an updated biography of Rasulzada see *Odlar yurdu,* no. 8 (August 1990) 3–4. For a biography of Amuoghli, see A. Hesabi, *Mujahid-i bozorg Haidar Amuoghli* (Teheran: Nashriyyat Hizb-i Tudeh), 1327; see also: H. Nava'i, "Haidar Amuoghli va Muhammad Amin Rasulzadeh," *Majalleh-yi yadegar* no. 1/2 (1948): 43–67.

22. Abrahamian, *Iran Between Two Revolutions* 247.

23. Rasulzade, "Vospominaniia o I. V. Staline," *Vostochnyi Ekspress* 1 (Moscow 1993): 49.

24. M. W. Shuster, *The Strangling of Persia* (New York, 1912), 220.

25. On Russo-Azerbaijani trade, see Sh. Tagiyeva, *Natsional'no osvoboditel'noe dvizhenie v iranskom Azerbaidzhane v 1917–1920 gg* (Baku: Izdvo ANAzSSR, 1956), 32; on the labor migration after 1911, see Issawi, *The Economic History of Iran,* 51; for the biographies of prominent Iranian Azerbaijanis of the period, see M. Mojtahidi, *Rejal-i Azarbaijan dar asr-i mashrutiyyat* (Teheran, 1327).

26. For a monograph on the Young Turks' Revolution, see Feroz Ahmad, *The Young Turks: The Committee of Union and Progress in Turkish Pol-*

itics, 1908–1914 (New York: Oxford University Press, 1969); J. Landau, *Pan-Turkism in Turkey: A Study in Irredentism* (London, 1981).

27. Alakpär Sabir, *Hophopnama* (Baku: Elmler Akademiyasi Nashriyyati, 1962), 171.

28. On Oghusianism, see Z. Gökalp, *The Principles of Turkism* (Leiden: Brill, 1968), 17.

29. *Türk yurdu* 14 (1912): 419.

30. *Türk yurdu* 17 (1912): 545.

31. I. I. Vorontsov-Dashkov, *Vsepoddanneishii otchet za vosem' let upravleniia Kavkazskim Kraem generala ad'iutanta grafa Vorontsova-Dashkova* (St. Petersburg, 1913), 9.

32. On founding of the Musavat, see M. A. Resuloğlu, "Musavat Partisinin kuruluşu," *Musavat Bülteni* 4 (1962): 9–14; M. Aliyev, "Azärbaijan Milli 'Musavat' Khalq Partiyasi. Yaranmasinin 80 illiyi garshisinda." *Odlar yurdu* 14 (June 1991).

33. Mehmet Mirza-Bala, *Milli Azerbaycan hareketi: Milli Azerbaycan Musavat firkasinin tarihi* (Berlin, 1938), 64; Mirza Daud Guseinov, *Tiurskaia Demokraticheskaia Partiia federalistov v proshlom i nastoiashchem* (Tiflis, 1927), 9.

34. I. Ratgauzer, "Sotsial'naia sushchnost' musavatizma," in *Pervaia vsesoiuznaia konferentsiia istorikov-marksistov* (Moscow, 1930), 501–20.

35. *Diriliq* 3 (1914).

36. *Füyüzat* 21 (1907).

37. For a recent discussion of the rise of linguistic particularisms among Turkic communities of Russia, see Nadir Devlet, *Rusya Türklerinin milli mücadele tarihi (1905–1917)* (Ankara: Türk Kültürünu Araştirma Enstitusu, 1985), 63–71, 180–216. See also Baldauf, *Schriftreform*, 110–21.

38. "Ana dili," *Molla Nasr al-din* 22 (1913).

39. *Shälälä*, nos. 21, 37 (1913).

40. Zenkovsky, *Pan-Turkism,* 127–28; for the discussion of the political goals of Turkey in the war against Russia, see G. Jäschke, "Der Turanismus der Jungturken," *WI* 23:1–2 (1941): 55–69; also Stanford Shaw, *History of the Ottoman Empire and Modern Turkey* 2 (Cambridge: Cambridge University Press, 1988), 314.

41. On World War I at the Caucasus Front, see A. E. D. Allen and Muratoff, *Caucasian Battlefields* (Cambridge: Cambridge University Press, 1953); E. F. Ludshuveit, *Turtsiia v gody pervoi mirovoi voiny* (Moscow: Izd-vo Moskovskogo Universiteta, 1966); W. Bihl, *Die Kaukasuspolitik der Mittelmachte: Ihre Basis in der Orient-Politik und ihre Aktionen, 1914–1917* (Vienna, 1975).

42. For recent works discussing Ottoman policy toward the Armenians in 1915 see Walker, *Armenia, 197–240;* for a differing view, see Shaw, *History of the Ottoman Empire* (vol. 2), 315–17.

43. On the volunteers from Iranian Azerbaijan who fought for the Ottomans, see, Kasravi, *Tarikh-i hejdah saleh,* 199–200.

44. On the significance of Iranian Azerbaijan for the Ottoman strategic planning, see U.S. National Archives, RG 256, 8891.00/14 (December 23, 1918). For the survey of 1915 military operations in Iranian Azerbaijan, see Allen and Muratoff, *Caucasian Battlefields,* 296–99.

45. Tekin Alp, *Turkismus und Pan-Turkismus* (Berlin, 1915), 89.

46. U.S. National Archives, RG 891.0014, *W. I. Westerman to E. L. Dresel [correspondence]* (February 21, 1919). On Pan-Islamic Ottoman propaganda in Iran, see A. A. Sepehr, *Iran dar jang-i bozorg* (Teheran: 1956), 237–75; for examples, consult *Kaveh* (Berlin) 12, 15 (1916).

47. On the mission of Aslan Khoiskii, see Jäschke, "Der Turanismus der Jungturken," 16; Bihl, *Die Kaukasuspolitik,* 70–71.

48. *Achiq söz* 1 (1915).

49. *Pervaia vsesoiuznaia konferentsiia istorikov-marksistov* 512. On the Ganja Federalists and their unification with Musavat, see N. Keykurun, "Türk Ademi Merkeziyet Firkasinin faaliyeti ve Musavat Partisiyle birleşme-si," *Musavat Bülteni* 4 (1962): 19–21.

50. Mirza-Bala, *Musavat,* 85–86.

51. For a recent discussion of the Ittihad's leader, see "Karabäy Karabäkov," *Odlar yurdu* 11 (1990). On Ittihad, see also D. B. Guliev, *Bor'ba Kommunisticheskoi Partii za osushchestvlenie leninskoi natsional'noi politiki v Azerbaidzhane* (Baku, 1970), 143–44; Mirza-Bala, *Musavat,* 155. For the results of the elections to the Constituent Assembly of Russia, see Hovannisian, *Armenia on the Road,* 108.

52. On the rise of Ädälät, see Ibrahimov, *Iran Kommunist,* 121–33; Ravasani, *Sowjetrepublik Gilan,* 248–51; for an account of a founding member, see Sayyid Jafar Pishevari, *Sechilmish Äsärläri* (n.d.), 371–404.

53. KPAz. Institut Istorii Partii, *Bol'sheviki v bor'be za pobedu sotsialis-ticheskoi revoliutsii v Azerbaidzhane. Dokumenty i materialy, 1917–1918 gg* (Baku, 1957), 1. On the rebirth of Himmät see also "O deiatel'nosti organizat-sii Gummet" in Nariman Narimanov, *Izbrannye proizvedeniia* (Baku: Azerb. Gos. Izd-vo, 1988) 195–97. For a survey of Himmät's history, see Swieto-chowski, "The Himmät Party."

54. Hovannisian, *Armenia on the Road,* 108.

55. Kasravi, *Tarikh-i hejdah saleh,* 705 (713).

56. Kasravi, *Zandegani-yi man* (Teheran, 1946), 86; see also Abrahamian, *Iran Between Two Revolutions,* 219.

57. M. A. Gilak, *Tarikh-i Enqelab-i Jangal* (Rasht, 1371), 15. Shövkät Taghiyeva, *1920-ji il Tabriz üsyani* (Baku: AzSSR Elmler Akademiyasi), 44.

58. For Ussubäkov's statement, see Iurii Semenov, "Zakavkazskaia

respublika," *Vozrozhdenie* 1 (Paris 1949), 146; for the Austrian report, see also Bihl, *Die Kaukasuspolitik* (1917–1918), 235.

59. For a discussion of the Transcaucasian Federation, see Hovannisian, *Armenia on the Road* 159–85; for a collection of official records, see Gruziia, *Dokumenty i materialy po vneshnei politike Zakavkazia i Gruzii* (Tiflis, 1919).

60. On the March 1918 massacre of the Baku Muslims, see Stepan Shaumian, *Izbrannye proizvedeniia* 2, 209. This figure differs sharply from the Azerbaijani claims of 12,000 lives lost. See *La Republique de l'Azerbaidjan du Caucase* (Paris, 1919), 19. For an estimate of 600 Iranians killed, see Bihl, *Die Kaukasuspolitik* (1917–1918), 71.

61. See Suny, *The Baku Commune*, 214–33; Hovannisian, *Armenia on the Road*.

62. For monographic works on the Baku Commune, see Suny, *The Baku Commune*; for a Soviet treatment, see Suren Shaumian, *Bakinskaia Kommuna* (Baku, 1927).

CHAPTER 4

1. On the debate over federation with the Ottoman State, see A. Şeih-ul-Islam, "Azerbaycan nasil kuruldu," *Azerbaycan* 2 (1952): 6.

2. For the Russian text of the declaration, see Aydin Balaev, *Azerbaidzhanskoe natsional'no-demokraticheskoe dvizhenie, 1917–1920 gg* (Baku: Elm, 1992), 28.

3. *Jangal* 24 (1918). The copy of the article was kindly supplied to the author by Cosroe Chaqueiry.

4. G. Jäschke, "Der türkisch-aserbaidschanisch Freundschaftsvetrag vom 4 Juni 1918," *Vorderasien: Studien zur Auslandkunde* 1 (1944): 64. See also Mammäd Ämin Räsulzadä, *Azerbaycan Cumhuriyeti*, 61.

5. On the Army of Islam, see K. Rüştü, "Büyük harpte Kafkas yollarinda 5-nci piyade firkasi," *Askeri mecmua*, no. 92 (Tarih kismi, no. 32) (1934); see also Allen and Muratov, *Caucasian Battlefields*, 470.

6. Rüştü, "Büyük harpte," 5.

7. For details on the Ottoman-Azerbaijani crisis of June 1918, see "Istoriia vozniknoveniia Azerbaidzhanskoi Respubliki. Iz adresa- kalendaria Azerbaidzhanskoi Respubliki," *Khazar* 2:3 (1990), 120–21; see also Balaev, *Dvizhenie*, 40; Mirza-Bala, *Musavat*, 148; Guliev, *Bor'ba komunistichskoi partii*, 74–75.

8. Cosroe Chaqueri, *The Revolutionary Movement in Iran Versus Great Britain and Soviet Russia* (Florence: Mazdak, 1979), 985.

9. On the cirumstances of Khiabani's exile, see Atabaki, *Azerbaijan*, 48; Zurrer, *Kaukasien 1918–1921*, 85.

10. On the 1918 Ottoman occupation of Tabriz, see Kasravi, *Tarikh-i hejdah saleh*, 261; on the language and literary impact of the Ottoman occupa-

tion, see Berengian, *Azeri and Persian Works*; for a contemporary account of the Ottoman policy in Iranian Azerbaijan, see *Der neue Orient* 3 (1918): 378.

11. On Dunsterville's expedition to Baku, see L. C. Dunsterville, *The Adventures of Dunsterforce* (London, 1932); see also A. H. Arslanian, "Dunsterville's Adventure: A Reappraisal," *IJMES* 12 (1982): 199–216.

12. Kazemzadeh, *The Struggle*, 143–44, gives the total of 9,988 persons killed, the figure based on Armenian sources. Other authors give much higher figures: Korganoff, p. 204, estimates the number of killed at 15,000 to 30,000; Walker, p. 261, at 20,000. For works on the September 15 massacre in Baku, see also National Archives, RG 256, "The Caucasus" *Confidential Volume*, "Massacres in Baku," 861.K.00/5.

13. For hypotheses on the Ottoman intentions, see Bihl, *Die Kaukasuspolitik* 2, 229–35; see also S. S. Aydemir, *Makedonyadan Orta Asyaya* (Istanbul: Remzi Kitabevi, 1978) 3, 426–28.

14. E. Kurtulan, "Türk ordusunun Azerbaycanda kalmasi meselesi," *Azerbaycan* 4:6 (1964); Mirza-Bala, *Musavat*, 149–50.

15. Kasravi, *Zandegani-yi man*, 89.

16. On the views of the British military on the need for the strategic defence of India, see UK FO, "Outline of the Events in Transcaucasia," 371/1 7729, May 31, 1922; for a Western proposal of uniting North Azerbaijan with Iran, see National Archives, RG.256.86900/00/2, Memorandum of Samuel Edelman, December 12, 1918.

17. UK FO, CAB 45/107.

18. On the Azerbaijani-Armenian agreement on Nagorno-Karabagh, see Hovannisian, *The Republic of Armenia* 2, 195, 211.

19. On the British policy on Azerbaijan, see Richard M. Ullman, *Anglo-Soviet Relations, 1917–1921, vol. 1, Intervention and War* (Princeton: Princeton University Press, 1961), 78–78; see also UK FO "Outline of Events" 371/E 8378/308; U. S. National Archives, RG 256, 861, K. 00/5, "The Caucasus," and RG 256, 184.02102/6 App. A, Harbord Report. For a Soviet view, see A. Raevskii, *Angliiskie "druz'ia" i musavatskie "patrioty"* (Baku, 1927).

20. Mirza-Bala, *Musavat*, 151; see also A. Baikov, "Vospominaniia o revoliutsii v Zakavkaz'ii," *Arkhiv russkoi revoliutsii* 9 (1923): 91–194.

21. On the Azerbaijani Parliament, see Nasibzadä, *Azärbaijan Demokratik*, 71–83; see also V. Chiragzade, "Deiatel'nost' parlamenta Azerbaidzhanskoi Demokraticheskoi Respubliki (1918 -1920)," *Novruz* 7/23 (1991).

22. For the names of the ministers of all Azerbaijani cabinets, see Nasibzadä, *Azärbaijan Demokratik*, 87–88.

23. Balaev, *Dvizhenie*, 40.

24. For extensive excerpts from Räsulzadä's declaration, see Mirza-Bala, *Musavat*, 159–64.

25. Baikov, "Vospominaniia," 156.

26. Mirza-Bala, *Musavat*, 68, 87.

27. On the establishment of the Baku University see, A. M. Atakishiev, *Istoriia Azerbaidzhanskogo Gosudarstvennogo Universiteta* (Baku: Izd-vo Azerbaidzhanskogo Universiteta, 1989), 28–60. On the alphabet reform projects, see Baldauf, *Schriftreform*, p. 365.

28. For a recent discussion of the Azerbaijani army, see N. Nasibzadä, "AKP vä milli ordu mäsäläsi," *Azarbaijan* 10:11 (1991); see also E. Kurtulan, "Azerbaycan ordu teşkilati," *Azerbaycan* 7:8 (1954): 13–15; Mirza-Bala, *Musavat*, 163.

29. Baikov, "Vospominania," 174.

30. Parvin Darabadi, *Voennye problemy politicheskoi istorii Azerbaidzhana nachala XX veka* (Baku: Elm, 1991), 132.

31. Narimanov, *Izbrannye*, 222.

32. UK FO, "Report on the Republics of Transcaucasia," 371/3662, May 12, 1919.

33. Republic of Azerbaijan, *Economic and Financial Situation*, 7; For Western views of Azerbaijan's economic potential, see UK FO, 371/3662/72735; National Archives, RG 256, 184.011602/2.

34. Republic of Azerbaijan, *Economic and Financial Situation*, 9.

35. UK FO, "Outline of Events," 13, 371/E 8378/808.

36. *Claims of Persia Before the Conference of the Preliminaries of Peace at Paris* (Paris, 1919), 9.

37. For Topchibashev's report, see A. Raevskii, *Musavatskoe pravitel'stvo na versal'skoi konferentsii. Doneseniia predsedatelia azerbaidzhanskoi musavatskoi delegatsii* (Baku, 1930), 50.

38. Ishtiaq, *Anglo-Iranian Relations*, 320.

39. UK FO, November 13, 1919 371/152743.

40. UK FO, November 19, 1919, 371/155188.

41. UK FO, November 19, 1919, 371/155188.

42. *Azerbaijan. Arkhiv Noveishei Istorii, Fond 211s, Edn. 99*, November 24, 1919.

43. Ishtiaq, *Anglo-Iranian Relations*, 219.

44. A. A. Cruinkshank, "The Young Turk Challenge in Postwar Turkey," *MEJ* 22:26 (Winter 1968): 31–46.

45. UK FO, "Outline of Events," 19, 371/E 8378/808. On the Soviet-Kemalist rapproachement, see G. Jaschke, "La role du communisme dans les relations russo-turque," *Orient* 2:26 (1963): 31–46; Richard Hovannissian, "Armenia and the Caucasus in the Genesis of the Soviet-Turkish Entente," *IJMES* 4:2 (1973): 227–92.

46. Kazim Karabekir, *Istiklal harbimiz* (Istanbul), 328–30.

47. National Archives, RG 184, 01.602/191/2, Bristol to Churchill, April 11, 1919.

48. Karabekir, *Istiklal*, 466–67.

49. U.S. National Archives, RG 184, 01602/23, Report on Transcaucasia, April 15, 1919.

50. Narimanov, *Izbrannye* 2, 185.

51. Guliev, *Bor'ba*, 284.

52. Ia. Ratgauzer, *Bor'ba za sovetskii Azerbaijan* (Baku, 1928), 61. On the dispute in the Kraikom, see A. G. Karaev, *Iz nedavnogo proshlogo* (Baku: Bakinskii Rabochii, 1926), 54–55.

53. KPAz Institut Istorii Partii, *Ocherki Istorii KPAz*, 324.

54. KPAz Institut Istorii Partii, *Bor'ba za pobedu sotsialisticheskoi revoliutsii v Azerbaidzhane. Dokumenty i materialy* 314 (Baku: Izd-vo ANAzSSR, 1957), 262.

55. N. Narimanov, *Izbrannye*, 205.

56. KPAz Institut Istorii Partii, *Ocherki Istorii KPAz*, 326–57.

57. For documentary evidence of the appointment of Serebrovskii, see H. Alibayli, "Arkhivlar achilir," *Azadliq* 8:4 (1990). On the Kavbiuro, see R. Pipes, *The Formation of the Soviet Union: Communism and Nationalism, 1917–1923* (Cambridge: Harvard University Press, 1964), 224.

58. For the full text, see Karabekir, *Istiklal*, 610. On the rise of the Turkish Communist organization in Baku, see G. S. Harris, *The Origins of Communism in Turkey* (Stanford: Hoover Institution, 1967), 58. For a Soviet source on the role of Turkish Communists in the downfall of the Azerbaijan Republic, see ANSSSR, *Internatsionalisty* (Moscow: Nauka, 1971), 216–25.

59. *Bakinskii Rabochii* 93 (1925): 4/23. For a detailed discussion of the Republic's downfall, see Swietochowski, *Russian Azerbaijan*, 165–90; Mammad Amin Räsulzadä, *Azarbaijan Jumhuriyyeti* (Baku: Elm, 1991), 66–78.

60. Iskenderov, *Iz istorii Kommunisticheskoi Partii Azerbaidzhana za pobedu sovetskoi vlasti* (Baku: Azgosizdat, 1958), 440.

61. KPAz Institut Istorii Partii, *Bor'ba za pobedu sotsialisticheskoi revoliutsii,* 541, 461–62.

62. For the full text of the declaration, see Humayounpour, *L'affaire d'Azerbaidjan*, 34.

63. Kasravi, *Tarikh-i hijdah sal*, 110. On the Public Commiitee, see Sh. Taghiyeva, *Natsional'no-osvoboditel'noe dvizhenie*, 85–86.

64. A. Azari, *Qiyam-i Shaikh Muhammad Khiabani dar Tabriz* (Tabriz: 1362), 465.

65. Chaqueri, *The Revolutionary Movement*, 982.

66. Kasravi, *Zandegani-yi man*, 110–13.

67. Shaikh Muhammad Khiabani (Berlin: Iranshahr, 1926), 56.

68. On Khiabani's position toward Ädälät, see Cosroe Chaqueri, *Le movement communiste en lian* (Florence: 1979), 120–28.

69. Shövkät Taghiyeva, *1920-ji il Tabriz usyani* (Baku: Elm, 1990), 93.

70. Berengian, *Azeri and Persian Literary Works*, 72–76; see ibid. for the discussion of Taqi Khan and Azeri-Turkish modernism. For a monographic work on literary manifestations of the Khiabani movement see M. Manafi. "Khiabani harakäti vä dövrun ijtimai-siyasi mäsäläläri," in *AzSSR, EA, XX asr Jänubi Azärbaijan ädäbiyyatinda demokratik ideyalar (1900–1985)* (Baku: Elm, 1990), 62–89.

71. Tagieva, *Natsional'no-osvoboditel'noe dvizhenie*, 107.

72. N. S. Fatemi, *Diplomatic History of Persia 1917–1923*, 247.

73. Azari, *Qiam-i Khiabani*, 538.

74. For further discussion of Khiabani and the 1920 Tabriz uprising, see A. Vishnegradova, "Revoliutsionnoe dvizhenie v persidskom Azerbaidzhane," *Novyi vostok* 2 (1922): 249–55; G. Nollau and H. J. Wiehe, *Russia's South Flank* (London, 1963), 156–58. *Shaikh Muhammad Khiabani* (Berlin: Iranshahr, 1926).

75. V. Abbasov, "Razdum'ia v zale vystavki," *Azarbaijan* 27 (1990).

76. Näsib Näsibzadä, "Ganja Üsyani," *Azärbaijan* 7:12 (1990); for a Soviet view of the Ganja uprising, see Kadishev, *Interventsiia i grazhadnskaia voina v Zakavkaz'e* (Moscow, 1960), 294.

77. Abbasov, *Razdum'ia*. On the executions of the army officers, see also Gasan B. Agaev, "Pis'mo Enver Pashe," *Kavkaz* 9 (1937), 25–29.

78. Kadishev, *Interventsia*, 292.

79. Kadishev, *Interventsia*, 301.

80. For the overview of the 1920 anti-Soviet uprisings, see Kadishev, *Interventsia*, 304–51; for the non-Soviet view, see Allen and Muratoff, *Caucasian Battlefields*, 511.

81. Kadishev, *Interventsia*, 350; see also Guliev, *Bor'ba*, 552.

82. For documentary evidence on activities of the underground organizations, see also the same author's *Gänj Azär (Istintaq materiällari üzre)* (Baku, 1993).

CHAPTER 5

1. *Zhizn' natsional'nostei* 18:70 (1920).

2. For a recent collection of documents on the Baku Congress, see John Riddell, ed., *To See the Dawn: Baku, 1920: First Congress of the Peoples of the East* (New York: Pathfinder, 1993).

3. *Atatürkün söylev ve demeçleri* 2 (Istanbul: Maarif Matbaasi, 1945), 18.

4. I. Baghirov, *Iz istorii sovetsko-turetskikh otnoshenii v 1920–1922 gg.* (Baku, 1965), 87.

5. Richard Hovannisian, "Caucasian Armenia Between Imperial and Soviet Rule: The Interlude of National Independence," in Suny, *Transcaucasia*, 291. On the Nakhichevan dispute, see also Altstadt, *The Azerbaijani Turks*, 127–28.

6. KPAz Institut Istorii Partii, *K istorii obrazovaniia Nagorno-Karabakhskoi Avtonomnoi Oblasti Az.SSR., 1918–1925. Dokumenty i materialy* (Baku: Azerbaidzhanskoe Gos. Izdatel'stvo, 1989), 41.

7. Ibid., 64.

8. *Azerbaijan* (Baku) 5 (1989). For a glasnost-period Soviet discussion of conflicts within the CPAz during the 1920s, see "Partiya häyäti: 20-ji illärin problemleri," *Kommunist* (Baku) August 24, 1989.

9. Pipes, *The Formation of the Soviet Union*, 252.

10. *Azärbaijan* (Baku), nos. 9-10, 4/4(1990).

11. For a discussion of the surrogate proletariat notion, G. Massell, *The Surrogate Proletariat: Moslem Women and Revolutionary Strategies in Soviet Central Asia: 1919–1929* (Princeton: Princeton University Press, 1974), 93–123. For a discussion of the Bolsheviks' policy toward the Muslim intelligentsia, see A. Bennigsen and C. Lemercier-Quelquejay, *Islam in the Soviet Union* (New York, 1967), 123–29.

12. *Odlar yurdu* (Baku) (August 1990). On the Soviet nationality policies toward the Muslims, see Tadeusz Swietochowski, "Islam and Nationality in Tsarist Russia and the Soviet Union," in *Soviet Nationality Policies*, H. Huttenbach, ed. (London: Massell, 1990), 221–34.

13. Ziya Buniatov, "Pervye poselentsy sovetskikh kontslagerei," *Tarikh* 3 (1990).

14. For the discussion of the national contract on the scale of the Soviet Union, see B. Nahaylo and V. Svoboda, *Soviet Disunion: A History of the Nationalities Problem in the USSR* (New York: Macmillan, 1990), 44–60. On the beginnings of korenizatsiia, see George Liber, "Korenizatsiia: Restructuring Soviet Nationality Policy in the 1920's," *Ethnic and Racial Studies* 14:1 (1991): 15–23.

15. Joseph Stalin, *Works* 5 (Moscow, 1953), 263.

16. For the full text of the report by the head of the Azerbaijan GPU, see B. Rafiev, *Gänch Azär (Instintaq materiallär üzre)*, Baki Azärbaijan Dövlet Nashriyyat, 1993, 39. On the Musavatist prisoners in the Solovki Islands, see "Solovkide sürgünlerimiz haqqinda," *Azeri Turk* 12 (1928): 4–6.

17. Azade Ayşe Rorlich, "The 'Ali Bayramov' Club, the Journal Sharg Gadini, and the Socialization of Azeri Women: 1920–30," *CAS* 5, 3:4 (1986): 221–39; see also R. R. Ragimova, "Nachalo sozdaniia tvorcheskikh literaturnykh organizatsii v Azerbaidzhane v pervye gody sotsialisticheskogo stroitel'stva, 1920–1927," *AN AzSSR, Izvestiia Ser. Its. Fil.Pr.*, 1 (1987): 18–26; Audrey Altstadt, "Azärbaijanda 'mädäni ingilab'," *Azärbaijan: adabi-badii jurnal* 9:10 (1993): 79–82.

18. J. M. Väkilov, "1920–46ji illärda Azärbaijan SSR-in Sovet-Iran alagalarinda ishtiraki," *Az.SSSR Elmler Akademiyasi, Jänubi Azärbayjan tarikhi mäsäläläri* (Baku, 1989), 6–17.

19. Mammäd Ämin Rasulzadä, *Chaghdash Azärbayjan tarikhi* (Baku: Gänjliq, 1991), 95. For a recent discussion of Khanbudagov, see L. Polonskii, "Inakomyslie," *Bakinskii Rabochii* 5:6 (1989).

20. A. Atakishiev, *Istoriia Azerbaidzhanskogo Gosudarstvennogo Universiteta*, 149.

21. Ibid., 153.

22. For a recent and comprehensive monograph on the alphabet reform, see Baldauf, *Schriftreform*. For earlier works, see Ettore Rossi, "Questione dell' alfabetto per le lingue turche" *OM* 7 (1927): 295–310; J. Castagne, "La latinisation de l'alphabete turc dans les republiques turco-tatares de l'URSS," *Revue des etudes islamiques* 1 (1927): 321–53; G. Imart, "Le mouvement de 'latinisation' en URSS," *CMRS* 4 (1967) 223–39. On Aghamalioghli, see G.Imart, "Un intellectuel azerbaidjanais face a la Revolution de 1917: Samad Aga Agamalioglu," *CMRS* 8:4 (1967): 528–59.

23. Castagne, "La latinisation," 326. On the Turcology Congress, see Baldauf, *Schriftreform*, 398–458.

24. ANAzSSR, *Istoriia Azerbaidzhana*, 2:1, 426.

25. Poland AAN MSZ, *6692/102*, (n.d).

26. T. K. Kochärli, "Bor'ba Kommunisticheskoi Partii za sotsialisticheskuiu industrializatsiu i podgotovku sploshnoi kollektivizatsii sel'skogo khoziaistva (1926–1929)," *KPAz, Institut Istorii Partii Trudy*, no. 23 (1959): 27–28. On anti-Islamic campaign, see Rafiev, B. "Mozhno li ubit' natsional'nyi dukh?" *Vyshka* 3/16/1993; Bennigsen and Lemercier, *Islam in the* Soviet Union, 138–52; W. Kolarz, *Religion in the Soviet Union* (London: Macmillan, 1962), 420; J. Hajibeyli, "Ten Years of the Bolshevist Rule in Azerbaijan," *AR* 27 (1931): 122–30.

27. For the Cheka sources on the Baku Muslim clergy, see Republic of Azerbaijan, *Arkhiv Politicheskikh i Obshchestvennykh Dvizhenii*, F. 1, op. 83, d. 345, A 184. Bakhtyar Rafiev, "Mozhno li ubit' natsional'nyi dukh," *Vyshka*, 3/16/1993.

28. Joseph de Gobineau, *Les religions et philosophies dans l'Asie Centrale* (Paris: Didiere et Cie, 1865), 15–16.

29. Bennigsen and Lemercier-Quelquejay, *Islam in the Soviet Union*, 150.

30. Akhundov, *Äsärläri* 2, 92.

31. On the formation of the Communist Party of Iran, see S. Zabih, *The Communist Movement in Iran* (Berkeley: University of California Press, 1966), 26–30; T. A. Ibrahimov, *Iran Kommunist Partiyasinin yaranmasi* (Baku, 1963).

32. For the full text of the treaty, see N. S. Fatemi, *Diplomatic History of Persia, 1917–1923: Anglo-Russian Power Politics in Iran* (New York: Russell Moore, 1952), 319.

33. *Azerbaijan* (Baku), 5/11/1989, 4.

34. On Lahuti, see Lenczowski, *Russia and West*, 63; Zurrer, *Kaukasien*, 428; on his writings, see M. Kiazimov "Tema Azerbaidzhana v tvorchestve Abul'Kasema Lahuti," *ANAzSSR, Izvestiia Ser. Lit. Iaz. Isk* 2 (1982): 47–51.

35. See M. Afshar, "Mas'aleh-yi melliyat va vahdat-i melli-yi Iran," *Ayandeh* 2:20 (1926–27), 566. Taqi Arani, "Azarbaijan, ya yak masaleh-yi hayati va mamati Iran," *Frangistan* 1:5 (1303): 254.

36. See Ahmad Kasravi, *Azari ya zaban bastan-i Azarbaijan* (Teheran, n.d.); on Kasravi, see Ervand Abrahamian, "Kasravi: The Integrative Nationalist of Iran," in *Toward a Modern Iran: Studies in Thought, Politics, and Society*, E. Kedourie and S. Haim, eds. (London, 1980), 96–131. S. Aliev, "Obshchestvennaia i publitsisticheskaia deiatel'nost' Akhmeda Kasravi Tabrizli v 1932–1946 gg.," *ANAzSSR, Izvestiia, Ser.Ob.N.* 6 (1958), 121–33.

37. On Agabekov's revelations and their impact in Iran, see D. N. Wilber, *Riza Shah Pahlavi: The Resurrection and Reconstruction of Iran, 1878–1944* (Hicksville, NY: Exposition Press, 1975), 136–37; M. Rezun, *The Soviet Union and Iran*, 174–82.

38. F. Fatemi, *The USSR in Iran* (New York: Barnes, 1980), 16; see also Issawi, *Economic History of Iran*, 111.

39. Abrahamian, *Iran Between Two Revolutions*, 345; For an Iranian view of the Persianization campaign, see Atabaki, *Azerbaijan*, 53–61.

40. Poland AAN MSZ, *Poselstwo w Teheranie, 1/p/s/66/1*, 1938.

41. L. Polonskii, "Namestnik vozhdia," *Bakinskii Rabochii* 15:6 (1989).

42. On Beria's relationship with Baghirov, see A. Antonov-Ovseenko, "Beriia," *Iunost'* 12 (1988): 67. See also C. H. Fairbanks, "Clientelism and Higher Politics in Georgia, 1949–1953," in Suny, *Transcaucasia*, 349. For published Soviet court records, see *Mir Jäfär Baghirovun Mähkämäsi* (Baku: Iazichi, 1993), 20–28.

43. On the tenor of the accusations against the CPAz leaders, see Räsulzadä, *Chaghdash Azarbaijan tarikhi*, 101.

44. Atakishiev, *Istoriia universiteta*, 186. On 186, this source contains the names of Azeri scholars who were victims of the purges. For archival sources on Baghirov's role in the purges, see Azerbaijan, Ts. GAPPODAzR, Prigovor Voiennoi Kollegii Verkhovnogo Suda SSSR po delu. M. D. Baghirova, F. 1, op331, d.22.

45. Nahaylo and Svoboda, *Soviet Disunion*, 76; for a detailed discussion of the show trials in Azerbaijan, and bibliographical guidance, see Altstadt, *The Azerbaijani Turks*, 141–50.

46. Atakishiev, *Istoriia universiteta*, 5.

47. *Istoriia Azerbaidzhana* 2:2, 43–4.

48. "O perevode azerbaidzhanskoi pismennosti s latinskogo na russkii alfavit," *Elm*, 7/14/1990 no. 29.

49. Poland AAN MSZ, *Poselstwo w Teheranie 6690, sign. 32*, April 29, 1931.

50. Poland AAN MSZ, *Poselstwo w Teheranie 6690, sign. 32*, April 29, 1931.

51. Robert Conquest, *The Harvest of Sorrow: Soviet Collectivization and the Terror Famine* (New York: Oxford University Press, 1986), 156–57.

52. On the Azeri émigré press, see E. Rossi, "Publicazioni di musulmani anti-bolscevichi dell'Azerbaigian Caucasico," *OM* 4:6 (1924): 401–8; J. Benzing, "Berliner politische Veroffentlichungen der Turken aus der Sowjetunion," *WI* 18 (1936) 122–31. L. Bezanis, "Soviet Muslim emigrés in the Republic of Turkey" *CAS* 13 (1994) 59–180.

53. Poland AAN MSZ, *Poselstwo w Teheranie 6992/73/1933.*

54. Poland AAN MSZ, *Poselstwo w Teheranie 6692/101* (n.d.).

55. For a chronological review of émigré activities, see ibid., *Poselstwo w Teheranie 6690, sign. 163*, Azerbaijani National Center in Exile.

56. For a discussion of the Promethean Movement, see Sergiusz Mikulicz, *Prometeizm w Polityce II Rzeczypospolitej* (Warsaw: Książką i Wiedza, 1971); Rezun, *The Soviet Union and Iran*. On the émigré Caucasian unity movement see D. Vachanadze, "Hariçte Kafkasya birligi hareketi tarihi," *Birleşik Kafkasya* 3:4 (20/21) (1953): 9–11. Also consult *Prometheé*, a periodical published from 1926 on in Paris.

57. Poland, *Records of the Consulate General in Jerusalem* (in possession of Wlodzimierz Bączkowski, Washington D.C.).

58. Joachim Hoffman, *Kaukasien 1942/43. Das deutsche Heer und die Orientvolker der Sowjetunion* (Freiburg: Rombach Verlag, 1991), 220.

59. On military operations of the Azeri troops, see ibid.

60. For Räsulzadä's reminscences on his wartime stay in Berlin, see his *Chaghdash Azärbaijan tarikhi*, 106–7.

61. On the political activities of the émigrés on the German side, see Patrick von zur Mühlen, *Zwischen Hakenkreuz und Sowjetstern. Der Nationalismus der sowjetischen Orientvolker in Zweiten Weltkrieg* (Düsseldorf: Bonner Schriften zur Politik und Zeitgeschichte, 1971); A. Fatalibeyli, "Medzhlis i politika Reykha," *Svobodnyi Kavkaz* 1/2 (1952): 51–53; *Svobodnyi Kavkaz* 3 (1952): 23–26.

CHAPTER 6

1. Avery, *Modern Iran*, 333.

2. Winston S. Churchill, *The Second World War* 3 (London-Boston, 1948–54), 424.

3. Churchill, *The Second World War*, 3, 428.

4. David Nissman, *The Soviet Union and Iranian Azerbaijan: The Uses of Nationalism for Political Penetration* (Boulder: Westview, 1987), 30.

5. UK FO 371/40171 xc 154. 884; see also P. Homayounpour, *L'Affaire d'Azerbaidjan* (Lausanne, 1947), 54.

6. UK FO 371/E3824, no. 10, "Tabriz Diary," June 1–14, 1944.

7. UK FO 371/40171 xc 154. 884.

8. UK FO 1E3824, no. 10, "Tabriz Diary," June 10, 1944.

9. UK FO 371/E 35512, no. 9, "Tabriz Diary," May 31, 1944.

10. On Ibrahimov's work in promoting the Azeri literary revival in Tabriz, see Afshar Jahanshahlu, *Ma va biganegan* (Düsseldorf, 1973), 306–8. For Ibrahimov's narrative of events in Iranian Azerbaijan, see "1945–1946 illärda Jänubi Azärbaijan milli-demokratik harakat haqqinda," see his *Äsärläri* 7, 72–115 (Baku: Iaziji Näshriyyäti, 1982).

11. On the Azeri Soviet cultural activities in Tabriz, see Nissman, *The Uses of Nationalism*, 31–34; Dzh. Vekilov, "Rol' tebrizskogo filiala obshchestva kul'turnykh sviazei Irana s SSSR i Sovetskogo Doma Kul'tury v Tebrize v razvitii sovetsko-iranskikh kul'turnykh sviazei," *AN AzSSR, Izvestiia, Ser. Lit. Iaz.* 1 (1989): 101–6.

12. Abrahamian, *Iran Between Two Revolutions*, 390.

13. Luise Estrange-Fawcett, *Iran and the Cold War: The Azerbaijan Crisis of 1946* (Cambridge: Cambridge University Press, 1992), 46–47: see also Abrahamian, *Iran Between Two Revolutions*, 392.

14. Robert Rossow, "The Battle of Azerbaijan, 1946," *MEA* 10 (Winter 1956): 18. P. Lisagor and M. Higgins, *Overtime in Heaven: Adventures in the Foreign Service* (Garden City: Doubleday, 1964), 149.

15. For biographical information on Pishevari, see Ervand Abrahamian, "Communism and Communalism in Iran: The Tudah and the Firqah-i Dimukrat," *IJMES* 1 (1970): 310; see also Mojtahidi, *Rejal-i Azerbaijan*, 47–50; for autobiographical reminiscences, consult Pishevari's *Sechilmish Äsärläri*, 1956/1344.

16. George Lenczowski, *Russia and the West in Iran: A Study in Great Powers Rivalry, 1918–1948* (Ithaca, N.Y.: Cornell University Press, 1968), 286; on the economic condition of Azerbaijan in the period, see Turaj Atabaki, *Azerbaijan: Ethnicity and Autonomy in Twentieth-Century Iran* (London: British Academic Press, 1993), 85–87.

17. Homayounpour, *L'Affaire d'Azerbaidjan*, 129. On the preparatory work for creation of the Democratic Party of Azerbaijan, see also M. M. Cheshmazar, "S. J. Pishävarinin Azarbaijan Demokrat Partiyasi vä Azärbaijan milli hokumätinin yaranmasi ughrunda mubarizadä rolu hagginda," *Jänubi Azarbayjan tarikhi mäsäläläri* (Baku, 1989), 30; H. M. Hasanov, "Azärbaijan Demokrat Firgasinin yaranmasi tarikhindan," *KPAz Institut Istorii Partii, Äsärlär-Trudy* 23 (1959): 183–98. On the Democrats' relationship to the Tudeh, see Abrahamian, "Communism and Communalism."

18. Cheshmazar, "Pishävarinin rölu," 33.

19. Estrange-Fawcett, *Iran and the Cold War*, 40.

20. Atabaki, *Ethnicity and Autonomy*, 107.

21. *Azarbaijan* 15, 9/28 (1945).

22. Ibid., 9/28 (1945).

23. Ibid., 5/9 (1945).

24. For the full text of the proclamation, see Abrahamian, "Communism and Communalism," 309.

25. Homayounpour, *L'Affaire d'Azerbaidjan*, 66.

26. UK FO 371/4537 XC 154884.

27. UK FO 371/4537 XC 154884.

28. For a detailed review of Iranian reactions, see Abrahamian, *Iran Between Two Revolutions*, 218–19.

29. Atabaki, *Ethnicity and Autonomy*, 139.

30. A. Roosevelt, Jr., "The Kurdish Republic of Mahabad," *MEJ* 1 (1947): 250–54; see also R. Ramazani, "The Autonomous Republic of Azerbaijan and the Kurdish Republic: The Rise and Fall," in *The Anatomy of the Communist Takeover*, T. Hammond, ed. (New Haven: Yale University Press, 1975), 456–58.

31. For the full text of the treaty see W. J. Eagleton, *The Kurdish Republic of 1946* (New York, Oxford University Press, 1963), 82.

32. William O. Douglas, *Strange Lands and Friendly People*, 44.

33. On the autonomous Azerbaijan's army, see Homayounpour, *L'Affaire d'Azerbaidjan*, 136–40; see also Afshar, *Ma va biganegan*, 249.

34. For a review of the educational and cultural policies of the Pishevari regime, see Berengian, *Azeri and Persian Literary Works*, 138–82. On the Azeri literature of the period, see Jafar Mujiri, "Ikinji dunya muharibasi va milli azadlig harakati dövrunda ädäbiyyät (1941–1953)," *AzSSR, EA, XX äsr Jänubi Azärbayjanda demokratik ideayalar*, 136–94; J. M. Väkilov, *Azärbaijan respublikasi va Iran: 40-ji illär* (Baku: Elm, 1991), 78–114.

35. Rossow, "The Battle of Azerbaijan, 1946," 19. For biographic information on Biriya and the discussion of his work as the education minister, see M. Cheshmazar, "Mashaggatli ömür," *Adäbiyyät v injä sänäti* 11/25 (1988).

36. UK FO 371/6169 (1947).

37. UK FO 371/6169 (1947).

38. For a detailed discussion of the Soviet impact on the cultural policies of the Tabriz regime, see Berengian, *Azeri and Persian Literary Works*, 146–50.

39. For archival sources see Azerbaijan, Ts. GAPPODAzR, F. 1, op 220, d.48.1.73, Protokol 407, 437, 444, 507, 521.

40. On hypotheses about Baghirov's role in the relations between the two Azerbaijans, see Afshar, *Ma va biganegan*, 306–8; see also Estrange-Fawcett, *Iran and the Cold War*, 97; Atabaki, *Ethnicity and Autonomy*, 142-43.

41. *Azarbaijan*, April 17–26 (1946), 393.

42. Rossow, "Battle of Azerbaijan," 17. For a recent monograph on Azerbaijan in the big powers' diplomacy, see Estrange-Fawcett, *Iran and the Cold War*. On the U.S. reaction, see Bruce R. Kuniholm, *The Origins of the Cold War in the Near East: Great Power Conflict and Diplomacy in Iran, Turkey, and Greece* (Princeton, Princeton University Press, 1980), 319–24; on Rossow's telegraph bills, see Lisagor, *Overtime in Heaven*, 157.

43. F. Azimi, *Iran: The Crisis of Democracy* (New York: St. Martin's Press, 1989), 150.

44. Homayounpour, *L'Affaire d'Azerbaidjan*, 156.

45. For the full text, see Atabaki, *Ethnicity and Autonomy* 185–9.

46. Homayounpour, *L'Affaire d'Azerbaidjan*, 160.

47. UK FO 371/6169 (1947).

48. Ibid. For a discussion of the economic condition of Azerbaijan in the 1946, see also Estrange-Fawcett, *Iran and the Cold War*, 68–80; also see I. Meister, "Soviet Policy in Iran, 1917–1950: A Case Study in Techniques," (Ph.D. dissertation, Tufts University, 1954), 355.

49. UK FO 371/6169 (1947).

50. Azimi, *The Crisis of Diplomacy*, 161.

51. Kuniholm, *The Origins of the Cold War*, 394.

52. Homayounpour, *L'Affaire d'Azerbaidjan*, 171.

53. Lenczowski, *Russia and the West in Iran*, 308.

54. Homayounpour, *L'Affaire d'Azerbaidjan*, 175; see also A. Zanganeh, *Khatirat-i az mamuriyatha man dar Azarbaijan* (Rasht, 1335).

55. Rossow, "Battle of Azerbaijan," 29–30.

56. U.S. Central Intelligence Agency, *Research Report. The Current Situation in Iran* (20 October 1947). For the estimate of the figures on the refugees, see Atabaki, *Ethnicity and Autonomy*, 175.

57. For a comprehensive discussion of international aspects of the post–World War II Azerbaijani crisis, and bibliographical guidance, consult Estrange-Fawcett, *Iran and the Cold War*.

CHAPTER 7

1. U.S. Central Intelligence Agency, *Research Reports, The Middle East: Developments in Azerbaijan* (June 1947), 6.

2. Douglas, *Strange Lands, Friendly People*, 50.

3. A. Tude, "Pishavari," *Adäbiyyat vä Injä Samati 6/17 (1988)*. On Pishevari's relations with the Soviets consult Afshari, *Ma va bineganan*.

4. *Mir Jäfär Baghirovun Mähkämäsi*, p. 98. On the circumstances of his death see also Keshavarz, *Man mottaham mikonam*, pp. 64–66.

5. M. Chesmazer, "Muhammad Biriya," *Novruz 5/22 (1991)*. On the dispersion of the refugees, see Azerbaijan. Ts. GAPPODAzR, F.I.op220,d.50; Protokol 581.

6. For a detailed discussion of and extensive excerpts from Radio Azerbaijan's broadcasting, see Meister, "Soviet Policy in Iran," 620–26.

7. Kamran Mahdi, "Tasalli," trans. by Nissman, *The Uses of Nationalism*, 199.

8. On Azerbaijani unity as a theme in contemporary Azerbaijani literature, see David Nissman, "The Origins and Development of the the Literature of 'Longing,'" *Azerbaijan, Journal of Turkish Studies* 8 (1984): 197–207.

9. For a survey of the Soviet-Iranian relations after 1946, see A. Z. Rubinstein, *Soviet Policy Toward Turkey, Iran, and Afghanistan: The Dynamics of Influence* (New York: Praeger, 1982), 62–96.

10. Abrahamian, "Communism and Communalism," 316.

11. Mammmäd Jafar, *Azärbayjanda romantizm* (Baku: Izd-vo ANAzSSR, 1966), 140; also consult Nissman, *The Uses of Nationalism*.

12. S. Z. Bayramzadä, "Iran hakim dairalarinin Jänubi Azärbayjanin maarifi va mädaniyyat sahasindaki siyasati (1947–1978-ji illär)," in *ANAzSSR, Jänubi Azärbayjan*, 51; for an Iranian survey of the history of educational system in Azerbaijan, see *Tarih-i farhang-i Azarbaijan* (Tabriz: 1332).

13. Abrahamian, *Iran Between Two Revolutions* 443.

14. For the data on ethnic composition of the power elite in Iran, see Marvin Zonis, *The Political Elite of Iran* (Princeton: Princeton University Press, 1971), 79, 180.

15. On post-1946 Iranian Azeri literature, see Berengian, *Azeri and Persian Literary Works*, 189–211.

16. Nasib Nasibzade, "A. R. Nabdel i A. Tabrizli: dva uklona v ideologii natsional'no-osvoboditel'nogo dvizheniia azerbaidzhantsev v Irane," *ANAz. SSR. Izvestiia, Ser. Ist. Fil, Pr.* 2 (1988).

17. V. V. Trubetskoi, "K voprosu o vliianii burzhuaznykh reform 60-kh i pervoi poloviny 70-kh godov na natsional'nye protsessy v Irane," 105.

18. A. R. Nabdel, *Azarbaijan va mas'aleh-yi melli* (Aden, 1356), 20.

19. Nasibzade, "Nabdel i Tabrizli," 27. On Tabrizli, see also V. K. Mustafayev, "Jänubi Azärbayjanlilarinin milli shuuru haqqinda ba'zi geidler," in *ANAzSSR, Jänubi Azärbaijan tarikhi masalari*, 182.

20. Bayramzadä, "Iran hakim dairalarinin," 55.

21. Trubetskoi, 'K voprosu o vliianii," 92.

22. Lowell Tillet, *The Great Friendship: Soviet Historians on the Non-Russian Nationalities* (University of North Carolina Press, 1969), 169.

23. On Beria's work for the Azerbaijani counterintelligence, see N. Keykurun, *Azerbaycan istiklal mücadelesinin hatiralari* (Istanbul: Azerbaycan Genclik Dernegi, 1964).

24. L. Polonskii, "Namestnik vozhdia," *Bakinskii Rabochii* 15/6 (1989).

25. *Bakinskii Rabochii* 5/27 (1956). For the transcript of the trial see Azerbaijan TsGAPPOD. Prigovor Voennoi Kollegii Suda SSSR po delu M.

D. Baghirova, F.I.op331,d.22. For the published and abbreviated version in Azeri, see *Mir Jäfär Baghirovun Mähkämäsi.*

26. On the "Gulistan" poem, see *Molodezh-Ganjliev*, September (1988), 10–3.

27. Leonhard, *The Kremlin since Stalin*, 345; for a discussion of post-Stalin Azerbaijan, see Altstadt, *The Azerbaijani Turks*, 161–76.

28. Alexandre Bennigsen and Enders Wimbush, *Muslims of the Soviet Empire: A Guide* (Bloomington: Indiana University Press, 1986), 140.

29. Bennigsen and Lemercier, *Islam in the Soviet Union*, 175–76.

30. Bennigsen and Wimbush, *Muslims*, 143.

31. Näsib Näsibzadä, "1960–1970-ji il illärda Jänubi Azärbaijanin sosial -igtisadi inkishafinin ba'zi mäsäläri hagginda," *Jänubi Azärbaijan*, 91.

32. E. Rouleau, "Iran: The Myth and Reality," *The Guardian*, October 24, 1976. On the Oil Revolution in Iran, see Abrahamian, *Iran Between Two Revolutions*, 472–78. For sceptical evaluations of its prospects, see R. Graham, *Iran: The Illusion of Power* (London: Croom Helms, 1978).

33. Näsibzadä, "1960–1970-ji illärda" 92; on the Azeri migrations to Teheran, see Shövkät Taghiyeva, "1978–1979-ju illär Iran ingilabindan sonra milli huguglar ughrunda mubarizä," *Jänubi Azärbaijan*, 168 n.7.

34. For a general discusssion and statistics on the Transcaucasia's economy of the period, see Alastair McAuley, "The Soviet Muslim Population: Trends in Living Standards, 1960–75," in *The USSR and the Muslim World*, Yaacov Ro'i, ed. (London: George Allen & Unwin, 1984). G. Schroeder, "Transcaucasia Since Stalin: The Economic Dimension," in Suny, *Transcaucasia*, 397–414.

35. M. Ismailov, "Azerbaijan," *CACC* 8/3 (1989), 5.

36. Schroeder, "Transcaucasia Since Stalin," 415.

37. Ismailov, "Azerbaijan," 5.

38. O. Zinam, "Transcaucasus," in *Economics of Soviet Regions*, I. S. Koropeckyi and G. Schroeder, eds. (New York: Praeger, 1981).

39. A. Nove, and J. A. Newth, *The Soviet Middle East: A Communist Model for Development* (New York, Praeger: 1966), 122.

40. Alastair McAuley, "The Soviet Muslim Population: Trends in Living Standards, 1960–75," in *The USSR and the Muslim World*, Yacov Ro'i, ed., pp. 96–116.

41. On the impediments to labor migrations from the Muslim parts of the USSR, see Michael Rywkin, *Moscow's Muslim Challenge: Soviet Central Asia* (Armonk, N.Y.: 1990), 71–81; see also Murray Feschbach, "Prospects for Massive Outmigration from Central Asia During the Next Decade," *Paper for the U.S. Department of Commerce, Bureau of Economic Analysis*, February 1977.

42. B. D. Silver, "Population Redistribution and Ethnic Balance in Transcaucasia," in Suny, *Transcaucasia*, 377.

43. USSR, Peoples' Deputies from Azerbaijan, *On Forcible Deportation of Azerbaijanis from Armenia* (n.d.), 2.

44. For statistics on the Azerbaijani population see USSR, Peoples' Deputies from Azerbaijan, *On Forcible Deportation of Azerbaijanis*; see also Ronald G. Suny, "Transcaucasia: Cultural Cohesion and Ethnic Revival in a Multinational Society," in *The Nationalities Factor in Soviet Politics and Society*, L. Hajda and M. Beissinger, eds. (Boulder: Westview Press, 1990), 236–37.

45. On the 1965 Erivan demonstrations, see Nahaylo and Svoboda, *Soviet Disunion*, 147–48; on the petitioning campaign, see Radio FE, *RAD Background Report 39*, March 11, 1988; Claire Mouradian, "The Mountainous Karabagh Question: An Inter-Ethnic Conflict or Decolonization Crisis?" *Armenian Review* 43/2–3, 9–12. R. G. Suny, *Looking Toward Ararat: Armenia in Modern History* (Bloomington: Indiana University Press, 1994), 185–91.

46. Suny, "Cultural Cohesion," 231.

47. For the discussion of Aliyev, see Altstadt, *The Azerbaijani Turks*, 177–91; on the transformations of the Azerbaijani nomenklatura, see J. P. Willerton, "Patronage Politics in the Soviet Union" (unpublished Ph.D. dissertation, University of Michigan, 1985), 141–69.

48. Suny, "Cultural Cohesion," 239. V. I. Kozlov, *Natsional'nosti SSR. Etnodemograficheskii obzor* (Moscow: Finansy i Statistika, 1982), 228.

49. Kozlov, *Natsional'nosti SSR. Etnodemograficheskii obzor*, 232.

50. Bakhtiar Vahabzade, "Dva kryla," *Bakinskii Rabochii* 10/11 (1988). For a comprehensive discussion of the issue see Paul Henze, "The Significance of Increasing Bilingualism Among Soviet Muslims," in *The USSR and the Muslim World*, Yaacov Ro'i, ed., 117–28.

51. On Tabriz in the Iranian revolution of 1978–79, see E. Ch. Babaev, "Jänubi Azärbayjan 1978–1979-ju illär Iran ingilabinda," *ANAzSSR, Jänubi Azärbaijan*, 98–142.

52. A. Bennigsen and M. Broxup, *The Islamic Threat to the Soviet State* (New York: St. Martin's Press, 1983), 115.

53. On the signs of Islamic revival in Soviet Azerbaijan, see Bennigsen and Wimbusch, *Muslims*, 140–42. Bennigsen and Wimbusch also offers bibliographic guidance to the Soviet sources.

54. Bennigsen and Broxup, *Islamic Threat*, 116–17; Y. Ro'i, "The Impact of the Islamic Fundamentalist Revival of the Late 1970s on the Soviet View of Islam," in *The USSR and the Muslim World*, Yaacov Ro'i, ed., 167–68.

55. F. Agamaliev, "Mezhdu polumiesiatsem i krestom," 1.

56. Sh. Akhavi, "Soviet Perceptions of the Iranian Revolution," *Iranian Studies* 19/1 (1986): 3–23.

57. For a review of the Azeri press publications of the period, see M. Ahrali, "Inkilabdan sonra Azärbaijan dilinda matbuat" *Azärbaijan sesi* 5

(Tabriz) (n.d.); Khuraman Guliyeva, "Diktaturanin devrilmäsi vä ingilabdan sonraki illärda ädäbiyyät (1978–1984)," in *AzSSR EA, XX äsr Jänubi Azärbaijanda demokratik ideyalar*, 195–220; On the Azeri cultural associations, see Taghiyeva, "1978–1979-ju illär," 150–58.

58. On political associations in Iranian Azerbaijan, see Taghiyeva, "1978–1979-ju illär," 158–59.

59. V. V. Trubetskoi, "Osobennosti natsional'noi situatsii v Islamskoi Respublike Irana," in *AN SSSR, Natsionalnyi vopros v stranakh vostoka* (Moscow, 1982), 258.

60. Taghiyeva, "1978–1979-ju illär," 162.

61. On the 1979 Tabriz disturbances, see S. Bakhash, *The Reign of the Ayatollahs: Iran and the Islamic Revolution* (New York: Basic Books, 1984), 89–90; Taghiyeva, "1978–1979-ju illär," 160–68.

62. Näsib Näsibzadä, "Vahid Azärbayjan: Ideali va gerchäklik," *Elm*, March 17, 1990. On the return of Biriya, see M. Chezmazar, "Muhammad Biriya," *Novruz* 21 (1991): 3–4.

63. Nissman, *The Uses of Nationalism*, 71.

64. On the "one Azerbaijan" campaign, see Nissman, *The Uses of Nationalism*, 73–77. On Aliyev's statement to the foreign diplomats, see *The Times* (London) November 29, 1982.

65. For a comprehensive restatement of these views under the Islamic Republic, see M. Azari, *Azärbaijan va naghme'ha-yi tazeh este'margaran* (Teheran: Sazman-i Intisharat-i Hafta, 1341), 52–54.

CHAPTER 8

1. On the Sumgait riots, see Ziya Buniatov, "Pochemu Sumgait. Situatsionnyi analiz," *Elm*, no. 19 (1989) ; for an Armenian view, see *The Sumgait Tragedy: Pogroms Against Armenians in Soviet Azerbaijan* (Cambridge, Mass: Zoryan Institute, 1990).

2. On the impact of the Nagorno-Karabagh dispute on the Armenian national movement, see Claire Mouradian, "The Mountainous Karabagh Question: An Inter-Ethnic Conflict or Decolonization Crisis?" *The Armenian Review* 43:2–3 (1990): 1–34. For an Armenian view of the dispute's historical background, see *The Karabagh File: Documents and Facts on the Question of Mountainous Karabagh, 1918–1988*, Gerard J. Libaridian, ed. (Cambridge, Mass: Zoryan Institute, 1988); Suny, *Looking Toward Ararat*, 192-212.

3. Mark Saroyan, "The Karabagh Syndrome and Azerbaijani Politics," *Problems of Communism* (September-October 1990), 16–17.

4. Tamara Dragadze, "Interview with Neimat Panakhov," *CACC* 8:5 (1989): 2.

5. On the refugee problem, see I. Mardanov and V. Rasulov, "Gachynlar v igtisadiyyätimiz," *Vätän säsi* 11 (1990): 5.

6. Leyla Iunusova, "Pestraia palistra neformal'nykh dvizhenii v Azerbaidzhane," *Russkaia mysl'* 22/9 (1989), 7.

7. Anonymous, "Azerbaijan: Takie my segodnia," Samizdat publication.

8. For a list of unofficial and opposition publications, see Altstadt, *The Azerbaijani Turks*, 228–30; see also Raoul Motika, "Glasnost in der Sowjetre-publik Aserbaidschan am Beispiel der Zeitschrift Azerbaycan," *Orient* 32:4 (1991): 573–90.

9. Leyla Iunusova, "End of the Ice Age: Azerbaijan, August-September 1989," *CACC* 8:6 (1989): 12.

10. M. Ibragimov, "Zavtra budet pozdno," *Vyshka* 9/2 (1989).

11. "About the Events in Nagorno-Karabagh; or, the Karabagh Adventure of the Armenian Nationalists," *CACC* 8:2 (1989): 4.

12. Tofiq Gasymov, "The War Against the Azeri Popular Front," *Uncaptive Minds* 3:5 (1990): 12.

13. Aydin Balaev, *Apercue historique du Front Populaire d'Azerbaidjan* (n.d.), 2.

14. "Program of the People's Front of Azerbaijan" (English translation), *CACC* 8:4 (1989): 7–10.

15. Ibid., 9.

16. Ibid., 8.

17. Full text of the law, in *Kommunist* (Baku) 17/9 (1989).

18. Elizabeth Fuller, "Moscow Rejects Azerbaijani Law on Sovereignty: A Moral Victory for Armenia?" *RFE/RL Research Institute, Report on the USSR* (December 1, 1989), 16–18.

19. Iunusova, "The End of the Ice Age," 13.

20. Ibid., p. 13.

21. Balaev, *Apercue historique*, 12.

22. "Ob istoricheskom edinstve Severnoi i Iuzhnoi chastei Azerbaidzhana," *Azerbaijan* 2, 1/11 (1990).

23. Gasymov, "The War," 13.

24. Ibid., 13.

25. Eldar Namazov, "Antiislamskii fundamentalizm," *Elm*, 1 /9 (1990).

26. Gasymov, "The War," 13.

27. For an account of the ethnic violence, see Helsinki Watch, *Conflict in the Soviet Union: Black January in Azerbaidzhan, Memorial Report, May 1991*; see also "Baku. Khronika sobytii," *Gazeta "B"* 4 (1990).

28. On the Soviet Army intervention see "January in Baku: Private Investigation," *Moscow News Weekly* 33 (1989).

29. For an official Azerbaijani account of the Baku January Days, see Azerbaidzhanskaia SSR, Verkhovnyi Sovet, *Zaiavlenie Kommissii po rassle-dovaniu sobytii imevshikh mesto v gorode Baku 19–20 ianvaria 1990 goda* (Baku, 1990); see also *Chernyi ianvar: Dokumenty i materialy* (Baku, 1990).

30. *Chernyi ianvar*, 86.

31. *CACC* 2 (1990): 7.

32. For the full text in the language of the original, see *Kommunist sahar*, 3–4–5, 1/25 (1990).

33. *Armenian Update* 3 (March 1990).

34. "L'Occident regrettte mais comprend," *Le Monde* 22/1 (1990).

35. FBIS-WEU 90–014,1/22/90.

36. *Iran Times*, February 2, 1990.

37. For Iranian reactions, see FBIS-NES-90, January-February, 1990.

38. "Le drame azeri divise la Turquie," *Le Monde Diplomatique* (March 1990), 10.

39. "Une frontiere glaciale dilue l'identite des Azeris," *Journal de Geneve*, 6/2–3/1990.

40. Ibid., 6/2–3/1990.

41. See U.S. Commission on Security and Cooperation in Europe, *Report on the Supreme Soviet Elections in Azerbaijan*, October 23, 1990.

42. *Komsomol'skaia pravda* 10/4 (1991).

43. U.S. Commission, *Report*, 5; see also Leyla Iunusova, "Kto stal deputatom. K itogam vyborov v Azerbaidzhane," *Ekspress-Khronika*, 10/23 (1990), 6.

44. U.S. Commission, *Report*, 14.

45. *Stolitsa* (Moscow), 1 (1990).

46. *Komsomol'skaia pravda*, 10/13 (1990); see also "Byvshyi," *7 s pliusom 6, Research Report* 2:5, January 23, 1993, 6–11.

47. On the return to Latinization of the alphabet, see Audrey Altstadt, "Azerbaijan Moves Toward the Latin Alphabet," *RFE/RL Research Institute, Report on the USSR* 2:29 (July 20, 1990), 24–26; "Elifba nece olacak," *Odlu yurd* 8:8 (1990).

48. *Elm* 8/25 (1990).

49. FBIS, NES–90–015.

50. FBIS, NES–90–019.

51. On Aliyev's foreign policy in Nakhichevan see Fuller, "Geidar Aliyev's Comeback," 9.

52. FBIS, NES–90–27.

53. *New York Times*, September 4, 1991.

54. Elizabeth Fuller, "The Azerbaijani Presidential Elections: A One-Horse Race," *RFE/RL Research Institute, Report on the USSR* 3:37 (September 13, 1991) 9/13, 12–14.

55. Helsinki Watch, *Bloodshed in the Caucasus: Escalation of the Armed Conflict in Nagorno-Karabagh* (September 1992), 6.

56. For a discussion of Azerbaijani army, see Elizabeth Fuller, "Paramilitary Forces Dominate Fighting in Transcaucasus," *RFE/RL Research Institute, Report on the USSR*, 2:25 (June 18, 1993), 74–83.

57. On the Khojaly massacre, see Helsinki Watch, *Bloodshed in the Caucasus*, 19–24. For an Azeri analysis, see Arif Iunusov, "Tragediia Khojaly. Opyt chastnogo issledovaniia," *Zerkalo* 25, June 13, 1992.

58. For an analysis of the Mutalibov's resignation, see Arif Iunusov, "Azerbaidzhan segodnia" *Ekspress-Khronika*, 10 (240), 3/9, (1992).

59. Commission on Security and Cooperation in Europe, *Human Rights and Democratization in the Newly Independent States* (January 1993), 110; on the political implications of the fall of Susha, see Arif Iunusov, "Karabagh War. Another Year Passed. What next?" *Express-Chronicle* 14, March 29, 1993.

60. *New York Times*, June 9, 1993.

EPILOGUE

1. For the numerical strength and dislocation of the Russian forces in Transcaucasia, see Fuller, "Paramilitary Forces," 75.

2. For the outline of the military operations, see Helsinki Watch, *Bloodshed in the Caucasus: Indiscrinate Bombing and Shelling by Azerbaijani Forces in Nagorno Karabagh* 5:10 (July 1993), 3–8; for a detailed discussion, see Arif Iunusov, "Karabakh War: Another Year Passed. What Next?" *Ekspress-Chronicle 14, 4/5/, 1993*.

3. *Azadliq* (Baku), July 19, 1991, 9; see also *Nezavisimaia Gazeta* 1992.

4. *Iran Times*, June 15, 1993.

5. For an Azeri view of the condition of the oil industry, see *Vyshka*, 3/1/1993; for a discussion of Turkey's interest, see *Milliyet* (Istanbul), 4/11/1993.

6. "Oil Fuels Azeris Hopes for Future," *Christian Science Monitor*, January 13, 1993.

7. For a detailed account of the coup, see Arif Iunusov, "Giandzhinskii taifun," *Ekspress-Khronika*, June 25, 1993; see the same author's analysis of the political condition of Azerbaijan on the eve of the coup in "Bezmolstvuet li narod? Obshchestvenno-politicheskaia situatsiia v Azerbaidzhane," *Ekspress-Khronika* 19, May 13, 1993.

8. For a Turkish evaluation of the coup, see Gün Kut, "Elçibey'in sonu, Türkiye modelinin sonudur," *Cumhuriyet*, June 24, 1993.

9. For an official Azerbaijani publication describing the oil agreement, see *Century's Contract* (Baku: Azerbaijan Publishers, 1994).

10. For the foreign press reports and commentaries on the October 1994 Azerbaijani crisis, see "Azerbaijan—Who'll Stop the Russians?" *The Washington Post*, October 11, 1994; "Azeriler darbeye geçit vermedi," *Cumhuriyet*, October 6, 1994.

BIBLIOGRAPHY

This bibliography is divided into three sections: Archival Sources, Official Publications and Collections of Documents, and Secondary Sources.

ARCHIVAL SOURCES

Azerbaijan

Central State Archives of Modern History
Central State Archives of Political Parties and Social Movements

Poland

Archiwum Akt Nowych

Ministerstwo Spraw Zagranicznych

United Kingdom

Public Records Office

Cabinet Office Archives
Foreign Office Archives
War Office Archives

United States

National Archives

General Records of the Department of State
Records of the American Commission to Negotiate Peace

OFFICIAL PUBLICATIONS AND
COLLECTIONS OF DOCUMENTS

ANAzSSR. Institut Istorii i Filosofii. *Rabochee dvizhenie v Baku v ody pervoi russkoi revoliutsii, Dokumenty i materialy.* Baku, 1956.

ANSSSR. Institut Istorii. *Kolonial'naia politika rossiiskogo tsarizma v azerbaidzhane v 20–60 gg. XIX veka.* Moscow: Izd-vo ANSSSR, 1937.

Azerbaidzhanskaia SSR. Verkhovnyi Sovet. *Zaiavlenie Kommissii po rassledovaniiu sobytii imevshich mesto v gorode Baku 19–20 ianvaria 1990 goda.* Baku, 1990.

Chernyi ianvar.' Dokumenty i materialy. Baku: Azernashr, 1990.

Kavkazskaia Arkheograficheskaia Komissiia. *Akty sobrannye Kavkazskuiu Arkheograficheskuiu Kommissieiu.* Tiflis: 1866–1885.

Kavkazskii Statisticheskii Komitet. *Sbornik svedenii o Kavkaze.* Tiflis: 1871.

K istorii obrazovaniia Nagorno Karabakhskoi Avtonomnoi Oblasti Azerbaidzhanskoi SSR, 1918–1925. *Dokumenty i materialy.* Baku: Azernashr, 1989.

Kommunisticheskaia Partiia Azerbaidzhana, Institut Istorii Partii. *Bor'ba za pobedu sotsialisticheskoi revoliutsii v Azerbaidzhane. Dokumenty i materialy.* Baku: Izd-vo ANAzSSR, 1967.

————. *Nagornyi Karabakh: Razum pobedit. Dokumenty i materialy.* Baku, 1989.

————. *Bol'sheviki v bor'be za pobedu sotsialisticheskoi revoliutsii v Azerbaidzhane. Dokumenty i materialy.* Baku, 1957.

Libaridian, Gerard, ed. *The Karabagh File Documents and Facts on the Question of Mountainous Karabagh, 1918–1988.* Cambridge: Zoryan Institute, 1988.

Mir Jäfär Baghirovun mähkämäsi. Arkhiv materriallari. Baku: Yaziji, 1993.

Obozrenie rossiskikh vladenii za Kavkazom v statisticheskom etnograficheskom i finansovom otnosheniiakh. St. Petersburg, 1836.

People's Front of Azerbaijan. Program (English translation). *CCAC* 8/4 (1989).

Persia, Delegation to the Paris Peace Conference. *Claims of Persia before the Conference of the Preliminaries of Peace at Paris.* Paris, 1919.

Pervaia Vseobshchaia Perepi's Rossiiskoi Imperii, 1897. *Raspredeleniie rabochikh i prislug po gruppam zaniatii i mestu rozhdeniia.* St. Petersburg, 1905.

"Pis'ma I. I. Vorontsova-Dashkova Nikolaiu Romanovu, 1905–1015," *Krasnyi Arkhiv* 16 (1928): 97–126.

Raevskii, A. *Musavatskoe pravitel'stvo na versal'skoi konferentsii: Doneseniia predsedatelia azerbaidzhanskoi musavatskoi delegatsii.* Baku: Azgnin, 1930.

Rafiev, Bakhtyar. *Ganj Azär (Istintaq materiallari üzre)*. Baku, 1993.

Republic of Armenia, Delegation to the Peace Conference. *Donnes statistique des population de la Transcaucasie*. Paris, 1919.

_____. *La republique Armenienne et ses voisins: Questions territoriales*. Paris, 1919.

Republic of Azerbaijan. *Le 28 Mai 1919*. Paris, 1919.

_____. *Claims of the Peace Delegation of Caucasian Azerbaijan*. Paris, 1919.

_____. *Composition antropologique et ethnique de la population de l'Azerbaidjan du Caucase*. Paris, 1919.

_____. *Economic and Financial Situation of Caucasian Azerbaijan*. Paris, 1919.

_____. *La Republique de l'Azerbaidjan du Caucase*. Paris, 1919.

Republic of Georgia. *Dokumenty i materialy po vneshnei politike Zakavakaz'ia i Gruzii*. Tiflis, 1919.

USSR, Ministerstvo Inostrannykh Del. *Dokumenty vneshnei politiki SSSR*. Moscow, 1957.

Vorontsov-Dashkov, I. I. *Vsepoddanneishaia zapiska po upravleniu Kavkazskim Kraem generala ad'iutanta grafa Vorontsova-Dashkova*. St. Petersburg, 1907.

_____. *Vsepoddanneishii otchet za vosem' let upravleniia Kavkazom*. St. Petersburg, 1907.

SECONDARY SOURCES

Abbasov, V. "Razdum'ia v zale vystavki," *Azärbaijan* 7/39 (1990): 5.

Abdullaev, Gasi. *Iz istorii Severo-Vostochnogo Azerbaidzhana v 60–80 gg XVIII veka*. Baku: Izd-vo ANAzSSR, 1958.

_____. *Azerbaidzhan v XVIII veke i vzaimootnosheniia s Rossiei.*. Baku: Izd-vo ANAzSSR, 1965.

Abrahamian, Ervand. *Iran Between Two Revolutions*. Princeton: Princeton University Press, 1982.

_____. "Kasravi: The Integrative Nationalist of Iran." E. Kedourie, S. Haim, *Towards a Modern Iran: Studies in Thought, Politics, and Society*. London, 1980, 96–131.

_____. "Communism and Communalism in Iran: The Tudah and the Firqah-i Dimuqrat," *IJMES* I.4 (1970): 291–316.

Adamiyat, Feridun. *Fekr-i demokrasi-yi ejtemâi dar nahzat-i mashrutiyat-i Iran*. Teheran: Payam, 1363.

_____. *Andishaha-yi Mirza Fath 'Ali Akhundzadeh*. Teheran: 1349.

Afshar, Jahanshahlu. *N. Ma va biganegan*. Düsseldorf, 1973.

Afshar, M. "Mas'aleh-yi milliyat va vahdat-i melli-yi Iran." *Ayandeh* 2/20 (1926): 557–69.

Agamaliev, F. "Mezhdu polumesiatsem i krestom." Samizdat.

Agaoğlu, Ahmet (Aghayev). *Iran ve inķilabi*. Ankara, 1941.

_____. *"La societe persane." Nouvelle revue* (1893).

Akademiia Nauk Az. SSR, Institut Istorii. *Istoriia Azerbaidzhana, 3 vols.*. Baku: Izd-vo ANAzSSR, 1958–1963.

Akhavi, S. "Soviet Perceptions of the Iranian Revolution." *Iranian Studies* 19:1 (1986): 3–24.

Akhundov, Mirza Fathali. *Äsärläri*. Baku, 1958.

Akhundov, Y. *Azärbayjan sovet tariķhi romani*. Baku: Yazichi, 1979.

Alaskerov, M. "Mezhdunarodnaia protivopravnost' giulistanskogo i turk-menchaiskogo dogovorov." *Khazar* 1 (1990): 133–34.

Algar, Hamid. *Mirza Malķum Khan: A Study in the History of Iranian Modernism*. Berkeley: University of California Press, 1973.

_____. "Malkum Khan, Akhunzade, and the Proposed Reform of the Arabic Alphabet." *Middle Eastern Studies* 5/2 (1969): 116–30.

Allworth, Edward. *Nationalities of the Soviet East-Publications and Writing Systems: A Bibliographical Directory and Transliteration Tables for Iranian and Turķic-Languages Publications, 1918–1945, Located in U.S. Libraries*. New York: Columbia University Press, 1973.

Altstadt, Audrey. *The Azerbaiajni Turķs: Power and Identity Under Russian Rule*. Stanford: Hoover Insitution Press, 1992.

_____. "Azerbaijan Moves Toward the Latin Alphabet." *RFE/RL, Report on the USSR* 2/29 (20/7/1990): 24–28.

_____. "Muslim Workers and the Labor Movement in Pre-War Baku." In *Turķic Culture: Continuity and Change*, S. M. Akural, ed. Indiana University Press, 1987.

_____. "The Azerbaijani-Turkish Community of Baku before World War I." Ph.D. Dissertation, University of Chicago, 1983.

Amanat, A. *Resurrection and Renewal: The Making of the Babid Movement in Iran, 1844-1850*. Ithaca: Cornell University Press, 1989.

Äminzadä, A. A. *Böyüķ oķtyabr sosialist ingilabinin Iranda demokratiķ fiķrin inķishafina ta'siri (1917–1925 illar)*. Baku: Azerbayjan SSR Elmler Akademiyasi Nashriyyäti, 1964.

Amir-Khizi, I. *Qiam-i Azärbaijan va Sattar Khan*. Tabriz: Shafaq, 1960.

Arani, Taqi. "Äzarbaijan va yak mas'aleh-yi hayati va mamat-i Iran." *Frangestan* 1:5 (1303).

Arjomand, Said A. *The Turban for the Crown: The Islamic Revolution in Iran*. New York: Oxford University Press, 1988.

Arsharuni, Arshaluis and Khadzhi Z. Gabidullin, *Ocherki panislamizma i pantiurķizma v Rossii*. Moscow: Bezbozhnik, 1931.

Atabaki, Touraj. *Azerbaijan: Ethnicity and Autonomy in Twentieth-Century Iran*. London: British Academic Press, 1993.

Atakishiev, Aslan. *Istoriia Azerbaidzhanskogo Gosudarstvennogo Universiteta.* Baku: Izd-vo Azerbaidzhanskogo Universiteta, 1989.

Atkin, Muriel. *Russia and Iran, 1780–1828.* Minneapolis: University of Minnesota Press, 1980.

Avery, P. *Modern Iran.* New York: Praeger, 1956.

Azärbaijan SSR Elmlar Akademiyasi. *Sovet Azärbayjani va khariji sharq.* Baku: Elm, 1980.

_____. *XX asr Jänubi Azärbaijanda ädäbiyyatinda demokratik ideyalar (1900–1985-ji illär).* Baku: Elm, 1990.

_____. *Jänubi Azärbaijan tarikhinin ocherki (1828–1917).* Baku: Elm, 1985.

_____. *Jänubi Azärbaijan tarikhi mäsäläläri.* Baku: Elm, 1989.

Azari, M. *Azarbaijan va naghma'ha-yi tazeh este'margaran.* Teheran: 1361.

Azari,'Ali, *Qiam-i Shaikh Muhammad Khiabani dar Tabriz.* Teheran: 1342.

Azimi, F. *Iran. The Crisis of Democracy.* New York: St. Martin's Press, 1989.

Baddeley, J. F. *The Russian Conquest of the Caucasus.* London, 1908.

Bagirov, Iu. *Iz istorii sovetsko-turetskikh otnoshenii, 1920–1922, (Po materialam Azerbaidzhanskoi SSR).* Baku: Izd-vo ANAzSSR, 1965.

Balaev, Aydin. "Kak dobit'sia realizatsii gosudarstvennogo statusa Azerbaidzhanskogo iazyka." *Khazar* 2 (1990): 150–53.

_____. *Azerbaidzhanskoe natsional'no-demokraticheskoe dvizhenie (1917–1920).* Baku: Elm, 1990.

_____. *Aperçu historique du Front Populaire d'Azerbaijan: 1988–90.* No publication data.

Baldauf, Ingeborg. *Schrifreform und Schriftwechsel bei den Muslimischen Russland und Sowjettürken (1850–1937): Ein Symptom ideen-gesichtlicher und kulturpolitischen Entwicklungen.* Budapest: Akademiai Kiado, 1993.

Bayat, Mangol. *Mysticism and Dissent: Socio-Religious Thought in Qajar Iran.* Syracuse: Syracuse University Press, 1882.

_____. *Iran's First Revolution: Shi'ism and the Constitutional Revolution of 1905–1909.* New York: Oxford University Press, 1991.

Baykara, Hüseyin. *Azerbaycanda yenileşme hareketi. XIX yüzil.* Ankara: Türk Kültürünü Araştirma Enstitüsü, 1966.

Baziiants, A. "V. A. Gordlevskii i reforma pis'mennosti tiurskikh iazykov." *Sovetskaia tiurkologiia* 5 (1976): 74–76.

Belova, N. K. "Ob otkhodnichestvie iz severo-zapadnogo Irana v kontse XIX veka." *Voprosy Istorii* 1 (1956).

Bennigsen, Alexandre. "Un temoignage francaise sur Chamil et les guerres de Caucase." *CMRS* 6/3 (1966): 311–22.

Bennigsen, Alexandre and Marie Broxup. *The Islamic Threat to the Soviet State.* New York: St. Martin's, 1983.

Bennigsen, Alexandre and Chantal Lemercier-Quelquejay. *Islam in the Soviet Union.* New York: Praeger, 1967.

———. *Les mouvements nationaux chez les musulmans de Russie: Le Soultan-galivisme au Tatarstan*. The Hague: Mouton, 1960.

———. *La presse et mouvements nationaux chez les musulmans de Russie avant 1920*. The Hague: Mouton, 1964.

Bennigsen, Alexandre and Enders S. Wimbush. *Muslim National Communism in the Soviet Union: A Revolutionary Strategy for the Colonial World*. Chicago: University of Chicago Press, 1979.

Benzing, J. "Berliner politische Verofentlichungen der Turken aus der Sowjetunion." *Die Welt des Islams* 18 (1936): 122–31.

Berengian, Sakina. *Azeri and Persian Literary Works in Twentieth-Century Iranian Azerbaijan*. Berlin: Klaus Schwarz Verlag, 1988.

Bezanis, L., "Soviet Muslim Emigrés in the Republic of Turkey" *CAS* 13 (1994) 59–180.

Bihl, Wolfdieter. *Die Kaukasus-Politik der Mittelmächte. Teil I. Ihre Basis in der Orient-Politik und ihre Aktionen, 1917–1917*. Vienna: Veroffentlichungen der Kommission fur neure Geschichte Osterreichs 61, 1975.

———. *Die Kaukasus-Politik der Mittelmachte. Teil II. Die Zeit der versuchten kaukasischen Staatlichkeit (1917–1918)*. Vienna: Bohlau, 1992.

Blank, Stephen. "Bolshevik Organizational Development in Early Soviet Transcaucasia." In *Transcaucasia: Nationalism and Social Change*, Ronald C. Suny, ed. Ann Arbor: The University of Michigan Press, 1983, 305–38.

Bor-Ramenskii, E. "Iranskaia revoliutsiia 1905–1911 gg. i bol'sheviki Zakavkaz'ia." *Krasnyi Arkhiv* 5 (1941): 33–70.

Bournoutian, George. "The Ethnic Composition and the Socio-Economic Condition of Eastern Armenia in the First Half of the Nineteenth Century." In *Transcaucasia: Nationalism and Social Change*, Ronald C. Suny, ed. Ann Arbor: The University of Michigan Press, 1983, 69–86.

———. *Eastern Armenia in the Last Decades of Persian Rule 1807–1828: A Political and Socioeconomic of the Khanate of Erivan of the Eve of the Russian Conquest*. Malibu, Calif.: Undena Publications 1982.

Brands, H. W. *Aserbaijschanische Volksleben und modernistische Tendenz in den Schauspielen Mirza Fathali Ahundzades*. The Hague: Mouton, 1958.

Browne, E. G. *The Persian Revolution, 1905–1909*. London: Cambridge University Press, 1914.

Buniatov, Ziya. *Istoricheskaia geografiia Azerbaidzhana*. Baku: Elm, 1987.

———. "Pervye poselentsy sovetskikh kontslagerei." *Tarikh* 3 (1990).

Castagne, J. "La latinisation de l'alphabet turc dans les republiques turco-tatares de l'URSS." *Revue des etudes islamiques* 1 (1927): 321–53.

Chaqueri, Cosroe. *The Revolutionary Movement in Iran Versus Great Britain and Soviet Russia*. Florence: Mazdak, 1979.

_____. "Sultanzade: The Forgotten Revolutionary Theoretician." *CAS* III/2 (1984): 57–74.

_____. *Le movement communiste en Iran*. Florence: Mazolak, 1979.

_____. "The Role and Impact of of Armenian Intellectuals in Iranian Politics: 1905–1911." *Armenian Review* 41, nos. 2–4 (1988).

_____. *Victims of Faith: Iranian Communists and the Soviet Russia, 1917–40*. Forthcoming.

_____. *The Socialist Republic of Iran, 1920–1921: Birth of Trauma*. Pittsburgh: University of Pittsburgh Press, 1994.

Cheshmazar, Mir Gasim. "Muhammad Biriya." *Novruz* 21 (1991) :24.

_____. "S. J. Pishävarinin Azärbaijan Demokrat Partiyasisnin va Azärbaijan milli hokumatinin yaranmasi ughrunda mubarizäda rolu hagginda." *Jänubi Azärbaijan tariḳhi mäsäläläri*. Baku: Elm, 1989.

_____. "Mashaggätli ömür." *Ädäbiyyät va injä sanaati* 25/11 (1988).

Churchill, Winston. *The Second World War:* Boston: Houghton Mifflin Co. 1950.

Conquest, Robert. *The Harvest of Sorrow: Soviet Collectivization and the Terror-Famine*. New York: Oxford University Press, 1986.

Cottam, Richard. *Nationalism in Iran* (updated through 1978). Pittsburgh: Pittsburgh University Press, 1979.

Curzon, George. *Persia and the Persian Question*. London: Longmans, 1892.

Darabadi, Parvin. *Voennye problemy politicheskoi istorii Azerbaidzhana nachala XX veḳa*. Baku: Elm, 1991.

Devlet, Nadir. *Rusya Türḳlerinin milli mücadele tarihi (1905–1917)*. Ankara: Türk Kültürünu Araştirma Enstitüsu, 1985.

_____. *Çağdas Türḳ dünyasī*. Istanbul: Marmara Universitesi Yayinlari, 1989.

Douglas, William O. *Strange Lands and Friendly People*. New York: Harper, 1951.

Dzhafarov, Imran B. *Russḳii iazyḳ-iazyḳ druzhby i bratstva*. Baku: Azerbaidzhanskoe Gosudarstvennoe Izdatel'stvo, 1982.

Eagleton, William. *The Kurdish Republic of 1946*. New York: Oxford University Press, 1963.

Emeni-Yeghaneh, J. "Iran vs. Azerbaijan (1945–46): Divorce, Separation, or Reconciliation?" *CIS* 3/2 (1984): 1–28.

Fasa'i, Hasan. *History of Persia Under Qajar Rule*. Trans. by Heribert Busse. New York: Columbia University Press, 1972.

Fatemi, Nasrollah S. *Diplomatic History of Persia: 1917–1923. Anglo-Russian Power Politics in Iran*. New York: Russell Moore. 1952.

Fawcett-L'Estrange, Louise. *Iran and the Cold War: The Azerbaijan Crisis of 1946*. Cambridge: Cambridge University Press, 1992.

Fuller, Graham. *The "Center of the Universe": The Geopolitics of Iran*. Boulder: Westview, 1971.

Gadzhizade Kh. (Hajizadä). *Azerbaijan. Takovy my segodniia.* Samizdat.

Gasymov, Tofiq. "The War Against the Azeri Popular Front." *Uncaptive Minds* (November-December 1990): 12–16.

Gobineau, Joseph de. *Religions et philosopies dans l'Asie Centrale.* Paris: Didier, 1865.

Guseinov, Mirza Daud. *Tiurskaia Demokraticheskaia Partiia Federalistov "Musavat" v proshlom i nastoiashchem.* Baku: Zakkniga, 1927.

Henze, Paul. "The Significance of Increasing Bilingualism among Soviet Muslims." In *The USSR and the Muslim World,* Yaacov Ro'i, ed. 117–128.

Hoffmann, Joachim. *Kaukasien 1942/43. Die deutsche Heer und die Orientvolker der Sovietunion.* Freiburg: Verlag Rombach, 1991.

Homayounpour, Parvis. *L'affaire d'Azerbaidjan.* Lausanne: Payot, 1967.

Hovannisian, Richard. *Armenia on the Road to Independence: 1918.* Berkeley, University of California Press, 1969.

_____. "The Armeno-Azerbaijani Conflict over Mountainous Karabagh: 1918–1919." *Armenian Review* 24 (Summer 1971): 3–24.

_____. "Caucasian Armenia between Imperian and Soviet Rule: The Interlude of National Independence." In *Transcaucasia: Nationalism and Social Change,* Ronald C. Suny, ed. Ann Arbor: The University of Michigan Press, 1983, 45–68.

_____. *The Republic of Armenia: The First Year, 1918–1919.* Berkeley: University of California Press, 1971.

_____. "Armenia and the Caucasus in the Genesis of the Soviet Turkish Entente" *IJMES* 4/2 (1973): 45–68.

Ibrahimov, Mirza. "1945–1946 illarda Janubi Azärbaijan milli-demokratik harakat haqqinda." In his *Äsärläri* vol. 7. Baku: Iaziji Nashriyyati, 1982, 72–115.

Ibrahimov, T. A. *Iran Kommunist Partiyasisin yaranmasi.* Baku, 1963.

Imart, G. "Un intellectuel azerbaidjanais face a la Revolution de 1917: Samad-Aga Agamalioglu." *CMRS* 8/4 (1967): 528–59.

_____. "Le mouvement de 'latinisation' en URSS." *CMRS* (1967): 223–39.

Ischanian, B. *Nationaler Bestand berufmässige Gruppierung und Gliederung der Kaukasischen Völker.* Berlin: G. J. Goshen, 1914.

Issawi, Charles, ed. *The Economic History of Iran, 1800–1914.* Chicago: University of Chicago Press, 1971.

Iunusova, Leyla. "Pestraia palistra neformal'nykh dvizhenii v Azerbaidzhane." *Russkaia mysl',* September 22, 1989.

_____. "Mera otvetstvennosti politika." *Istiqlal* 4 (1990).

Javadi, Abbas Ali. *Azarbaijan va zaban-i an. Oza' va moshkelat-i Turki Azari dar Iran.* Piedmont, Calif.: Jahan Book Co., 1989.

Kadishev, A. B. *Interventsia i grazhdanskaia voina v Zakavkaz'e.* Moscow: Voennoe Izd-vo, 1960.

Karabekir, Kazim. *Istiklal harbimiz*. Istanbul: Turkiye Yayinevi, 1960.

Karaev, Gaidar. *Iz nedavnogo proshlogo*. Baku: Izd-vo Bakinskii Rabochii, 1926.

Kasravi, Ahmad. *Zandegan-i man*. Teheran, 1946.

_____. *Zaban-i azari ya zaban-i bastan-i Azarbaijan*. Teheran, 1926.

_____. *Tarikh-i hejdah saleh-i Azarbaijan ya dastan-i mashruteh-yi dar Iran* Teheran: 1313–20 (1934–40).

_____. *Tarikh-i mashruteh-yi Iran*. Teheran: 1317. Annotated translation by Evan Siegal. Manuscript.

_____. *Zandegani-yi man*. Teheran 1946.

Kaukasielli, *Der Kaukasus im Weltkrieg*. Weimar: Verlag Gustav Kiepenheuer, 1916.

Kazemzadeh, Feridun. *The Struggle for Transcaucasia (1917–1921)*. New York: Philosophical Library, 1951.

_____. *Russia and Britain in Persia, 1864–1914*. New Haven: Yale University Press, 1968.

_____. "Russian Penetration of the Caucasus." In *Russian Imperialism from Ivan the Great to the Revolution*, Taras Hunczak, ed. New Brunswick: Rutgers University Press, 1974.

Keddie, Nikki. *Sayyid Jamal "al-Afghani": A Political Biography*. Berkeley: University of California Press, 1972.

Keshavarz, F. *Man mottaham mikonam*. Teheran: Ravaq, 1980.

Klimovich, L. *Islam v tsarskoi Rossii*. Moscow: Izd-vo Bezbozhnik, 1936.

Kochärli, T. K. "Bor'ba Kommunisticheskoi Partii Azerbaidzhana za sotsialisticheskuiu industrializatsiiu i podgotovku sploshnoi kollektivizatsii sel'skogo khoziaistva (1926–1929 gg.)." *KPAz. Institut Istorii Partii, Trudy*. 23 (1959): 3–33.

Kolarz, Walter. *Religion in the Soviet Union*. London: Macmillan, 1962.

Kozlov, Viktor I. *Natsional'nosti SSSR. Etnodemograficheskii obzor*. Moscow: Finansy i Statistika, 1982.

Kuniholm, Bruce R. *The Origins of the Cold War in the Near East: Great Power Conflict and Diplomacy in Iran, Turkey, and Greece*. Princeton: Princeton University Press, 1980.

Landau, J. M. *Pan-Turkism in Turkey: A Study of Irredentism*. London: Hurst, 1981.

Larcher, M. *La guerre turque dans la guerre mondiale*. Paris: Berger-Levrault, 1926.

Lenczowski, George. *Russia and the West in Iran: A Study in Great Powers Rivalry: 1918–1948*. Ithaca, N.Y.: Cornell University Press, 1968.

Liber, George. "Korenizatsia: Restructuring Soviet nationality policy in the 1920s." *Ethnic and Racial Studies* 14:1 (1991): 15–23.

Lisagor, P., and M. Higgins. *Overtime in Heaven: Adventures in the Foreign Service*. Garden City: Doubleday, 1964.

McAuley, Alastair. "The Soviet Muslim Population: Trends in Living Standards 1960–1975." In *The USSR and the Muslim World*, Yaacov Ro'i, ed. London: George Allen and Unwin, 1984, 95–116.

McKay, John. "Baku Oil and Transcaucasian Pipelines, 1883–1891, a Study in Tasrist Economic Policy." *Slavic Review* 43:4 (1984).

Mammadov, M. "O perevode azerbaidzhanskoi pis'mennosti s latinskogo na russkii alfavit." *Elm* 29 (1990): 237.

Mammädov, M. *N. Narimanov va ana dili*. Baku: Elm, 1971.

Mammadzadä, Hamid. *Mirza Fathali Akhundov va sharg*. Baku: Elm, 1971.

Meister, I. "Soviet Policy in Iran: 1917–1950: A Case Study in Techniques." Ph.D. Dissertation, Tufts University, 1954.

Menzel, Theodor "Der 1 Turkologische Kongress in Baku." *Der Islam* 16 (1927): 1–169.

Mikulicz, Sergiusz. *Prometeizm w polityce II Rzeczypospolitej*. Warsaw: Ksiazka i Wiedza, 1971.

Mil'man, Aron. *Politicheskii stroi Azerbaidzhana v XIX-nachale XX veka*. Baku: Azerneshr, 1966.

Mirza-Bala, Mehmet. *Milli Azerbaycan Musavat Halk Firkasinin tarihi*. Berlin: Firka Divani, 1938.

Mojtahedie, M. *Rejal-i Azarbaijan dar asr-i mashrutiyat*. Teheran, 1327.

Motika, Raoul. "Glasnost in der Sowjetrepublik Aserbaidschan am Beispiel der Zeitschrift Azärbaycan." *Orient* 32/4 (1991): 573–90.

Mouradian, Claire. "The Mountainous Karabagh Question: An Inter-Ethnic Conflict or Decolonization Crisis?" *Armenian Review* 43/2–3, 1–34.

Muhlen, Patrik von zur. *Zwischen Hakenkreuz und Sowjetstern: Der Nationalismus der sowjetischen Orientvolker im Zweiten Weltkrieg*. Dusseldorf: Droste Verlag, 1971.

Nabdel, A. R. *Azarbaijan va mas'aleh-yi melli*. Aden, 1356 (1977).

Najafov, Kh. S. *Aghamalioghlunun ijtimai-siyasi va ateist qörushläri*. Baku: Azärbayjan Dövlet Näshriyyäti, 1968.

Namazov, Eldar. "Stalin, Kavbiuro, Nagornyi Karabagh." *Bakinskii rabochii* 11/22 (1989).

Narimanov, Nariman. *Izbrannye proizvedeniia*. Baku: Azgosizdat, 1989.

Nasibzade, Nasib. "A. Nabdel' i A. Tabrizli: Dva uklona v ideologii natsional'no-osvoboditel'nogo dvizheniia Azerbaidzhantsev v Irane." *ANAz.SSR Izvestiia, Ser. Ist. Fil. Pr.* 2 (1988): 60–65.

_____. "1960–1970-ji illärda Jänubi Azärbayjanin sosial-igtisadi inkishafinin ba'zi mäsäläri hagginda." *ANAz.SSR Elmlar Akademiyasi, Shargshunaslig Instituti, Jänubi Azärbayjan tarikhi mäsäläläri*. Baku: Elm, 1989.

_____. "Vahid Azärbayjan. Ideal va qerchaklik." *Elm* 3/17 (1990).

_____. *Azärbayjan Demokratik Respublikasi. Magalälär va sanädlär*. Baku: Elm, 1990.

Nava'i, 'Abd ul-Husain. "Haidar Amuoghli va Muhammad Amin Rasulzadeh." *Majalleh-yi Yadegar* 1/2 (1948): 43–68.

Nissman, David B. *The Soviet Union and Iranian Azerbaijan. The Use of Nationalism for Political Penetration.* Boulder: Westview Press, 1987.

_____. "The Origins and Development of the Literature of 'Longing' in Azerbaijan." *Journal of Turkish Studies* 8 (1984): 197–207.

Nove, Alec and J. A. Newth. *The Soviet Middle East. A Communist Model for Development.* New York: Praeger, 1966.

Ordubadi, Mammad Said. *Ganli illar.* Baku: Karabagha Yardim Komitäsi, 1991.

Pishävari, Mir Jafar. *Sechilmish äsärlär.* Baku, 1986.

_____. *(Javadzadä Halkhali) Sechilmish Äsärläri.* Azärbaijan Ruznamäsinin Näshriyyati 1965, H. 1344.

Polonskii, L. "Namestnik vozhdia. Mir Dzhafar Bagirov. Put' k vlasti. Prestupleniia protiv naroda." *Bakinskii rabochii* 6/15 (1988).

_____. "Inakomyslie." *Bakinskii rabochii* 5/6 (1989).

Raevskii, A. *Angliiskiie druz'ia i musavatskie "patrioty."* Baku, 1927.

_____. *Angliiskaia interventsiia i musavatskoe pravitel'stvo. Iz istorii interventsii i kontrrevoliutsii v Zakavkaz'e.* Baku: Krasnyi Vostok, 1927.

_____. *Partiia Musavat i ee kontrrevoliutsionna rabota.* Baku, 1929.

_____. *Bol'sheviki i mensheviki v Baku v 1904–1905 godakh.* Baku: Azgnin, 1930.

Rafiev, Bakhtyar. "Set' nelegal'nykh organizatsii deistvovala v Azerbadzhane v dvadtsatye gody." *Vyshka* 3/10, 11, 12/1993.

_____. "Mozhno li ubit' natsional'nyi dukh," *Vyshka* 3/10/1993.

_____. "Ternovyi venets kul'tury." *Vyshka* 3/10, 11, 16, 18, 20 /1993.

Ra'in, Ismail. *Haidar Khan Amu Oghli.* Teheran: Amir Kabir, 1973.

Rasulzade, (Räsulzadä) Mehmet Emin. *O Panturanizme v sviazi s kavkazskoi problemoi.* Oxford: Society for Central Asian Studies, 1985.

_____. *Asrimizin Siyavuşu.* Istanbul, 1339 (1923).

_____. *Azerbaycan Cumhuriyeti.* Istanbul, 1339 (1923).

_____. "Iran Türkleri." *Türk yurdu* 4 (1911).

Ravasani, S. *Sowjetrepublik Gilan. Die sozialistische Bewegung in Iran seit Ende des 19 Jhdt bis 1922.* Berlin: Basis Verlag, 1973.

Rezun, Miron. *The Soviet Union and Iran: Soviet Policy in Iran from the Beginning of the Pahalvi Dynasty Until the Soviet Invasion in 1941.* Boulder: Westview, 1988.

Rorlich, Azade-Ayşe. "The 'Ali Bayramov' Club, the Journal 'Sharg Gadini,' and the Socialization of Azeri Women: 1920–30." *Central Asian Survey* 5/3-4 (1986) 221–40.

_____. "Not by History Alone: The Retrieval of the Past Among the Tatars and the Azeris." *Central Asian Survey* 3/2 (1984): 91–97.

Rossi, Ettore. "Publicazioni di musulmani anti-bolscevichi dell' Azerbaigian Caucasico." *Oriente moderno* 4/6 (1924): 401–8.

_____. "Questione dell'alfabetto per le lingue turche." *Oriente moderno* (1927): 295–310.

Rossow, Robert. "The Battle of Azerbaijan: 1946." *MEJ* 10 (Winter 1956).

Rozhkova, M. K. *Ekonomicheskaia politika tsarskogo pravitel'stva na Srednem Vostoke vo vtoroi chetvert'i XIX veka i russkaia burzhuaziia.* Moscow: Izd-vo ANSSR, 1949.

Rywkin, Michael. *Moscow's Muslim Challenge: Soviet Central Asia.* Armonk: M. E. Sharp, 1990.

Samedov, Viacheslav. *Neft i ekonomika Rossii (80–90 gody XIX veka).* Baku: Elm, 1988.

Saray, Memhet, ed. *Kafkas araştırmaları.* Istanbul: Acar Yayinlari, 1988.

_____. *Gaspirali Ismail bey (1851–1914).* Ankara: Türk Kültürünü Araştırma Enstitütsü, 1987.

Schroeder, Gertrude. "Transcaucasia Since Stalin: The Economic Dimension." In *Transcaucasia: Nationalism and Social Change*, Ronald C. Suny, ed. Ann Arbor: The University of Michigan Press, 1983, 397–416.

Seidzade, Dilara. *Iz istorii azerbaidzhanskoi burzhuazii v nachale XX veka.* Baku: Elm, 1978.

_____. *Azerbaidzhanskie deputaty v Gosudarstvennoi Dume Rossii.* Baku: Azerbaidzhanskoe Gosudarstvennoe Izd-vo, 1991.

Sepehr, *Iran dar Jang-i Bozorg: 1914–1918.* Teheran, 1959.

Shahriyarin on ikisi, 1324–1325. Azärbaijan Dimukrat Firqasinin birinji yildönümü münasebetile. Tabriz: 1325.

Silver. Brian. "Population Redistribution and the Ethnic Balance in Transcaucasia." In *Transcaucasia: Nationalism and Social Change*, Ronald C. Suny, ed. Ann Arbor: The University of Michigan Press, 1983, 373–96.

Simon, Gerhard. *Nationalismus und Nationalitatenpolitik in der Sowjetunion: Von totalitaren Diktatur zu nachstalinischen Gesellschaft.* Köln: Bundesinstitut fur Ostwissenschaftliche und Internationale Studien, 1986.

Strigunov, I. V. "Baki proletariatinin tashäkkülu mäsäläsinä dair." *ANAzSSR, Trudy* 10 (1955).

Sumbatzade, A. S. *Promyshlennost' Azerbaidzhana v XIX veke.* Baku: Izd-vo ANAzSSSR, 1964.

_____. *Azerbaidzhantsy-etnogenez i formirovanie naroda.* Baku: Elm, 1990.

_____. *Sel'skoe khoziaistvo Azerbaidzana v XIX veke.* 1958. Azerneshr, Baku.

Sumbatzade, A. S., ed. *Qorkämli ingilabchi Sattarkhan.* Baku: Azarnashr, 1972.

Sumbatzade, A. S. and G. Mekhtiev, *Prisoedinenie Azerbaidzana k Rossii i ego progressivnye posledstvia v oblasti ekonomiki i kul'tury.* Baku, 1995.

Suny, Ronald G. *The Baku Commune, 1917–1918: Class and Nationality in the Russian Revolution.* Princeton: Princeton University Press, 1972.

_____. *Looking Toward Ararat: Armenia in Modern History*. Bloomington: Indiana University Press, 1993.

_____. *The Making of the Georgian Nation*. Bloomington: Indiana University Press, 1988.

_____. "Transcaucasia: Cultural Cohesion and Ethnic Revival in a Multinational Society." L. Hajda and M. Beissinger, *The Nationalities Factor in Soviet Politics and Society*. Boulder: Westview, 228–53.

Swietochowski, Tadeusz. *Russian Azerbaijan, 1905–1920: The Shaping of National Identity in a Muslim Community*. New York: Cambridge University Press, 1985.

_____. "The Himmat Party: Socialism and the Nationality Question in Russian Azerbaijan, 1904–1920." *CMRS* 19 (1978): 119–42.

_____. "National Consciousness and Political Orientations in Russian Azerbaijan, 1905–1920." In *Transcaucasia: Nationalism and Social Change*, Ronald C. Suny, ed. Ann Arbor: The University of Michigan Press, 1983, 209–83.

_____. "Islam and Nationality in Tsarist Russia and the Soviet Union." In *Soviet Nationality Policies. Ruling Ethnic Groups in the USSR*, Henry Huttenbach, ed. New York: Mansell Ltd., 1990, 221–34.

Tagieva, Shövkät. *Natsional'no osvoboditel'noe dvizhenie v iranskom Azerbaidzhane v 1917–1920 gg*. Baku: Izd-vo ANAzSSR, 1956.

_____. "Nariman Narimanovun 1905–1911-ji illär Iran ingilabi alagadar faaliyyati hagginda." *ANAzSSSR Izvestiia, Ser. Ist. Fil. Prava* 3 (1973): 38–49.

_____. "Tebrizskoe vosstanie 1920 g." *ANAzSSR, Trudy* 7 (1955): 89–134.

_____. *1920-ji il Tabriz üsyani*. Baku: Izd-vo ANAzSSR, 1990.

Tairbekov, B. G. "O traditsiiakh i novshestvakh v pis'mennoi fiksatsii tiurskoi rechi." *Khazar* 2 (1991): 145–50.

Tillet, Lowell. *The Great Friendship*. Chapel Hill: University of North Carolina, 1969.

Tolf, R. W. *The Russian Rockefellers: The Saga of the Nobel Family and the Russian Oil Industry*. Stanford: Stanford University Press, 1976.

Trubetskoi, V. V. "K voprosu o vliianii burzhuaznykh reform 60-kh-pervoi poloviny 70-kh godov na natsional'nye protsessy Irana." *Natsional'nye problemy sovremennogo Vostoka*, 81–113.

_____. "Osobennosti natsional'noi situatsii v Islamskoi Respublike Irana." *ANSSR, Natsional'nyi vopros v stranakh Vostoka*. Moscow: Izd-vo Nauka, 1982, 249–68.

Vekilov (Väkilov), Dzhavanshir. "Rol' tebrizskogo filiala obshchestva kul'turnykh sviazei Irana s SSSR i Sovetskogo Doma Kul'tury v Tebrize v razvitii sovetsko-iranskikh kul'turnykh sviazei." *ANAzSSSR Izvestiia, Ser. Lit. Iaz.* 1 (1989): 101–6.

_____. "1920–1940-ji illärdä Azärbaijan SSSR-in Sovet-Iran mädäni ala-gadarinda ishtiraki." *ANAzSSR, Jänubi Azärbaijan tarikhi mäsäläläri*. Baku: Elm, 1989.

_____. *Azärbaijan respublikasi vä Iran: 40-ji illär (mädäni alagalar)*. Baku: Elm, 1991.

Willerton, J. "Patronage and Politcs in the Soviet Union." Ph.D. Dissertation, University of Michigan Press, 1985.

Yüksel, Ibrahim. *Azerbaycan fikir hayati ve basin*. Acar Yayinlari, n.d.

Zabih, Sephr. *The Communist Movement in Iran*. Berkeley: University of California Press, 1966.

Zanganeh, Ahmad. *Khaterati az mamuriyatha man dar Azärbaijan Rasht* 1366.

Zarcone, Thierry. "Une source pour l'histoire de la revolution iranienne de 1905–1911 et de la communaute iranienne d'Istanboul." *Toplumbilim* 1 (1992): 54–79.

Zenkovsky, Serge. *Pan-Turkism and Islam in Russia*. Cambridge: Harvard University Press, 1960.

Zinam, O. "Transcaucasus." In *Economics of Soviet Regions*, I. S. Koropeckyi, G. E. Schroeder, eds. New York: Praeger, 1981.

Zonis, Marvin. *The Political Elite of Iran*. Princeton: Princeton University Press, 1971.

Zürrer, Werner. *Persien zwischen England und Russland, 1918–1925*. Grossmachteinflusse und nationaler Wiederaufstieg am Beispiel des Iran. Bern: Peter Lang, n.d.

_____. *Kaukasien, 1918–1921: Der Kampf der Grossmachten um die Landbrucke zwischen Schwarzen und Kaspischen Meer*. Dusseldorf, 1978.

INDEX